MASK IMPROVISATION

for Actor Training & Performance

W. T. Benda and Friends, Greenwich Village Studio, New York, 1936. Courtesy of Glena Benda Shimler.

MASK

IMPROVISATION

for Actor Training & Performance

THE COMPELLING IMAGE

Sears A. Eldredge

Northwestern

University

Press

Evanston,

Illinois

Northwestern University Press

Evanston, Illinois 60208–4210

Printed in the United States of America

10 9 8 7 6 5 4 3 2

ISBN 0-8101-1365-1

Library of Congress Cataloging-in-Publication Data

Eldredge, Sears A.

Mask improvisation for actor training and performance :

The compelling image / Sears A. Eldredge.

p.   cm.

Includes bibliographical references.

ISBN 0-8101-1365-1 (pbk.)

1. Masks.   2. Improvisation (Acting)   I. Title.

PN2071.M37E43   1996

792'.028 — dc20   96-22440

CIP

The paper used in this publication meets the

minimum requirements of the American National

Standard for Information Sciences — Permanence of

Paper for Printed Library Materials, ANSI Z39.48–1984.

FOR PAT

An actor's motivation doesn't come from a sort of technical understanding of his body; it comes from his capacity to create an incredibly powerful image in himself that he's convinced by. Now to a degree the two fit together, but not at their root and you will see this phenomenon of young actors who have prepared themselves marvelously, but whose performances are not at all interesting. Yet if the inner image is incredibly strong, an actor can transcend his physical limitations. Then the ideal comes when the two go together, when a real actor also prepares his body. . . . For a real actor, the right school is not the school of learning to make the body expressive; the right school is making the body a very closely concerned, free instrument through which an acting impulse—the acting imagination—can pass and not be blocked on the way.

PETER BROOK,

"The Physical Life of the Actor"

Contents

Exercises

Illustrations

Acknowledgments

This book has had a long gestation and birthing. It grew out of my previous investigation into masks and methods of training actors with masks that took place twenty years ago. I welcome the opportunity to thank once again those teachers and artists who participated in that original research for their generosity in sharing their invaluable knowledge of the mask and mask training with me. They are Bari Rolfe, Jacques Lecoq, Carlo Mazzone-Clementi, Peter Schumann, Jeremy Geidt, Leonard Pitt, Estelle Spector, Libby Appel, Peter Frisch, Rolland Meinholt, and Joy Spanabel. Special appreciation must be given to Marie-Hélène Dasté and Mrs. Glena Benda Shimler for their willingness to let me examine documents and masks and/or to publish photographs in their possession. I also thank Tom Leabhart for his encouragement of this project over the years.

Peter Layton, founder and executive director of The Drama Studio, London, provided me with an opportunity to test my own methods of teaching mask improvisation with students at that institution on several occasions. I am most grateful for his support.

I also want to thank those faculty who field-tested an earlier draft of this text, thus providing me with indispensable feedback on its strengths and weaknesses. They will see the effects of their comments reflected in the text. These people are Jackie Davis, University of New Hampshire; Patrice Egleston, DePaul University; Colleen Kelly, University of Virginia; Barbara Sellers-Young, University of California, Davis; and Robert Amsden, Ripon College.

Perhaps those who have taught me the most about the mask and its effectiveness in actor training are the many students who have participated in my classes and workshops over the years. Their willingness to experiment, as well as their resistance at times, have been very instructive. I especially thank Tom Luce, Lars Myers, Tom Lommel, Elena Giannetti, Elee Wood, and Megan Odel, who, as student preceptors, assisted in teaching the course with talent and enthusiasm.

Earlham College was gracious in granting me a faculty development grant to begin this text. My colleagues in the Department of Dramatic Arts & Dance at Macalester College have been very supportive during the long writing process. Beth Cleary offered insightful comments on the opening chapter; Daniel Keyser's skill provided the computer-drawn templates for the masks, and Tom Barrett, photographs.

Much appreciation is also due to Susan Harris, editor-in-chief at Northwestern University Press, for her guidance and encouragement and to Angela G. Ray for her careful editing of the manuscript.

Finally, much gratitude is due to Patricia Reid Eldredge for her partnership in this project over the years and for the many conversations about masks and masking in which her insights greatly illuminated my own.

Prologue

Jake pulled obsessively at his collar button. It was obvious that he was very anxious about being interviewed. He had not wanted to be approached and had kept himself in a corner, trying to hide from the rest of us. But he seemed to be an interesting character with a rich personal history and therefore ripe for an interview. I approached him carefully. Jake was a stocky, imposing person with a menacing aura about him. From his stance and physical traits I guessed he was in his late forties or early fifties. He cringed as I sat down on a chair near him. And I wasn't sure that he wouldn't strike out at me if I made the wrong move or said the wrong thing.

"Hi!"

No answer.

"Would you come over here and sit down by me?"

He huddled into a tighter ball and trembled all over.

"Wouldn't you like to sit here beside me? I'm not going to hurt you. I only want to ask you a few questions."

"Why?"

"I just want to be your friend, to ask you a few questions about yourself."

Jake moved cautiously toward the chair beside me and sat down. There was so much tension in his body that he was shaking. His eyes were filled with fear and suspicion. "Why do you want to talk to me? What are you trying to find out about me?"

"Nothing. I just thought that you looked like an interesting person that I would like to get to know. You can trust me. I only want to be your friend."

Silence.

"What's your name?"

After a pause, he said, "Jake."

"Where are you from?"

"Around here."

"Are you married?"

"No."

"What do you do for a living?"

"Nothin'. I ain't got no job." Jake started pulling at his collar button again. He was clearly a troubled person. I wanted to find out what was bothering him if I could.

"Then what do you do with yourself all day?"

"Not much . . . I like to sit in the park and watch the children play."

"And why do you enjoy doing that?"

"I don't know . . . I liked to play tag as a kid."

"Who played tag with you?"

"There were five of us."

"What were their names?"

"Bobby . . . Jimmy . . . Carolyn . . ."

"I thought you told me there were four friends you played tag with."

"Yeah."

"But you only named three."

Silence.

"You only named three."

Silence. For some reason Jake did not want to acknowledge this fact. Why? What was the mystery about the fourth person?

"Where did you play tag?"

"In an abandoned warehouse."

This sounded intriguing, so I continued my probing. "Tell me about playing tag in an abandoned warehouse."

Pause. Jake tugged more insistently at his collar button. "We used to play in this abandoned warehouse. The windows were all broken, and it was dark inside. There were signs all around warnin' people to keep out, that it was dangerous to be there. The warehouse had different rooms and levels. We'd run up and down the stairs inside. One time Suzy . . ."

Suzy. Is she the fourth person, I wondered, the missing playmate?

"Suzy and I were bein' chased by the person who was it. I heard this voice behind us yelling, 'I hear you! I hear you! I'm coming to get you!' We were runnin' ahead of him through the warehouse on an upper floor . . . It was the second or third floor . . . And we came to a section that we'd not been in before. It got darker, but we kept runnin'. Suzy was ahead of me. She stopped suddenly." He stopped tugging at his collar button. Jake raised both hands in front of him, palms out, and started a pushing motion. I sensed that we were getting close to something important in Jake's past.

"What happened next?"

"I heard the others gettin' closer, comin' up behind us . . ."

"So then what happened?"

Jake kept pushing with his hands. He seemed to be pushing against a weight that wasn't there. Jake's eyes glistened with pain and fright. His body was still now, but taut.

"Tell me what happened next."

"I ran up to Suzy. I told her, 'Keep goin'! Keep goin'! He's comin'! He's comin'!' . . . And then I found out the reason she had stopped so quickly. The floor had given out there."

"And?"

There was a long pause. Jake did not go on. But his hands continued to make the pushing motion against the air in front of him. Recalling this memory was causing him great anguish.

"You pushed her, didn't you?"

Jake acknowledged this with a single slow nod of his head.

"And she fell."

"Yeah. I stood there with my arms still out, listening to her scream as she fell through the hole and landed on the cement down below."

"Was she killed?"

With a deep release of breath, he slowly lowered his hands to his lap.

"I didn't see the hole."

"And you've been carrying this story around for a long time?"

"I never told anyone else."

A pause. "I feel privileged that you've been willing to share this story with me."

We sat there silently for a while. It was getting late, and I knew that it was time for me to end the interview. But I wanted to reach out and touch Jake in some way so that he would know I cared about him.

"Jake, it's time for me to leave now. I am grateful for your willingness to share your life with me. Would you shake hands good-bye?"

He looked at my outstretched hand. The distrustful, questioning look returned to his eyes. He pulled his body slightly away from me.

"I would like to shake your hand good-bye," I said. "Would you do that, as a friend?"

Jake looked searchingly into my eyes. Then he took my right hand in his and moved it over his heart. With his head bowed, he held my hand tightly against his chest as if he didn't want to let go. Tears came to my eyes. I let him hold my hand there a while.

"Thanks, Jake, for your friendship. But I've really got to go now."

Jake slowly let go of my hand. He watched as I got up and backed a short distance away from him.

"Freeze! Close your eyes, relax, and come out of the mask."

Introduction

1

The Ubiquitous Mask

It is a fact that all mankind wears or has worn a mask. This enigmatic accessory, with no obvious utility, is commoner than the lever, the bow, the harpoon or the plough. Whole peoples have been ignorant of the most ordinary tools. They knew the mask. Complete civilizations, some of them most remarkable, have prospered without having conceived the idea of the wheel, or, what is worse, without using it even though it was known to them. But they were familiar with the mask. . . . There is no tool, no invention, no belief, custom or institution which unites mankind so much as does the habit of wearing a mask.

—Roger Caillois, The Mask of Medusa

Origins

No one knows where or when the first human being picked up an object and decided to cover his face with it.[1] But wherever it was, and whenever it happened, the effect on the mask wearer and his audience must have been immediate and powerful. Masks and masking have long been ubiquitous in human society. As the anthropologist Harry Shapiro asserts, "The mask is among the oldest items in our present culture. As far back as the Upper Paleolithic Era, perhaps 50,000 years ago—its use was already known."[2]

One of the earliest visual records of a human figure wearing a mask, engraved and painted on the wall of a prehistoric cave in southern France, is known as the Sorcerer.[3] What is remarkable about this figure, and other like figures, is the fact that it seems to represent a human being wearing a mask and costume made from animal skins. The identification of the skins, however, appears to depend upon the viewer's perception. According to the religious historian Mircea Eliade, the figure "has a stag's head topped with immense antlers, an owl's face, ears like a wolf's, a long goat's beard, uplifted arms ending in bear paws, and a long horse's tail."[4] John Pfeiffer, however, has perceived that the figure has the "ears and antlers of a stag." He writes, "Close up, the feet as well as the legs and body appear human, and so is the penis except that it is drawn in a position more appropriate for a feline than for a man. The figure has a horse's tail and a vaguely beak-shaped nose."[5] Eliade's "owl's face" has another possible interpretation: perhaps, staring at the viewer out of the empty eye sockets of the skin covering the face are the apotropaic eyes of the human wearer of the mask.

Lest we dismiss this figure as a fantasy on the part of the prehistoric artist, the British Museum displays an actual Antler Mask from North Yorkshire, made from the skull of a red deer (c. 7500 B.C.E.). So most observers have assumed that the Sorcerer represents a human equivalent, involved in some unknown shamanistic activity in the cave.

Many ancient and modern cultures around the world have employed masks and masking practices. Masks are global, but not universal. They have not been found, for instance, among the aboriginal groups in Australia. But the highly developed use of facial and body paint, with feather, cane, and clay embellishments, speaks to a masking complex among these peoples.

The impulse to mask takes us back to earliest human history. The mask seems to be, as the phenomenologist Gaston Bachelard suggests, "the object of a veritable instinct of the human race."[6] This observation raises the most important and intriguing question of all: Why have human beings felt a need for masks and masking, unless these objects and activities have been recognized as somehow necessary for survival?

Abbé Breuil's drawing of "The Sorcerer." Negative #329853. Courtesy Department of Library Services, American Museum of Natural History.

Theories abound concerning the origins and purposes of masks and masking. Myths about masks and masking from preliterate societies often describe their origin in women's ritual activities that were then stolen by or transferred to men. In European culture, serious interest in the purpose and function of masks did not occur until the nineteenth century.[7] Since then, writers have composed numerous essays and books about the possible religious, social, and psychological reasons for masking. People have most frequently used masks in conjunction with rituals involving communion with animals and ancestors. Was our Sorcerer, then, engaged in some sort of sympathetic magic preparatory to a hunt? Or was his entranced state part of an initiation rite? Was he instructing new believers about their animal totems? We will never know, and our conjectures probably tell us more about ourselves than about the object studied.

The complementary and contradictory critical theories about the origins and purposes of masks and masking in human society demonstrate that these objects and activities function in the imagination as archetypal images. What you see depends upon who you are and what you are looking for. So rather than search for one paradigmatic origin and purpose, we might profitably turn to Henry Pernet's proposal, that masks and masking activities may have originated independently in different times and places and for different reasons.[8]

The Five Major Functions of Masks

It is important for us to investigate the ways in which the mask may operate in the interstices between the mask wearer and the audience, and between the mask wearer and the mask. By examining the writings of anthropologists, sociologists, psychologists, folklorists, and philosophers, we can identify five major functions that masks perform in society, as well as in individuals.[9] These functions are given metaphorical designations: *frame, mirror, mediator, catalyst,* and *transformer.* We shall briefly examine each of these. As we shall see, however, the problem with isolating these functions in separate categories is that such a scheme suggests that the functions form a hierarchy and a sequence, when in fact they operate simultaneously. They are, to use anthropologist Elizabeth Tonkin's term, "metaphors-in-action," constantly metamorphosing into each other's zone of meaning.[10] They are like the sculptured facets of a single mask that, when turned in the light, suggest different impressions of the whole.

Mask-as-Frame. The most common type of frame with which we are familiar is the literal one that surrounds a painting or photograph. This frame, often wooden or metal, functions at its most basic level to hold the prized image we have chosen to place within it. We carefully select the frame to highlight what is placed within it and to focus our attention inward on the contents. The frame also functions as a boundary marker, in that it creates a demarcation between that which is being framed and that which is not.

Conceptually, framing marks off the boundaries for a separate and unique way of seeing and knowing. As anthropologist Marjorie Halpin knows from her study of masks, it is the framing that determines our perspective on what the frame contains. "The effect of framing," she writes, "is to allow or permit the participants to step into the other reality of the frame. This requires a willingness to step out of the realm of the ordinary— to be dispatched, displaced."[11] Our considering the mask as a frame or framing device, then, means that we look not at the mask and masking behavior in themselves, but at an object and an activity that are set apart from the normal and the everyday. We also need to recognize that the very act of framing implies that a choice is being made about what is to be framed and what is not. We usually frame only those things that have the greatest significance to us.

Mask-as-Mirror. What this mask-as-frame encloses is a mask-as-mirror. A mirror reflects either a virtual or a refracted image of the world, depending upon the type of mirror. But this mask-as-mirror is one that allows you not only to see a surface reflection of yourself and your world but also to see *through* into another reality. Werner Muensterberger observes:

> Rather than mirror nature in a photographic sense, the mask confronts us with a portrait more or less removed from the world of reality. It is a visible expression not merely of a human or animal face but a portrayal of an inner image responding more to the emotional needs of the maker, the wearer, and the community of spectators in general. Considered thus as a spiritual manifestation the mask can be said to symbolize concretely what so frequently must be regarded as transcendental, or, as an observation, not of outer, but of inner nature; an effective bridging of the emotional experience through its visible manifestation.[12]

Given this double perspective, then, it would be appropriate to consider the mask-mirror as a "two-way mirror," as Ron Jenkins calls it.[13] For Ronald Grimes, this dual-purpose mirroring must be understood as societal as well as personal: "Masking is not always a personally expressive activity in which people wear masks of themselves. It may be a culturally reflexive activity in which the collective unconscious—that is, the ambivalences and contradictions latent in a culture—are acted out. In ritual contexts masked acting is seldom a matter of performing an individual's repressions."[14]

From her ethnographic research on masks and masking activities in preliterate cultures, Margaret Mead hypothesizes about the complex reflexive (mirroring) interrelationships involving the mask, the wearer, and the observers. "The wearer of the mask reflects the terror or delight, the wonder or awe or panic in the eyes of those who were, until a few moments ago, his neighbors—perhaps his wife and children. His audience, responding not to him but to the mask he wears, gives him new clues, and he in turn becomes in feeling temporarily transformed into the creature whose image has been fashioned of wood or straw, of bark cloth or leather."[15]

Thus, masks and masking activity allow for a contingent and reciprocal reality to come to the fore and to possess the minds of the wearer and observers, while everyday actualities are suspended.

Mask-as-Mediator. Yet as the anthropologist Claude Lévi-Strauss perceives it, this two-way mirroring function of the mask permits the mask to serve as a mediator between opposing worlds. "Imbued with life by its wearer," he writes, "the mask brings the god on earth, it establishes his reality, mingles him with the society of men; inversely, by masking himself, man testifies to his own social existence, manifests it, classifies it with the aid of symbols. The mask is both the man and

something other than the man: it is the mediator par excellence between society, on the one hand, and Nature, usually merged with the Supernatural, on the other."[16] For Tonkin, however, the more important realization is that masks "mediate and direct the flow of power within a system," at the same time as they function as "conductors, exemplars and operators in those innumerable initiation sequences which enact the death of the old self and the rebirth of a new one."[17]

Mask-as-Catalyst. The mask-as-mediator is not only "a potent metaphor for the coalescence of the universal and the particular, immobility and change, disguise and revelation," but in another guise functions as a "catalyst for transformation," in that it stimulates change, especially during times of transition.[18] In his masterful text *Masks, Transformation, and Paradox,* A. David Napier theorizes:

> Throughout the anthropological literature, masks appear in conjunction with categorical change. They occur in connection with rites of passage and curative ceremonies such as exorcisms. . . . their predominance during transitional periods attests to their appropriateness in the context of formal change. The special efficacy of masks in transformation results, perhaps, not only from their ability to address the ambiguities of point of view, but also from the capacity to elaborate what is paradoxical about appearances and perceptions in the context of a changing viewpoint. Masks, that is, testify to an awareness of the ambiguities of appearance and to a tendency toward paradox characteristic of transitional states. They provide a medium for exploring formal boundaries and a means of investigating the problems that appearances pose in the experience of change.[19]

Mask-as-Transformer. Napier conflates the ideas of mask-as-mediator/catalyst with that of mask-as-transformer. Psychologist Carl Kerényi, in his Jungian study "Man and Mask," also fuses these roles. He asserts that the "principal function" of the mask "is to transform and thereby to unite, or, perhaps more fundamentally, to unite and thereby transform." This function of the mask as an agent of transformation is the most recognized and discussed aspect of masks in the literature. "Man's need to extend and transform himself," says Muensterberger, "must be seen as the prime motivation behind the invention of the mask and its wellnigh universal use in magical and religious ceremonies."[20]

Masks and Faces

This focus on transformation leads to an important question. What needs transformation? One's body? One's role? One's status? One's relationship to someone or something else? All of these kinds of changes are subsumed in changing what is perhaps the most important semiotic signifier of all—one's face. Jurgen Ruesch and Weldon Kees, in their book *Nonverbal Communication,* state that "from the beginning of recorded history, men have been guided in their judgments by the observation of facial expression."[21] But why the face? What is there about the human face that predestines it to be the primary locale for the placement of the covering mask, the substitute face?

For Lévi-Strauss, the face is the location of the "socialising" functions. For the psychologist Charlotte Wolff, the face has primacy over the rest of the body because "four of the five senses are concentrated in the face—seeing, hearing, smelling, and tasting—which makes the head the region *par excellence* of emotional expression." Wolff also believes that the single human face contains within it two seemingly disparate elements: "The face can be considered as the mirror of the two poles of the inner life: primary emotion and lucid intelligence."[22]

The novelist Robert Brechon writes that "the face is obscene. More naked than the naked body because the expression and the eyes betray the soul. Man is caught in the trap of his own face, but at the same time he wears it like a mask of the image that he thinks he is. One can be ashamed of one's face more than of one's body because one is responsible for it; it has meaning."[23]

If these feelings and beliefs about one's own face exist, then what effect does the confrontation with someone else's face have on us? The French philosopher Max Picard, in his study *The Human Face,* answers this question: "He who looks upon a human face is moved to the very core of his being; his emotions, his understanding, his will are affected, and even to the very depths of him, where his emotions, intelligence and will coexist in that dark formlessness which we call presentiment or foreboding, he feels the face which he looks upon. His whole being is plowed up."[24]

From a different perspective but with a similar awareness, Lévi-Strauss infers a possible motivation for masks and masking: "It is by reason of the face and by the face that man communicates with man. It is by disguising or transforming his face that he interrupts that communication, or diverts it to other ends."[25] It is Bachelard, however, who makes an additional and shocking allegation about our observation of the face of another human being: "Whenever we want to read a person's face, we tacitly accept that face as a mask."[26] The art critic E. H. Gombrich, in his article "The Mask and the Face," makes some observations that may help us understand Bachelard's assertion: "We generally do take in the [face as a]

mask before we notice the face. The mask here stands for the crude distinctions, the deviations from the norm which mark a person off from others. . . . For it is not really the perception of likeness for which we are originally programmed, but the noticing of unlikeness, the departure from the norm which stands out and sticks in the mind."[27]

We all know that a mask changes our perception of what a face is. But what perception about the face does a mask change? For Stefan Brecht, "a mask alters the face by reversing the relationship of universals to particular." He writes that "in the masked face, the false face, perceived as false, but even so as face, the extrojected individual we supply it with is imagined or perceived as individuation of universals. The mask carries its representational character into the face it becomes for us."[28]

The "boundary shifts" that change the face to mask to face in the observer's perception transform not only the mask wearer but also his audience. Tonkin writes that "the observer of Masks [masks of actions] is by no means passive, but a participator caught up in a drama through which he or she is sometimes actually changed."[29] As we have already noted in comments by Mead and Tonkin, not only wearers and audiences are transformed; events are changed as well. Roger Caillois, in his important study *Man, Play, and Games,* says that "the use of masks is supposed to reinvigorate, renew, and recharge both nature and society."[30]

As Henry Pernet cautions us, and as the Sorcerer illustrates so effectively, we need to be careful about overemphasizing the face alone. Instead, we should enlarge our notion of what constitutes a mask. Pernet writes: "The mask must . . . be considered from a larger perspective, so as to include the costume, the headdress, the possible accessories, as well as immaterial factors such as the behavior, the dance steps, and the songs or texts pertaining to the mask."[31] Therefore, when we speak of the *mask,* we need to remember that it presupposes a whole context of related movements, activities, and paraphernalia. It is not just a covering for the face.

Masks and Time

Masks are intimately connected with time. Eliade recognizes this truth:

The mask's capacity for existence on another time level perhaps explains its dual function: alienation of the personality (ritual and theater masks), and preservation of the personality (death masks and portraits). Both cases exemplify a reactivation of past time: primordial time in the case of ritual and spectacle masks; historic and personal time in the case of death masks and portraits. Primordial mythological time, reactualized by ritual and spectacle masks, can be *lived*, but only by means of changing the personality and becoming "other." On the other hand, death masks and portraits reactualize historical time, which is not only past but dead, for no one can relive the inner life of anyone else. In either case, the time implied by the mask is ecstatic time, removed from the here and now. Whatever its type, every mask proclaims the presence of some being who does not belong to the everyday world.[32]

For Eliade, then, the mask is an "instrument of ecstasy" that allows the wearer to transcend earthly time, "even when the mask is his own portrait."[33]

Masks and Power

Whatever the reasons proposed for masks and masking, writers would almost universally agree that the fundamental issue in masking is power—power over the individual wearing the mask and power over the viewers of the masked activity. N. Ross Crumrine, in his introduction to *The Power of Symbols*, defines masks as "power-generating, -concentrating, -transforming, and -exchanging objects."[34]

Masks and masking have offered both a means of defense and protection as well as a means of offense and intimidation. They have been, and still are, used in a variety of ritual activities: for initiation, healing, hunting, death rites, and fertility practices. These are, of course, not mutually exclusive activities. The actual prehistoric shaman that the Sorcerer may depict could have participated in any or all of these kinds of ceremonies.

Tonkin rightly suggests that the power of the mask for users and observers should be understood to reside not in the mask or in the wearer, but in the interstices between the masked performer and his audience. She writes, "The Mask [mask of action] takes meanings on itself and appears charged with Power because it is the focus of concentrated symbolism, whose associated meanings and emotions reverberate off one another. . . . A study of Masks suggests that we must see Power in relation to human imagining; Power is not just the unstructured, nor the absence of structure."[35] For Bachelard, this understanding must also include the powerful transactions occurring between the mask wearer and the mask itself: "Between the masked person and the mask there is a flux and reflux—two movements reverberating alternately in consciousness. The phenomenology of the mask gives us insights into this process of duplication in a person who wants to appear other than he is and ends up revealing himself in and through his dissimulation."[36]

Masks and Trance

Many writers have commented on the mask's power to possess the wearer, compelling him to action over which he has little if any control. In some traditions, the mask wearer claims to enter an ecstatic trance that dissolves the boundary between the Self and the Other, as the power he projects as residing in the mask takes over, transforming him into a visible manifestation of that power. For Caillois,

> the eruption of strange powers terrifies and captivates the individual [mask wearer]. He temporarily reincarnates, mimics, and identifies with these frightful powers and soon, maddened and delirious, really believes that he is the god as whom he disguised himself, cleverly or crudely in the beginning. . . . After the delirium and frenzy have subsided, the performer lapses to a state of dullness and exhaustion that leaves him only a confused, blurred memory of what has transpired.[37]

Elias Canetti, however, doubts this loss of self-consciousness. He claims that the mask wearer is always conscious of his duplicity:

> As long as he wears it he is two things, himself and the mask. The more often he has worn it and the better he knows it, the more of himself will flow into the figure it represents. But there is always one part of him which necessarily remains separate from it: the part that fears discovery, the part which knows that the terror he spreads is not his due. . . . He must manipulate it, remaining his everyday self, and at the same time, must change into it as a performer. While he wears the mask he is thus two people and must remain two during the whole of his performance.[38]

Is Caillois right, or is Canetti? Does the wearer lose total consciousness of Self, or is there "always one part of him which necessarily remains separate"? How should we understand the phenomenon of Jake?

Jake was a character that appeared in a workshop session, during the exercise "The Interview." He was such a powerful manifestation that those of us who were present have never forgotten him. Greg, the actor in whom Jake became embodied, when quizzed afterward, had no idea where this personage came from. During the exercise Jake appeared to be in charge. No one was aware of Greg's secret presence behind the mask making the situation happen. My interview with Greg afterward demonstrated that Greg also knew that Jake was in charge.

This is not at all an unusual occurrence in mask improvisation training or in people's experiences with masks. In every workshop that I have conducted, whether with actors, art teachers, therapists, or others, at least one person (usually more than one) has a compelling experience with a mask. Of course, not everyone embodies a personage with such an intense personal history as Jake's. If the participant can relax, let go of himself (his Self), and let the mask take over, then a whole life history of the character will flow from the actor's unconscious during the prompting of an exercise like "The Interview."

A corroboration of this potential effect of a mask on a sensitive wearer is found in the memoirs of the German writer Carl Zuckmayer. He describes the astonishing effect an artist friend had on his observers when he donned a mask.

> But suddenly he put the mask on, tying it behind his ears with the leather thongs attached to the sides—and instantly everyone fell silent. For a while his head swayed; we saw only the mask and his expressive hands poking out of his shirt sleeves, looking strangely naked. Suddenly he said: "Oh, I'm terribly sad. There's nothing I can do about it. I have to weep. I am filled with sorrow. I could weep for the rest of my life." He spoke almost in a monotone. But we all saw the mask weeping. He went on like that for a while. He told a story about the death of his sweetheart. He defended himself in a dialogue with an invisible person who held him guilty of that death. He admitted it. "Yes, I know, it is my fault, I caused it," and the mask took on an expression of utter despair, of terrible incurable unhappiness. Then he suddenly gave an embarrassed chuckle and removed the mask. But he himself seemed to have no face. His eyes, ordinarily a radiant blue with a sly twinkle in them, were as if switched off and not looking at anyone. "You're wonderful," I said, handing him a glass of wine. "Go on." He drained it, leaned back, replaced the mask, and suddenly—without laughing, without uttering a sound—slapped his thigh. He merely drew in his breath like someone so amused that he is choked with laughter. Then, "Fellows," he gasped, "what a joke!" And I could swear, like everyone else at the table, that the mask grinned, that laughter spread across its whole face.

> It went on that way for a long time. He played out scenes of comedy, happiness, lies, avarice, anger, uncompromising hatred, distrust, and fear with the most economical movements of his hands—and with the mask—always accompanied only by perfectly simple cue-like words. When he leaned his head to the side and suddenly said, "Now I'm angry!"—with an almost childlike intonation like he sometimes used for Franz Moor—it was frightening. When he laughed or played the blockhead, it made us laugh till our sides ached. It was like being at a hypnotic or magical seance. At those times I blocked out the mask.[39]

How are we to understand what was happening here? Was the artist in some sort of autohypnotic trance state, one that provides proof of "past life" experience or an authentication of the idea that we are all secretly "multiple personalities"? I don't know. I only know that these kinds of things happen with masks, and that such an event can be a powerful tool in the training of an actor.

What is significant is that this process of transformation seems to follow a definite pathway into and out of the actor's unconscious. It starts with the external object of the mask, a physical image that activates a strong answering reflection in the actor's imagination. This reflected image seems to be a conflation of embryonic mental, emotional, and physical states and actions. Once such a conflation occurs, a character has become manifest in the actor. This character will exhibit a particular behavioral pattern in the present and will "remember" his life story.

The cultural historian Walter Otto, in his pioneering investigation into the ecstatic worship of the ancient Greek god Dionysus, discerned what he called a "primal phenomenon of duality," a correspondence between the mask wearer's experience and the believer's encounter of Dionysus. "The wearer of the mask is seized by the sublimity and dignity of those who are no more," wrote Otto. "He is himself and yet someone else. Madness has touched him—something of the mystery of the mad god, something of the spirit of the dual being who lives in the mask and whose most recent descendant is the actor."[40]

In the British theatre a phrase refers either to the actor's loss of consciousness of Self onstage or to the awareness that the actor is in a heightened state during the performance and his conscious self is not in control. In both cases, though, all the lines and stage business are correctly and effectively performed. This state is called the moment when "the god descends."[41]

Perhaps this question of whether the masker loses awareness of his Self and goes into an ecstatic trance state or is always conscious of himself should be understood not through a bipolar "either/or" construct but as an experience of convergence—a "both/and" duality of divided consciousness. Throughout this book, we will consider the possible psychophysical relationships between the actor and his role, between the face and the mask.

Masks in Western Theatre

Numerous theatrical performances around the world have used, and still use, masks. Many of these performances retain strong vestiges of their ritualist origins. One has only to think of Japanese Noh, Indian Krishnattam, Yoruban Gelede Masquerades, and Kwakiutl Winter Dances, among others. Here, though, we will focus on the use of masks in Western theatre, because what has happened in the European cultural tradition has most influenced attitudes and beliefs about masks in the West.

Egyptian and Near Eastern Sources of Western Theatre

Many people now speculate about the beginnings of Western culture, which has traditionally been placed in ancient Greece. But what about the Babylonian, African, Egyptian, Minoan, and Mycenaen cultures that preceded it? How much influence did they have on the formation of Greek civilization and culture, including theatre? Written archeological records describe yearly ritual dramas in the ancient Hittite, Canaanite, and Egyptian cultures. Especially interesting is an Egyptian drama focused on the death and resurrection of Osiris.[1] The Egyptian pantheon, particularly, is peopled with human figures wearing animal masks, which are usually described as animal-headed gods. There are dancing floors and other performance spaces at Minoan sites on Crete, where celebrants masked as bulls invoked the mythological story of the Labyrinth, occupied, so Minoan mythology tells us, by the Minotaur—a man with the head of a bull. These and other precursors of ancient Greek culture may well have influenced its development.

Masks in the Ancient Greek and Roman Theatre

For the ancient Greeks, the god of theatre was Dionysus—the "god of the mask."[2] Initiation into the mysteries of Dionysus was a passage through ecstatic possession and transformation into the mysteries of identity—appearance and reality, death and rebirth. This god with many faces was also the "god of confrontation" whose entranced eyes "cannot be avoided."[3] In this role Dionysus confronted paradoxes, uniting opposites by promoting the experience of a double consciousness.

It is not surprising, then, that Dionysus is the god of the theatre, where the experience of transformation and double consciousness is a requisite for both the actors and the audience. Nor is it surprising that masks, the most paradoxical and symbolic of handmade objects, are the emblems for both Dio-

9

nysus and the theatre. What Stefan Brecht says about the effect of a mask on the viewer is also true about the effect of theatre on its audience: we are in "the grip of an illusion we know to be an illusion and yet can't dispel."[4]

The presence of masks in ancient Greek theatrical performance, with their reactivation of ancestors, makes palpable the ecstatic time that Mircea Eliade noted. Many cultural historians have puzzled over the relationship between the origins of Greek tragedy and rituals for the dead. So what we can detect in the ritual cum civic performances in the Theatre of Dionysus at the foot of the Acropolis is a fusion of more than one religious tradition, not the enactment of one alone.

The masks in the ancient Greek theatre appear to have inspired the performer, transforming him into characters that produced powerful impressions on his audiences. We know, as the classicist F. B. Jevons emphatically declared, that it would have been unthinkable for a Greek actor to perform without a mask: "To wear a mask is to act."[5]

We also know that playwrights identified each character in their plays, whether these were mythological or historical, as a *prosopon* (mask). This term, though, is somewhat ambiguous in ancient Greek, implying more than a specific character with a particular personality and behavior. As A. David Napier notes, "The word *prosopon* could mean the mask, the dramatic part, the person, and the face."[6] Henry Pernet, in his study of masks in preliterate cultures, supplies some additional insights: "In most cases the mask does not simply represent a particular figure; it contextualizes it as well. That is, it evokes the paradigmatic events in which the figure in question has played a role." Pernet goes on to note that "the use of masks can be derived as much from the will to enact certain events as from the desire to portray certain figures." He says that "the mask is thus closely linked to the founding events of the society and its institutions, as well as to its values. It is, therefore, easy to understand why among many peoples the mask is linked to conservative forces and plays an important role in social control, assuming even a quasi-police function."[7]

The first part of Pernet's statement is relevant to the ancient Greek theatre, but the conclusion he draws from his observation does not seem to apply to the function of the masks in Greek theatre, although it might apply to the masked rituals out of which the theatrical performances may have evolved. With the use of masks for theatrical performance in ancient Greece, masks and masking activity were employed more for "service" to the community than for "liberation" of the individual wearer.[8] We know next to nothing about the acting practices of ancient Greek actors, but it seems reasonable to assume that they could not have gone into ecstatic trance states to perform the carefully constructed and choreographed plays.

Perhaps this is one reason for the modern criticism that the theatrical performances had "nothing to do with Dionysus."[9]

I do not mean to imply that the ancient actor did not identify with his characters and become caught up in his roles. Many artistic representations have survived from ancient times, showing actors contemplating their masks before performance. As we shall see, this is a well-known method for "getting into character" when working with masks.[10]

In the ancient Greek theatre, something fundamental began to shift in Greek consciousness with regard to perceptions about masks and masking. This shift concerned the mystery and power of masks. Masks in the Greek theatre were involved in a process of demystification and therefore a loss of power, because they were losing, or had lost, their ability to instill fear. The story that has come down to us from an ancient biography about the reactions of audience members when the masked Furies appeared in Aeschylus's *Eumenides* (i.e., "children died" and "women suffered miscarriage") probably reflects more hype than history, although it may also bespeak a residue of power that could still be activated in the audience's psyche in the first half of the fifth century B.C.E., when the *Oresteia* was performed.[11] But by the latter half of that century, masks in theatre were becoming, or had already become, aesthetic objects. This does not mean that they had no potency. Their power, as Roger Caillois admits, may be "held in check, on a rein, but it is not gone." It is just that masks were no longer so useful for inspiring genuine "intimidation and political power."[12]

The fifth-century Greeks were at one of those transitional points in history that Caillois discusses in *The Mask of Medusa*, his investigation of the mask in human society. His hypothesis that "peoples belong to history and civilization the moment they give up the mask, when they reject it as a vehicle of personal or collective panic and strip it of its political function," may carry too many suggestions of a European ethnocentric viewpoint. Nevertheless, it does describe a transitional phase when a loss of faith in a traditional identity and belief system occurred, as others came to the fore.[13]

If this hypothesis has merit, then the playwright's obligation as a devotee of Dionysus was to re-create for the audience an experiential confrontation with the god's "double truths" by means other than the mere presence of masked actors on the stage. According to Renate Schlesier, the playwright must express through the masks and through the embodiment of the text in performance "two very different kinds of 'masks,' and . . . two different modes of looking at them."[14] It is through the audience's experience of dual consciousness that the ironic "other" mask is to be seen through the frame of the first. Schlesier continues:

Tragedy, then, I think, presents both the concept of truth and the mask in a different way. There is not one single truth but two (or even more) truths that are simultaneously operative and equally valid. . . . One kind of mask, the one that is only verbally applied, is indeed not a mask that can actually be touched or that can be grasped by an ordinary kind of looking. It is evoked by means of words, which are able to engender a sight or vision that emerges as a nonmaterial image before the eyes of the spectators. . . . The described evocation of complementary "imaginary" masks is, I believe, a procedure consciously inflicted by the tragedians upon the spectators in order to lead them to a distinctive, and to some extent religious, experience.[15]

For the ancient Greeks, as for other ancient societies, the theatrical event was itself understood as a mask.

The use of masks in the festival performances in the Theatre of Dionysus may have had ideational and emotional resonances that are impossible for us to comprehend fully. They may also have been, as Schlesier posits, doubles and signifiers, along with the chosen text, of more important imaginary "masks" created through performance. Did the use of Homeric heroes and Theban "others" in the plays allow the ancient Greek audience to "see through" the mirror of performance into a reflexive recognition of parallel events? Indeed, it could be argued that the purpose of the second "imaginary" mask was to *unmask,* or to reveal the truth behind the first. If so, these playwrights would only be the first in a long line of writers in difficult political circumstances to use past events to comment on the present, recognizing that time as experienced onstage in performance is always "now."

During the course of the enormous changes in political, philosophic, and cultural realities from the fifth century B.C.E. to the fourth, the tragic theatre experienced a shift away from the actors' use of more realistic human-scale masks to the outsized and grotesque masks of the Hellenistic period. At the same time, the comic theatre abandoned the increasingly dangerous caricature masks of actual living individuals in favor of innocuous stereotypes sanitized of political import. A corresponding shift also occurred, away from the importance of the mask as an initiator of Dionysian experience to the importance of the actor and his ability to play many roles.

Masks were used in theatrical performances throughout the rest of the ancient Greek and Roman periods (with a hiatus of sorts in Roman practice until the Greek model for theatre became the norm). The Latin word for mask, *persona,* referred "not only (and some suggest even secondarily) [to] a mask used by a player, [but] could also refer to one who plays a part or to characters acted."[16] The Roman masks still signified character,

but they had become identified, if Pollux's catalog of masks (second century C.E.) is any indicator, as an assortment of stock character types useful for any Roman situational comedy or hyperbolic tragedy.

Masks and the Drama of the Christian Church

With the political triumph of the Christian Church over the Roman Empire in the fourth century C.E., dramatic activities, and especially masks, were discouraged if not forbidden in the West under the jurisdiction of the Roman Church. Masks were seen as associated with pagan practices and polytheism and therefore challenging to the Christian churches' monotheistic theological position about the essential natures of the One God and of humankind.[17] Masks and masking activities did not disappear, however, as the many invectives against them during the next several centuries testify.

Masks did not begin to reappear in Western dramatic performance until after the ninth century, with the rebirth of drama within the Church itself. By the time that the Church officially encouraged the great medieval mystery play cycles in the fourteenth century, masks had already regained some of their vitality in secular mummings and disguisings (in which animal masks associated with pre-Christian rituals for the dead were popular).[18] But interestingly enough, in the mystery plays themselves, masks were employed primarily for representations of devils—disguised evil that could take many shapes.

Masks in the Renaissance Theatre

It was during another major transitional phase in Western culture, the Renaissance in sixteenth-century Italy, that a form of masked theatre developed from indigenous folk and classical roots. This was the commedia dell'arte, the "theatre of the professional artists," as compared with that of amateur performers in the universities. The hallmark of this new theatre was the use of masks for some characters, women performers in the troupes, and the actors' abilities to improvise dialogue and business within the confines of a set scenario. One characteristic of the commedia dell'arte that allowed this freedom to improvise was that all the roles were based on stock types, the masked characters of Pantalone, the Dottore, Arlecchino, Brighella, Pulcinella, and Capitano being the most representative.

The Italian word *maschera* (mask) refers not only to those characters actually masked but also to a fixed role, personality, vocal quality, movement, and behavior established for each of the characters. As Bari Rolfe says, "The miser is always miserly, the lovers are always in love, and the doctor is always pedantic. You see, there are no variations among that permitted."[19]

The iconography of the masks worn by the masked characters—played only by men, incidentally—suggested animal identifications and correspondences:

The mask of Capitano is the result of a coupling between a beagle and a Neapolitan mastiff that bears the face of a man. . . .

Another famous mask, the classical Arlecchino, is part-cat, part-monkey, and in some cases is referred to as the "Arlecchino-Gatto," or Cat-Harlequin. The actor who wears this mask must be able to leap gracefully through the air and reveal the utmost agility in his arms and legs as he saunters about the stage.

The turkey and cock give rise to Pantalone, not to mention Brighella, who is half-dog and half-cat, or the Dottore, who . . . is derived from a pig. These are all courtyard animals, from the lower court, where the servants and others eked out a precarious living doing odd jobs for the court.[20]

The actual masks used in the commedia dell'arte are made of leather, and without exception, they are partial; that is, they do not cover the whole face of the actor as did the ancient Greek and Roman theatre masks. We do not know who devised this type of mask, but certainly these partial coverings allow greater freedom for the mouth and jaw, permitting the significant intake of air necessary for the verbal and physical agility required for playing these energetic roles. The physical requirements of active characters may have inspired the creation of the partial mask, but the fixed but somewhat flexible leather mask juxtaposed with the mobile exposed face made audiences constantly aware of the simultaneous "interface" between the human and the mask, the human and the animal, the living and the dead.

Troupes of Italian commedia dell'arte performers became all the rage at courts and in marketplaces throughout Europe from the late sixteenth to the eighteenth century. These actors traveled as far north as Scandinavia and Russia. Their brilliance and attraction were so great that they influenced professional playwrights such as Shakespeare in England, Lope de Vega in Spain, and Molière in France. Molière himself at one point in his career even sought training in acting from a famous commedia actor. And many of Molière's major characters, such as Harpagon, the Miser, are rooted in commedia stock figures. Themes of masking and unmasking, illusion and reality, permeate the plays of this age.

During the decline in popularity of the commedia dell'arte in the eighteenth century, the Venetian playwright Carlo Goldoni borrowed the plots of commedia plays, removed the more objectionable and obscene material—as well as the opportunities for potentially uncontrolled and disruptive improvisation—and transformed commedia into a literary and genteel product for more refined tastes. It is Goldoni who has the dubious distinction of being the one who banished masks from the legitimate stages of the Western theatrical world.[21]

Masks in the Modern Western Theatre at the Turn of the Century

Not until the latter half of the nineteenth century did the Western world rediscover the mask as more than a decorative ornament. With its rebirth in the modern world, the mask became so ubiquitous in the fine and performing arts that detailing its history and significance here would become an end in itself. Other publications about the history of the mask in the modern theatre explore this subject, so my purpose will be to present a brief outline of the modern theatre's experiments with the mask in performance and to explore how it came to be utilized in actor training programs.[22]

Because of renewed interest in the mask, a revival of interest occurred in earlier forms of Western theatre that employed masks, such as ancient Greek drama and the commedia dell'arte, and in Asian theatrical forms, particularly Japanese Noh drama. Playwrights, directors, and designers also attempted to create new forms of masked theatre bearing little or no relationship to earlier models.

Whatever their inclination, the recovery of the old or the discovery of the new, theatre artists who adopted the mask struggled to break out of the stranglehold of the staging and acting requirements decreed by adherents of realism and naturalism. They wanted to "retheatricalize the theatre," and the mask became symbolic of this antirealist movement. Such artists saw in the mask a new and profound metaphor for the composition of the human psyche and the nature of societal relationships.

In 1872 Friedrich Nietzsche published *The Birth of Tragedy,* a work infused with the concept of masking—masks of Apollonian order and control and masks of Dionysian chaos and release. He declared that tragedy was born out of a conjunction of these two forces but appeared especially when the Dionysian spirit assumed the mask of Apollo.[23] In this work, Nietzsche was not only concerned with writing dramatic criticism but also with propounding a view of the nature of humankind. Both in *The Birth of Tragedy* and a later work, *Beyond Good and Evil* (1886), Nietzsche's "insistence upon looking behind physical phenomena for more profound truth" and his "conception of the Dionysian and Apollonian forces within human beings foreshadows Freud's conception of the human psyche."[24] Both Nietzsche and Freud, who published *The Interpretation of Dreams* in 1900, sought to demonstrate that a human being's outer appearance and behavior and inner needs and longings were not necessarily one and the same—that the outer aspect was frequently a mask behind which the true being lay hidden.

The work and writings of Carl Jung gave this concept further credence. With the publication of *Psychology of the Unconscious* in 1912, Jung began to revise Freud's concept of the unconscious. Jung perceived another part of the human psyche that Freud had failed to explore. He called this the collective unconscious. Jung claimed that an individual's collective unconscious revealed, and readily responded to, archetypal images and patterns of experience.[25] In the process of defining what he meant by the relationship between the individual and the collective unconscious, Jung employed the ancient Latin word for mask, *persona*.

> This arbitrary segment of collective psyche—often fashioned with considerable pains—I have called the *persona*. The term *persona* is really a very appropriate expression for this, for originally it meant the mask once worn by actors to indicate the role they played. . . . It is, as its name implies, only a mask of the collective psyche, a mask that feigns individuality, making others and oneself believe that one is individual, whereas one is simply acting a role through which the collective psyche speaks.
>
> When we analyze the persona we strip off the mask, and discover that what seemed to be individual is at bottom collective; in other words, that the persona was only a mask of the collective psyche. Fundamentally the persona is nothing real: it is a compromise between the individual and society as to what a man should appear to be.[26]

In *Beneath the Mask*, Christopher F. Monte's text on theories of personality employing the metaphor of the mask, Monte states the standard interpretation of Jung's somewhat opaque and more complex statement: "The metaphor of the actor and his mask was used by Carl Jung . . . to indicate the public self of the individual, the image he presents to others, as contrasted with his feelings, cognitions, and interpretations of reality anchored in his private self."[27]

Both Freud and Jung emphasized the surface, but not superficial, nature of the mask behind which the more vulnerable and authentic individual was necessarily concealed (they believed) for personal protection and survival. For the performance critic Walter Sorell, Jung's concept means that "the formation and wearing of our mask is a general experience and a seeming necessity for life in our society. The *persona* is the mask which protects us not only against the other people behind their masks, but also against our own real self."[28]

These twentieth-century philosophical and psychological concepts encouraged the already active antirealist movement in the arts that was trying to express a reality not observable by objective scientific means. Antirealists would accomplish the manifestation of this reality not through the accumulation of surface details, like the realists, but through a direct presentation of the inner and subjective life of human beings.

Yet in contrast to the way in which the metaphor of the mask was being defined by philosophers and psychologists such as Nietzsche, Freud, and Jung, these antirealists had themselves revived and adopted the mask for precisely the opposite reasons. For these artists, the mask represented not a human being's outer condition but her inner state of mind. The mask was not to be considered a false face; it was the true face. The ancient theatrical device of the mask allowed these artists to abstract and externalize in concrete fashion this inner subconscious world. The antirealists rediscovered the old powers of the mask living still "in the blood and in the bones," only waiting to be revived.[29]

Masks from the Turn of the Century through World War I

Before and during World War I, artists and theatre practitioners all over Europe manifested tremendous interest in the mask. It is not my purpose here to detail the varied and exciting experiments of theatre artists such as Alfred Jarry, Edouard Autant, and Louise Lara in France; Stanisław Wyspiański in Poland; Vsevolod Meyerhold, Leonid Andreyev, and Nikolai Evreinov in Russia; William Butler Yeats in Ireland; and Oskar Schlemmer and Yvon Goll in Germany. These people, among others during this period, pursued the rebirth of the mask for the revitalization of the modern theatre. Much of their thinking about masks in theatre was influenced by the remnants of knowledge about commedia dell'arte performance and/or their research into traditional Asian masked dance-drama forms.

It was the English stage designer and theorist Edward Gordon Craig, in his influential theatre journal, *Mask*, who was most instrumental in spreading this gospel of the mask as the salvation of the theatre: "The mask must return to the stage to restore expression . . . the visible expression of the mind. . . . the inspiration which led men to use the mask in past ages is the same now as it ever was and will never die. It is this inspiration that we shall act under and in which we trust. Therefore let no one attempt to put this thing aside as being of the antique, or an eccentric explosion of 'L'Art Nouveau.' "[30]

In order to train artists for this theatre of the future, Craig opened the School for the Art of the Theatre at the Arena Goldoni in Florence, Italy, in 1913. In his curriculum, investigation and experimentation with the mask were to occur only in those sections dealing with the past and the development of future forms, as he thought that the "mask would be out of place in the modern theatre. It has to do with the Future."[31] Craig also attempted to recover and incorporate training in commedia dell'arte masks and improvisation techniques into his school's program of study. But 1913 was an inopportune time to initiate any new ventures. Craig's school was closed a year later with the outbreak of war.

During the war the German expressionist Yvon Goll wrote,

The mask is rigid, unique, and impressive. It is unchangeable, inescapable; it is Fate. Every man wears his mask, wears what the ancients called his guilt. Children are afraid of it and cry. Man, complacent and sober, should learn to cry again; the stage serves that purpose. And do not the greatest works of art, a Negro god or an Egyptian King, often appear to us as masks?

In the mask lies a law of the drama. Nonreality becomes fact. For a moment, proof is given that the most banal can be mysterious and "divine," and that herein lies Sublime Truth.[32]

The kinds of masks Goll advocated were not realistic, but mechanical and abstract—extensions of the human bodymind. "Therefore," he said, "the new drama must have recourse to all technological props which are contemporary equivalents of the ancient mask. Such props are, for instance, the phonograph, which masks the voice, the denatured masks and other accoutrements which proclaim the character in a crudely typifying manner: oversized ears, white eyes, stilts. These physiological exaggerations, which we, shapers of the new drama, do not consider exaggerations, have their equivalents in the inner hyperboles of the plot."[33]

So, during the second decade of the twentieth century, while horrible destruction was occurring on the battlefields of Europe, the mask emerged for many artists as a symbol of the dislocation between Western humanity's inner and outer worlds and of the anarchy occurring within each of those worlds.

Masks in the Interwar Period

If the mask was an important metaphor or symbol for artists before and during World War I, then after the war the image of the mask appeared everywhere, as if by spontaneous generation. Sorell, in his history of the mask in the twentieth century, *The Other Face,* reflects on the reasons for this enthusiasm for the mask:

After the First World War, when all the old values collapsed with the empires and traditional ideas, the search went on for the forgotten primitive forms and sources which were resurrected in basic modern dance, in the volcanic stammering cries of Expressionistic despair, in the Dadaistic fury of self-defiance, and in phantasmagoric Surrealism with its glazing of Freudian imagery. The mask returned, reflecting and revealing the savage instinct of man let loose again, the old demonic spirits in new clothing, the spirits man feared and tried to escape while falling prey to them. The mask triumphed in leading man back to its cruel sources and projecting its influence with a sophisticated gesture, often hiding as a mask behind non-masklike masks.[34]

Meyerhold continued his exploration of the mask in his actor training program, but he was forced to abandon his research under growing political pressure against experimentation in the arts. Craig never reopened his school. Schlemmer continued his research on masks at the Bauhaus in Germany until it too was closed by the Nazis. It was Schlemmer, along with Mary Wigman in Germany; Luigi Pirandello in Italy; Eugene O'Neill, Kenneth MacGowan, and W. T. Benda in the United States; and Jacques Copeau and Léon Chancerel in France, who were in the forefront of theatrical experiments with masks and masking concepts during the turbulent interval between World War I and World War II.

For these artists, the mask had become a more complex icon and no longer represented only the chaos of the internal world. The American playwright Eugene O'Neill proclaimed that modern drama was "an exercise in unmasking," and in his play *The Great God Brown* (1926), he tried to use the mask "as a means of dramatizing a transfer of personality from one man to another."[35]

The Italian playwright Luigi Pirandello, aware of relative truths and the fluidity of human identity that lead to the construction of simultaneous realities, extended the concept of masking to questions of seeming and being. He attempted to disrupt his audience's ability to tell the difference between illusion and reality in their experience of his plays. For Pirandello, though, as Sorell notes, "masks are not psychological or symbolic but philosophical devices. . . . [His] masks only suggest being masks."[36] The insights from the research that these artists and many others conducted concerning the significance of the mask—the effect of the mask on the performer and on the audience—are essential understandings in the use of the mask in actor training and performance. We will explore them more fully later.

By the mid-1930s interest in the mask for theatrical performance had declined sharply because of the tacit acceptance of realism as the "correct" form in both democratic and socialist countries. Only two major performance groups continued to explore mask drama on a continuing basis: Art et Action and Léon Chancerel's Comédiens Routiers. Masks on the stage had been explored and exploited in every conceivable manner and found wanting, except, perhaps, in their influence on Bertolt Brecht's "alienation" theories. The mask had been revived only to decline again before the onslaught of World War II.

Masks in the Theatre after World War II

It would be the 1950s before a significant renewal of interest in mask drama would again occur. This time it was sparked by Giorgio Strehler's production of *Arlecchino; or, The Servant of Two Masters* in Milan in 1951, a production of *The Caucasian Chalk Circle* by Bertolt Brecht's Berliner Ensemble in 1954, Tyrone Guthrie's *Oedipus the King* at Canada's Stratford Shakespearean Festival in 1954, and Jean-Louis Barrault's *Oresteia* (1955) and Jean Dasté's *Caucasian Chalk Circle* (1957) in Paris.

It was also during this period that Michel Saint-Denis, Jacques Copeau's son-in-law, would mandate mask improvisation training in the various actor training schools he founded both in Europe and the United States. And Jacques Lecoq would open his school in Paris, where a regimen of mask training was central to the program of study. This renewal of interest in the use of masks in theatre for performance percolated into an explosion of theatrical experiments in the 1960s and early 1970s, only to decline again until recently.

In this time of global change and transition, at the end of the twentieth century and the beginning of the twenty-first, the world is experiencing an identity crisis. Complex and sometimes paradoxical questions about individual and collective identity within a pluralistic society, informed by a threatening global political, economic, and media-driven hegemony, engage our attention. On all sides, and for all peoples, urban or rural, challenges to cherished beliefs and values are emerging. Napier observes, "Masks are, without a doubt, heresy to any sort of positivistic psychology, because they suggest a sensibility for multiplicity and for saltatory change. They also challenge our perceptions of what is ethical. How do we attribute intentions and responsibility to personages whose images of themselves literally shift from plane to plane, in and out of focus?"[37]

My primary concern in exploring the rebirth of the mask in the modern world has been to provide a brief context for the rediscovery of the mask for performance and the realization of its potential for actor training. As Eugenio Barba rightly claims, "The study of the performance practices of the past is essential. Theatre history is not just the reservoir of the past, it is also the reservoir of the new, a pool of knowledge that from time to time makes it possible for us to transcend the present."[38] The twentieth-century theatre artists mentioned, and many others less well known, recognized and reawakened the forces latent within the mask. They discovered that the mask contained a dynamic revelatory power to which their psychophysical and spiritual beings readily responded. For the most part, however, the theatrical experiments they conducted were solitary, scattered, and abortive, as there has been little interest in establishing an ongoing tradition of mask theatre in the West.

Only Jacques Copeau and his followers were able to conduct a serious investigation of the effects of the mask on the performer and to develop a teaching method through which the irresistible powers of the mask could be put into service, training young actors and inspiring new modes of performance.

In the first two chapters, we have surveyed a number of theories about the possible origins, purposes, and functions of masks and masking activities in human society. We have also surveyed the use of masks and their changing representation of outer and inner states of being in Western theatrical practice.

Masks engage us in a series of doubling encounters, flux and reflux. They attract us, pulling us toward them, and yet, at the same time, they distance us and repel us. They are engaged in making present a presence and making present an absence. The mask's fixity immerses us not only in a process of projection but also in a predestination. A mask may be a "conclusion," as Elias Canetti believes, but paradoxically, for Gaston Bachelard, it can also "help us to *face* the *future*."[39] Jean-Louis Barrault observes:

A mask confers upon a given expression the maximum of intensity together with an impression of absence. A mask expresses at the same time the maximum of life and the maximum of death; it partakes of the visible and of the invisible, of the apparent and absolute. The mask exteriorizes a deep aspect of life, and in so doing, it helps to rediscover instinct. This kind of simultaneous exteriorization of the inner and outer aspects of life, of the relative and of the absolute, of life and death, makes it possible to reach through incantation a better contact with the audience.[40]

Masks *are* necessary for our individual and collective survival. As this brief overview of the history of masks in Western theatre and culture has shown, new masks appear in times of psychic upheaval and transition, unmasking the power of the old "truths," only to retreat again once these "new truths" have been assimilated into the individual and social psyches. Then the cycle repeats itself as the "invisible" masks of these new truths themselves become rigid and inflexible while creating the illusion that any new masks are nonessential. As Claude Lévi-Strauss warns us, "A society which believes it has dispensed with masks can only be a society in which masks, more powerful than ever before, the better to deceive men, will themselves be masked."[41]

The mask's ability to conceal and reveal, to function in multiple capacities as frame, mirror, mediator, catalyst, and transformer both of individuals and of societies, commands our attention. We want to reappropriate this source of potency and prophecy for our theatre. As the psychologist Robert Landy acknowledges, "To let go of the mask, which points to the notion of two realities, is to let go of a profound conception of man."[42] Edward Sullivan writes:

> Whatever primitive man did learn through his use of symbol masks remains an integral part of human culture. . . . The residue remains in a state of availability in the subterranean reserves of the imagination and the passions. They serve their purpose in ways that bear the marks of the old nocturnal state, defying our logical analysis to a great extent. Now, they serve as background for discovery, for invention, and what concerns us here, for artistic creation. As we can discern in our modern masks, the insights of the past still live in the blood and in the bones, almost reluctant to serve a daylight master.[43]

Mask Improvisation for Actor Training and Performance is about regaining access to those residues of inspiration and empowerment for actor training and for theatrical performance.

3

Mask Improvisation

An Introduction

For the training of the actor, the knowledge and practice of performing masked in school exercises *seems to be indispensable. In depriving the apprentice actor of the use of his face, the mask requires him to perform with his entire body; to do away with making faces; to get outside himself; to deeply, physically and psychologically, understand the value of a position, of a gesture, of a step; to develop within himself the pure dramatic instinct: the sense of play, of character, of situation; to depart from photography in order to raise himself to the level of sculpture; to understand that* art interprets nature but does not copy her.

—*Léon Chancerel, "Notes personnelles"*

A Brief History of Mask Improvisation Training

The brilliant French critic, director, and teacher Jacques Copeau first employed mask improvisation training for the actor as an important and necessary procedure for his young students at the Ecole du Vieux-Colombier in Paris between 1920 and 1924. He discovered in the mask a compelling image for releasing the psychophysical being of his students and a potent agent for teaching them how to transform into their characters. Copeau was not interested in teaching actors to impose their own psychological needs and physical idiosyncracies onto every role they were to play, turning their performance into another presentation of themselves. He wanted, instead, to develop actors who would be willing to cultivate their imaginations, their minds, bodies, and emotions, to receive the psychophysical needs of their characters. It is from Copeau and his students, particularly Michel Saint-Denis (Copeau's nephew) and Jacques Lecoq (a student of Copeau's son-in-law, Jean Dasté), that all modern mask improvisation training has descended.

Copeau well understood that while a mask conceals the wearer, it also reveals the wearer. In this book we will fully explore these contrary and paradoxical effects of the mask on the actor, as they offer essential lessons in acting training. Mask improvisation training is not mime training, nor is it movement training per se. Mask improvisation is an actor training method that sensitizes and frees the imagination stored in the psychophysical being of the performer.

The Benefits of Mask Improvisation Training

This text has a double purpose: the first is to train actors to be more effective in their acting *without* masks. This was Copeau's original intention, and it is still the primary purpose of mask improvisation training taught in schools of theatre. The second purpose is to provide those performers interested in alternative performance styles, such as nonrealistic acting, solo performance of multiple roles, or mask theatre, with a foundational method for their experiments. Any explorations in those forms will benefit from the concepts and procedures detailed here. Indeed, performers in mask theatre must have prior training and experience in mask improvisation.[1]

This text does not focus on the psychological processes of the actor, as do most books on the realistic acting style. Instead, it emphasizes the physical presence and performance of the actor, since I believe that the actor must learn to communicate a truthful physical manifestation of the character's inner states of being through his external actions. It is *in* and *through*

Michel Saint-Denis as Knie, Suzanne Bing as Célestine, and Jean Dasté as M. César, in Jacques Copeau's L'Illusion, *1926. Bibliothèque de l'Arsenal, Paris. Courtesy of Marie-Hélène Dasté.*

his body that the actor communicates with his audience. The audience responds by living in and through the actor's body in return. As E. H. Gombrich realized, "We interpret and code the perception of our fellow creatures not so much in visual but in muscular terms."[2] Therefore, there should be no sense of separation between the emotional, the psychological, the verbal, the physical, and the mental life of the character as it is portrayed. All these aspects should be embodied in as well as enacted through the *one* bodymind of the actor (unless, of course, the character is itself playing a role or is lying, or the actor is purposefully creating an alienation effect). This unity of the character's bodymind requires that the actor's bodymind be transformed in order to reveal and release the life of the character. Ariane Mnouchkine, a French director and acting teacher, has said that the greatest law operating in theatre around the world is "the one that governs the mystery between inside and outside, between the state of being (or the feeling as [Louis] Jouvet would say) and the form."[3] She asks:

How do you give form to a passion? How do you exteriorize without falling into exteriority?

How can the autopsy of the body—I mean the heart—

be performed by the body? My slip of the tongue is revealing because the autopsy of the heart must be performed by the body. And the actor or actress worthy of the name is a kind of autopsy-er. His or her role is to show the inside.[4]

What resolves this mystery between the inside and the outside is the metamorphosis effected through the actor's identification with an image: the compelling image of the mask.

Before this transformation can be accomplished successfully, however, the actor must first discover how he manifests himself physically in space and what signals his body consciously or unconsciously sends about his own inner life, so he can learn to get himself out of the way. Clive Barker, a British acting trainer and author of *Theatre Games,* identifies the central problem facing young actors: "They are unable to transform themselves into other characters or perform effectively other functions, such as symbolic or metaphoric actions. They have not been 'broken down'—have not learned the systematic stripping away, which Laban considered essential, of all inauthentic action to find the core of the person from which all authentic action springs."[5]

This preliminary and necessary "breaking down" of the

actor as a precursor to learning methods of transformation is exactly what training in mask improvisation accomplishes. In addition, at the same time that the actor is brought to a profound awareness of his own psychophysical being through this training process, he is also made aware of the essential dynamic possibilities of space, line, color, rhythm, movement, gesture, sound, texture, and so on, as well as the rudiments of dramatic composition—all of which are indispensable to his final effectiveness as a performer. Mask improvisation training should be understood as a complement to, not a contradiction of, other actor training methods.

How to Use This Text: Instructions for the Teacher

This text is designed so that the concepts and techniques of mask improvisation are taught in a laboratory setting. That means that the only place that one can learn what this method has to teach is with others in a workshop. The participants must be there not only watching and analyzing each other—learning to see—but also experiencing what is happening *in* and *through* themselves. In a tangible way, once the actors have become sensitized to themselves and the potential life in the masks, the masks themselves become the participants' real teachers, and the comments of others only confirm or deny the lessons that the masks are teaching.

The complete implementation of the training techniques detailed in this text assumes that participants will spend approximately two to three hours in a workshop three or four times a week. Most of that time will be spent in improvisation, much of it in silence. Of course, there should be time for discussing and evaluating the discoveries made in the training process, but always *after* the exercises and improvisations are completed. Never discuss the purpose or expected results of an exercise beforehand, or you will put the student in the analytic mode instead of the intuitive mode for the exercises that follow.

If you are going to incorporate mask-making as part of the workshop, then time must be set aside for lecture and demonstrations on these techniques and procedures as well as actual mask construction. Instructions for the design and construction of masks for this course are included in Appendix A. This book also contains a series of recommended assignments for the students to complete outside the workshop hours.

The ideal training program would devote one workshop series (in an educational environment, a semester or term) to the Neutral Mask and another to the Character Masks. This text contains enough material for a complete training program. But perhaps you want to concentrate only on the Neutral Mask. Or perhaps you wish to devote time only to the Character Masks (Beginning Character, Life, Totem, Found Object, and Complex Character Masks). Or maybe you need to train actors in preparation for a masked theatre performance. Or maybe you, as a performer, want to explore an alternative performance style—mask improvisation illuminates the Brechtian approach—or to create a new theatrical form. The text can be used in a variety of ways, according to your needs. Therefore, before you begin, it would be wise to review the whole text, note the important lessons and their sequence, and then choose what is important for your situation.

If you have the opportunity to offer only one course in mask improvisation, as in many school situations, then you can incorporate both the Neutral Mask and the Character Masks in the same program of study. Although this scheme ensures some distinct losses, some definite advantages can be gleaned from such an approach. In a combined course you can integrate the Neutral and Character Mask exercises, playing them off each other in a way impossible in a separate workshop setup. This integrated approach teaches the participants, in a most provocative and lasting fashion, that the work in the Neutral Mask always underlies the work in the Character Masks—and, in fact, all performance work, with or without masks.

The integrated training begins with the Neutral Mask—in many ways the most difficult mask. As you move on to the other masks, always reserve time for continuing improvisations in the Neutral Mask, since this work forms the foundation for all the later explorations. This text presents the Neutral Mask and the Character Masks separately, as if the two types of work are being taught in separate courses of study. I have chosen this approach because many teachers will want to teach mask improvisation this way, and because this format offers greater clarity than combining the two types of mask work.

During this intensive workshop course, students improvise in a variety of masks, such as the Neutral, Beginning Character, Life, Totem, Found Object, and Complex Character Masks. Each mask becomes in turn the basis for a new area of exploration, as each type of mask evokes different responses, teaches new concepts and techniques, and challenges the students in new ways. This does not mean, though, that the class must improvise in all the masks, or do them in sequence, to gain the benefit of what mask improvisation has to teach. You can examine the training for each type of the mask and apply its techniques and lessons to whichever mask you are using.

To experience the full training program as detailed in this text, you will need six different types of masks. Having a mask sculptor provide you with the sets of masks that you need would be the best solution to this problem. If a mask sculptor is not available in your area or if your budget for this workshop is limited, these requirements may seem like insurmountable obstacles, but never fear. Templates for the Neutral and Beginning Character Masks are provided in Appendix B. The support forms for the Beginning Character Masks can function as the Neutral Mask. Make sure that you copy them onto a buff, tan, or off-white paper so that you do not work with white Neutral Masks. If there is enough preparation time before the course or during it, then either you or the participants can provide the rest of the masks needed. The assignment for participants to sculpt and construct some of their own masks for use in the course can be a very important part of their learning experience about masks. Either the Totem Masks or the Complex Character Masks, or both, can be sculpted by the participants. The Life Masks are made from casts of the participants' own faces. The Found Object Masks can be provided either by the participants or the teacher.

Be forewarned! Mask design, sculpting, and construction is enormously time-consuming and should be done outside the scheduled workshop hours. If mask-making is to be incorporated into the program of study, then very early in the sessions, make a plaster cast of each participant's face to serve as a negative mold for the Life Mask and as the mold for pouring the plaster form that functions as a positive mold on which to sculpt the final Character Masks (see Appendix A).

Personal Note. This text should be considered as a *guide* to your work. There are many principles and procedures described, sometimes in great detail, but they are not meant, finally, to be prescriptive! I have tried to give the reader the benefit of my perceptions about working with masks in improvisation and performance and working with students in masks. But I have discovered that every time I use my prior description of an exercise as "the right way," I want to adapt it to meet the immediate situation. My best advice is to use the text as authoritative the first time through, and afterward only as a resource for your own explorations. Any "truths" in the text will prove themselves in your own creative improvisation!

Establishing the Working Atmosphere

The nature of the experiential workshop in mask improvisation may be quite different from anything students have experienced in the past, but it is actually quite typical of acting and improvisation courses. Some clarification of the roles and relationships in the workshop should be made, though, so that everyone understands the expectations and responsibilities.

The Role of the Participant-Student. It should be evident by now that each student must enter this study as an "explorer"—a self-motivated participant, eager to learn all that this journey into unchartered territory has to teach him about himself and the craft and art of performing.

If the student is a person who expects a teacher to tell him how to do an exercise or improvisation so that he will not risk failure or embarrassment, then this course of study is not for him. The teaching method expects the student to discover that he has the imaginative resources within himself to accomplish the tasks. If, on the other hand, the student is a person willing to experience new ways of doing things, even if that means abandoning some previously held concepts and self-images along the way, then this workshop will help him grow into a more imaginative, flexible, and effective performer. As one of my former students said to a prospective participant who was somewhat anxious about the workshop, "There are no mistakes you can make. You only learn more about yourself."

Participation in the workshop requires commitment and discipline, because what is happening *in* and *through* the participant is the primary subject matter of the course. The participant has to be present in the studio, undergoing the training experiences watched by the experienced eye of the observer-teacher, in order to learn what this course has to teach. Reading the text will only give him "head" knowledge, which is practically worthless for his growth as a performer. This text alone cannot give him the intimate, subjective experience and, therefore, personal understanding. He must be willing to venture into unknown territory. As the poet Theodore Roethke suggests, "I learn by going where I have to go."[6] As Josette Féral realized from her workshop in masks with Ariane Mnouchkine,

> During the course of the workshop it was shown that the mask is essential for training the actor because it does not allow lies and it uncovers all the weaknesses of the actor: lack of imagination, knowing how to act more than how to be, lack of presence, lack of listening power, etc. By its very nature, the mask uncovers all complacencies, all weaknesses. It goes against the actor who doesn't enter it and uses it to hide herself. Inversely, it can become sublime and bring forth theatrical moments of rare intensity. Behind the mask, thanks to it and its support, characters emerge and are led into extraordinary adventures.[7]

At times the work will be frustrating, as the participant-student discovers resistances, or blocks, within himself, as he discovers the limitations of his body and his blocked imagination. But these resistances are exactly what he needs to know about in order to work through them. As Shomit Mitter interprets it, "The explicitly somatic agency of masks permits the simultaneous operation of both literalism and otherness. Indeed, it is because the mask is so physically, and therefore unambiguously, 'other' (as that more multifarious phenomenon, the role, is not), that the actors can, when they wear masks, become themselves. It is the ability of masks completely, concretely and concurrently to induce and efface otherness that allows the actors to be themselves by discovering within themselves an otherness that they had not previously had reason to imagine."[8]

Training in mask improvisation is like creating and giving yourself your own Rorschach test. The participant is simultaneously the pattern and the interpreter. For "as the actor is identified with the mask, the self becomes an external attribute that can be studied."[9] At the same time, the work will be fun—exhilarating and rewarding. The success of the training depends on the participant's attitude and commitment to the process and to his own development.

The Role of the Observer-Teacher. In this course the teacher's role would be best described as that of guide, facilitator, or informed observer. In any journey into unknown territory, the guide is a person who has been there before and/or knows how to read the map and understands what to look for. The guide knows what the symbols on the map mean and can interpret them in order to get the explorer where he wants to go. As informed observer, the teacher functions as the external, objective, critical eye, sympathetic but encouraging the exploration to continue.

If you have taught mask improvisation before, then this text will give you new techniques and insights to make your teaching more effective. If you have not been involved in mask improvisation before, then this text will provide you with a detailed chart of those unexplored territories, and it is up to you to watch carefully for the markers along the route. You will also learn in the doing. This is where your own ability to develop skills as an informed observer come into play. (The Teacher Observation Notes, located throughout the text, will provide you with some guidance.) If you have training in acting, mime, movement, or dance (or in any of the other bodymind systems, such as Alexander, Lessac, Laban, Feldenkrais, Authentic Movement, and so on), then you will discover that you are already trained to observe many of the skills needed for this course.

At the same time as you operate as the "objective" informed observer, you will also be subjectively inside the work as well. The participant's work should not just be observed from the outside; it must be felt by you from the inside, through your empathy with the performer. The teacher is therefore an informed coparticipant, *subjectively knowing* when the work is honest and when it is not. In some mysterious way, as audience to the embodiment enacted before him, the teacher actually functions in the double capacity as a participant-observer, having both subjective and objective responses to the work.

The observer-teacher cannot make the journey of discovery for any one of the participants. Each student can only make the journey on his own with assistance and encouragement. Each participant is a unique individual and will progress at a personal rate; each will begin at a different starting place, and each will end at a different stopping place. The responsibility of the guide is to keep all the explorers on the trail, moving toward their own destinations. The effectiveness of this mask improvisation workshop depends on the student and teacher working together as participants and observers.[10]

The process is incremental and cumulative—later exercises build on earlier experience and understanding. The process of learning never finishes. Even the series of suggested workshop presentations should not be seen as finished products but as works in progress that are also part of the educational process.

The Workshop Process as an Ensemble Process. Participants in the group must feel that each member of the group is interested in and supportive of every other member. This does not mean that they have to love each other, but they must *trust* each other. Only if a basic level of trust is established will all the individuals in the group take risks that will allow each of them to learn and grow.

As is usual in this kind of workshop, the students will get to know each other well, observing each other's work in class closely and carefully. Everyone must be on the lookout to see that each one is asking the right questions about his work, taking risks with encouragement from each other when resistance and blockage occurs (as they surely will), and requesting appropriate feedback concerning what was observed about his progress or any recurrent habitual choices being made.

Workshop Size and Space Requirements. For the most effective learning environment, the size of the group in the workshop should be limited to ten to twelve participants at most. You will need a space with a sealed wooden floor large enough for the group to move in easily and not hurt themselves, as some of the work gets quite physically demanding. But your work space should not be a dance studio where the surface has to be carefully maintained and you cannot bring furniture onto it. For the Neutral Mask work, the space should be empty most of the time, except for chairs for the class to sit on. Occasionally a few chairs or stools will be needed in the work space. If tumbling mats are available, they can be very useful in some of the Neutral Mask identification exercises. For the Character Mask work, a variety of furniture and props are needed—anything interesting to sit on, at, or under—for the actors to use in their improvisations.

Mirrors are not used for the Neutral Mask work, but they are necessary for training with all the other masks. What is ideal for this workshop is a mirrored wall that can be curtained off when the mirrors are not needed. If this is impossible, then you can purchase some inexpensive door mirrors and set them up when needed. One of these door mirrors should be provided for every two to three participants in the workshop.

Unless the work space will be used exclusively for mask improvisation, so that the mirrors and furniture can be left in place, allow time at the beginning and end of the sessions to deal with the necessities of setting up and clearing the space. In my experience, it is a healthy "ritual" for the participants to sweep the floor and to set up and dismantle the space for the classroom sessions each day. It encourages them to value and take responsibility for their work space.

The Learning Objectives

The overall learning objectives for this workshop program in mask improvisation are twofold: to teach actors how to perform effectively *without* masks, and to teach actors how to perform effectively *with* masks.[11] The specific learning objectives can be described as follows:

1. to experience the mask as an agent for psychophysical release.
2. to discover how images (actual or fictional) can transform the total psychophysical being of the actor.
3. to acknowledge and release the cast of characters within.
4. to experience release from the tyranny of the analytic, the critical, and the logical in the flow of the improvisation.
5. to discover how to develop an appropriate psychophysical existence for each character created.
6. to discover that masks demand total commitment (physical, mental, emotional) to make them come alive.
7. to recognize and learn how to use the actor's divided consciousness.
8. to discover the external world (as well as the internal world) as rich with potential resources for the imaginative actor-creator.
9. to discover how to use the total bodymind economically and appropriately, and therefore effectively, to communicate.
10. to discover idiosyncrasies in personal movement and habitual movement patterns so that they can be employed or eliminated in developing a characterization.

11. to discover habitual psychological choices and patterns of behavior so that they will not be projected onto every characterization. (In other words, the actor learns how to get the Self out of the way.[12])
12. to discover and utilize the techniques of playing with and against the mask (text), thereby creating and developing mask and countermask, public face and private face.

In mask improvisation the performer will experience *dedoublement*—the "double vision" of a simultaneous subjective and objective perception that occurs in the chemistry of the creative process. The experience of this doubling both constructs and deconstructs the central paradoxes of the mask (which also seem to be at the heart of what acting is about and what theatre is about).

The mask conceals *and* reveals, controls *and* releases, depersonalizes *and* essentializes, the actor *and* the audience.

Workshop Requirements

Uniform. After the introductory session, all participants come to class dressed in black leotards and tights, or unitards. These are to be plain, solid black leotards and tights (no designer leotards, please!), so that the outlined "calligraphy of the body" of the actor can be clearly visible at all times.[13] Men will want to purchase a black dance belt or support briefs. No jewelry is to be worn during the workshop, and the hair is to be pulled back out of the face and off the neck, if necessary with a nonreflectant barrette or tie.

These severe restrictions help to strip away from the actor everything that is not essential to the work of the class and may draw attention away from the shape and movement of the participant's body. The actor's body must be the focus of our attention at all times—and through it our perception of the actor's identification with the image and manifestation of it in the body.

Many people are initially disturbed by the fact that they must wear leotards and tights as their work outfit for the workshop. Our self-image is inextricably tied up with our body image, and we are not used to exposing our bodies for close examination by others in a class situation. So it is important that the group be sensitive to this issue. What anxious participants will quickly learn is that everyone in the group has similar anxieties coming into the workshop, but after the first two sessions in leotards and tights the problem will evaporate.

Depending upon the composition of the workshop floor, participants may want to buy tights without feet or stirrup tights. If footed tights are bought, the student can undo the seam on the bottom of each foot, being careful not to damage the tights themselves, and roll up the tights around the ankles.

If the workshop is to take place in a black box-type studio, participants may want to consider purchasing similarly colored leotards and tights of a lighter neutral shade so that their bodies will be seen well in the space against the dark background. Whatever the case, it is wise to contact a local store and ask the manager to preorder the leotards and tights, so that the participants will have them when needed. Dance stores do not always stock the number of leotards and tights you will need for the participants in the workshop, and you don't want to wait while the outfits are special-ordered after you have started the course.

Journal. The primary function of a journal in the workshop is to serve as a record of the student's discoveries in the course: what the participant learned about himself physically, emotionally, and psychologically; what the participant learned about movement by observing others; and what he learned about the processes and techniques of bringing the masks to life. The journal is not a diary of how the participant *felt* about the work. A periodic review of the journal by the instructor allows an ongoing dialogue to be established between the teacher and each student. A loose-leaf notebook of standard size will be adequate for notes, worksheets, research assignments, and journal entries. It should always be available during a workshop session.

Sculpting Tools and Materials. If participants will be sculpting any of their masks, then see the list of supplies in Appendix A.

Assessment

The problems of evaluating the students' work in this course are the same as in any performance laboratory workshop: how frequently? how rigorously? how subjectively? Students must be given frequent feedback on their performance and progress in the course. It is also important that the students be engaged in the evaluation of their own work, as they are finally responsible for it. They must learn how to evaluate the effectiveness of their own work from the outside as well as to understand how it felt from the inside. If handled properly, students can also evaluate each other, an approach that will increase their learning experience. But the voice and eye of the experienced teacher, the informed observer, is crucial.

Observation and discussion questions are provided in the text after most of the exercises, to assist in prompting an awareness about the experience in the mask. These questions should be used sparingly during class time—only when the teacher believes a discussion would be useful for the class. The workshop session should not become focused on thinking instead of doing. The questions are best used, perhaps, to guide reflective comments in the journals after the day's workshop ends.

A series of specific individual presentations that should occur during the workshop are suggested in the text. These individual presentations function as assessment "markers," demonstrating whether the student has assimilated the lessons or not. The instructor should provide an in-depth evaluation of each student's work following these demonstrations.

The rigor of the feedback will depend on what the teacher (and the students) want to achieve in the course and what value is attached to process over product. Too rigorous, and you inhibit the student's willingness to risk; too lenient, and the workshop becomes an exercise in self-expression where anything goes. Find the proper balance between these two extremes that is right for your situation.

How subjective? The experienced observer's response should be seen as most valuable to the students' perceptions about their own work. (I have a vivid memory of sitting in on "crits" at the Drama Studio in London when a teacher responded to a student's unhappiness with her notes with this: "You are paying me a great deal of money to tell you these things. If you don't want to hear them, then you should leave the program!") An acting teacher has great responsibilities to the students to be fair and honest in his perceptions, but of course the feedback is always "as he sees it."

If equipment and resources are available, you can create a videotape portfolio for each student by videotaping each session and then editing each student's work onto a separate tape for review. But a simple stationary camera does not always capture the experience, and a series of editing and review sessions can take an enormous amount of time. An alternative approach would be to set aside one workshop session to videotape while repeating a number of the key exercises. Then the tape can be shown to the group for review and evaluation.

Some suggested general, but important, criteria for evaluation are the following:

1. A positive attitude and commitment to the work.
2. Willingness to risk ("nothing to gain and nothing to lose").[14]
3. Willingness to play.
4. Ability to allow the nonanalytic, nonlogical, and noncritical aspects of the bodymind to lead in the creative process.
5. Evidence of growth in the work during the workshop.
6. Ability to recognize and acknowledge strengths and weaknesses and demonstrated progress in problem areas. (It should be understood that later work in the course "carries more weight" than earlier work.)[15]

A STARTING CLUSTER EXERCISE: MASKS OR FACES?

OBJECTIVE: to reveal thoughts and feelings about "masks" and "faces."

PARTICIPANTS: full group.

INSTRUCTIONS: Take a piece of paper and write the word *mask* in the center of it. Then start writing other words around this central term, conveying what the word *mask* means to you. Draw a line connecting these satellite words back to the core word. If a new word sets off another association, then add that word to the previous one, again connecting it with a line. Try to make a distinction between those words that are derived from definitions or denotations and those that grow out of associations or connotations.

Create a "generic" cluster on a blackboard from the group's individual clusterings. Discuss what we mean by the word *mask* and what associations seem to be connected with it.

Now ask the group to repeat the cluster exercise using the word *face*.

Compare the meanings you have uncovered about the two words.

Supplemental Texts

Barba, Eugenio. *The Paper Canoe.* Trans. Richard Fowler. New York: Routledge, 1995.

Barba, Eugenio, and Nicola Savarese. *A Dictionary of Theatre Anthropology: The Secret Art of the Performer.* Trans. Richard Fowler. London: Routledge, 1991.

Herrigel, Eugen. *Zen in the Art of Archery.* New York: Vintage Books, 1971.

James, Thurston. *The Prop Builder's Mask-Making Handbook.* White Hall, Va.: Betterway Publications, 1990.

Landau, Terry. *About Faces.* New York: Doubleday, 1989.

"Mask and Metaphor: Role, Imagery, Disguise," *Parabola* 6, no. 3 (Aug. 1981). Special issue.

Minton, Sandra Cerny. *Body and Self: Partners in Movement.* Champaign, Ill.: Human Kinetics Books, 1989.

Moore, Carol-Lynne, and Kaoru Yamamoto. *Beyond Words.* New York: Gordon and Breach, 1988.

Nachmanovitch, Stephen. *Free Play: Improvisation in Life and Art.* Los Angeles: Jeremy P. Tarcher, 1990.

Sher, Antony. *Year of the King: An Actor's Diary and Sketchbook.* New York: Limelight Editions, 1992.

Getting Started

A Note on Warm-ups

Always begin the workshops with a series of warm-ups and exercises designed to instruct the participants in techniques for body relaxation and stretching of the different muscle groups. Lead these warm-ups for part of the course, and then put participants on their own, so that they are responsible for getting themselves warmed up and ready to work. Each participant should know what special warm-ups she needs to perform to prepare for the class. It is valuable for the teacher to warm up before each class too, as it helps clear the consciousness and focus concentration and also provides the students a good model.

Warm-up exercises can become boring and tedious if they are not done for the right reasons. If they are performed only to get to the work for the day, then they are a chore to get past. If you live in and into the exercise, then the warm-ups become engaging each time you do them, as you are always checking and testing your achievements in the present against the previous time.

When each person is working individually in a group warm-up, it is helpful for her to develop her own specific kinesthetic image context for the exercise. Visualize an animal stretching, for instance, or the accomplishment of some purpose or task for each stretch (e.g., pushing the wall away). In this way the participant warms up not only her body but her imagination as well.

Using taped music as background to some of the warm-up sessions can also be helpful. Try three minutes each of three very different kinds of music, sidecoaching the participants to work both individually and collectively. At first the students should move as the music suggests. Later, when the concept of the countermask is being explored, they can be coached to move in opposition to the music. Finally, of course, during a warm-up session they should move both with and against the music. At all times students should be sidecoached to explore levels, scale of movement, and leading with different parts of the body.

Basic Terminology and Techniques

Body memory (muscle memory). Edward S. Casey defines *body memory* as "an active immanence of the past in the body that informs present bodily actions in an efficacious, orienting, and regular manner."[1] Body memory occurs through the conscious and/or unconscious training that the body has received, and it seems not to depend upon imaging to be reactivated. For instance, once you have learned how to ride a bicycle, you do not need consciously to image how to do it each time before you ride again. Rehearsing the blocking or movement pattern of a show should be understood as actually training the actor's body memory. See *dark consciousness* and *mental rehearsal* below.

Bodymind. A term used for speaking holistically about the unity of the physical, the emotional, the mental, and the psychological within the individual.[2]

Bodyscan. To conduct a bodyscan is mentally to travel inside and outside the body to "see" and "feel" how the total body or individual body part is positioned, or where tension and relaxation are located.

Bright consciousness. Yuasa Yasuo uses this term to describe the conscious mind, the acts of thinking and willing. "The bright consciousness is reflective," he says. "It takes time to deliberate."[3]

Dark consciousness. Yuasa uses this term to describe the spontaneous and impulsive part of the bodymind that is trained by the "bright consciousness" to perform certain physical and mental behaviors until they become "second nature," allowing the doer to "act creatively and responsively without deliberation."[4]

Feel/feeling. At times these terms are used to refer to a tactile sensory experience (to feel the table). At other times they refer to an emotional state (to feel happy). There is yet a third way in which we use the word that is most important for our purposes in this course. We use the word *feeling* to suggest a "primal awareness taking place in the organism-as-a-whole," an awareness in which "meaning is felt and expressed without words, by the total gesture of the body."[5] Actors, directors, and choreographers use this bodymind sense of the word all the time when they say that a scene in rehearsal or performance "felt right."

Freeze. A sidecoaching instruction. When the students hear the command "Freeze!" they "freeze" in place, holding their position (but continuing to breathe, of course). They are then issued new instructions that will change the context of the improvisation in some way when it continues. *Freeze* will be used to end an improvisation and will be followed by the instructions "Close your eyes, relax, and come out of the mask."

Improvisation. The spontaneous and intuitive response to a set of conditions or instructions. For Viola Spolin, "true improvisation re-shapes and alters the student-actor through the act of improvising itself."[6]

Mask. A tangible object designed to cover the face in order to disguise it and transform the wearer.

Mental rehearsal (mental practice). This is an important technique to understand and employ for mask improvisation and all acting work. After a student has worked through the

details and sequence of an action, she uses a combination of visual and kinesthetic imagery to "rehearse" it in her bodymind without physically performing the action. Mental rehearsal is to be employed just before repeating the action or for rehearsal outside the workshop. Scientific studies show that a mental rehearsal actually prepares the body's muscles—as well as the total bodymind—to perform the action as imaged.

Mirroring. To consciously, or unconsciously, imitate someone else's behavior.

Sidecoaching. Any instructions given while the participant is in the process of improvising. Most of the time sidecoaching will be given to the participant as her character, not as herself. The intent of the sidecoaching is not to make the actor stop and think about what she is doing, thereby stepping outside of the action and analyzing it, but rather to have the character incorporate the additional instructions into what she is presently doing. This involves the actor in utilizing her divided consciousness (see chapter 5). Sidecoaching may also be directed at one individual in the group rather than the full group. In that case the sidecoaching instruction is preceded by the character's or participant's name (e.g., "Anne, you need to increase the size and impact of your physicalization. Make it bigger . . . bolder!").

Wipe away/erase. To switch the performer's focus or concentration from the image onto her breathing in order to dissolve the image.

Terminology and Techniques in Action

What is spontaneity? How do we recognize spontaneity when it happens? What is the difference between a planned or performed moment and a spontaneous moment? Can we *feel* the difference (as participant)? Can we *see* the difference (as observer)?

EXERCISE 1: THE FOLDING CHAIR

A chair presupposes an action: to sit. But here students will alter that expectation into others as they manipulate the object with their transforming imaginations.

OBJECTIVE: to discover the qualities of spontaneity.

PARTICIPANTS: one person at a time.

PREPARATION: Take a simple folding chair (one without a padded seat and back) and place it in the center of the space. The other students stand around it in a large circle.

INSTRUCTIONS: One volunteer at a time goes to the center and sees the chair in her imagination, not for what it is but for what it might become. Through her manipulation of the flexible structure of the chair, she transforms it into as many different useful objects as possible, each time demonstrating the new manifestation. The challenge is to see how many different imaginative uses she can find for the chair in thirty seconds.

TEACHER OBSERVATION NOTE: Once you have given these instructions in front of the whole group, the students' minds will start to play with the possibilities of the object. So you want to make sure that you get *beyond* the preplanning that the student has done before she goes in to do the exercise. To accomplish this goal, lengthen the time for improvisation (if the first few participants get thirty seconds, then later participants get forty-five seconds). Making the exercise a fun contest between participants helps to fuel the imagination and focus the concentration.

OBSERVATIONS/DISCUSSION: After a number of students have improvised for thirty seconds each, ask the group what they saw, felt, and experienced as observers with their body-minds.

1. (To observers:) Could you the tell the difference between the preplanned uses of the object and those transformations found spontaneously in the doing? If so, how were they different? (To participant:) What was the difference for you between the preplanned and the spontaneous moments?

a) *The preplanned usages.* The chair might be used in quite imaginative ways, but you realize that the imaging process has taken place *before* handling the chair. The focus is in the head of the actor on a series of predetermined images that she is performing.

b) *The usages planned during action.* You are very aware of the participant's mind being in the way. The actor is thinking, trying to come up with ideas about how the chair might be transformed into other uses rather than letting her imagination be transformed in the flow of the ongoing kinesthetic experience. The participant's concentration is on coming up with ideas rather than letting her mind play with images aroused by the visual, tactile, kinesthetic experience of the object. The participant is trying to make transformations happen.

c) *The spontaneous response usages.* These responses take place in the flow of the ongoing kinesthetic experience while the student is manipulating the object. An instantaneous response to an image "pops" into the consciousness from a "holographiclike" concentration on the total visual, tactile, kinesthetic experience of the object. The participant's transforming imagination is released, wide-open, and available—allowing transformations to happen. This is an "ah-ha!" in-the-moment experience.

d) A response can be planned or spontaneous, but the next image or usage of the chair is not a totally new transformation of the object but an *extension* of the previous image or usage (e.g., if the folding chair is seen as a tray, then placing something on or taking something off the tray is not a transformation of the tray into a new image, but an extension of the image already established).

e) A response can be planned or spontaneous, but you sense the body *performing* the image or usage on automatic pilot while the mind has already moved onward, anticipating, searching for, an image and/or trying to plan the next transformation. The mind is not living in the flow of the moment.

2. (To both participant and observers:) How does the *sense* of energy, flow, engagement, and so on change between a planned moment and a spontaneous moment? Does this sense change for both the participants and the observers?

3. Did observers experience the discovery moment of the new image and/or the transformation?

The truly spontaneous moment is an experience of *entrainment,* one in which the observers are experiencing the discovery of the new image from *within* the action along with the participant in the moment it is happening and yet simultaneously continue to be outside observers of the action.

Exercise 1a: Folding Chair Revisited

Repeat the Folding Chair exercise with new participants. If you need to aid concentration, shorten the time span for the number of discoveries.

Exercise 1b: Testing Spontaneity

Repeat the Folding Chair exercise with new objects that have movable parts until all students have fulfilled the exercise and have both seen and felt the difference between the planned or illustrated and the spontaneous.

In Japanese Noh theatre, an actor's folding fan can be transformed by his imagination into many different objects by the ways it is manipulated within the context. It can be, for example, a tray, a dagger, a sword, a mountain.

Exercise 1c: Spontaneity in Performance

Repeat the Folding Chair exercise, only this time the student must *perform* it—as if for the first time—capturing the illusion of the discoveries made spontaneously but adding nothing new to the sequence of images. In this exercise we confront the difference between spontaneity in improvisation and spontaneity in scripted theatre. Actors need to perform on dual tracks: performing as planned, but allowing for spontaneous nuanced variations to occur in speech and movement in response to the changing in-the-moment realities.

TEACHER OBSERVATION NOTE: It is quite possible that not everyone in the group will have the experience of a truly spontaneous moment. You will have to make a judgment call about whether or not to prod everyone to try and have one. You could send a student back in to do the exercise again. But you will probably have some students who find it very difficult to "let go" enough at this point in front of others to experience real spontaneity. What you have done in this exercise, besides focusing on the issue of spontaneity, is to identify where people are in their abilities to be spontaneous. Those who cannot be spontaneous do not need to be branded as failures if they cannot achieve it right now. They need to think about what "blocks" are preventing them from being truly spontaneous in the moment. And they need reassurance that they are already spontaneous improvisers in much of their everyday life and that they can learn to be more spontaneous in front of each other.

"Getting to Know You": Beginning Exercises

These beginning exercises have multiple purposes. They will provide exposure and experience in imaging, sidecoaching, and freeze-framing. At the same time, they will also help the participants get to know each other and begin to form a cohesive group, or ensemble. More exercises are provided here than are necessary, so look them over and choose the ones that best fit your situation. The few that are essential are marked with an asterisk.

EXERCISE 2: NAME GAME*
OBJECTIVE: to help the participants become acquainted with each other.

PARTICIPANTS: full group.

INSTRUCTIONS: Form a circle. Go around the circle, asking everyone to give her first name. Repeat this three times. Then, moving clockwise around the circle, ask each participant to name all the other persons in the circle. Repeat this exercise at the next workshop session to confirm that everyone has learned everyone else's name.

Exercise 2a: Name Game Repeat
Repeat the Name Game, but this time ask each student to designate an image for herself when she gives her name. Ask each participant to repeat the names and the images for the others in the circle.

Exercise 2b: Name Game Repeated Again
Each student creates a gestural shape in space as her name. The others must repeat it.

EXERCISE 3: MIRROR EXERCISE*
OBJECTIVE: to create an ensemble.

PARTICIPANTS: full group.

INSTRUCTIONS: Participants stand in two equal rows facing each other. One row is designated the initiators, the other row the mirrors. The person opposite is the partner. The goal for the mirror is to imitate as closely and as simultaneously as possible the movements of the initiator—as if the initiator were looking in a mirror. The goal for the initiator is not to try and "fake out" her partner, as in a contest, but to work together with the partner to fulfill the exercise.

The initiator should avoid "mimetic gestures" (e.g., brushing teeth, combing hair) but should use her whole body to create abstract gestures in space. The initiator and the mirror keep their eyes focused on each other's eyes and rely on their peripheral vision while completing the exercise. At some point the teacher will call out, "Change leaders!" and the initiator and the mirror will change roles.

SIDECOACHING
Any questions? Ready? Go!
(Time lapse) Change leaders!
(Time lapse) Change leaders again!
(Repeat this change in leadership back and forth a few more times.)
(For any initiators who are moving so quickly that their partners cannot mirror them:) If your partner cannot stay with you, then change what you are doing so that can happen.
(Time lapse) Freeze! Relax.

Exercise 3a: Mirror Exercise Repeat*
PARTICIPANTS: full group, with new partners.

INSTRUCTIONS: Each new partner is a new challenge to completing the exercise. The instructions are the same, but this time an additional sidecoaching instruction will be given at some point during the exercise.

SIDECOACHING
(Repeat sequence for the Mirror Exercise.)
(Time lapse) Change leadership at your own will. Be willing to lead and to follow. Make it difficult for me to tell who is leading at any one point. Make it difficult for you to tell who is leading at any one point.
(Time lapse) Freeze! Relax.

OBSERVATION/DISCUSSION
1. Did you achieve the goal of simultaneity? How did it feel when you did?
2. How did you achieve it? Where was your concentration when you achieved it?
3. Did you feel at any point that your physical choices seemed to be quite limited?
4. *Reflect on* (pun intended) the concept of "mirroring." How do we mirror others in life? What do we mirror?

Do we learn about life by mirroring others? Does mirroring others help us to determine who we are? Is our mirroring of someone else an exact reflection or our own interpretation (refraction) of the other's behavior?

TEACHER OBSERVATION NOTES: The Mirror Exercises offer an excellent way to find out some things about the members of your workshop. Who in the group anticipates her partner's move? Who seems to have a problem maintaining eye contact? Who has a concentration problem, seeming to be focused more in her own head than on the partner? (This is evident with those students who appear unaware of what their partners are doing.) You will also note those participants who incorporate the goals of the exercise and work hard to share themselves with their partners.

EXERCISE 4: FREEZE-FRAME

OBJECTIVE: to employ the technique of bodyscan.

PARTICIPANTS: full group.

INSTRUCTIONS: When participants are settling down at the beginning of a workshop, say, "Freeze! Even your eyes! But do not stop breathing!"

SIDECOACHING

During the freeze, conduct a bodyscan, to locate where you have areas of tension in your body. Do not relax those areas of tension right now; just locate them.

Check your neck . . . shoulders . . . torso . . . hips . . . hands . . . feet . . . eyes . . . tongue . . . jaw . . . stomach. Be aware of the alternating rhythm of tension and release in your breathing.

Without actually looking at yourself, imagine stepping outside yourself and observing your whole body from this perspective. See it as a statue that someone else has sculpted. Walk around this statue, and see it from all angles. Even notice its facial features and expression. After observing this statue in detail, give it a title.

Now wipe away this image by refocusing your concentration on your breathing.

Conduct another bodyscan, relocating those areas of tension in the body. Now every time you find an area of tension, talk to it, telling it to relax.

(You will need to repeat the possible areas of tension listed above and remind the participants to relax each area as they locate it. If the students follow through on the full completion of this exercise, they will slowly collapse to the floor.)

Relax, and come out of the freeze!

Go to your journals and write down the title of your statue and a description of its body position and facial features. Also note where you located distinct areas of tension in your body during your bodyscan. You will check these notes later to see

if you tend to store tension in a particular part of your body. If so, that will be an area to spend extra time on in your individual warm-ups.

OBSERVATIONS/DISCUSSION: When the group has finished writing, discuss the term *tension*. We tend to use the term *tension* with negative connotations, to mean an excess of *unnecessary* energy bound up or concentrated in the total body, or isolated in a body part, or in the mind, preventing the release of the *necessary* energy to operate. But what about the need for a balance and interplay of differing or contrasting tensions and relaxations in the body to make the body operate? Also discuss the possible positive role of "tension" in the creative act.

EXERCISE 5: BREATHE!*

OBJECTIVE: to investigate the movement pattern of breathing.

PARTICIPANTS: full group.

INSTRUCTIONS: Stretch out on the floor on your back, with your knees bent and your feet flat on the floor. Your eyes should be open and alive. Breathe normally. Concentrate on your breathing. Note that your breathing pattern has four parts to it: an intake of air rising to a peak; a slight hesitation when all the air is in place; an expelling of air, sinking to the lowest point; and another hesitation and adjustment before the new air is brought in.

Continue on into the next exercise.

Exercise 5a: Breathing and Doing*

OBJECTIVE: to test how the tempo and rhythm of breathing changes according to the physical task a person is performing and/or an emotional state.

SIDECOACHING

Raise and lower your right arm easily. Keep repeating this simple action. What is the relationship between your inhaling and exhaling when are you raising and lowering your arm? Do you raise it on an intake of breath? Do you lower it on an exhalation of breath?

Imagine you are raising a heavy object in one hand vertically over your head. Focus on feeling the size and weight of the object. How does the tempo and rhythm of your breathing change?

Now place your hands over your eyes and imitate sobbing over a very sad event. How does your breathing tempo and rhythm change?

OBSERVATIONS/DISCUSSION: After you have completed these exercises, discuss first the possible connections between breathing and physical action, and then between breathing, emotion, and physical action. What were the similarities and/or differences in breathing between sobbing and laughing? What happens when you work against the natural inclination to inhale before beginning a physical action? What happens when you add more resistance between breathing and doing?

EXERCISE 6: FACEOFF*

OBJECTIVE: to investigate the unique architecture of a face.

PARTICIPANTS: full group, working in pairs.

PREPARATION: Produce a handout that details the areas for investigation, such as

a) skin texture
b) the *round* versus the *square* versus the *triangular* areas of the face
c) the soft and fleshy places versus the taut and muscular places
d) the places where the planes of the face intersect, especially around the areas of the eyes, cheeks, nose, and mouth.

INSTRUCTIONS: Taking your notebook and pencil with you, choose a partner. Stand or sit facing each other and close enough to touch. One person closes her eyes, and the other person explores her partner's face with her hands. Using your handout, write down your notes on the areas for investigation.

SIDECOACHING

Note the distance between the hairline and the center of the eyebrows.

Notice the distance between the center of the eyebrows and the tip of the nose.

Note the distance from the tip of the nose to the chin.

How do these distances compare?

Draw an imaginary line down the center of the face. Do you find that the two sides of the face are symmetrical in shape and mass, or asymmetrical? How are they alike? How are they different?

Observe the face in profile from each side. Do you notice any distinct difference between the two profile views?

Now compare the profile views with a full front view. What differences do you note here, if any?

Standing on one side, ask your partner to open her eyes and focus on a distant point. Observe the intricate musculature around the eyes when they are open. What change, if any, does having the eyes open make in your reaction to the total face?

When you have completed your survey, have your partner relax. Using your notes for reference, describe what you saw and felt.

Repeat the exercise, with your partner exploring your face in the same way.

OBSERVATION/DISCUSSION: When the exercise is completed, the students should compare notes with the rest of the class. Use Max Picard's statement below as the basis for beginning the discussion. Pay particular attention to the questions of symmetry versus asymmetry and front versus side views.

JOURNAL ASSIGNMENT: In *The Human Face,* the French philosopher Max Picard makes these observations about actors' faces:

> On the actor's face the profile and front face are so much strangers to each other that they seem not to belong to the same face. It is as if the actor had put his face together out of the profile of one face and the front of another. And now the actor hunts for these people, he hunts for the faces that will complete him, he changes himself into a thousand characters, and searches their faces for the features that belong to him. He stands before his thousand characters and seeks the features that would help him establish concord with himself.[7]

Now that each of you has examined your partner's face and had your own face explored, respond to Picard's observations. Is there actually a difference between an actor's face and a nonactor's face? How might an actor find Picard's observations useful?[8]

EXERCISE 7: MAKING FACES

OBJECTIVES: to investigate the sculptural details of the human face, and to become acquainted with another member of the group.

PARTICIPANTS: full group, working in pairs.

INSTRUCTIONS: Choose a partner, and sit facing each other on the floor. Decide who will be the sculptor and who will be the clay for the first round. The clay closes its eyes, and the sculptor tries to sculpt this facial clay into a primary emotional state. The clay must allow the sculptor to model it, trying to hold the position. The sculptor may also want to sculpt the eyes open to complete the sculpture. The clay must hold the facial position, as it is on exhibit for the rest of the group.

When you are finished sculpting your partner's face, ask your sculpture (partner) to create a pose with her body that will support and complete the facial expression. When she has done this, release your sculpture and discuss.

Exercise 7a: Making Faces Repeat

Repeat the Making Faces exercise, switching roles.

EXERCISE 8: BODY SCULPTING

OBJECTIVE: to investigate the possible dependence between the expression of the face and the rest of the body.

PARTICIPANTS: full group, working in pairs.

INSTRUCTIONS: Extend the Making Faces exercises. This time the sculptor shapes the whole body—but not the face—in space to communicate an emotional state. When you have finished, ask your partner to make the facial expression that completes the body you have sculptured. When completed, relax out of the sculpture and discuss.

Exercise 8a: Body Sculpting Repeat

Repeat the Body Sculpting exercise, switching roles.

OBSERVATIONS/DISCUSSION

1. What physical changes, if any, occurred in the face when the sculpture correctly identified the emotional state and filled it from the inside?
2. Were these actual physical changes that you could identify, or were they "felt" changes?
3. What significance might these sculpting exercises have for future mask improvisation work?

EXERCISE 9: WALKING IN ANOTHER'S SHOES*

OBJECTIVE: to begin the investigation of another person's movement as other than one's own.

PARTICIPANTS: two people at a time.

INSTRUCTIONS: One person in the group volunteers to walk in a wide circle. Everyone observes the walk and movement of this individual. Another person volunteers to go up and walk behind the first participant, trying to assume her walk and movement. The person imitating the walker may also take time out to observe the walker's movement from the side, front, and from behind before going back into the other's walk. As the two continue circling, the imitator explains verbally what the walker's movement that she has tried to assume feels like in her own body. Where are the areas of tension? relaxation? What are the tempo and rhythm?

Then the first person drops out, and the imitator reverts to her own walk. Another volunteer enters and repeats the exercise.

All the students should get a chance to participate in this exercise, both imitating others and having their own walks imitated. To accomplish this, more than one circle walk can occur simultaneously, or the exercise can be spread out over several sessions.

EXERCISE 10: PLAY BALL!*

This is an exercise borrowed from Viola Spolin's pioneering work on improvisation, *Improvisation for the Theater.*[9]

OBJECTIVE: to begin to explore the effects of imaging on the bodymind's response.

PARTICIPANTS: full group.

INSTRUCTIONS: Everyone stands in a circle. The leader creates an imaginary ball, tells the group what kind of ball it is (e.g., a softball) and tosses it to someone else in the circle. That person catches it and tosses to another person, and so on. The members of the group are sidecoached to concentrate on the *size* and *weight* of the ball, not on whether they can fake someone else out.

At some point in tossing this imaginary ball back and forth, the leader calls out a change in the size and weight of the object being tossed (e.g., the softball is now a bowling ball, or a balloon, or a feather—be imaginative!). The group is sidecoached to maintain focus on the size and weight of the new imaginary object. The leader continues to call out other changes in the object.

OBSERVATIONS/DISCUSSION

1. What adjustments did you feel in your bodymind in response to the size and weight of the various objects being tossed about?
2. What did your muscles do?
3. What changes in breathing did you notice? When did you breathe in? When did you exhale?
4. What does this suggest about the relationship between mental imagery and physical responses?

TEACHER OBSERVATION NOTES: Notice how the bodies of the participants adjust physically to the size and weight of the images being visualized. What they have learned is that the bodymind automatically makes psychophysical changes in response to strong visual and kinesthetic images. They have also learned that we tend to inhale when preparing to initiate an action, and to exhale as we start to fulfill the action.

5

The Lesson of the Mask

Whoever, having a mask in his hands, and the ambition to play with it, isn't seized by an emotion which suddenly detaches him from his own humanity and plunges him into a "state" which he cannot define but where he suddenly enters into a sort of quasi-magical, mysterious, fever; whoever, having hidden his face behind a mask of a given character, doesn't feel himself immediately possessed by an irresistible force, burlesque or tragic, from head to foot, that one will perhaps be able to interpret "the roles" agreeably; he is assuredly not and never will be a true dramatic "creator."
—*Léon Chancerel, "Notes personnelles"*

Introduction

Now the participants in the workshop will get their first opportunity actually to experience working with masks . . . and it will be in the celebration of a masquerade party! The party context sets up a low-risk situation so that the students can enter the initial encounter playfully. The only overt goal is to have fun! Only when the party is over will we examine the experience more closely for what the participants have learned about masks and about themselves.

EXERCISE: THE PLUNGE!*

OBJECTIVE: to initiate the students into the magic and mystery of the mask.

PARTICIPANTS: full group.

PREPARATION: For this exercise you will need to have a collection of masks, costumes, and props on hand for the actors to play with. The best masks for this exercise are masks from previous productions (not seen or used by any of the participants in the group), masks you may have collected, and possibly even inexpensive plastic Halloween masks available at your local costumer. You can even use full-head latex masks, a Lone Ranger domino, or Carnival masks.

You should not use masks that members of the group have recently seen onstage. Performances will have "fixed" an image of how those masks are to be used that will be difficult to shed. You should also not use masks from other cultures that were not created for theatrical purposes. Some cultures use masks for sacred rituals, and that use should be respected.

Place the masks on a table, allowing the participants to crowd around as you are laying them out. The costumes can be hung on a rack in the room. An assortment of props can be placed on another table.

Mirrors are necessary for this exercise. Set some interesting furniture around for the actors to improvise with.

Have a variety of party music tapes playing in the background during the party.

INSTRUCTIONS: (As you are setting out the masks:) Why is a masquerade party fun?

(When the masks are all set out:) When I finish giving these few beginning instructions, go and play with the masks. Choose one that fascinates you. Let the mask dictate what you will do and say. Find a costume for the mask. Find a prop. Have fun! See if you can fool us about who you are. Other than one ground rule, there are no restrictions on what you can do or say. The ground rule is this: *When you are told to stop and come out of the mask, you will do so.*

When you get tired of playing in one mask, take it off and

try another one. Try masks that are completely different. Try different mask and costume combinations.

SIDECOACHING

(Allow students time to play and to explore a series of masks.)

Feel free to make sounds or talk with each other as your characters.

(One way to help them release the verbal aspects of the masks is to walk among them, observing them. When you spot a student who has really connected to his mask, start talking to that student as his character, first asking if you may talk to him. Ask simple interview questions, such as "What is your name?" "Where do you live?" "Are you married?" "Do you have any children?" "What are their names?" Concentrate on the mask's answers to pick up clues about where to take these mini-interviews. Let the mask lead you too! Encourage the masks to interact. Try to make contact with as many masks as possible.)

(When all students have tried a number of masks:) Freeze! Close your eyes, relax, and come out of the mask.

OBSERVATIONS/DISCUSSION: The experience that students have in this "plunge" exercise is very important in initiating them into the possibilities and problems of mask improvisation. The questions below will provoke their thinking about masks and masking. These questions relate to more extensive sets of observations given later in this chapter, detailing the important lessons that can be learned from the exercise.

1. What was your experience in the masks? Did you feel as if you "plunged" into another world? Did you experience release from your normal self and your everyday world? If you didn't, why do you think that didn't happen?

2. How did you choose the costumes and props for your various masks? Did you feel that a mask in any way chose the costume or prop for itself or that the costume or prop chose the mask?

3. How did you know what to do or say in the mask? Where did that knowledge come from? Did you discover that you had a cast of characters within you who had thoughts and voices of their own?

4. Did you find that certain of your characters popped into being as complete characterizations and others you had to work at a bit? If so, what made the difference?

5. While you were improvising in the masks, were you aware of experiencing multiple levels of consciousness?

6. While you were improvising, were you at any time aware of the effect your character was having on you? On others? If so, how did that affect what you did?

7. Do you still have any images of your characters in your mind's eye? What residue of the experience of those characters

do you still feel in your bodymind? Do you think you could now re-create any of those characters without their masks?

8. When you were improvising in the masks, did you experience a strong inner voice telling you not to do or say something? Did you allow that critical voice to take control of your behavior?

9. Conversely, did you experience the effect of an inner guide prompting you to do and say certain things without judgment?

10. When you were in the mask, did you feel that you were not in control, or were in danger of losing control?

11. Did the experience of being in a mask disturb or frighten you in any way? Did you feel trapped in any one of the masks? If so, it is important to acknowledge these feelings and ask yourself why you felt this way.

12. What do you think about the evaluation of actors and their potential contained in the quotation from Léon Chancerel that begins this chapter?

Lessons from "The Plunge!" Exercise

If any of the students have experienced a powerful engagement with the masks (or even a single mask), as Greg did with "Jake," they have learned a great deal, if not all, that the mask has to teach them about acting. Unfortunately, they won't understand the full implications or the application of that experience for their acting without masks (or with masks). So for these students, the training is really about unpacking this initial experience, and they need to be reminded of how this rush felt in their bodyminds as they continue on through the training.

Not all students will have connected deeply with a mask in the masquerade. These students need to learn what it is in their mental or emotional being that is preventing this identification from taking place and how they can learn to set this block aside so that the spontaneous encounter can be kindled.

Lesson 1: Acknowledging Psychophysical Release

W. T. Benda writes: "When our masquerader unmasks, he may tell us what strange experience he had behind the mask: how he was released from all constraint of self-consciousness and conventions, how irresistible was the urge to act like the creature the mask portrayed, how indeed he imagined himself to be that creature."[1]

One of the most important lessons that "The Plunge!" exercise is meant to teach is what happens when the wearer releases the intuitive, spontaneous, image-making part of the brain to work for him in the workshop, and, indeed, in all of his acting. The students' experience in this exercise should be comparable with Malte Laurids Brigge's reactions to his own "plunge" into a mask for the first time:

I had never seen any masks before, but I immediately understood that masks ought to exist. . . . I put on the clothes, and in the process I completely forgot what I had intended to dress up as. All right, it was new and exciting not to decide until I was in front of the mirror. The face I tied on had a peculiarly hollow smell; it fitted closely over my own face, but I was able to see through it comfortably, and only after the mask was on did I choose all kinds of materials, which I wound around my head like a turban, in such a way that the edge of the mask, which extended downward into a gigantic yellow cloak, was almost completely hidden on top also and on the sides. Finally, when there was nothing more to add, I considered myself adequately disguised. To complete the costume, I picked up a large staff and walked it along beside me at arm's length, and in this way, not without difficulty but, as it seemed to me, full of dignity, I trailed into the guest-room toward the mirror.

It was really magnificent, beyond all expectation. And the mirror repeated it instantly: it was too convincing. It wouldn't have been at all necessary to move; this apparition was perfect, even though it didn't do a thing. But I wanted to find out what I actually was, so I turned around slightly and lifted both arms: large gestures, as if I were a sorcerer, were (as I saw immediately) the only appropriate ones.[2]

What the participants and Malte Laurids Brigge discover is that the bodymind is inspired by compelling images!

This release from self-consciousness on the part of the performer is one of the most important lessons of mask improvisation. Paradoxically, because the face is concealed, the actor can risk more, physically and psychologically, without being concerned with what others might think of him. The British director Peter Brook observes:

The moment the mask absolves you in that way, the fact that it gives you something to hide behind makes it unnecessary for you to hide. That is the fundamental paradox that exists in all acting: that because you are in safety, you can go into danger. It is very strange, but all theater is based on that. Because there is a greater security, you can take greater risks; and because here it is *not* you, and there-

fore everything about you is hidden, you can let yourself appear. And that is what the mask is doing: the thing you are more afraid of losing, you lose right away—your ordinary defenses, your ordinary expressions, your ordinary face that you hide behind; and now you hide a hundred percent, because you know that the person looking at you doesn't think it is *you,* and on account of that you can come right out of your shell.[3]

Lesson 2: Acknowledging the Cast of Characters Within

In answer to an interviewer's question about how she was able to play so many different roles, the British actor Edith Evans remarked, "I don't really know, except that I seemed to have an awful lot of people inside me. Do you know what I mean? If I understand them I feel terribly like them when I'd be doing them." Another British actor, Sybil Thorndike, said: "When you're an actor you cease to be male or female, you're a person, and you're a person with all the other persons inside you."[4]

It is interesting that a number of playwrights, too, readily acknowledge the presence of this cast of characters within and their inspiration of creative work. The playwright Sam Shepard, as far as I know, has not undergone mask improvisation training, but his experience in discovering the verbal life of his characters is similar to a participant's experience in the masks. He says that "language can explode from the tiniest impulse. If I'm right inside the character in the moment, I can catch what he smells, sees, feels and touches. In a sudden flash, he opens his eyes, and the words follow. . . . I begin to get the haunting sense that something in me writes, but it's not necessarily me."[5] Can we say, then, that Shepard is actually inspired by imaginatively "wearing the masks" of his characters? This ability to wear the character's mask imaginatively will become important later in the workshop.

Playwrights August Wilson and Tina Howe also explain the effects of this phenomena on their process of creation. Wilson says that in his writing he does not use autobiographical details. "These are entirely invented characters," he says. "They are not modelled along anyone. But at the same time they are all myself. I make them all up out of myself. If Troy [the dogmatic patriarch of *Fences*] is anyone, he is me. And so is Rose and so is Lyons, and Cory and Gabriel. They are all different aspects of myself."[6] Howe says: "I think it's true of most playwrights that their characters—male and female, young and old—are just aspects of themselves. When I people the stage with all these souls, what I do is split myself up. I implode and all these little fragments tear around inside me like crazy and become the characters."[7]

William Mastrosimone, the author of *Extremities* and other plays, has thought, perhaps, even more extensively about this cast of characters within and their influence on his creative process. Mastrosimone probes a bit further in identifying the origin of this cast of characters in the human psyche:

> I have a theory that we are filled with hundreds of personalities, possibilities of personalities, who never had a chance, because of pure accident. The personality that we manifest to the world is the one that was necessary, or the one that was most adaptable to the situation in which we were born. The other ones never had a chance, but they didn't die. They remained dormant. Certain situations bring them out, and you'd think about them in your dreams or you write about them. All the characters that I write about are other personalities of mine. When I put my ego aside I'm able to see my other masculine and feminine personalities much better. They really are there and they're quite distinct sometimes. They cut across race and culture.[8]

What these actors and playwrights suggest, and what the participants in the workshop have just experienced, is that we all have multiple voices within us that can easily be evoked. Mask improvisation training teaches us not only to acknowledge their presence but also how to tap this reservoir within ourselves as a resource for our creative work. We could claim, I believe, that the more imaginative and successful actors or writers are the ones who not only acknowledge the presence of this cast of characters within but also allow them to "speak with their own voices" in the creative process. This is exactly what the director Claude Purdy asserts about August Wilson's method: "His characters come out of voices. . . In trying to discover how to write dialogue he allows his characters to talk instead of making them talk."[9]

Lesson 3: Recognizing Dual Consciousness

With the recognition of the presence of the cast of characters within and/or the critical voice, we may realize that at many times when we are improvising or performing we experience a *divided consciousness*. It is as if one part of us was sitting back, watching what the other part was doing and allowing it to happen—at least, most of the time. You have other observer-selves within you too, not just the inhibiting critical voice. As Joseph Roach comments in *The Player's Passion*, "At any given moment the actor's mind must retain his cues, his lines, his blocking, his gestures, some idea of the similar assignments of his cohorts (lest they forget), audience reaction, the location of properties and their heft, the precise timing of complex business, and if he works that way, his motivation."[10]

It is common for actors to recognize the presence of this divided consciousness while they are performing. Fanny Kemble, for example, wrote:

> The curious part of acting to me, is the sort of double process which the mind carries on at once, the combined operation of one's faculties, so to speak, in diametrically opposite directions; for instance, in the very last scene of Mrs Beverley, while I was half dead with crying in the midst of *real* grief, created by an entirely unreal cause, I perceived that my tears were falling like rain all over my silk dress, and spoiling it; and I calculated and measured most accurately the space that my father would require to fall in, and moved myself and my train accordingly in the midst of the anguish I was to feign, and absolutely did endure. It is this watchful faculty (perfectly prosaic and commonplace in nature), which never deserts me while I am uttering all that exquisite passionate poetry in Juliet's balcony scene, while I feel as if my soul was on my lips and my colour comes and goes with the intensity of the sentiment I am expressing: which prevents me from falling over my train, from setting fire to myself with the lamps placed close to me, from leaning upon my canvas balcony when I seem to throw myself all but over it.[11]

Interviewer Derek Hart once asked Ralph Richardson, "Are you fully inhabiting the character, or are you stepping aside and having a look at him from the outside?" Richardson responded:

> Part of it is stepping aside and controlling it, that's the first thing. You're really driving four horses, as it were, first going through, in great detail, the exact movements which have been decided upon. You're also listening to the audience, as I say, keeping, if you can, very great control over them. You're also slightly creating the part, in so far as you're consciously refining the movements and, perhaps, inventing tiny other experiments with new ones. At the same time you are really living, in one part of your mind, what is happening. Acting is to some extent a controlled dream. In one part of your consciousness it really and truly is happening. . . . Therefore three or four layers of consciousness are at work during the time an actor is giving a performance.[12]

Laurence Olivier said that "a good actor is working on at least three levels at all times: lines, thought and awareness of the audience." Charles Janasz remarked, "Even when you give yourself totally to the character, it's still your own soul inside the creation. It's as though your mind were outside watching the creation happen, observing it; two minds working in tandem, that of the character and that of the actor."[13]

As these actors affirm, an actor can have a divided consciousness, or *co-consciousness,* of his performance while he is performing. He is functioning on dual tracks, as participant and observer simultaneously. Indeed, Richardson's and Olivier's testimony suggests that there may be more than two layers of awareness! But we will simplify and consolidate the multiple layers of consciousness within the performer into our two functions of observer and participant.

What is the possible relationship between these parts of your consciousness during performance? Does this relationship remain constant? No. The term *divided consciousness,* or *co-consciousness,* does not mean that you have two or more impulses or thoughts of equal force or weight pulling against each other simultaneously. That would cause *stasis*—the inability to act. I suggest that these participant- and observer-selves exist in a dynamic multidimensional relationship; a continually flowing interchange operates between different layers of consciousness. Yuasa Yasuo would say that the spontaneous action of the character (the participant) operates out of the actor's "dark consciousness," not his unconscious. He would also say that the "dark consciousness" has been trained by the "bright consciousness" (the reflective mind) through the rehearsal process in what to do and say. All of us, actors and doers in our daily lives, have experienced just such a co-consciousness and operated out of our dark consciousness without realizing its full significance.

At times the actor will be more aware of an attentive, encouraging, but silent, observer-self who is audience to his participant-self. As noted in the comments by actors above, this observer-self can also subtly and quietly intervene as a personal inner guide to direct or coach the participant-self (e.g., "Cross to the couch").

Let me use a homely metaphor to try and explain the various relationships that can occur within the divided consciousness. Suppose you are driving a car and talking to someone at the same time. When you first learn to drive, you can't hold a conversation with anyone, because you need both hands on the wheel and all your concentration on the act of driving itself. But as you gain experience and confidence, you realize that you can relax, trust yourself, and drive carefully and converse at the same time.[14]

That part of your bodymind that is securely driving the car is on automatic pilot, operating out of the driver's dark consciousness. It is relaxed and "in flow" because it has had extensive mental and physical training and experience. It knows all

it has to do to drive the car properly: shift gears, stop at stop signs, watch traffic lights, and so on. This bodymind is alert to any unusual changes in the routine and will automatically respond to sudden danger *before* the bright consciousness, the reflective mind, can take conscious control again. In an emergency, as Thomas Kasulis explains, it will be "the body, not the mind, that decided the action."[15]

In making an analogy with acting, we can say that the actor's bodymind in performance (memorized dialogue, the pattern of the character's mental, motivational, and physical activity, etc.), which has become scored, and therefore imprinted, through rehearsals, is like our habitual bodymind driving the car. The actor's spontaneous, in-the-moment awareness of the nuances of change—in fellow actors and the audience—is the flow of his trained subtextual bodymind response, which conditions how he responds at any moment. This is like the driver's automatic response to changing road conditions.

An actor never wants to live permanently as a totally self-conscious student driver with a learner's permit, because there the observer-self becomes the totally intrusive critical voice, commenting on or even inhibiting the participant-self's proposed behavior. In this state, the actor does not allow himself to let a dynamic multilayered interchange occur, either within himself or between himself and the world outside. Rather, he is being dictated to by the critical voice (which means that the actor will in turn program the mask in what it must do or say). Because of this need for control, the mask will be lifeless, an object stuck on the actor's face. The masked performers of Balinese Topeng say of inexperienced and inept mask wearers that they "are pushing the wood around."[16] When this happens, the actor is tightly holding on to his steering wheel in order to keep himself safe and in total control. As Roach interprets this behavior, the actor has not yet released into the character:

> In the early stages of an actor's efforts—either as a beginner or at the start of rehearsals for a new role—his body resists his will; his gestures die still-born, words fail him, his rhythms sputter and lurch like a new machine whose parts do not quite fit. As he repeats himself in rehearsals and exercises, however, testing the pulses of his imagination, probing his physical and mental limits, these hesitancies tend to fall away one by one; his assurance generates energy, until he seems more thoroughly alive than ever before. The paradox is evident: the actor's spontaneous vitality seems to depend on the extent to which his actions and thoughts have been automatized, made second nature.[17]

Kasulis's explanation of how the dark consciousness is trained to perform has an astounding parallel to Roach's description of the process an actor undergoes:

The initial step in all these disciplines [meditation, acting, etc.] is that the mind (the bright consciousness) deliberately places the body into a special form or posture. Whether learning a golf swing or learning to sit in mediation, the beginning phase is awkward. The body is uncooperative or inert and one feels, we say, "self-conscious." The self-conscious bright consciousness is imposing its form on the dark consciousness. Gradually, through, the posture becomes natural or second nature. It is *second nature* because the mind has entered into the dark consciousness and given it a form; it is an acquired naturalness. Once the transformation takes place, however, there is no further need for the self-reflective bright consciousness and one can act creatively and responsively without deliberation.[18]

What is important in both analyses is the *inscribing* and *imprinting* of mental and emotional forms onto the actor's "other" consciousness through physicality.

Some actors are like drivers who seem to drive just this side of being out of control, cruising where the conscious self isn't quite connecting with what it is doing or saying—but it is not driving in a state of total unconsciousness either. This situation is evident in rehearsal or performance when the actor plays for a moment as if he is functioning only on automatic pilot and no fresh "conversation" is occurring. Nothing is changing the nuance of his behavior, not his partner and not his environment, since the last time he performed the scene. This condition is called "phoning it in." When an actor reaches this point, he has lost contact with his participant-self who lives in the moment and is outside the action. This is another condition the actor wants to avoid.

We don't issue driving licenses to those people in a state of total unconsciousness of the world around them either. (We try to keep drunks off the road—and off the stage—also.) These people are too dangerous to be on the road. People who experience a real psychic split, a dissociation, and cannot choose but live in this other state are, of course, in need of professional psychiatric help. The actor cannot live in this state of total unconsciousness of the world outside himself.

The mask awakens and prompts the wearer's active imagination that resides in his dark consciousness. It is the form (image) of the mask that constellates in the dark consciousness of the individual wearer, prompting the totality of his psychophysical response onstage. For, as Yuasa writes, "behind this dark consciousness lurks a capacity unifying all acts of consciousness, such as thinking, willing, emotion, and perception in their differentiating development."[19]

Paradoxically, the actor has to learn to step aside and allow this active imagination to flow through him without becoming totally engulfed by it. As we acknowledged at the close of chapter 1, there are those moments onstage when "the god descends," when an actor does lose total contact with his observer-self and becomes completely engulfed by the participant-self—even to the point at which he comes offstage and has no consciousness about what he just said or did. It is as if another being or consciousness totally took over his will, inhabiting his bodymind (but, interestingly enough, saying all the right lines and performing all the right movements!). Usually this happens for a brief moment, and it can perhaps be best understood as a momentary low-level autohypnotic trance state. Most actors have experienced this state to some degree. But actors should not try to induce this condition, thinking it will make them more effective performers. In fact, trying to make it happen will guarantee that it won't!

Where an actor wants and needs to live most of the time in improvisation (and performance) is at a center point between the extremes of being totally in control and totally out of control. He should be able to move freely back and forth between his multiple layers of consciousness. In this state he can allow himself to be led by the character without being overly aware of his participant-self. In a dimly lit back row of his consciousness, though, his observer-self sits, silently watching and guiding his performance.

Conversely, when the actor becomes so aware of the divided consciousness itself that it begins to solidify into a barrier between his Self and the mask's self, he must use his imagination and will to *choose* to enter the bodymind of the mask. He must let go of his Self and commit to the mask by attending to, and living in, the present and presence of his physical actions.

Any sidecoaching that the teacher does during exercises will evoke this divided consciousness to some degree, although most sidecoaching is directed to the actor-as-character.

Participants in this workshop will discover that mask improvisation promotes more understanding of this experience of co-consciousness than regular acting training. The important value for the actor in acknowledging and utilizing this experience of divided consciousness was best explained by the great acting teacher Michel Saint-Denis. "Mask work," he said, "is central to the training precisely because it enables the student to warm his feelings and cool his head; at the same time it permits him to experience, in its most startling form, the chemistry of acting. At the very moment when the actor's feelings beneath the mask are at their height, the urgent necessity to control his physical actions compels him to detachment and lucidity."[20]

We might summarize Lesson 3 as follows: What needs to happen in the actor's bodymind most of the time is a ready oscillation between his multiple layers of consciousness, the driver's ongoing conversation of his rehearsed and unrehearsed dialogue with himself and the world.

Lesson 4: Living in and through the Image of the Mask

In the opening chapters of Konstantin Stanislavski's book *Building a Character,* he has his fictional teacher, Tortsov, ask his fictional students to participate in a masquerade—just as we have done. This was Stanislavski's attempt to explain the mysterious but effective process of how an image affects the development of a characterization and the actor's awareness of a double consciousness. One of the students, Kostya, found the exercise most rewarding—and most revealing about the process of acting:

> As I was taking my bath I recalled the fact that while I was playing the part of the Critic [the character he had created earlier that day in class] I still did not lose the sense of being myself. The reason, I concluded, was that while I was acting I felt exceptionally pleased as I followed my own transformation. Actually I was my own observer at the same time that another part of me was being a fault-finding, critical creature.
>
> Yet can I really say that that creature is not a part of me? I derived him from my own nature. I divided myself, as it were, into two personalities. One continued as an actor, the other was an observer.
>
> Strangely enough this duality not only did not impede, it actually promoted my creative work. It encouraged and lent impetus to it.[21]

What Stanislavski was trying to teach his students through the example of Kostya was that in order to create a full characterization, they needed to learn to let themselves "live in the image" of the mask and discover the divided consciousness.[22] Kostya gets high marks from Tortsov for his ability to do this:

> We have seen how a modest youth, who would scarcely even speak to a woman, suddenly becomes insolent and from behind a mask exposes his most intimately secret instincts and features—things he would not dream of mentioning even in a whisper to anyone in ordinary life.
>
> What makes him so bold? The mask and costume behind which he hides. In his own person he would never dare to speak as he does in the character of this other personality for whose words he does not feel himself responsible.
>
> Thus *a characterization is the mask* which hides the actor-individual. Protected by it he can lay bare his soul down to the last intimate detail.[23]

This is true—provided other things aren't in the way! Unfortunately Stanislavski did not follow up on this awareness of the mask's effectiveness on the actor to explore further possibilities for using masks in training, although he did finally see the value of images and "physical actions" in affecting the actor's psychological life.

Lesson 5: Recognizing the Presence of the Critical Voice

Rather than allowing the mask to prompt his actions, the wearer may have experienced his critical-analytic self dictating his behavior. His persona may have been trying to protect him from doing something unacceptable or saying something stupid or foolish. It was censoring his behavior, protecting his self-image. The actor must learn to let the mask impose what it wants to do or say, and then go with it! It is the self-critical, inhibiting voice that we want to confront, the voice that tells us not to do something unless it's "right," or not to do anything that might make us look silly or stupid. In this course it is important to say to this hypercritical self: "Go sit in the corner for the time being, keep quiet, and just watch what is going on!" This is not always easy to do, and we can use certain techniques to help us tackle this problem.

We don't want to ignore the critical voice entirely, however. We want to encourage its transformation into its other possible manifestation, a supportive, caring voice—the actor's own inner guide! Before we can do that, we have to contemplate another, and important, lesson to be learned from "The Plunge!" exercise.

Lesson 6: Dealing with Issues of Control

Losing Control. It may be that some who underwent "The Plunge!" exercise were brought face to face with some old and disturbing fears. It is all very well to be told to let the mask dictate your behavior and "go with it," but what happens when the mask suggests violent thoughts and actions? Now is a good time to clarify the ground rule stated earlier: *It must be clearly understood that in this course violence toward one's self or others is not allowed!*

Actors *do* need to acknowledge the violent feelings and impulses within themselves, even though they are not permitted to carry them out. They must not be ashamed to have or admit these thoughts and feelings. The playwright Maria Irene Fornes, who has created very violent characters, has this to say about the cast she has discovered within herself:

When you are writing purely from imagination, you let the characters move and behave as *they* want; they find their own parameters, their own lives. . . . When you follow the characters in your imagination there is not one truth but a number of possibilities, all of which are true.

The character that is completely imagined comes out of myself. Every character I imagine is part of me. I'm not embarrassed to put myself on stage. The sadistic captain in *The Conduct of Life,* and the victim of that sadistic captain—you can't write them unless you *are* them. If a character is brutal, it is because I am brutal. I take the blame and the credit. No writer can write a character unless she understands it thoroughly inside herself.[24]

Actors who will be asked to inhabit characters like those of Fornes will have to acknowledge the violence within themselves as well.

Remember, the voice of social control also lives in the actor's divided consciousness and will let him know when behavior is truly inappropriate and dangerous for him or the class. *Each participant is finally in control. He can always stop and take off the mask.* And the teacher is always present to intervene if necessary.

What we don't want is to allow the fear of possibly having these thoughts and feelings to inhibit the actor's experience of full release into the mask. For as Ronald Hayman acknowledges, "This is one of the most exciting sensations in all acting—the feeling of being in control and out of control at the same time, liberated from yourself and from all your normal inhibitions and anxieties. You are circumscribed only by the character. Something has been born for which you are both responsible and not responsible."[25]

Getting Trapped in the Mask. Another aspect of this fear of loss of control is the feeling of being dissolved or trapped in the mask. Rilke's character Malte, whose "plunge" into the mask we examined earlier, went on to experience just such a disturbance. Hearing a "multiple, complicated noise" somewhere in the building, Malte responds:

Hot and furious, I rushed to the mirror and with difficulty watched, through the mask, the frantic movements of my hands. But the mirror had been waiting for just this. Its moment of revenge had come. While I, with a boundlessly growing anguish, kept trying to somehow squeeze out of my disguise, it forced me, I don't know how, to look up, and dictated to me an image, no, a reality, a strange, incomprehensible, monstrous reality that permeated me against my will: for now it was the stronger one, and I was the mirror. I stared at this large, terrifying stranger in front of me, and felt appalled to be alone with him. But at the very moment

I thought this, the worst thing happened: I lost all sense of myself, I simply ceased to exist. For one second, I felt an indescribable, piercing, futile longing for my self, then only *he* remained: there was nothing except him.[26]

A participant in this workshop will discover that dissolving into, or being trapped in, the mask so that only it remains will not happen. His fear of this occurrence, however, might be quite real. As with the experience of violent impulses, acknowledging this fear allows the participant to begin to overcome it. Acknowledgment alone, of course, will not make the fear disappear instantly, as if by magic. It is an old and deeply rooted fear. But it is not an unusual reaction to the experience of being encased in a mask. By continuing to deal with this fear as he performs the exercises, the participant will find that as he adjusts to the work, his fear will lessen. He will discover in its place his more integrated self, his creative self.

Some Additional Comments

If there was a difference between what the student thought the mask would look like on his body when he picked it up and the way it appeared when he checked himself in the mirror, he should always go with the image that comes back at him in the mirror.

If students find they are improvising some characters that are stereotypes, they should not discourage that behavior at this point. They need to discover what catalog of stereotypes they carry around within them. Through the course of the workshop, they will learn to develop characters beyond the stereotype into original creations. If a participant avoided vocalizing and verbalizing in his series of masks, then he was manifesting another "letting go" problem that needs to me acknowledged and monitored.

For the receptive and willing bodymind, the mask acts as a compelling image, stimulating the imagination, suggesting and even dictating psychophysical changes in the behavior of the wearer. The external, physical object of the mask becomes a potent image that convinces the sensitized wearer to do its bidding.

Jacques Copeau, the founder of this method of training actors, well understood the efficacy of the mask. He wrote,

The actor who performs under a mask, receives from this papier-mâché object the reality of his part. He is controlled by it and has to obey it unreservedly. Hardly has he put it on when he feels a new being flowing into himself, a being the existence of which he had before never suspected. It is not only his face that has changed, it is all his personality, it is the very nature of his reactions, so that he experiences emotions he could never have felt or feigned without its aid. If he is a dancer, the whole style of his dance, if he is an actor, the very tones of his voice, will be dictated by the mask—the Latin "persona"—a being, without life till he adopts it, which comes from without to seize upon him and proceeds to substitute itself for him.[27]

Masks and Countermasks

The masks make terrible and unyielding demands. . . . The mask is not makeup. It is not a nonentity. Everything is at its service. If you use it wrong it will denounce you right away. You are the one to yield to the mask, it will never yield. So you have to respect it, love it. If not, it is as though you don't recognize that these masks have a history, a past, a divinity. Instead of wishing to rise toward them, you bring the masks down toward you, you make them banal. You have to make a journey toward them. You do not use a mask in any which way. You do not use just any mask, either. Our relationship to the mask is one of magnanimity.
—Ariane Mnouchkine

Masks

The theoretical foundation on which all mask improvisation training and mask theatre stands is this: *The mask is the reality.* What does this mean? It does not mean that we are dealing with a superficial concept of the mask as an object to hide behind, or something to put on in order to "trick or treat" another person. Nor are we dealing with a common psychological understanding of a mask as a false face behind which the "real" person resides.

We are dealing with a more ancient and mysterious concept of the mask, the mask as agent of transformation or locus of the presence of an Other. In this view, the mask *is* the reality. The wearer's task is to allow herself to be taken over by this presence in the mask. Like the text of a play, the physical object of the mask provides both the inspiration and the boundaries for the actor's work on a role. In this case, however, there are not words but sculptural features (hills, valleys, crevices, plateaus, intersecting planes), colors, and textures to "read" in order to release the imagination. If the mask is to live and breathe, it must live and breathe in and through the wearer's bodymind. Its face must become her face, its body her body, its mind her mind.

Mask improvisation is not solely about evoking the actor's subjective life, however. That can be done by putting a paper bag over your head. Mask improvisation is about evoking and experiencing *dedoublement,* an objective *and* subjective psychophysical response by actor and observer to the external object of the mask.

In "The Plunge!" exercise the actor discovered that she has a whole cast of characters within waiting to be released by the various masks in which she will improvise or perform. Let us take a moment and contemplate this mysterious process and phenomenon: A sculptor has a vision of an essential personality, an archetype, or a spiritual force and tries to incarnate that presence in a sculpted object that will affect the physical senses and imagination of the wearer and observers. Correspondingly, the actor-wearer is a person gifted to respond sensitively to the potent and compelling image of the mask, allowing it to transform her psychophysically into the character of the mask.

As we saw with Jake, the mask awakens in the wearer a correspondence—a new personality constellation that has a physical, mental, and emotional presence as well as a life history of its own. In a way the mask acts as a "psychic template" that releases through its cutout form only that corresponding pattern of the wearer's physical, emotional, and mental life that will complete it. To paraphrase Marshall McLuhan's famous dictum, we make our masks, and afterward our masks make us.

Countermasks

Countermasks are not a new set of masks, but a new way of playing with a given set of masks. Countermasking describes the technique of "playing against" the givens of the mask after they have first been discovered by the actor. Thus an actor can play against the physical, vocal, emotional, and/or mental characteristics that she has first established as harmonious with the mask. It is a way of enriching the characterization. The countermask work refers only to work in the Character Masks. There is no countermask for the Neutral Mask.

In order for effective countermasking to occur, the countermask training must *follow* the discovery and exploration of the bodymind that is in harmony with the mask. It is not a substitute for that initial experience and should not be introduced into the training until that work has been explored and well understood.

See chapter 11 for information and exercises that explain the concept and techniques of the countermask. Initial exercises in exploring the countermask are given at the end of the training in the Beginning Character Masks. Further countermask explorations are included in the chapters on Life Masks, Totem Masks, Found Object Masks, and Complex Character Masks. Chapters 13 and 15 also contain exercises for investigating the possibilities for vocal and verbal countermasks.

Ground Rules for Mask Improvisation

These ground rules apply generally to all the masks used in this workshop. Additional instructions will later be established for certain masks before improvisation is done in them.

1. *Have respect for the mask.* The mask is an affective artifact—a power-filled image. It will affect the wearer according to the respect given it. A workshop participant should not carry it around by sticking her fingers through its eye or nostril holes. Handle it properly—masks can be fragile. When putting the mask down, place it face up, with the back of the mask on the surface.

2. *Work on yourself and for yourself until told to do otherwise.* Participants should focus on developing strong and clear physicalizations from their heads to their toes. Nothing should be left out of these physicalizations. Participants should not relate to others until told to do so, even though they may have strong impulses to interact.

3. *Work in silence.* Much of the exploratory work is done in silence. The voice and speech are taken away so that they are not a crutch or a substitute for first finding the masks' physicalizations with the body. Later the participants will learn to discover the appropriate vocal qualities for their characters coming forth from those bodies. According to the dancer Mary Wigman, the power of the mask "is felt in its living silence and its demands."[1]

All performers need to learn the value of silence and stillness onstage. Jacques Copeau, the originator of mask improvisation training, wrote, "To start from silence and calm. That is the very first point. An actor must know how to be silent, to listen, to answer, to remain motionless, to start a gesture, follow through with it, come back to motionlessness and silence, with all the shadings and half-tones that these actions imply."[2]

4. *Avoid touching the mask while wearing it.* Once the participant has the mask in place and as comfortable on her face as possible, she should not touch it during the exercises unless she is going to take it off. Touching the mask breaks the illusion the participant is creating for herself and others by making direct contact with the material object. If she needs to make a gesture, such as wiping her eyes in crying, she should keep her hand slightly away from the surface of the mask.

5. *Keep the separation clear between your Self and your mask.* A participant should not speak in her own voice in the mask. The mask does not talk with her voice; it has its own voice. If she needs to ask a question of clarification, she should raise the mask to the top of her head. After she has asked her question and been given an answer, she should follow the basic procedures for going back into the mask (see below). In the Totem and Complex Character Masks, participants will be exploring the voice and diction of their masks.

If the image of the mask dries up in a participant's bodymind, or she wants to work out a movement problem without being in character, she should take off the mask. There is no need to pretend that the mask image is alive in her when it isn't. The situation will be readily perceived by the observers anyway, so she should take the mask off, work on her problem, and then go back into the mask. Then she should contemplate the mask again, allowing herself to recapture the potency of the image with her bodymind.

6. *When you are told to stop and come out of the mask, you will do so.* This ground rule was given in chapter 5. Sometimes masks release behavior that is not appropriate, and this ground rule is the safeguard against that eventuality.

Objectives

The first objective is to use the whole body to physicalize the mask, fingertip to fingertip, toe to scalp, leaving no part of the bodymind out.

The second is to bring the bodymind into harmony with

the mask, not just the mind and not just the body. Make sure the focus is on the physical, not the psychological. Participants should feel the incipient unfolding movements in the intuitive responses to the images that the masks awaken in them and follow where they lead. Franco Ruffini writes: "The physical and the mental are not two different paths but only two different starting points which necessarily have to meet."[3]

Carrying the Mask

Form. Bringing one's body "into harmony" with the mask means that the actor's physicalization supports, reinforces, and echoes the sculpted design features of the mask. It is *appropriate* for the mask. This aspect of carrying the mask is known as "carrying the form." The shape and configuration of the dominant lines (for two-dimensional masks) and sculptured contours (for three-dimensional masks) should be extended and imitated (harmonized) in the physicalization by the actor's body. But the actor must not *illustrate* the apparent emotional signification of those lines or contours, as this results in playing an attitude, not a physicalization.

For example, if curved, circular forms are dominant in the mask, then the actor's body must also exhibit this "roundness," both in her silhouette and in her movement through space. If the mask has sharp diagonals, the body must also reflect this angularity in its silhouette and in its movement. In freeze-frame moments, the physicalization should be complete—appropriate and filled—as in a snapshot or a still frame from a film.

Start with the body. In mask improvisation, discovering the appropriate and harmonious body should always come first. The emotion and characterization should flow from that strong physical identification. We are not seeking a surface imitation but a deep identification with the physical.

Level. Carrying the mask also means that the actor must discover the appropriate level of the mask. Both the participant and the teacher-observer are involved in this discovery. Much of this discovery will happen naturally if the actor has allowed herself to work spontaneously, following the impulses of her bodymind evoked by the image of the mask. But it is good to check it out, just in case. What does the expression *level of the mask* mean? First, it means that the *size* and *strength* of the physicalization should be appropriate to the size and strength of the design or sculptural features of the mask—as big and bold as the dominant features of the mask, or as simple and subtle. It means that the *weight* of the physicalization should match the thickness of the lines or the mass of the sculptured forms. Does the mask suggest heaviness or lightness? Also, the

tempo or *rhythm* of the gestures and movement through space should correspond to the *energy level* expressed by the mask. Is the actor underenergizing or overenergizing the mask? Finally, the *intensity* of the psychic or emotional state and the physical movement is connected to, and determined by, the energy level, size, strength, and weight of the mask. Is the actor truly connected to the inner life of her mask?

These remarks on carrying the mask are not meant to imply that there is only one way to physicalize a mask. Participants will discover that masks can effectively come to life in many ways, depending upon the actors' personal responses to them. The participants do not want their observers to be aware that they are actors wearing masks—an awareness of the separation between actor and mask—but rather, the participants want to maintain the illusion that they have been transformed into totally new beings—an awareness of unity or merger. This is, in fact, the manifestation of a "double negation." Just as the mask negates the face of the wearer, so the actor must live into the mask, making the observer forget the presence of the mask and see a face. The Noh actor Kunio Komparu expressed this seeming paradox thus: "By first denying all raw facial expressions in the act of donning the mask and then denying the existence of the mask, the performer constantly seeks a higher degree of sensitivity in the presentation of an infinite number of sentiments."[4]

It is no good for the actor to say that she "feels it" when the body does not exhibit any change. She must find how to *embody* ("in-body") it. Observers must see and experience the physical transformation. The internal can only be made manifest through the external!

Basic Procedures

Contemplating (Watching) the Mask. These are the basic procedures to follow when contemplating and assuming a mask. Some variation in these procedures will occur, depending upon the type of mask an actor is working with at the time. Those variations will be noted when necessary. Participants should memorize these procedures! They must become part of the preparation each time the participants work in masks.

1. *Observe the masks available for use.* The participants should note which ones pique their interest the most. Which ones would be the most intriguing to try? Those masks have already begun to inspire the students' imaginations, and the students are already unconsciously putting them on.

2. *Choose the mask that is most intriguing.* Given the number of participants, this may not always be possible. Each participant should always notice more than one intriguing mask. Any

mask that intrigues is fine for the improvisational work. If participants do not get their first choices in one session, they will have another chance.

3. *Take the mask and find a private place in the space to contemplate it.* Max Picard says: "Every object has a hidden fund of reality that comes from a deeper source than the word that designates the object. Man can meet this hidden fund of reality only with silence. The first time man sees an object, man is silent of his own accord. With his silence, man comes into relationship with the reality in the object which is there before ever language gives it a name."[5]

4. *Contemplate the mask by holding it at arm's length, observing the overall design and sculptural features of the mask as it is turned slowly from side to side and up and down in the light.* Participants should squint their eyes to shut out any peripheral images in the space as they focus totally on the masks. They should note any asymmetrical characteristics in the face, but they should concentrate on the "global impression" of the mask, not its individual parts.[6] As they manipulate the masks, they should let the masks activate their imaginations, letting the masks come alive in their hands. They must be open to letting their imaginations play with all the sensory impressions.

Participants must trust their impulses! They must not analyze! They need to allow themselves to be spontaneous in their visual and tactile responses to the masks. They do not want to screen their impulses or to let their critical minds intervene, telling them what to do or not do. They must follow where the masks lead them without reservation, even if they think that the mask is leading them to do "stupid" or "foolish" things. As we have seen, these negative evaluations of impulses come from the critical voice, not the spontaneous imagination.

Contemplating the mask is not an inspection, a critical evaluation of the design and sculptural features of the mask. Contemplating the mask is watching the mask for its life to reveal itself and then beginning to participate in the imagined life of the mask. Contemplation involves an emotional and physical commitment to what is seen and felt. Participants have already been receiving strong psychophysical impulses from the masks. If they trust those impulses, the physicalizations will be appropriate, and the masks will live.

TEACHER OBSERVATION NOTES: "Trusting one's impulses" can actually be more complicated than it sounds. It depends on what those impulses are and where they are coming from. If the actor's own habitual compulsions are getting in the way, then you will note little if any change in the physicalization from mask to mask. In discussion, you may learn that the actor mistakenly believes she was physicalizing the masks quite differently. So, there are impulses and impulses, and . . . not all impulses are created equal!

Some impulses are freeing, creative, and risky. Others are inhibiting, repetitious, and safe. Sometimes the riskier choice is just to be silent and still; loudness and assertiveness can actually be a very comfortable choice. It all depends on where an actor is and where she needs to go.

A participant needs to treat herself with respect. She should be encouraged not to impose on the Self old habits of thought and behavior that give it no room for discovery and growth. A very important part of the process of mask improvisation training is diagnostic: the actor discovers how she has psychophysically "sculpted" her own persona—her mask—so that she can either use it or dispense with it when it gets in her way.

Some students may be confused about how to tell the difference between a healthy, spontaneous impulse and an unhealthy, habitual impulse. That's okay. Distinguishing between the types of impulses is part of your function as observer-teacher and the self-diagnostic aspect of mask improvisation. For the moment, coach the participants not to analyze and screen their impulses, but to trust them! Habitual impulses will be sorted out from original creative ones as we go along.

As we saw in chapter 5, there is only one exception to the students' not following their impulses when being led by the mask: that is the impulse to violence. It is important for them to realize and own that they have violent feelings, but they may not act them out against themselves or others in the class.

5. *Image the mask.* In order to fix the mask in her bodymind, the participant needs to take a moment before she dons the mask, close her eyes, and see the mask in her mind's eye. She should feel it taking over her bodymind. Then she should open her eyes and glance at the mask again as she starts to put it on.

TEACHER OBSERVATION NOTES: If you find a student taking noticeably longer than others in the contemplation stage, then it is quite likely that that student is blocking the impulses already received from the mask and is analyzing ways to physicalize the mask so as to complete the exercise successfully. This will result in illustrating the mask, not living it. The student is trying to control the situation. She either has not trusted that she will receive impulses that spark her imagination or is screening the ones she is having, searching for those she can approve for herself to perform in the class.

Those students who go into the mask and illustrate their analysis will quickly tire, as they are doing all the work. The mask has not energized them by inspiring their imaginations and prompting their behavior. Pay particular attention to the moment when the participants come out of the masks. If their eyes and faces are shining, or it takes them a few minutes to recover, then the masks have been working on them. If not, this is another indication that they have been illustrating the masks.

Assuming (Donning/Shoeing) the Mask. When working

with the Character Masks, the students should stand in front of a mirror when they assume the masks. The Neutral Mask work does not use mirrors.

1. Participants should stand with their weight on both feet, with the body centered. They will come to know this stance as the neutral body position.

2. They should take the mask in one hand, the elastic in the other.

3. As they start to raise the mask into position on their faces, they should close their eyes and inhale.

4. With their eyes shut, they put the masks on their faces, adjusting the elastic around the back of the head to make it as comfortable as possible.

If anything goes awry at this point (e.g., the elastic is too tight or not tight enough, the mask cuts into the eyes), then the participant should remove the mask, open her eyes, and fix the problem. When ready, the participant can begin the procedures again.

5. When the masks are firmly fixed on the students' faces, they should exhale and open their eyes. As they exhale, they should imagine that they are clearing and emptying their bodyminds.

6. (For Character Masks only:) Students should see their new selves in the mirror and let the shock of that discovery affect their bodyminds.

At this point in the process, the linear sequence of assuming the mask changes into an all-at-onceness, where many doors into the discovery of the character can open simultaneously. So procedures 7 and 8 may happen spontaneously, and the participant can move to 9 and 10 if appropriate.

7. The next breaths they take are the masks' (the characters') breaths. Each participant should each find the appropriate breath or breathing patterns for her mask. (These can be shallow or deep, relaxed or constricted, quick or slow, regular or erratic.)

8. They should let the discovery of the breathing patterns of the masks begin their transformations into the physicalizations that they feel are appropriate for their masks, leaving no part of themselves out!

9. (For Character Masks only:) Participants should try backing away from the mirror, exploring some possibilities for the physicalizations. The should also try moving toward the mirror.

10. (For Character Masks only:) Once a psychophysical image of the character begins to emerge and take over the bodymind, the participant should turn away from the mirror and discover the movement of the character in space without the visual crutch of the mirror.

Sidecoaching by the teacher for the different mask explorations occurs at this point.

Different Routes through the Training

With an understanding of these basic concepts, ground rules, objectives, and procedures, participants are now ready to start the mask improvisations. But at this point a decision about the route to follow through the training must be made. That will be determined by the purpose in using this text.

For actor training, I recommend the full course (two twelve-to-fourteen-week series), exploring the Neutral Mask, the Beginning Character Masks, the Life Masks, and so on, in sequence. For this approach, follow the text as written. Alternatively, the workshop can follow an Integrated program (one twelve-to-fourteen-week course). For this approach, follow the instructions given at key junctures in the text.

For preparation for mask theatre, consult chapter 17 and then refer back to appropriate parts of the training.

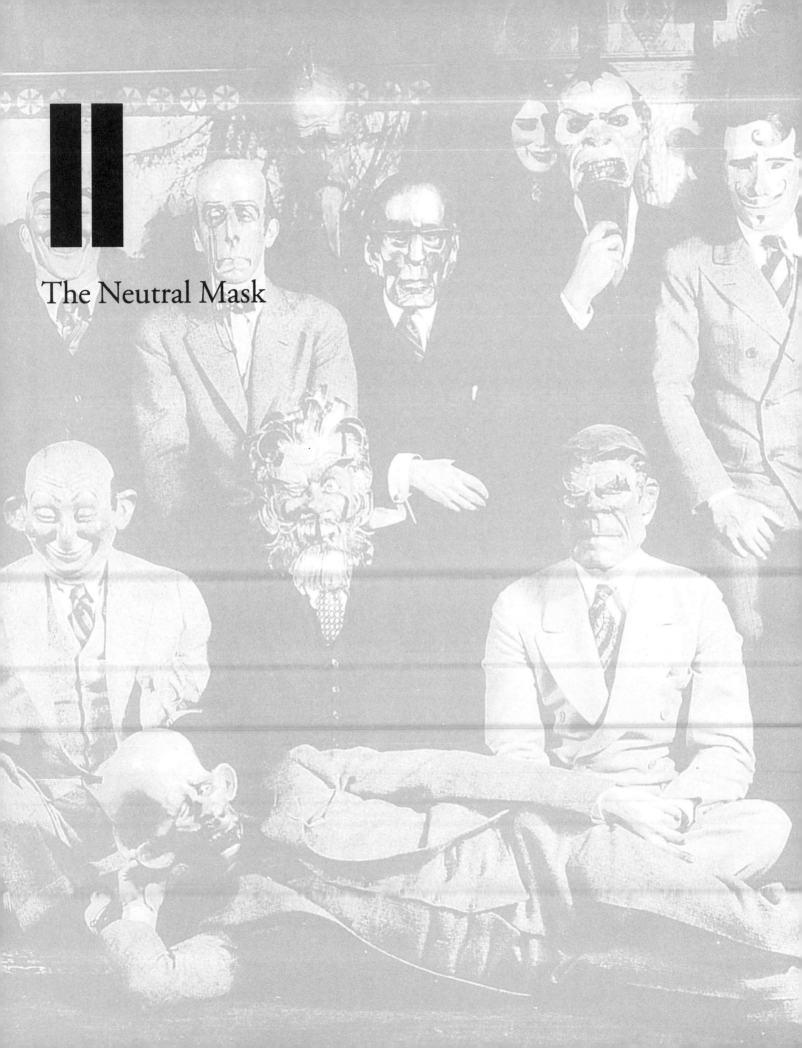

II

The Neutral Mask

7

The Concept of Neutral

What do we mean by the word *neutral*? In what other instances do we use the term? Do we mean "disinterested," "uninvolved," "bland," or do we mean something more like "impartial" or "open-minded"? Why is Switzerland traditionally neutral in international conflicts? Is it because it is "disinterested" and "uninvolved"? What is the function of the neutral gear in an automobile? Bari Rolfe at one point in her work with American students changed her use of the term *neutral* to *universal* because her students connected the idea of "neutral" with "being neutered"![1] But the term *universal* has now become even more unacceptable.

Students may initially resist the concept of neutral. They know that nothing in nature is truly neutral. And they're right! The concept of neutral is an intellectual and imaginative construct. Once it is consciously, or unconsciously, applied, like any concept it conditions how we look at the world: through its lens we notice things that we might not see otherwise. The best way to understand what *neutral* means and what the concept of neutral (and the Neutral Mask) can do for the actor is to discuss the idea after some contemplation and exploration. Participants are asked to set aside any objections they have to this concept for the time being.

The Neutral Mask suggested for this workshop is unlike any other in use. It is a simple paper mask with only holes for eyes and a cone shape for a nose. There is no indication of a mouth or any other unique features of the face. Most Neutral Masks in use are three-dimensional masks based on the leather ones sculpted by Amleto Sartori for use in Jacques Lecoq's training program. (Until recently I too used this type of mask.) These are wonderful masks, but they have become increasingly questionable in our multicultural age because their physiognomy immediately signals their European heritage.[2]

Trying to sculpt a Neutral Mask is, I think, an impossible task, as the sculptor immediately realizes that nothing we do or make is "neutral." No one Neutral Mask is appropriate for everyone in our diverse culture. The advantage of the simple paper Neutral Mask is that it is more abstract. It signals "human face" but has less indication of a particular nationality; the nose of the mask, for instance, is unlike any nose ever lived in! Instructions for constructing this type of Neutral Mask can be found in Appendix A, and a template appears in Appendix B.

EXERCISE 1: CONTEMPLATING THE NEUTRAL MASK*

OBJECTIVE: to contemplate the distinct characteristics of a Neutral Mask.

PARTICIPANTS: full group.

PREPARATION: Set the Neutral Masks out on a table so that everyone can see them as you discuss the concept of neutral.

INSTRUCTIONS: Following the instructions in chapter 6 for contemplating and imaging the mask, the participants take one of the Neutral Masks and go away by themselves in the space. They can set their Neutral Masks upright on a chair or table and observe them from different angles and distances. As they contemplate the masks, they should ask themselves how the face of a Neutral Mask differs from a human face. They should not rush this time for contemplation. They also need to make notes about their perceptions in their journals.

OBSERVATIONS/DISCUSSION: After the time allowed for individual contemplation has been completed, reassemble the Neutral Masks on the table in front of the group. As you collectively contemplate the row of Neutral Masks, ask yourselves the following question: What unique qualities or characteristics have you observed about the Neutral Mask?

Possible responses include:

"It has little or no expression." Therefore it is capable of revealing all expressions.

"It has no mouth indicated for speaking." Therefore the Neutral Mask work is done in silence. This is done so that the participants will concentrate fully on the physical. Much acting training concentrates on the verbal and ignores the physical. Here this is impossible.

"It is symmetrical in shape." Yes, in the Neutral Mask, one half of the face is identical to the other half. As participants discovered in an earlier exercise, no actual human face is symmetrical. Our faces are asymmetrical: one half is in a constant silent dialogue with the other half.

"It gives no clues about its gender." There are, perhaps, only larger and smaller sizes to fit the face sizes of the different wearers.

"All the Neutral Masks are identical in structure. Does that mean that we should all end up looking identical when wearing the masks and moving though space?" Again, yes . . . and no. The intent of the Neutral Mask is to *depersonalize* the wearer, stripping away the idiosyncratic movement or behavior that is "you." Peter Brook, among others, has noted the value of mask work on the wearer's psyche: "The moment you take someone's face away in that way [in this case with the Neutral Mask], it's the most electrifying impression: suddenly to find oneself knowing that that thing one lives with, and which

one knows is transmitting something all the time, is no longer there. It's the most extraordinary sense of liberation. It is one of the great exercises that whoever does for the first time counts as a great moment: to suddenly find oneself immediately for a certain time liberated from one's own subjectivity." [3]

There is a sense in which people wearing Neutral Masks will tend to look and move more uniformly. Paradoxically, though, at the same time that the Neutral Mask depersonalizes the wearer, it also *essentializes* the wearer. You discover more of what is distinctly "you." On each wearer, in fact, the Neutral Mask adapts itself to that wearer. Therefore, what is elicited is actually your *individual* neutral. As Shomit Mitter explains it, "As the actor is identified with the mask, the self becomes an external attribute that can be studied." [4] What neutral *is* is not easy to define. What is interesting, though, is that we seem to have an idea, a concept of what neutral is in our imaginations. And the acknowledgment of this concept is crucial for our training in mask improvisation.

It is easier to see what neutral is not than what it is. Jacques Lecoq, the foremost living authority on the Neutral Mask, says that you discover the "yes" of neutral by a series of "noes." He also explains neutral by using the image of a seesaw. Neutral is the fulcrum—the point of perfect balance—when the seesaw is tilting neither to one side nor to the other. [5] This image of the seesaw and the idea of the perfect balance point will become important in our understanding of neutrality.

Interface: Individual Movement Analysis

The Neutral Mask is used in the exercises that follow, but the participants should not make any attempt to contemplate the mask in order to bring their bodies into harmony with it. The Neutral Mask is worn here not to affect the wearer so much as to influence the viewer's perceptions. In these exercises, students are taught to observe closely the movements of their classmates playing against the Neutral Mask.

It is best to spread these individual movement analyses out over several class sessions, combining them with the "Getting to Know You" exercises from chapter 4. Too many of the movement analyses in one session can dull the concentration. Use the Individual Movement Analysis Form, found in Appendix C.

Caution: Each of us intimately connects our self-image with our body-image, and the movement analysis can be a very threatening experience for some people. The exercises should be taken seriously and conducted with respect for the personhood of each individual in the class. A great element of personal risk can be involved in this procedure, and therefore the exercises should offer a time for the group to demonstrate concern and trust for each other. Each member of the workshop should have complete trust that no person's body or movement will be the subject of private comment within the class or of gossip outside it.

EXERCISE 2: PERSONAL MOVEMENT ANALYSIS*

OBJECTIVE: to analyze each person's physical being, standing still and in movement, in order to determine what is unique about it. How do we recognize Tom, for instance, by the way he stands and moves through space?

PARTICIPANTS: full group, one at a time.

PREPARATION: No mirrors are used during these exercises.

INSTRUCTIONS: Do not begin with extended warm-ups, as you want to see the bodies of the students as they function normally in daily life.

Half the class sits at one end of the room, and the other half sits along one side of the room. The participants are therefore observed from two perspectives.

One participant at a time goes into the space, dons a Neutral Mask, without contemplating it, and walks up and down in front of the group as himself. He moves parallel to the observers on the side and perpendicular to the observers at the end of the room.

SIDECOACHING

Walk normally as you do in everyday life.

(The teacher, sharing the space with the participant, watches from both angles of observation and makes notes on an Individual Movement Analysis Form. Everyone observes silently.)

TEACHER OBSERVATION NOTE: One procedure you can use to help identify what is happening in the student's body is imaginatively to "put on" the part of the student's anatomy and/or movement that puzzles you and live inside it for a few moments while you are observing it in action.

(When the teacher is finished taking notes on the subject as he moves:) Please stop in the center of the space, standing at a right angle to the main body of student-observers.

(Now the student's body is observed in stillness. Here the teacher makes further notes about the person's body alignment. At the conclusion of this procedure:) Please walk up and down the room again.

(As the student does so, the teacher points out to the subject and to rest of the class the idiosyncratic movements of the subject, starting with his feet and moving upward.)

A CAUTIONARY NOTE: Watch your use of unconscious judgmental language when you analyze someone else's movement. Say, for instance, that "the movement is fast for the size and weight of your body in space," not "your movement is too fast." Or say that the person is "more aligned," not has "good alignment."

Exercise 2a: Personal Movement Analysis Repeat

After one or two times of doing the Personal Movement Analysis exercise with different participants, the teacher should ask the class to assist in commenting on the movement and alignment of the subjects. One important aspect of this exercise is to train the eyes of the observers to analyze other people's bodily movement.

At the next class session, the teacher will give each student a copy of his Individual Movement Analysis Form to put in his journal for future reference. It will become an important part of his Actor's Psychophysical Profile.

Why do we use a mask for this exercise? Couldn't it be done without a mask? Yes . . . and no. Interestingly enough, using a mask helps both the participant and the observers concentrate on the body and the body's movement.

From the observer's point of view, the fact that the mask obscures the student's face seems suddenly and sharply to etch the silhouette of his body in space. As observers, we actually watch for the whole body of the actor to communicate. What the actor now learns is that when he is onstage, at a distance of twice his height from an audience, his face is not the primary communicator of what is going on. At that distance, the members of the audience can no longer "read" the actor's face clearly, even though they believe they can. The audience actually reads the signals sent by the actor's body and transfers them to his face. That is why in performance the physical and the verbal must send the same messages. The two aspects must be of one bodymind. *The mask reveals as it conceals.*

From the participant's point of view, the mask promotes the participant's concentration so that he has an enhanced awareness of his whole body moving through space. It also gives him a sense of protection—known in anthropological literature as the "anonymity function" of a mask—helping to hide any embarrassment he might feel in having his body and movement openly commented on.[6] A person can feel quite exposed and naked in the stripping-away process that goes on in this exercise. *The mask conceals as it reveals.*

Understanding Neutral: Part II

Why do we use a Neutral Mask for this exercise? Of crucial importance in the understanding of the concept of neutral is the observers' awareness of the Neutral Mask on each individual body. We are very aware of a person wearing a mask—a body wearing a mask that doesn't belong to it. As we have seen, this interface helps us identify the individual's idiosyncratic movements. And this occurs not just because the subject is wearing a mask, but because, in this case, the mask is symmetrical and the person's body and movement are not. Actually, what we are doing is taking our cues from the Neutral Mask, which tells us what the potential corresponding neutral body underneath the mask should be like. We superimpose or project an idealized neutral image of the participant's body—not of some universalized mythic human being—suggested by the Neutral Mask over the actual body of the participant in order to identify those unique physical and movement characteristics of the individual. Mitter writes: "It is impossible to view the self directly; the self cannot be both subject and object at once. But the moment an actor attempts to play a role [or, in our case, puts on a Neutral Mask] the self is objectivized. As the actor becomes another, the self can be brought to light as an intrinsic entity. . . . Aspects of the character that are easily portrayed suggest that they reflect something of the actor's own engagement with the world. Elements that are more remote define the self by negation."[7]

Participants can learn to bring their bodies more into alignment and harmony with the Neutral Masks so that the separation we sense so strongly is not as evident.

Repeat the Personal Movement Analysis until you have examined each member of the workshop.

EXERCISE 3: EXPLORING DIFFERENT MOVEMENT CENTERS*

We will now use the Neutral Mask as a device to increase the wearer's concentration and sense of protection in a series of exercises that will tell him more about his own and others' movement habits.

OBJECTIVE: to explore different movement centers in order to give students choices in creating characters.

PARTICIPANTS: full group, working individually.

INSTRUCTIONS: Begin by moving into the space and donning your Neutral Masks. Start moving around the space through a variety of paths, as yourselves.

When the first movement center is mentioned, continue walking, but begin to concentrate on that specific area of the body, allowing it to dictate how you now move through space. Do not thrust that part of the body forward to "show" that you are now moving from that center. Just concentrate on it. Visualize moving from that center.

The movement centers are the (fore)head center, the oral (throat) center, the chest center, the stomach center, the genital center, and the anal center.

SIDECOACHING

Imagine an energy source located in [name the movement center] that is leading the rest of your body through space.

(As students are moving from the announced center:) Don't let the emotion contained in that center remain excluded from your physicalization. Make an emotional commitment as well as a physical commitment to that center.

(Time lapse) Live *in* that center! Live *from* that center!

Sit down in a chair from that center!

(Time lapse) Stand up and walk around, exploring the world around you from that center.

(Time lapse) Relax out of that center by shifting your concentration to your abdominal breathing.

Now imagine an energy source located in [name a different center] that is leading the rest of your body through space.

Let your concentration and the energy source move to [the new movement center]. Allow it to lead you through space, making any adjustments in your movement you feel are necessary.

(Repeat sidecoaching, exploring different centers.)

(At end of exercise:) Freeze! Close your eyes, relax, and come out of the mask.

TEACHER OBSERVATION NOTE: Note the changes in physicalization that occur as students imagine moving from different centers. You can see that it is almost impossible for the image *not* to affect the body physically.

OBSERVATIONS/DISCUSSION

1. What changes did you feel happening in the body when you moved from each center?
2. Did the way you sat down change with different movement centers?
3. What feelings, attitudes, or emotions were aroused by each movement center?
4. What did incorporation of those feelings, attitudes, or emotions do to your movement from that center?
5. Should every character you create have the same movement center?
6. How might you identify a character's movement center from reading a playscript?

EXERCISE 4: MOVEMENT CENTER STEREOTYPES*

OBJECTIVE: to learn that we store in our unconscious an image library of movement stereotypes that we associate with different roles or personalities. We can easily retrieve these movement stereotypes. Once these have been brought to the attention of the actor, they can be used or avoided in creating a characterization.

PARTICIPANTS: half the group at a time. Assign an observer for each participant.

INSTRUCTIONS: Participants don Neutral Masks and start moving about the space. The teacher announces a series of roles or personalities. Each participant is to visualize the figure or character and see the figure moving through space. He should let the figure take over his body, allowing the image to suggest movement, gesture, attitude, and motivation or action.

Some possible stereotypes include wrestler, professor, movie star, store clerk, rock star, politician, priest, construction worker, talk-show host, criminal, jogger, and soldier.

TEACHER OBSERVATION NOTE: The transfer from image to movement should appear almost instantaneous. When a quick transfer does not occur, then the student is most likely analyzing, screening to decide on the "right" behavior.

SIDECOACHING

Image a [name one of the roles].

Image a stereotype of the character, enter it, and go with it, moving through space as that figure. Don't analyze the image that comes to you. Accept it. Commit to it physically and emotionally!

What attitude do you have about the people around you?

What do you feel about this space?

What's your biggest goal in life?

(Repeat twice, using different roles. After the first three roles are physicalized, stop the exercise:) Freeze! Close your eyes, relax, and come out of the mask.

(Have the participants and the observers compare notes in front of the class.)

Exercise 4a: Movement Center Stereotypes Repeat

Repeat the exercise with the other half of the group, but do not repeat the same roles, as the observers will have already "tried them on" imaginatively.

OBSERVATIONS/DISCUSSION

1. What center did you discover that each of the characters had?

   Some of these centers will be conditioned by the type of wrestler or movie star the actor imaged. Don't expect only one movement center possibility for each role. If you discover differences, examine the differences in the images further.

2. How did the quality of your movement through space change with each new character? Where was your movement center for each character? Where was your weight? What was your energy level? What was the focus or direction of your movement?

3. Did you have the image of a specific person in mind that you were physicalizing, or was the image a generic type?

4. Which do you think is the more compelling image to work with—a generic, stereotyped image or a specific, individualized image? Why?

Actors are normally taught to avoid stereotypes in their work. Stereotypes are seen as too clichéd, generalized, and un-

truthful. But since we so readily have access to them through our image library, perhaps we should think about them differently—as important starting points, not the ending points, in creating characterizations. The British actor Simon Callow, in his book *Being an Actor,* recommends this approach: "To begin with you'll probably conventionalize him [the character], see him as a type. You must do this, simply to separate him, stake out the territory. Then day by day, you particularize."[8]

The Neutral Body

Considering the earlier discussion of the term *neutral* and the concept of neutral, as well as the experience in Personal Movement Analysis and stereotyped characters' movements, what qualities could we say a neutral body might have that would bring it more into harmony with the Neutral Mask?

A neutral body would have at least six characteristics:

1. *A neutral body is symmetrical.* Each half of the body balances the other half; one half is a mirror image of the other half.

2. *A neutral body is centered.* The neutral body neither sinks into the floor nor tries to levitate. It does not lean back, avoiding life, or push headlong into it. The parts of the body do not work against each other but flow into each other; thus, we are not conscious of any one part "sticking out."

3. *A neutral body is integrated and focused.* Where is the movement center for the neutral body located? Is it the same place for everyone, or can it be in different places, depending on the individual?

4. *A neutral body is energized.* The neutral body has a sense of alertness and attention but not anxious anticipation or apathetic disengagement. It can be compared with the neutral gear of an automobile transmission when the engine is running, ready to shift into any gear. It is a level of energy full of potentialities, not overcharging or draining out.

5. *A neutral body is relaxed.* The neutral body should not appear tense and mechanical, but neither should it appear loose and floppy. The appropriate state is best described as "relaxed attention."

6. *A neutral body is involved in being, not doing.* The standing neutral body is not involved in any activity other than its own being state, "standing" within the action "to stand." It is only engaged in "making present," which means "making presence." I once had a student who was on the university swim team, and he described his understanding of neutral as the physically centered state that

his coach wanted him to achieve at the end of the diving board, the moment before he began his dive.

As we saw earlier, it is easier to characterize the concept of neutral by describing what it is not. If any descriptive quality can be attached to a person's stance, such as "imposing," "empty," or "stiff," then the stance is not neutral. These terms describe a physicalization that is not at the balance point of the seesaw, but already tilted to one side or the other. They are the beginnings of a characterization.

This fulcrum point, the state of perfect equilibrium—neutral—is rarely, if ever, achieved! All students can do is work toward it. We are not going to undo their unique and personal body formations and movement habits easily—certainly not in one workshop course. So why try at all? We'll try because in the process of moving toward neutral with their bodies and movements, they will discover more about themselves. In the Neutral Masks, they are engaged in the process of deconstructing themselves, of uncovering the construct of their own personal masks.

EXERCISE 5: DISCOVERING YOUR OWN MOVEMENT CENTER*

OBJECTIVE: to have each student discover his own personal movement center so that he can choose to move from it or from another one—whatever is most appropriate—for each of his future characterizations.

PARTICIPANTS: full group, divided into three subgroups (e.g., three groups of four participants).

INSTRUCTIONS: Divide the space into three equal work areas. Participants should go to the side of the room in their area and put on Neutral Masks. One at a time, they walk up and down the room in their area in front of their subgroup, as they did in the Personal Movement Analysis exercise.

Observers take notes on the location of the participant's personal movement center.

After a few minutes of walking up and down, the participant stops and removes his mask. He should then tell his observers where he believes his own personal movement center is located. Observers respond with what they witnessed. The participant and the observers may need to repeat the exercise if there is disagreement about the location of the person's movement center.

Repeat the exercise until everyone in each group has participated.

Exercises in Moving toward Neutral

EXERCISE 6: TO STAND*

Actors frequently believe that if their characters are not moving or talking onstage, they are not present. But an actor needs to learn that he can just be still onstage and be filled with the presence of his character. This exercise helps the actor to understand and promote "stillness" and "presence."

OBJECTIVE: to discover how to stand and generate presence with a neutral body.

PREPARATION: Warm-ups. Do not use mirrors! Divide the work space into two equal areas.

PARTICIPANTS: full group, in two subgroups (rotating as participants and observers), each with its own work area. The teacher floats from group to group as the students work.

OBSERVERS: Each participant gives his Individual Movement Analysis Form to one of the observers so that that person can check the progress on the identified problem areas.

INSTRUCTIONS

(For participants:) Before beginning the exercise, consult your Movement Analysis Form to refresh your memory of your own physical idiosyncrasies.

Take your Neutral Mask, find your own space in the room, and briefly contemplate your mask. Fix the image of the Neutral Mask in your mind's eye, and then assume the mask. Let the image of the Neutral Mask transform your bodymind.

First regulate your breathing, and then move your body toward neutral.

SIDECOACHING

Still fixed on the vivid image of the neutral body, conduct a bodyscan. Adjust any parts of your physicalization that you feel need changing.

As you continue to stand, move into a state of relaxed attention and just be!

(The teacher and the other half of the group observe this process carefully. After the participants are ready in their "neutral" positions, the partners observe them from all sides, making notes on what is and is not neutral.)

Freeze! Close your eyes, relax, and come out of the mask.

OBSERVATIONS/DISCUSSION: Hold a brief feedback session, comparing what was observed as neutral and not neutral from the outside with what was experienced by the participants from the inside.

Repeat this exercise until all the members of each group have participated.

EXERCISE 7: TO SIT*

When we sit down in a chair or stand up from a chair, we do not think about doing it as ourselves. We just automatically do it as ourselves. But how does the neutral figure sit or stand up?

OBJECTIVE: to discover neutral in sitting and standing.

PREPARATION: Place a straight-backed chair in front of the class. Prepare copies of the Observation Questions (below) for use in the exercise.

PARTICIPANTS: one volunteer. Divide the other students, the observers, into three groups: one group watches from the front, one from the right side, and one from the left side. Give each group a copy of the Observation Questions.

INSTRUCTIONS: The volunteer takes his Neutral Mask and stands in front of the chair. Before he puts on his mask, he tests sitting on the chair so that he will be secure about where the chair is located and the height of the seat. He should not lean against the backrest of the chair, but sit on the front half of the seat. The participant will decide when to sit and stand.

SIDECOACHING

Assume the Neutral Mask and move your stance toward neutral.

Matching your breathing to your movement, sit down, hold the sitting position briefly, and then stand up.

(Repeat this three times. Following the three sequences, critique the movement while the participant stands in the Neutral Mask listening.)

(To participant:) Try to incorporate the ideas you've just received from us, and repeat sitting and standing three more times, working on finding neutral.

(When the participant has finished this sequence, give further observations and then bring him out of the mask. The participant should note in his journal anything he needs to remind himself about what he needs to work on in the future.)

OBSERVATION QUESTIONS

1. Is the movement coordinated with the breathing? Does the person sit on an exhale and stand on an inhale?

2. Is the movement smooth, even, continuous, centered?

3. Are you aware of parts of the body not connected to the movement?

4. Is the neutral figure alive throughout, so that you do not sense separate "segments" of movement but experience a continuous flow?

5. When the participant sits down on the chair, do you sense that it is the end of the movement? It should be only one part of an ongoing movement sequence. As the participant sits in the chair, the energy must continue to flow, so that the standing will come out of it and not appear to originate as a wholly new impulse.

6. Is the neutral seated figure as centered as the neutral standing figure?

7. Does the participant anticipate the movement? There should be no separation between action and awareness, thinking and doing.

8. Does the neck move forward and the head tilt up in the standing and sitting down action? The head should be an extension of the spine and move with it, neither dropping forward nor tilting up in the process of standing or sitting.

9. Is the movement too fast or too slow for neutral?

10. Is the movement too rigid or too loose for neutral?

11. Does the participant's body adjust to the chair after sitting down? Watch for a collapse of the small of the back into the chair.

12. Where does the impulse for sitting and standing come from? From the chest? from the knees? Is it the same for sitting as for standing?

Exercise 7a: To Sit Repeat

Repeat the To Sit exercise with another student in front of the group.

Exercise 7b: To Sit Repeated Again

Repeat the To Sit exercise with the rest of the class in teams. Divide the class into two groups to work simultaneously, so that each student has observers watching from the front and from each side.

ASSIGNMENT: Practice the To Sit exercise on your own outside the workshop session.

Understanding Neutral: Part III

Anything that is not neutral is the beginning of a characterization—a turnout with the left foot, or a cocked-back pelvis, a head tilting down, or a loping walk, a movement center in the chin, or a shallow chest with hunched, curving shoulders. Each of these is a character!

The actor will discover through the work in neutral that he now has unlimited choices. He can bring this new knowledge to bear on each characterization. He will now be able to choose to use his left foot turnout, for example, as part of the physicalization of a character, or to realize that that body-image is not appropriate. His character may need his feet turned in and close together. The image of the individual neutral figure, like the concept of neutral, is obviously an intellectual construct— a compelling and powerful image that can function as an agent for the psychophysical transformation of the actor.

I-Not-I. As a student discovers his physical and movement idiosyncrasies and learns to move toward neutral, something wonderful happens. He finds that he has more presence and authority onstage. This presence and authority will be himself, but also more than himself. It will be him and other-than-him simultaneously. The actor and his double. As the director Ariane Mnouchkine observes, the actor's "presence increases with the capacity of the actor to be naked."[9]

In a 1976 interview with the critic John Lahr concerning his then-current production of *The Ik,* Peter Brook discussed the necessity for the actor to have the ability to create this quality of the not-I.

> The actor is what he is, but he projects an image which superimposes itself. This is the difference between an actor and a non-actor. The actor acquires this possibility (that everybody has to a certain degree) of making a certain concentration. He has to make a great concentration and from this concentration he then projects outwards something that is a suggestion to the other person. . . . And that's what we're working towards. A point of meeting in which you have what an actor is. The evocation has to go through the actor. The actor has to have sufficient self-knowledge to be able to whittle away the superficial excrescences and excesses of his normal personality simply because they have nothing to do with the pure line he wants to draw. He has to draw it in strict relation to what is his own specific nature.
>
> So there one has to distinguish between the mannerisms of personality and the essence. Therefore, if you are a fat person, you have to get rid of the personality characteristics that become the stock-in-trade of a big fat comic like Robert Morley and get down to the essence which can come in a flash in a performance of someone like Zero Mostel, who has the capacity in some of the things he does to look astonishingly light because of the conception of lightness which radiates through a heavy physique. An unprepared actor can't accomplish this. He has to get to know himself. He has to learn to free himself of a whole lot of mannerisms which lock him in. Having done that, he mustn't look for everything inside himself.
>
> The actor who tries, say, to bring Hamlet down to what he himself feels and understands is ridiculous. That is subjectivity and vanity gone mad. . . . The actor has to realize that what he's trying to create is not in himself, it's outside himself. But he can't understand it unless he can find an echo, point for point, a corollary with himself. If this is found, then he can immediately conjure that up before his audience.[10]

The exercises Contemplating the Neutral Mask, To Stand, and To Sit should be repeated at the next class session, if possible, as they help to confirm the students in the "just being" of neutral.

ASSIGNMENT: Practice standing and sitting in neutral on your own outside the workshop sessions.

EXERCISE 8: TO WALK*

OBJECTIVE: to discover how to walk with a neutral body.

PARTICIPANTS: The group is divided into two teams, with the teacher floating from group to group during the work. One person in each group volunteers to be observed trying to walk in neutral.

INSTRUCTIONS: Each participant takes a neutral stance and then starts walking up and down in the space.

SIDECOACHING

(For both participant and observers:) How does the Neutral Mask walk? Where is the Neutral Mask's center? What do you have to do to change your own personal movement habits to move toward neutral?

What energy level does a neutral walk use?

What is the purpose of your walking? Can you "just be" in your walking?

(The teacher and the other students carefully observe and make notes on this attempt to walk in neutral.)

The Neutral Body in Movement: Additional Qualities

What additional qualities characterize neutral when observed in movement?

1. *A neutral body is economical.* The neutral body uses only the energy that is appropriate and necessary to accomplish a task. When the neutral body moves through space, it can be characterized as neither fast nor slow. It is efficient.

2. *A neutral body is coordinated.* The movement should flow through all parts of the body, with every part engaged in a continuous and coordinated interrelationship.

Just as with the neutral body standing still, if the "doing"—the sitting, the walking—communicates anything other than the pure action "to sit" or "to walk," then it is not neutral. "Purposeful," "hesitant," "lackadaisical," "walking on eggs," "sauntering," "sluggish," "prancing," "fast," "slow"—these are not neutral. Only the appropriate energy needed to accomplish the task economically should be employed here.

Exercise 8a: To Walk Repeat

INSTRUCTIONS: Repeat the To Walk exercise. After the participant has walked for a few minutes, trying to bring his body into harmony with the Neutral Mask, the teacher and observers should comment on his movement, helping him be aware of parts of his movement that are not communicating neutral. The participant, hearing the comments, should try to make any adjustments necessary to bring his body into harmony with the mask.

When he has completed the exercise, the participant should go to his journal and write down any information he needs to help him remember how to accomplish moving toward neutral more effectively the next time.

Repeat this exercise until everyone in each group has participated.

EXERCISE 9: MAKING AN APPROPRIATE NEUTRAL GESTURE*

Is it possible to make a neutral gesture? This exercise examines that interesting question.

OBJECTIVE: to investigate whether one can make a neutral gesture.

PARTICIPANTS: Divide the group into three teams. The teacher floats from group to group. One student in each group volunteers to be observed.

INSTRUCTIONS: Once you have achieved a neutral stance, make a gesture that you believe is appropriate for neutral.

SIDECOACHING

You decide when to make the gesture.

Repeat the gesture three times, trying to refine it each time so that it becomes more neutral.

Can you "just be" in your gesture?

OBSERVATIONS/DISCUSSION

1. What is a neutral gesture? What type of arm movement does it entail? What configuration of the arm and hand is neutral? How does the arm move away from the body?

2. What images or associations did the gestures suggest by themselves? Did repeating the gesture begin to create a meaning beyond the gesture itself?

3. What happens to a gesture when we change the context in which it occurs?

4. Can there be a gesture without intention? What happens to a gesture when we give it a specific intention?

Context, intention, and a particular configuration to the relationships among the arm, hand, and finger give meaning to a gesture. We are trying to achieve a shape and a movement that communicates nothing but itself. Is that possible?

RESEARCH ASSIGNMENT: Observe very closely someone performing a simple, repetitive, work-related or sports-related physical action. Analyze the movement carefully to answer the following questions:

1. How much of the total body is involved in the simple action? Is it isolated in one part of the body only?

2. Where are the person's focus and concentration located?

3. What are the person's involvement and commitment to the task?

4. Is the simple physical action as efficient and economical as possible, or is there wasted effort? Does the body move toward neutral when a physical task is performed efficiently?

5. How much energy would be too much to accomplish the task? How much energy would be too little?

6. What type of space is needed to conduct the action?

7. How much time is needed to fulfill the action?

8. What is the pace, tempo, and rhythm of the simple physical action? Are there many tempos within the total action?

9. How neutral is the person's body in this action?

EXERCISE 10: PERFORMING A SIMPLE PHYSICAL ACTION

OBJECTIVE: to test the student's ability to analyze and duplicate a simple physical action.

PARTICIPANTS: full group, one at a time.

INSTRUCTIONS: After a brief warm-up period in which everyone can practice the simple action that he researched for the research assignment, the actions are shown one at a time to the class for identification and comments. The student should not inform the class what simple action he observed and analyzed.

OBSERVATIONS/DISCUSSION

1. What is the simple action being physicalized?

2. How do you know that?

(Repeat the questions asked in the Research Assignment.)

Summary. The qualities of the *being* and *doing* states of the Neutral Mask are symmetrical, centered, integrated, focused, energized, relaxed, economical, and coordinated. These will become important as guideposts in the training with the Character Masks as well. They also make an excellent starting point for becoming or presenting a character creation in any acting style without masks.

The Neutral Mind

Up to this point we have concentrated on finding neutral physically, in simple movement exercises. This last series of exercises raises the question that has been anxiously waiting in the wings—unless someone in the group has already raised it. If we have been talking a lot about the unity of body and mind, then where does the mind get involved in the neutral explorations? Can a person have a neutral mind?

We are now going to investigate this aspect of neutral. First, we need to refer back to the earlier discussion of the actor's divided consciousness in chapter 5. In that discussion we talked about two parts of the mind or consciousness: the knowing, experienced mind brings past knowledge and experience to bear in a new situation; and the innocent, inexperienced mind seems to experience everything as if for the first time and lives in the flow of the immediate present, in the here and now.

The neutral mind is this innocent, inexperienced mind or consciousness. The neutral mind has no memory, no past knowledge, and no experience. It is a *tabula rasa,* with no personal or collective history. It experiences everything it sees with new and innocent eyes without anticipation, as if for the first time. We know that no human mind is a *tabula rasa.* But this concept of the neutral mind is again a valuable construct that can reveal something important about ourselves to ourselves. Just as students learned a lot about the possibilities of their physical selves in attempting to move physically toward a neutral body, now they will learn a lot about the possibilities of their mental and emotional selves as they attempt to move toward a neutral mind. To do this, we will set aside our work with the neutral body for a while.

EXERCISE 11: DISCOVERING AN OBJECT FOR THE FIRST TIME*

OBJECTIVE: to explore and experience the neutral mind in discovering an object as if for the first time.

PARTICIPANT: one student. The teacher and the rest of the group will be observers.

PREPARATION: Before the class, gather together a collection of objects—try to have objects with working parts or compartments—and keep them out of sight of the class. (Otherwise, when they see them, their busy bodyminds will already be imaginatively exploring them, subverting the exercise.) The surprise element is important here.

INSTRUCTIONS

(To participant:) Assume your Neutral Mask and lie down on the floor on your side, facing the class. Don't worry at this point about whether this is a neutral position or not. We're setting aside the neutral body temporarily to concentrate on another aspect of the Neutral Mask work. Shut your eyes, and don't open them until given permission.

(To observers:) Watch closely to see if the participant communicates that he knows what the object is and how it is used by the way he handles it.

(Once the participant is lying on the floor in his Neutral Mask with his eyes closed, the teacher silently places an object on the floor in front of him.)

SIDECOACHING

When you are ready, open your eyes and discover the object placed in front of you *as if* for the first time.

Explore the object fully. You have never seen this object before in your life.

(While the participant is exploring the object, the teacher and observers make notes. After a specified time, end the exercise and bring the student out of the mask. Discuss the exercise with the students, using the questions below.)

OBSERVATIONS/DISCUSSION: Before beginning the discussion, look over both sets of questions and intersperse them in the discussion.

For observers:

1. Did the participant know the texture of the first part touched, or was it discovered? Of the second part, third part, and so on, if different from the first?

2. Did the participant discover the different surfaces of the object—dull, polished, matt, reflective—or were they ignored?

3. Did the participant know the temperature of the first part touched, or was it discovered? Of the second part, third part, and so on, if different from the first?

4. Did the participant know the weight of the object when picking up the object, or was it discovered?

5. Did the participant know the sound or noise the object would make when handled, or was it discovered?

6. Did the participant discover any working parts or compartments (e.g., a pocket, the inside)? Did the participant communicate a knowledge of these from past experience?

7. Did the participant discover the color(s) or smell(s) of object?

8. Did the participant show any emotional reaction, such as pleasure or apprehension, to the object that communicated past knowledge and/or experience?

9. Did the participant learn from discoveries in an orderly incremental progression (from effect to cause), without jumping any necessary steps in between?

10. Did the participant discover a whole new way to see and understand the object?

11. What happened to you as an observer when the participant was exploring the object in his innocent mind? Were you also seeing it as if for the first time?

For participants:

1. What was your experience in this exercise? Did you find you could see and explore the object for the first time?

2. When you first saw the object in front of you, you probably recognized what it was right away. Were you also able to disengage from the "knowing" mind and see it innocently?

3. As you began to explore and discover the object, what interface process was occurring between your knowing mind and your innocent, unknowing consciousness?

4. Did you discover anything about the object that you didn't know before?

5. Did you ever lose your awareness of the presence of the knowing mind? If so, was it when you found something about the object you had not previously known or noticed? Were you aware of us watching you at that moment? Of you watching you?

Exercise 11a: Discovering an Object Repeat

Repeat the Discovering an Object exercise with another student.

Exercise 11b: Discovering an Object Repeated Again

Repeat the Discovering an Object exercise with the whole group in three teams.

Now is the time to repeat the exercise so that the whole group has the experience of discovering an object as if for the first time. The group is divided up into three teams, with one member always functioning as participant and the rest as observers. The teacher is still the one to place the objects in front of the subjects, bringing each object out of hiding when the participant is ready. Repeat the instructions if necessary.

Observers carefully monitor the discovery process of their partners, making sure that each tiny increment in the discovery process is apparent. Place a time limit on the discovery process so the whole group will have a chance to participate during the workshop time. Team members discuss with the participants what they observed at the end of each round.

Repeat the exercise, rotating participants in each team, until each student has done the exercise.

JOURNAL ASSIGNMENT: Relate this experience of the neutral mind to your regular nonmasked performance work.

8

The Neutral Mask
Identifications

Introduction

The exercises in exploring the neutral body and the neutral mind prepared the workshop participants for the major training that occurs in the Neutral Mask: identifications. In the identification exercises that follow, we will combine the neutral body with the neutral mind. These identification exercises are based upon the training procedures used by Jacques Lecoq at his school in Paris, although the interpretations and commentary are my own.

Neutral Mask identification exercises depend upon the participant's ability to image: to understand and employ visualization. So first we need to define what we mean by *imaging* or *visualization* and then explore its technique.

Definitions. An *image* is a bodymind picture of something. It can be the recollection of an actual object or place, or a construct created by combining or superimposing real and/or fictional images. Imagery is based on sensory experience. Therefore, we have sight, sound, touch, taste, and smell images, although most of the time a nonvisual image is correlated with a visual image, such as the smell of a rose. Another kind of imagery also affects us constantly. We may not be too aware of this kind of imagery, but it is very important to mask improvisation. This is kinesthetic imagery, or a sense of movement and weight.

We need to remember that images and concepts are not the same thing and require different skills. As Gaston Bachelard so succinctly put it, "Whoever gives himself over to the concept with all his mind, over to the image with all his soul, knows perfectly well that concepts and images develop on two divergent planes of the spiritual life."[1]

Therefore, participants will have varying skills in imaging. All of us, however, can increase our abilities to operate "in our mind's eye." Visualization, or imaging, is not a mystical esoteric process. We employ it every day in order to live. Athletes have found it useful in enhancing their performance. In fact, the workshop participants have already employed visualization consciously or unconsciously in earlier exercises like Play Ball! and the Folding Chair.

To image is to be involved in the act of making images from the memory of sensory experience. It is also known as *visualization*. The noted British psychologist Rosemary Gordon explains *imagery:* imagery, she says, "serves several important biological and psychological functions: primarily it helps the organism to arrange the multiplicity of sensory stimuli into meaningful patterns which then make possible the release of instinctional reactions in the appropriate situations."[2]

Guided imagery occurs when the workshop leader side-

Eiko and Koma in "Tree." Photo by David Fullard. Courtesy of Pentacle.

coaches the participants into a more complete realization of the subject matter through suggestion of sensory images.

Imaging is the process of producing images.

Imagination can be defined as the ability of the bodymind to reproduce images from memory and/or the ability to create original images by combining, superimposing, or transforming previously experienced images. Imagination is the basis for our powers of creativity and discovery. Gordon's definition of the term is valuable. She views "imagination as a form of dramatization of images, a collection of images which have been brought together and 'produced' in association with other mental processes like thought, past experience, and intention. The special abilities upon which imagination depends are likely to come from the preconscious area, that is, that area or 'critical threshold of the conscious-unconscious border' which Rugg (1963) has called the 'transliminal state.' Clearly imagination is unthinkable in the absence of images, for they are its raw material." [3]

Imaging/Visualization Exercises

In the Play Ball! exercise, described in chapter 4, students learned how concentration on a specific image affects their bodymind responses. In the Folding Chair exercises, they experienced the difference between planned and spontaneous moments and tested their powers of visualization (imaging) and transformation. Now they will use what was learned there: they need to open themselves to let the spontaneous images flow into their bodyminds.

It is important in these imaging exercises that the participants become as specific as possible about what they are visualizing. The teacher should follow the procedures given for Group 1 below in all the other visualization exercises, using similar sidecoaching instructions to help the participants define the image for each exercise.

These visualization exercises can be divided between two workshop sessions. So Groups 1 and 2 could be performed before the first set of identification exercises, and 3 and 4 before the second set. At least the first round of visualization exercises should be followed with the discussion questions, or the

Eiko and Koma in "Wind." Photo by Tom Brazil. Courtesy of Pentacle.

teacher can allow time for the participants to write in their journals.

All participants should sit in a chair or on the floor in a neutral centered position. If a student is in a chair, then she should sit away from its backrest, with both feet on the floor and hands resting on her thighs.

VISUALIZATION EXERCISE, GROUP 1*

Close your eyes and concentrate on your breathing to help cleanse your mind.

When given the imaging instructions, visualize the image as vividly as possible.

See a bird flying across the sky.

Watch its flight pattern.

What kind of bird is it?

Now let the image fade out by shifting your concentration to your breathing again.

See a rose.

What color is it?

Bend over and smell the rose.

Now let the image dissolve by shifting your concentration to your breathing again.

Hear a bell ringing in the distance.

What does it sound like?

Now see the bell that is still ringing.

Let the image fade out by concentrating on your breathing again.

Touch a piece of velvet cloth.

What color is the velvet?

Let your fingers luxuriate in the pile of the fabric.

Now let the image dissolve by concentrating on your breathing again.

Taste mashed potatoes.

What is the consistency of mashed potatoes in your mouth?

What do they taste like?

Now let the image fade out by concentrating on your breathing again.

VISUALIZATION EXERCISE, GROUP 2*

Close your eyes and concentrate on your breathing to help cleanse your mind.

When given the imaging instructions, visualize the image as vividly as possible.

Walk through mud up to your shins.

Feel the pressure of the mud against the front of your legs.

What thickness is it?

What temperature is it?

Let the image dissolve by concentrating on your breathing again.

Stand up . . . and then sit down.

Imagine that you are walking around carrying a bowling ball in your right hand.

How is the rest of your body adjusting to this weight?

Let the image fade out by concentrating on your breathing again.

Balance a feather on your nose.

What is the rest of your body doing to keep the feather balanced?

Let the image dissolve by concentrating on your breathing again.

VISUALIZATION EXERCISE: GROUP 3*

Close your eyes and concentrate on your breathing to help cleanse your mind.

When given the imaging instructions, visualize the image as vividly as possible.

See a bug crawling on the ground.

How does it move through space?

Imagine that you are a camera and can focus in on it to see it close up.

What does it look like close up?

Let the image fade out by shifting your concentration to your breathing again.

Smell popcorn popping.

What does it smell like in your nostrils?

What does the smell taste like in your mouth?

Let the image dissolve by shifting your concentration onto your breathing again.

Hear footsteps coming toward you.

What kind of shoes is the person wearing?

Hear the footsteps getting closer . . .

and closer . . .

Let the image fade out by shifting your concentration onto your breathing again.

Touch the bark of a tree.

Let your fingers explore its unique texture.

What qualities does it have?

What does this texture remind you of?

Let the image dissolve by shifting your focus onto your breathing again.

Taste a slice of lemon.

What does the taste of it do to your mouth?

What qualities does the taste have?

Let the image fade out by shifting your concentration onto your breathing again.

VISUALIZATION EXERCISE: GROUP 4*

Close your eyes and concentrate on your breathing to help cleanse your mind.

When given the imaging instructions, visualize the image as vividly as possible.

Stand in the doorway of your bedroom at home.

What do you see from this angle?

Now shift your focus to the other side of the room, looking back at the doorway.

What do you notice from this angle?

See yourself in the doorway looking into the room.

Let the image dissolve by shifting your concentration onto your breathing again.

See your mother or father standing in front of you.

Rotate her or him slowly in front of you, seeing the sides and back of the person as she or he rotates.

What typical pose is she or he in?

What is she or he wearing?

What expression is on her or his face?

Let the image fade out by shifting your concentration onto your breathing again.

See a turtle crawling along the ground.

Watch its slow progress.

How do its legs move?

How does its neck stretch forward, leading the movement?

Now put wings on the turtle . . .

and watch it fly off.

Let the image dissolve by shifting your concentration onto your breathing again.

Hear the sound of a bass drum being struck repeatedly.

Feel the sound of it reverberate through your body.

See the sound of it in the air in front of you.

Let the image fade out by shifting your concentration onto your breathing again.

OBSERVATIONS/DISCUSSION

1. Which images were the strongest for you? Why?

2. Did you notice any slight physical changes or shifts in your body when you imaged? Where? When?

Experimental studies have shown that all imagery sets off a chain of minute psychophysical responses in the participant, whether acknowledged by the participant or not.

3. Did any images awaken memories or emotions?

Most memory imagery is also heavily charged emotionally, so it is even more effective in stirring psychophysical responses.

4. Did you find that imaging a single sensory subject brought other senses into play as well?

5. Where was your concentration when you imaged?

Students should discover during these visualization exercises that they have a vast image library stored within them that can be accessed at any time to feed them powerful and power-filled images. With Group 4 they discover that they also have the power to combine, superimpose, and synthesize images in their imaginations. This is exactly what happens when they dream. For mask improvisation, these are tremendously important skills to cultivate. Students will experience masks as *compelling* images that engage their senses and transform their bodyminds.

In the imaging exercises above, participants visualize the different images with the "eyes" of their bodyminds. Images make subtle changes in the physical being of the imager. It is this sensitive reaction of the body, as well as the mind, to visualization that the new exercises in the Neutral Mask will expand upon and explore.

General Instructions

In the Neutral Mask identification exercises, the neutral figure becomes what it sees. Its bodymind is totally transformed by its identification with the image of the subject matter.

The student's task is to visualize a series of given visual, tactile, and kinesthetic images as vividly as possible, letting each of them in turn take over her total bodymind. None of the subjects for identification are neutral in themselves, and all have unique physical properties and movement qualities.

Let's return to the imaging exercises for a moment and repeat some of them with an added identification component:

Close your eyes and concentrate on your breathing to help cleanse your mind.

When given the imaging instructions, visualize the image as vividly as possible.

See a bird flying across the sky.

What color is it?

What kind of bird is it?

Watch its flight pattern.

Now *become* the bird flying across the sky. Live *in* and *through* the visual/kinesthetic image, letting the image affect your bodymind.

What does the world look like below you as you fly over it?

Step out of the identification and see the bird continuing its flight.

Now let the image fade out by shifting your concentration to your breathing again.

Hear a bell ringing in the distance.

What kind of bell is it?

What does the ringing sound like?

Now *enter* that sound and become it. Live *in* and *through* the aural/kinesthetic image.

Feel yourself, as the sound, vibrating through the space.

Step out of the identification and hear the bell continue to ring in the distance.

Now let the image dissolve by shifting your concentration to your breathing again.

(Any of the other imaging exercises can also be handled in this same way, incorporating an identification with the image.)

OBSERVATIONS/DISCUSSION

1. How does the identification with the image affect the bodymind of the imager?

2. What happens to an image in your bodymind's "eye" when you become it?

The image that is other-than-you becomes you. The question is the same as "What happens to a character in a play when you become it?" The answer is the same: it becomes you as you become it. What we want to see in both cases is the image—or the character—living in front of us, not the actor playing the role. In other words, we want the image to move into the foreground as the actor moves into the background.

3. Imaging and identifying with an aural image is no different than imaging and identifying with a visual image. Remember, there are different kinds of images: sight, sound, smell, touch, taste, and kinesthetic—or any fanciful combination of these.

4. If there is a psychophysical reaction when visualizing the image as other-than-you, isn't there an even stronger impulse to physicalize the image when you become it?

The Transforming Imagination

Mask improvisation asks us to "see" with our transforming imagination. The procedure is simple. The all-at-onceness process can, perhaps, be separated into minute sequential components in the following manner:

Focus your "holographic" bodymind concentration on the visual, aural, tactile, kinesthetic experience of your image of the subject.

Surrender or abandon your body completely to the image when it comes, letting it flow from a mental image into the rest of your body.

Play with the image physically, letting it evolve and transform your bodymind and itself in your becoming of it.

Being versus Imitating/Illustrating

We must be careful to make a genuine distinction in evaluating the work between "becoming/being" the image by completely identifying with it and illustrating it. Konstantin Stanislavski was fond of quoting Nikolai Gogol's statement: "Anybody can imitate an image, but only a true talent can become an image."[4] An illustration is merely an *imitation* of the external characteristics of the image, successful though it may be.

General Guidelines for Identification Exercises

The identification exercises that follow can be physically demanding. Participants need a good physical warm-up and a great deal of clear space around them when they come to improvise. Elbow and knee protectors and tumbling mats, if available, should assist the more adventurous.

1. Don't worry about how to *do* the improvisation. That is analyzing, which will result in illustrating! Each subject for identification is general enough that it can be physicalized in many different ways.

2. Always move from the general to the specific in these exercises.

3. In these identification exercises, you are not asked to portray the whole of the subject in your physicalization. In fact, given the subjects, there is no way that you can do this. You are asked, instead, to become only a small part of a larger moving entity.

4. Once the subject for the improvisation is announced, visualize a vivid and specific moving image of it in your mind's eye. (Eyes can be closed for these exercises, if the participant so desires. Closing the eyes can sometimes aid concentration, especially if the participant is nervous about her physicalization.)

5. Accept the first image that comes spontaneously in the moment of visualization. Do not screen for other "better" possibilities here. If you do, your critical mind has already come between you and the work.

6. In the moment of visualizing the image, start to *become* it. As you move into the most appropriate starting position—standing, sitting, or lying down—let go of the image in your mind's eye and become it with your whole bodymind.

7. Sidecoaching will provide further help in identifying with the image.

8. Improvisations will end with a freeze-frame. In this freeze-frame do not let go of the image, but keep it alive in your bodymind.

To the Teacher. Give any unusual instructions for a specific exercise first. Then make sure the subject matter of each identification exercise is the *last* thing mentioned when you give the instructions to the students. Otherwise, their minds will be engaged in visualizing the subject at the same time as they are trying to listen to you complete the instructions.

The Four Elements

In all of the identification exercises that follow, the goal is to identify totally with, and fully become, the subject, leaving no part of the bodymind out of the physicalization.

EXERCISE 1: FIRE*

PARTICIPANTS: full group, working individually.
INSTRUCTIONS: Sidecoaching instructions, given when participants are doing the exercise, will ask them to utilize their divided consciousness. That is, one part of them hears the sidecoaching and adjusts, while the other part of them continues to live in the image.

Participants take their Neutral Masks and find a part of the space in which to work individually. They will need plenty of space around them so they don't come in contact with others.
SIDECOACHING

Assume your mask, moving into a neutral position.

Center your body in neutral.

Focus on your breathing to clear your mind.

The subject for identification is *Fire*.

(Time lapse) Be Fire with all of your bodymind.

Are you embodying Fire with all parts of your body? With your head? With your ankles and feet? With your chest? Stomach? Buttocks?

At what energy level is your Fire?

Where is the movement center of your Fire?

In what direction does the movement go away from that center?

What space does your Fire want to take up?

TEACHER OBSERVATION NOTE: Allow students to work for a short time on this element. Watch out for hyperventilation.

Freeze!

(Time lapse. During this brief freeze-frame, the teacher should check on the continuing embodiment of the image.)

Close your eyes, relax, and come out of the mask.

OBSERVATIONS/DISCUSSION: In discussing the identification with Fire, you will be addressing the distinction between the *universal* qualities of Fire—what all fires have in common that qualifies them as that entity—and the *particular* qualities of the specific type of fire that the participant has visualized. The particular fire imaged will have some effect on the universal qualities but will not contradict them.

1. What are the universal qualities of Fire that you have to communicate with your bodymind?

2. What specific image of Fire did you visualize, and how did your particular fire alter the universal qualities?

3. What are the challenges in identifying and physicalizing Fire?

Would using a film technique such as *stop motion* or *slow motion* help you to identify with and physicalize the element more effectively? You've all seen stop-motion photography that speeds up the imperceptible natural growth of a plant so that it blossoms miraculously before your eyes. That's one technique you may use: speeding up the actual kinesthetic developmental process inherent in the subject matter so that it is possible for you to physicalize the subject's movement through time and in space.

The other technique is like slow-motion photography that retards fast movement until you can see every part of the action. This is especially useful when the subject matter is moving too quickly for the human body to identify with it and physicalize it. With either one of these techniques, all the qualities of the image in movement must still be present.

4. How was Fire embodied in your body? Where is Fire's movement center?

5. What might be the most effective or appropriate beginning body position from which to physicalize this element?

6. What kind of breath or breathing pattern does Fire suggest? How can you connect your breathing to your physicalization to make it more an organic part of the whole?

The correspondence between breathing and movement in this exercise is a particular problem. Students must actually slow down their breathing and not try to match the surface breathing energy of fire. It is the powerful slower breathing pattern at the core of the fire that supports the more frantic activity at its outer edges. This is an important lesson for students to learn for their nonmasked acting as well: when the action is most energetic and intense, the actor should be most relaxed and should have her breathing most under control.

7. What's the form or shape of Fire? At its edges? At its center?

8. What's the energy level of Fire?

9. In what direction does the energy move?

10. What emotional state of being does Fire evoke?

11. What is the relationship between being and doing in Fire?

12. What is the relationship between inside and outside in embodying Fire?

These last two questions are important in effectively embodying these identification exercises (or for any effective acting, for that matter). Ariane Mnouchkine's comments in one of her workshops help us to understand the "rapport" that must be developed between these two entities. She is not directly discussing working with masks, but her observations are pertinent to our problem nonetheless.

One of your only weapons is action. But while you are in the doing alone, nothing can happen to you. You need states of being, presence. It is the state of being that justifies actions. The most important thing is to find your state of being. You need a *pure state of being,* a series of pure states of being. Is it enough to work on the state of being? Are we sure that if we work on a state of being, the state of being will follow? No!—a lot comes from what you believe or do not believe. But to *believe* is most important. You believe that space is outside of you. This is wrong, it is in you. I can only take in space if I see you take it in. I only see this distance by your look. . . . The problem is a rapport between the interior and the exterior. If you are not able to translate this rapport, you do little things, instead of daring to tell us, instead of making signs. Signs ask the question. If you haven't at a given moment felt both the emotion and the externalization by the sign, you haven't found it. Do not hide yourself, reveal yourself. You have to dare to discover. You are being figurative instead of metaphorical, instead of finding the sign.[5]

EXERCISE 2: WATER*

PARTICIPANTS: full group, working individually.

INSTRUCTIONS: Follow the sequence of procedures and instructions given for the Fire exercise.

SPECIAL SIDECOACHING FOR WATER

Be Water in all parts of your body. In your head. In your torso. In your stomach. In your ankles, your feet, your toes.

At what energy level is your Water?

Where is the movement center of your Water?

In what direction does the movement go away from that center?

What space does your Water want to fill?

OBSERVATIONS/DISCUSSION: Now that the students have physicalized the second element, they can compare this experience with their experience in the Fire exercise in answer to the observation/discussion questions (see Fire, above).

EXERCISE 3: AIR*

INSTRUCTIONS: Follow the sequence of procedures and instructions given for the Fire exercise.

SPECIAL SIDECOACHING FOR AIR

Be Air in all parts of your body. In your head. In your torso. In your hips. In your knees. In your ankles, your feet, your toes.

At what energy level is your Air?

Where is the movement center of your Air?

In what direction does the movement go away from that center?

What space does your Air want to fill?

OBSERVATIONS/DISCUSSION: Now that they have physicalized the third element, participants can compare this experience of Air with their identifications with Fire and Water in discussing the observation/discussion questions (see Fire, above).

EXERCISE 4: EARTH*

Identifying and physicalizing Earth is a unusual problem. All of the other elements are visibly in constant movement. We like to think that the earth is solid and unmoving, but we know from scientific investigations and natural phenomena that the earth is constantly in movement too. We are only aware of this movement when there is an "earthshaking" event. If students choose to image this violent movement of the earth, then they should use the technique of slow motion to help them physicalize it. This will be a real challenge to their ability to slow down the movement but still capture its essential qualities.

Other movements of the earth are more subtle, occurring over time. If students want to image these movements, then they can use the technique of stop motion to enable them to speed up their physicalization. This is also a challenge to their imaginations, as they must still maintain a continuous flow of movement. They need to remember that in these identifications they are only parts of larger moving entities.

PARTICIPANTS: full group, working individually.

INSTRUCTIONS: Follow the sequence of procedures and instructions given for the Fire exercise.

SPECIAL SIDECOACHING FOR EARTH

Be Earth in all parts of your body. In your head. In your chest. In your stomach. In your hips. In your thighs. In your ankles, your feet, your toes.

At what energy level is your Earth?

Where is the movement center of your Earth?

In what direction does the movement go away from that center?

What space does your Earth want to take up?

OBSERVATIONS/DISCUSSION: Now that they have physicalized the fourth element, students can compare this experience of Earth with their experiences with Fire, Water, and Air in discussing the observation/discussion questions (see Fire, above).

Movement Study

After the identification experiences with the four elements have been completed, students should work on the series of identifications, developing each of them into a movement study. Now they have the opportunity to rehearse aspects of their physicalizations without wearing the Neutral Mask, and they can also go back into the mask to incorporate the new work into the movement studies. Each student should receive a copy of the handouts entitled "Developing a Neutral Mask Movement Study," "Neutral Mask Movement Study Questionnaire," and "Determining the Form and Structure of the Movement Study" (see Appendix C) to aid her in fulfilling this extension of the identification exercises. At this time students can ask the teacher to observe their work in progress and give feedback.

The following procedures must be kept separate in the rehearsal process: When students are in the Neutral Mask, they are totally identifying with the subject, living it from the inside. When they are not in the Neutral Mask, they are watching their bodies function from the outside, as they work on refining isolated parts of the total movement, not the complete physicalization.

Students should not develop the movement study without using the Neutral Mask. The total identification with the element while in the Neutral Mask is part of the discovery process. In mask improvisation, participants learn in and through the flow of the improvisational moment, not just in any planning before or after it. In this rehearsal process, the total movement pattern of the element is inscribed, or habitualized, into the bodymind memories of the participants.

The realization of the movement study for presentation, therefore, proceeds by parallel yet interdependent methods: first, subjectively, by an identification and reidentification with the element while in the Neutral Mask, and, second, objectively, by an analysis and rehearsal of the movement phrase without the Neutral Mask.

TEACHER OBSERVATION NOTES: When the students are on their own working in the space, make sure that you observe their work from various sides, as their physicalizations must be three-dimensional. See the Observations/Discussion section under the Fire exercise for other notes.

Does the participant hold on to the image/visualization for too long before entering it? If so, watch for screening and the illustration or analysis of the subject rather than a total identification with it. The student will have usually made a choice with less risk.

Does the participant leave some part of her body out of the physicalized identification? Check the head, especially the eyes. Make sure that the eyes are not watching the rest of the body and that the hands, fingers, ankles, feet, and toes are totally involved.

Does the participant tend to isolate her physicalization into certain parts of her body? Is this a habitual behavior pattern?

One of my students said that in his imaging of the element of Fire he only saw the image as involving his head and the upper half of his torso. I reminded him that the instructions call for the total body to be identified with the subject, rather than an isolation of the image into a part of the body. Interestingly enough, the student's remark revealed his ongoing acting problem: his previous nonmasked characterizations had been criticized for being isolated in his head and upper torso. This provides an excellent example of how impulses from the unconscious can block a person's development. When I pointed this out to the student privately after class, he realized the connection between his remark and previous comments on his nonmasked acting. In the next workshop session, he actively involved his whole body in the identification exercises.

These identification exercises demand an abandonment of the Self on the part of the participant. Some students will have a difficult time allowing this and will resist the exercises, stating that they think the exercises are "silly." What they are really saying is that they think these exercises make them look silly. This protection of their personas and resistance to abandonment will most likely be a problem with their nonmasked performance work also. Check the eyes of the participants while they are working. The eyes will tell you immediately whether the students are living the image or just watching themselves perform it.

Does the student lose control of her physicalization? One way to prevent this is to tell the student that she may physicalize the identification in slow motion.

Does the student lose the image in the freeze-frame moment, or is the image embodied in the frozen physicalization?

Do not explain how to do an exercise. Some students have a tremendous need for approval. They need to know if what they are doing is "right." Your job is to tell them what you see, not how to do the exercise. Encourage them to try anything as long as they keep in mind the parameters of the exercise.

Watch out for participants sitting and thinking about how to do the exercise. They need to be exploring and discovering with their bodies, knowing that understanding will come in and through the being and doing.

Caution against storytelling in the exercise. We do not want to see the life history of the element, only a brief moment in time.

ORGANIZATION OF THE PRESENTATIONS

Plan A: After the warm-up period, the students work on each of the elements in turn (in any order). When one student is ready to show her work, she calls the teacher over to observe and comment. Depending on the time, the teacher may request that she continue to work on it and show it again.

Plan B: Before the warm-ups, the teacher meets with each participant individually to decide which elements are to be presented. The participant chooses one; the teacher another. The teacher should base her decision on the close observations of each student in the work session and should choose the element that will challenge the student most. Allow twenty minutes for warm-ups and another twenty to thirty minutes for the students to reconnect with and rehearse their images. Each participant will present both of her elements in sequence, without any comment in between. At the end of each student's presentation, ask the observers for comments using the following questions as a guide.

OBSERVATIONS/DISCUSSION

1. What qualities or properties did the movement study present?

2. Based on your experience of those qualities or properties, what element did you identify?

3. How did you know it was that element? Or, why were you confused about which element it was?

4. What qualities or properties were captured well?

5. What qualities or properties were missing?

6. Was the student doing only what was necessary to communicate the subject? Remember that two of the key principles of being neutral are economy and appropriateness.

7. Were all parts of the person involved in the identification? What were the most difficult parts to include?

8. Was the breath or breathing connected to or incorporated into the physicalization in such a way that it prompted and released it?

9. Did you experience a presentation of the being and doing state of the element, or an imitation and illustration of it?

10. Were the form and shape of the subject established well?

11. Was the level of energy or intensity appropriate for the image?

12. Was the direction of the energy or movement appropriate?

13. Did the movement phrase seem complete and organic to the particular form of the element?

14. Was the physicalization effective enough so that the presence of the human being performing the movement phrase moved into the background and the image of the element moved into the foreground?

15. Did the presentation tell a story—an event revealed through time and space—or was it simply a presentation of the "being state" of the element?

EVALUATION: These identification improvisations provide an

excellent opportunity for the evaluation of the psychophysical strengths and weaknesses of the workshop participants. Habitual patterns of doing and thinking are foregrounded by these exercises. When the improvisations of the four elements have been completed—including the movement study assignment—take time to evaluate each of the participants so that she is clear about what she is doing effectively and what needs more work.

The Four Elements Continued: Extension Exercises

In the exercises that follow, the identifications with each of the four elements are extended in new and exciting ways that will challenge the students' imaginations. Now participants will be involved in transforming an element from one state to another, combining the elements, expressing interactions between two elements, and transferring the element identifications to nonmasked improvisations. Only one exercise is given, in most cases, as an model for work with the remaining elements.

These exercises also involve the participants in a further investigation of structure as it evolves toward a more dramatic form.

EXERCISE 5: TRANSFORMATIONS*
In this exercise we extend further the exploration of the element of Water by exploring the ways it transforms from one permanent state to another.

PARTICIPANTS: full group, working individually.

INSTRUCTIONS: Begin by finding and establishing the form of the beginning permanent state of your element, and then discover the movement process from this beginning to the final permanent state.

Some subjects might include an ice cube in the beginning state, melting ice in the transitional state, and a puddle of water in the final state; or a pan of water on a stove in the beginning state, boiling water in the transitional state, and steam in the final state.

OBSERVATIONS/DISCUSSION

1. What are the problems in completing this exercise?

2. Does an inside force or an outside force catalyze the transformation from one state to another?

TEACHER OBSERVATION NOTE: Watch to see that the images are clear for the participants. For example, an ice cube does not melt all over at the same tempo.

EXERCISE 6: COMBINATIONS*
This exercise extends the process of identification and physicalization of combining the properties of different elements so

that they have a different form and composition, weight, spatial requirement, tempo and rhythm, center, and so on.

PARTICIPANTS: full group, working individually.

INSTRUCTIONS: Students choose one combined element to work on, following the procedures established in the identification exercises. Combined elements include mud (water and earth), lava (fire and liquid earth), and dust (earth and air).

OBSERVATIONS/DISCUSSION: How does the identification and physicalization of these combined elements differ from the work with elements treated separately?

EXERCISE 7: ENSEMBLES*
OBJECTIVES: This exercise extends the exploration of Fire, Water, Air, and Earth into ensemble improvisations where participants learn to identify collectively with each element while interacting and working off each other as part of a larger moving body.

PARTICIPANTS: full group, working together.

INSTRUCTIONS: These ensembles can be created with all improvising done simultaneously, or they can be created sequentially, with participants joining the ensemble one at a time. Place the members of the group in a configuration that is appropriate for each element; for example, for Air, they might be placed around the perimeter of the room facing inward.

If you are working simultaneously, then all participants begin improvising when the element is announced. Each improviser needs to adapt or adjust her movement to the rest of the group to establish a collective atmosphere and energy level.

If you are working sequentially, then one student should be designated to start the exercise by moving through the space lightly and easily at the lowest level of energy of the element; for Air, she begins as a zephyr. Then select another student to join the first participant, interacting with that student to increase and intensify the energy level. The level of intensity is not to reach its peak until the final student has entered the exercise. Indicate to all the remaining students one by one that they should join the moving ensemble. (Each new student should increase the intensity of the element as she enters—just by the fact of her entry.)

SIDECOACHING

Remember, you are all part of something that is larger than any one of you. Let the intensity, dynamic structure, and shape evolve spontaneously.

OBSERVATIONS/DISCUSSION

1. What are the problems and possibilities in fulfilling this ensemble exercise?

2. How did you feel as part of a collective identification with the element?

3. (For the sequential approach:) What happened to the

energy level of the element as more participants joined the ensemble?

4. (For the sequential approach:) What happened to the internal shape and structure of the element as more participants entered the ensemble?

TEACHER OBSERVATION NOTE: Watch for students who have difficulty giving up their individual movement to evolve a collective movement.

EXERCISE 8: INTERACTIONS*

What happens when one element interacts with another element? This exercise explores the actions and reactions that the elements have on each other when introduced into the same space. For example, if we bring together Water and Earth in a dialogue, what kind of physical development might occur during the interaction? Erosion!

We are aware of the movement of the earth when it has been sculpted or eroded by Air or Water. Here we have an outside force, Water, working upon and shaping the element Earth. Students must image and identify with their element, Earth or Water, experiencing the action and reaction of the other element that is working on them; for example, Earth does not erode the same way with Air as it does with Water. It is particularly important that each improviser identify with her own element and not that of the other person.

PARTICIPANTS: full group, working in pairs.

INSTRUCTIONS: All possible combinations need to be represented in the improvisation, so identify in advance which students will improvise which specific elements. The following combinations are needed: Air versus Fire, Air versus Water, Air versus Earth, Fire versus Earth, Fire versus Water, and Water versus Earth.

Students should have a chance to work on their elemental dialogue by themselves and then present it to the group for observation and comments. Make sure that the students do not just sit and talk but spend 90 percent of their time discovering through improvising. For this exercise, 90 percent perspiration plus 10 percent discussion equals inspiration!

OBSERVATIONS/DISCUSSION

1. Was each element established clearly before the dialogue began?

2. How was the relationship initiated?

3. How did the relationship develop? How was each element affected by the relationship?

4. What is the final result of combining these two elements? Did everyone explore the improvisation to this extreme? If not, why not?

5. What laws govern an element's behavior with another element?

6. What does this exercise suggest about dramatic activity and dramatic structure? (Give students a copy of the handout "Notes on Structure" in Appendix C.)

Transfers to Nonmasked Improvisations

These transfer exercises take place without masks.

In the previous exercise, it was difficult not to see the dialogues taking place in anthropomorphic terms. The elements provided the temperaments for human figures in a drama. One earlier understanding of these elements in Western culture identified the elements as psychological temperaments, or *humours*. Joseph Roach, in *The Player's Passion*, writes, "Each humour corresponds to both a characteristic passion and an element of nature; choler, like fire, dry and hot, fuels anger; melancholy, like earth, dry and cold, embodies grief; the sanguinary humor, like air, is moist and hot, and leads to amatory passions; the phlegmatic, like water, is wet and cold, and if not inert, shows itself as fear or astonishment."[6]

A new employment of this ancient correspondence between the elements and human psychology has now developed. In a recent article on the application of techniques of virtual reality to the transformation of theories of rhetoric and narrative, Sarah J. Sloane investigated the possibilities of building two distinct virtual reality body representatives, or narrative agents, that have the characteristics of Fire and Water, respectively.

Participants in virtual worlds would have the option of seeing themselves as a different kind of being in the artificial reality. The virtual world would help them imagine themselves as a blaze of fire or a wave of water.

Why fire and water? Fire is supple. A body representative of fire would show us a new way of putting hands through objects, a new understanding of our own edges. It would offer us the possibility of metaphors of heat, vacillation, disappearance. It would offer us a way of being in the world that was authentically antigravity; and it would offer us new sets of verbs—flickering, burning, inspiring (drawing in air), guttering, baking—to describe our active physical world.

Water, on the other hand, would provide an interesting counterpart to an avatar of fire. Water would likewise challenge human notions of edges, offering used metaphors of accommodation, verbs of seeping, steeping, waving, diluting, evaporating. While the possibility of being fire would offer users a weightless way of being in the world, the possibility of being water would offer a transparent identity. Both elements would offer users the possibility of assuming a wavering identity, a way of being in the world that could alter their human presence and that might have tangible effects on human expression. Specifically, these two body representatives modeled in a virtual world would afford a way of being in the world that is very different from what has previously been humanly possible.[7]

Now we will try to realize this correspondence more fully as we apply the Neutral Mask identifications with the elements to nonmasked acting.

EXERCISE 9: CHANCE ENCOUNTERS*

OBJECTIVE: to transfer the Neutral Mask identification understandings to improvising without masks.

PARTICIPANTS: full group, working in pairs without masks.

INSTRUCTIONS: Students work in pairs, each member basing her character in one of the elements (each pairing should represent contrasting elements). The students are now human figures that retain all the movement and other unique properties and qualities of their elements as the basis for their characters' beings and behavior.

The teams quickly decide on a location and an occasion for the chance encounter. When the encounter takes place, each student should engage her partner so that the elements interact and affect each other. The students should not decide the outcome of the encounter but should allow it to be discovered during the improvisation.

Each pair has thirty seconds to discuss the setup before presenting the improvisation to the class.

OBSERVATIONS/DISCUSSION: See questions under the Interactions exercise, above.

EXERCISE 10: COLD READING*

OBJECTIVE: to apply element identifications to scripted material

PARTICIPANTS: full group, working in pairs without masks.

INSTRUCTIONS: This exercise is similar to the Chance Encounters exercise, but this time scripts of two-character scenes are handed out for the actors to perform, after identifying each character with a specific element.

Each pair has two minutes to review the scene and choose an element for each character.

EXERCISE 11: "IT'S ELEMENTARY, MY DEAR WATSON!"*

Warning! This exercise should not be attempted until the students have experienced the countermasks training.

OBJECTIVE: to extend element identifications as a base for the creation of more complex characters.

PARTICIPANTS: half the group, unmasked.

INSTRUCTIONS: As an added complication to the Cold Reading exercise, this improvisation incorporates the concept of the countermask (private face versus public face) in an improvisation about a criminal investigation.

One student (playing the culprit) creates a character based on one element who disguises herself as one of the other elements to escape detection.

Two other suspects base their characterizations on contrasting elements but do not disguise themselves.

The rest of the participants play their characters as their elements.

The detective also must use an element as the basis for her characterization. She may also use a disguise of another element in order to apprehend the culprit. The detective should not know beforehand who the culprit is but should use detection devices to discover her identity.

The disguised characters—culprit, suspects, and detective—must include moments during the improvisation when the disguise or mask slips, revealing the true element beneath it.

Choose the location and the situation but not the outcome.

Exercise 11a: "It's Elementary" Repeat

Repeat the "It's Elementary" exercise with the other half of the class.

Key Juncture

For the one-semester integrated approach to mask improvisation, it is now time to shift to the Character Mask Improvisations. Some of the remaining Neutral Mask identification exercises will be incorporated into that training.

Continuing
Identification
Exercises

Introduction

These continuing exercises will explore the Neutral Mask's identification with various subjects in several categories: substances, colors, sounds, vegetation, and living creatures. There are many more exercise possibilities here than you will probably be able to incorporate into the workshop. If there is not enough time for everyone to explore these exercises fully, perform them with half the class at a time, with the other half observing. In this way all of the participants will be exposed to the full series of exercises and thus be made aware of their potential usefulness for nonmasked acting and their potential basis for original performance pieces. For students interested in exploring new performance modes and content, investigation of these exercises is required.

If your program of study does not allow time for these exercises at all, you *must* incorporate the human emotion exercises into the explorations of the Beginning Character Mask, as the integrated approach suggests.

Objectives. The subjects of these improvisations are to be explored in and through movement, by discovering what unique properties and movement qualities the subjects have, what inherent or external force compels or impels the movement, and what dynamic or dramatic qualities and structures are inherent in the particular movement qualities and in the sequence of movements.

Each exercise asks the student to investigate and discover within himself a whole range of imaginative psychophysical connections by identifying with subjects in each of the various categories. Two of the major goals of these exercises are to awaken the student's imagination and have him realize that the physical world around him is a tremendous resource for his future imaginative and creative work in the theatre; and to gather and store the experience of what is occurring in these identification exercises in his bodymind's imagination.

Pattern and Sequence of Exercises. These continuing identification exercises follow the same pattern and sequence as the identification with the elements exercises investigated previously, and in the interest of avoiding needless repetition, only sample exercises will be given in each category to serve as models. The sequence of exercises is identification (individual identification with the subject matter), transformation (individual transforming from one thing to another within the same category), combinations (two subjects merging to become a third), interactions (movement dialogues between two opposite subjects), ensemble (full group physicalizing the same subject or combinations of subjects within the same category), and transfers (application to nonmasked acting).

Procedures. Further instructions will involve only unusual

Erik Hawkins as Squash in original production of "8 Clear Places." Photograph by Peter Papadopolous.
Courtesy of the Erik Hawkins Dance Foundation, Inc.

information that needs to be provided for a specific exercise. Many of these exercises require half the group to observe the other half while evaluating the effectiveness of the explorations.

Identification with the World of Nature: Part I

These identification exercises explore identifications with substances, colors, and sounds. Then participants will combine the identifications.

EXERCISE 1: IDENTIFICATION WITH A SUBSTANCE*

Substances are interesting to imagine and physicalize. Either they have inherent dynamic qualities, or they are a force working on the environment around them, or they are moved and shaped by an outside force. The presence of this internal or external force must be accounted for in order to discover the movement possibilities.

OBJECTIVE: to identify with the dynamic qualities of a substance.

PARTICIPANTS: half the group, working individually.

PREPARATION: Print the names of substances on cards—one substance per card—to distribute to the participants. Possible substances include acid, glass, foam, oil, sponge, clay, steel, mercury, glue, rubber, honey, bread dough. Additional or different substances can be used.

INSTRUCTIONS: Assign each member of the group a different substance—one that will stretch that individual in a way that he needs to be stretched at the moment. The participants should not identify their substances to each other or to the observers.

Follow standard procedures for identification exercises (see chapter 8).

OBSERVATIONS/DISCUSSION

For observers:

1. What substance did you see?

2. Why did you identify it as that particular substance?

For participants:

1. What inherent dynamic qualities and overall structure did your substance provide for you?

2. What internal force did you exert on the environment? What external force did you feel working on you?

Exercise 1a: Identification with a Substance Repeat

Repeat with other half of group.

EXERCISE 2: TRANSFORMATION OF SUBSTANCES

Students are given two contrasting substances and asked to transform from one into the other.

EXERCISE 3: INTERACTION OF SUBSTANCES*

OBJECTIVE: to investigate the ways in which the behavior of one substance is modified by its interaction with another substance.

PARTICIPANTS: half the group, working in pairs.

INSTRUCTIONS: Each student takes the substance he has been investigating in a previous exercise and now works with a partner of a different substance, creating a silent movement dialogue or debate (see Interactions exercise, chapter 8). Use the previous discoveries of the inherent dynamic qualities in each substance to inspire and structure this dialogue. Develop an interesting and complex relationship.

When ready, present movement to the class.

OBSERVATIONS/DISCUSSION

1. How well did each student keep the integrity of his substance alive in the dialogue?

2. Was it a real dialogue in which the students worked off each other effectively? Or did each substance stay in its own little world?

3. Did the interaction with another substance modify the nature of each individual substance?

4. Did the structure of the developing dynamic relationship become dramatic? How did it begin? Where did it end?

Exercise 3a: Interaction of Substances Repeat

Repeat with other half of group.

EXERCISE 4: TRANSFER OF SUBSTANCES IN THE COLD READING*

As in the transfer exercise with the four elements, the students are asked to keep the qualities they have discovered in the substance alive as part of their human character's attitude and behavior. They work without masks and can verbalize.

PARTICIPANTS: full group, working in pairs without masks.

PREPARATION: Make copies of a variety of audition materials for the group to use.

INSTRUCTIONS: Hand out the audition scenes to the group to work on privately. When time is up, hold the audition. The actors must keep their substance alive physically as part of their own actor-personality, not as part of the role for which they are auditioning. A student who is "foam" and one who is "oil," for example, might audition for the roles of Hamlet and Ophelia in *Hamlet*. Let the substance also influence the vocal delivery.

OBSERVATIONS/DISCUSSION: See questions in the Interaction of Substances exercise, above.

EXERCISE 5: IDENTIFICATION WITH INDIVIDUAL COLORS*

PARTICIPANTS: full group, working individually.

PREPARATION: Prepare a series of cards with the name of a color printed on each of them. Colors can include red, blue, green, brown, purple, fuchsia, pink, yellow, orange, gray, black, chartreuse.

INSTRUCTIONS: Give one card to each student. The student is to develop a physicalization and movement phrase that captures the essence of the color named on his card.

OBSERVATION/DISCUSSION: See questions in the Interaction of Substances exercise, above. Additional questions can be asked about the work on this exercise:

1. How does the shade or intensity of the color affect the physicalization of it?

2. What is the difference between a primary and a secondary color? How can that difference be recognized physically?

EXERCISE 6: COMPLEMENTARY COLOR TRANSFORMATIONS

PARTICIPANTS: full group.

INSTRUCTIONS: Each participant is given two cards that list colors that are complementary to each other and asked first to establish one color and then to transform into the other color.

EXERCISE 7: COMBINING COLORS

Give each student two colors. Ask him to explore the physicalization of each one separately and then combine the qualities of each into one new "color." Alternatively, two students, each with his own color, merge to form a third.

EXERCISE 8: COLOR INTERACTIONS, A PAS DE DEUX*

PARTICIPANTS: full group, working in pairs.

INSTRUCTIONS: With each student taking the same color that he has previously worked on, pair the students with others of different colors. Students must create a brief pas de deux and present it to the rest of the class for evaluation.

EXERCISE 9: KALEIDOSCOPE ENSEMBLE

Everyone starts off by physicalizing the same color but changes as the teacher calls out different colors. Or, the change from one color to another can involve only a few of the students at any one time.

EXERCISE 10: COLOR TRANSFERS

Again, you can employ scripts for two-character scenes, as in the earlier Cold Reading exercise (see chapter 8). But you can certainly imagine your own original improvisations based on the identifications with colors. This exercise is done, of course, without masks.

OBSERVATIONS/DISCUSSION: Discuss the effectiveness of the students' individual and ensemble work following the improvisation. How did the dynamics of the scene change the intensity of the color of the physicalization?

EXERCISE 11: IDENTIFICATION WITH THE SOUND OF MUSICAL INSTRUMENTS*

This series of exercises is in three sequential parts, taking the participants through various permutations with their new identification.

OBJECTIVE: In this lesson the student identifies with and silently physicalizes the sounds of different musical instruments and then adds the composition dynamics, rhythms, and tempos.

PARTICIPANTS: full group, working individually.

PREPARATION: Prepare a set of cards with a different instrument noted on each of them. Some possibilities include piano, viola, trombone, violin, triangle, piccolo, trumpet, marimba, snare drum, flute, bass fiddle, oboe, kettle drum, harp.

INSTRUCTIONS: Each student picks a card out of a hat. He is to physicalize the instrument's sound qualities but not to mime how it is played.

After a time lapse, continue into the next exercise.

Exercise 11a: Dynamics, Rhythms, Tempos*

INSTRUCTIONS: As students are physicalizing the sounds of the musical instruments, the leader sidecoaches changes in the dynamics, rhythms, and tempos. Dynamic possibilities include crescendo, diminuendo, forte, pianissimo, piano. Possibilities for rhythms include pizzicato and syncopated. Tempos include allegro, vivace, lento.

After a time lapse, continue into the next exercise.

Exercise 11b: Combos*

Sidecoaching combines compositional elements (e.g., ask the participants to syncopate a diminuendo).

Discuss the challenges and effectiveness of the work at the completion of the improvisation.

EXERCISE 12: DUETS, TRIOS, AND QUARTETS

In this exercise the students work in teams of two, three, or four, with each participant continuing to perform the physi-

calized silent sound of the instrument with which he identified in the previous improvisation. The students improvise together to "play" a brief section of a well-known musical composition that employs differing dynamics, rhythms, and tempos.

When the groups are ready, they show their compositions to the rest of the class, who tries to guess the compositions.

EXERCISE 13: SOUND TRANSFERS

PARTICIPANTS: full group, working in pairs, without masks.

INSTRUCTIONS: Each pair of students takes a brief scene from a play and prepares a reading of it. They must employ the physicalization of the sound of the musical instrument developed previously to create their character. But now they must also create an appropriate vocal quality.

When they are ready, they present the reading to the class for comments.

EXERCISE 14: THE RAG BAG*

OBJECTIVE: Participants are asked to combine identifications to create a more complex improvisation. Because it is sometimes difficult to present various properties and qualities simultaneously, they can be explored and presented sequentially.

PARTICIPANTS: full group, working individually or in pairs.

PREPARATION: Gather together a collection of fabric materials in a bag (the costume shop is a gold mine here).

INSTRUCTIONS: Students one by one (or one from each pair) choose a piece of fabric from the bag without looking. Their task is to create a brief solo (or duo) movement piece that captures the properties and qualities of their fabric. When they are ready to present their movement piece, they hide their fabric so the observers will not know what to expect and will give them feedback based on what was experienced through the physicalizations.

SIDECOACHING

Take time to observe your piece of fabric carefully. Think about its properties and qualities: its color, its texture, its weight, its design, its flexibility, its weave.

These properties and qualities suggest the dynamics for your movement piece.

Here's an idea: if your fabric has a backing that is different from its surface, you have the potential for creating a dialogue between the two surfaces.

You must also keep any preconceived associations and/or emotional connections out of the physicalization or you will "illustrate" the significance of the fabric for you. This does not mean that you don't make an emotional connection with your identification with the fabric. For example, a piece of silk might suggest elegance to you. What you have to do is identify with and physicalize the inherent properties of the fabric that suggest those qualities, so that the observers are made to experience elegance.

When ready, present your movement piece to the rest of the class for comments.

Identification with the World of Nature: Part II

This set of exercises asks the students to identify with and gain bodymind knowledge of the world of nature: vegetation and living creatures. As a consequence of these exercises, students become fascinated with the world around them and have a deeper appreciation for it. These exercises, as we shall see, also have excellent possibilities for applications to performance.

EXERCISE 15: IDENTIFICATION WITH TREES*
OBJECTIVE: to identify with the configuration and growth pattern of specific trees.

PARTICIPANTS: half the group, working individually.

INSTRUCTIONS: Choose a specific mature tree to identify with and transform into.

SIDECOACHING: Ask the participants to live their trees through a cycle of the seasons as the seasons are announced.

OBSERVATIONS/DISCUSSION

For observers:

1. What kind of tree did each student embody?

2. Was the student fully identified in the process, or were parts of his body left out?

For participants:

1. What unique problems did you encounter in identifying with and physicalizing trees?

2. What forces were at work promoting your growth and development?

3. How did your tree react to the changing seasons? Did your changing physicalization also affect your emotional state?

Exercise 15a: Identification with Trees Extension
Repeat exercise with other half of class.

RESEARCH ASSIGNMENT: Go to the library and research the tree you worked on in class. Note specific references to the various stages of growth, and make sketches of any of those in your journal. See if you can locate a sample of your tree in the vicinity so that you can observe its structure and appearance closely. Then consider these questions:

1. What changes did your research produce in your understanding of the physicalization of your tree?

2. What is the value of this "academic" research for your imaginative life?

3. What possibilities do you see for creating a performance piece based on your subjective and objective research?

Dancers Eiko and Koma have created performance pieces out of identifications with nature—water, erosion, and so on—as well as a multifaceted identification with trees. Their choreography entitled *Tree,* according to Lynn Garafola, "celebrates the ripeness of nature in decline. An ode to autumnal pleasure, the piece has the quiet intensity of a last affair, its knowing eroticism, its savored textures, as distinct as the mosses surfacing the tree trunk around which the lovers twine. As in *Thirst,* they form part of nature's pattern, blending like camouflage into the leaves of their love nest. But they are also dehumanized by trompe l'oeil effects reducing their bodies to mysterious synecdoches—headless torsos, severed limbs, as beautiful in their strangeness as they are troubling."[1]

Examining this description of the content of Eiko and Koma's performance, we see that they use a seasonal reference that has deep emotional connotations, metamorphic transactions and correspondences suggested between tree, branches, and leaves and human shapes, and emotional and mental resonances evoked through embodied imagery.

Exercise 15b: Identification with Trees Repeat
Repeat exercise, creating a movement study incorporating your understanding gained from your inner and outer research. This time, physicalize the different aspects of the tree—roots, trunk, limbs, branches, leaves, and so on—in a transforming and metamorphosing sequence of your own devising.

EXERCISE 16: IDENTIFICATION WITH VINES AND VEGETABLES*
OBJECTIVE: to experience imaginatively the growth and movement of various vines and vegetables.

PARTICIPANTS: half the group, working individually.

INSTRUCTIONS: Each student chooses, or is given, a specific vine or vegetable with which to identify. The student explores the dynamics of its growth from seed to maturity. The rest of the class will observe and try to guess the plants from the physicalizations.

OBSERVATIONS/DISCUSSION

1. What plant did you see?

2. How well did the participant communicate the unique pattern and dynamic growth of his plant?

3. How well did the participant communicate the various stages in that process?

Exercise 16a: Identification with Vines and Vegetables Extension
Repeat exercise with other half of class.

RESEARCH ASSIGNMENT: Research your vine or vegetable

for more specific clues about the movement of its growth process.

Exercise 16b: Identification with Vines and Vegetables Repeat

Repeat exercise, creating a movement study incorporating the understanding gained from your research.

EXERCISE 17: NO ONE WANTS TO BE A WALLFLOWER

OBJECTIVE: to explore character creation and relationships using vegetation as an image base for the characterizations.

PARTICIPANTS: full group, working without masks.

INSTRUCTIONS: Assign a vegetation image for each characterization, based on the student's previous work, so that there is a mixture of trees, vines, and vegetables. Each participant must base his human characterization on the movement qualities of the assigned image. Let the unique growth and movement dynamics of the specific plant suggest movement, gesture, personality traits, motivations, and survival strategics. Vocalizations may be used, but they should be sounds coming out of the physicality of the image, not words!

The setting is a singles bar, where no one wants to go home alone. Assign bartender, waiters and waitresses, and customers. Ask the students to move into the space and take a neutral stance.

SIDECOACHING

Image your plant. Feel it in your bodymind, transforming it into the character. Establish its unique presence through the character's movement and vocal quality.

Enter the bar to accomplish your objective or task.

(Time lapse) Time is getting short. It's now only an hour until closing time.

(Time lapse) You now have only fifteen minutes until closing time.

(Time lapse) Five minutes 'til closing! You must get that date for tonight now if you haven't already done so.

(Time lapse) The bar is closed. Leave the bar and head home with your date, or deal with the fact that you don't have one.

OBSERVATIONS/DISCUSSION

1. How well were you able to keep your image alive in the exercise?

2. Did your image give you ideas for movement, personality traits, and motivations?

3. Name a character from a play you know well that might profit from a vegetation image base in your development of the characterization.

Identification with the World of Nature: Part III

In these exercises, participants will explore identifications with various nonhuman animals and then will identify with human emotions.

The exercises focusing on nonhuman living creatures could be extended to investigate all the different types of animals. Here we have limited ourselves to three: insects, fish, and birds. One of the interesting challenges of this exercise is identifying with and physicalizing these different orders of being. It is easiest to use the body to capture the form and movement of insects; it is hardest, perhaps, to physicalize fish and birds. The way to approach these exercises is not to try to manipulate the body into the literal shape of the creature but to suggest the essence of its form and motion. Just as in the earlier exercises, the images of the creatures, not the actor, should be foregrounded.

EXERCISE 18: IDENTIFICATION WITH LIVING CREATURES*

Each student chooses, or is assigned, a specific insect, fish, or bird to identify with through physicalization of it.

EXERCISE 19: TRANSFORMATIONS OF LIVING CREATURES*

OBJECTIVES: to develop bodymind knowledge of the world of living creatures as a basis for future creative work and character development; and to look at the world imaginatively from the point of view of different orders of being.

PARTICIPANTS: full group, working individually.

PREPARATION: Gather a variety of chairs, tables, and other furniture in the room to act as dens, perches, and hiding places for the creatures in this exercise.

INSTRUCTIONS: This is an extended three-part improvisation. Until told differently, students should work only on and for themselves. They should not relate to the other creatures as yet. Students don their Neutral Masks and go into the space, assume a neutral stance, and await the announcement of the first image.

SIDECOACHING

Image a specific insect, and begin the exercise.

(Time lapse) What possible range of movement does your creature have within it?

How does the size and weight of your creature affect its movement?

How does the shape or form of your creature facilitate its movement?

How much does the physical environment in which your creature lives condition its movement and behavior?

Try to physicalize moments when your creature is at rest or immobile.

How much space or territory does your creature need in order to live?

Discover and relate to all the other creatures in the space with you.

(Time lapse) Freeze! When you come out of the freeze, you will transform into a fish. Image a specific fish. Transform your insect into the fish and continue the exercise. Ready? Go!

(Repeat sidecoaching sequence above as applicable.)

(Time lapse) Freeze! When you come out of the freeze, you will transform into a bird. Image a specific bird. Transform your fish into the bird and continue the exercise. Ready? Go!

(Repeat sidecoaching sequence above as applicable.)

(Time lapse) Freeze! Close your eyes, relax, and come out of the mask.

OBSERVATIONS/DISCUSSION: Any of the sidecoaching instructions above can be turned into questions for discussion. The following questions can also promote discussion:

1. What unique challenges did you face in physicalizing a fish, an insect, and a bird?

2. How did it feel to "evolve" from one creature into the next?

3. How did you relate to the other creatures?

4. How did you know whether the other creature was a friend or a foe?

5. What did you do when you sensed danger? How did this change your behavior?

EXERCISE 20: METAMORPHOSIS*

OBJECTIVE: to explore the movement possibilities in transforming from one creature into another.

PARTICIPANTS: full group, working individually without masks.

INSTRUCTIONS: Borrowing a fascinating idea from Franz Kafka's short story "Metamorphosis" (as Steven Berkoff did for his stage adaptation), this exercise asks the participants to undergo a metamorphosis from human being into one of the three orders of living creatures and back again (e.g., human into insect into human; human into fish into human). The student may choose any of the three creatures—bird, fish, insect—to transform into, but he must always live for a few moments in one state, establishing that life before transforming back again.

The student should discover the "trigger" that begins the metamorphosis into the other creature and the trigger that reverses the process. Each image should be of a specific creature that exists, not some fantasy creature.

When the students are ready, the metamorphoses should be shown to the rest of the group for comments.

OBSERVATIONS/DISCUSSION

1. What was the nature of your metamorphosis?

2. What did you find most interesting, the full realization of the new creature once you had changed into it, or the transitional moments?

3. What trigger compelled the metamorphosis into the creature? What trigger compelled the metamorphosis into the human again?

4. What psychophysical connection could be made between the human and the creature?

NOTE: Further work with animals, including transfer exercises, is carried out with the Totem Masks. If you are only studying the Neutral Mask and want to conduct further animal identifications, see chapter 13.

The identification with human beings completes the Neutral Mask identification exercises. It would be well to explore the full pattern of exercises (identifications, transformations, combinations, interactions, ensembles, translations), though only a few of these are offered here.

EXERCISE 21: IDENTIFICATION WITH EMOTIONAL STATES*

OBJECTIVE: to explore the physicalization of various emotional states of being.

PARTICIPANTS: full group, working individually.

INSTRUCTIONS: Begin the exercise by having the students don their Neutral Masks and assume the neutral stance. When the teacher announces the specific emotional state, the participants transform themselves into kinetic sculptures that embody that emotion. Some emotional states of being—in no particular order—include fear, surprise, acceptance, anger, anticipation, disgust, happiness, sadness, awe, tranquillity, hope, disappointment.

Caution: Like any emotional work, these exercises can release real emotion from past experiences, images, and memories that have been stored in the muscle memory of the body, so be sensitive to that possibility and be careful to balance the "heavier" emotions with "lighter" ones. Also watch that you do not give all the "heavy" emotions to one group.

SIDECOACHING:

Your emotional state is one of [name an emotional state].

Communicate the emotional state with your whole body.

Make sure your hips are expressing the emotion.

Make sure your chest is expressing the emotion.

Feel the energy of the emotional state in your legs and in your fingertips.

(Sidecoach other areas of the body, if necessary.)

(Time lapse) Freeze! Close your eyes, relax, and come out of the mask.

OBSERVATIONS/DISCUSSION

1. What focus or directions—such as inner or outer, up or down, forward or back, twisting or thrusting—did the emotional state seem to have in its physicalization?

2. Did you discover that there are different ways to physicalize an emotional state? Why is that so? How would you characterize the difference?

3. Did you discover that you began to feel the real emotion in the act of physicalizing it? Were any specific images awakened in your mind? What does that tell you about the interrelationship of the physical and the emotional? The image and the emotion?

4. Did you find that your face under the mask was trying to express the emotional state also?

5. What emotional states were more difficult to physicalize than the others? Why? What emotional states were the easiest to physicalize? Why?

6. In what emotional state is the Neutral Mask? Does being neutral mean there is no emotional state present?

EXERCISE 22: EXPLORING THE RANGE OF AN EMOTION*

OBJECTIVE: to explore the physicalization of various emotional states through increasing levels of intensity.

PARTICIPANTS: full group, working in two equal teams. The teacher and the students not participating in the exercise at one moment serve as the observers.

INSTRUCTIONS: Divide the class in half and have the two groups line up at opposite ends of the room. Each group is involved on an alternating basis in this exercise. We will designate them Group A and Group B. The group's task is to increase the emotional intensity in equal steps over the number of participants in the group.

Group A goes into the Neutral Masks and the neutral stance. When ready, the teacher announces the emotional state they are to physicalize in the space. As they are identified by a tap on the shoulder, the students one at a time enter the space and create the emotional state or atmosphere through their physicalizations of it.

The first student into the space establishes a neutral atmosphere or state. The next student into the space establishes the lowest level of the emotional state. The first student already in the space must then join the second student in creating the lowest level of the emotional state. This does not mean that the first student has to imitate the exact physicalization of the emotion by the new person, but he should try to discover his own expression of the new intensity level.

The third student enters the space and raises the level of emotional intensity through his physicalization. The previous two students must join him in creating this new level.

This process continues until all the members of one group are in the space creating the emotion. The last person to enter has to raise the emotional level to its highest level.

After Group A has raised the emotional state to its highest peak, ask Group B: "Do you think that is the highest level at which that emotional state can be physicalized? In not, enter the exercise and raise it higher."

When the highest emotional state has been established, stop the exercise: "Freeze! Close your eyes. Let the emotion drain out of your toes into the floor. Come out of the mask."

Group A returns to its side of the room.

Ask the following questions:
1. What movement qualities did the emotion have that were unique to it?
2. Did the focus or direction of the emotion remain consistent with its static expression?

Then Group B dons the Neutral Masks and stands ready to receive the announcement of an emotional state. Repeat the exercise with a new emotion.

After each group has physicalized three different emotional states, gather everyone in a circle in the center of the space on the floor and discuss the discoveries made during the improvisation using the questions below, or give questions as assignments to be answered in the journals later.

OBSERVATIONS/DISCUSSION

1. What is the relationship between emotional level and energy level?

2. Did moving the physicalization of the emotion through increasing intensities awaken your own feelings of the emotional state more than the static expression?

3. At what level of emotion is the Neutral Mask?

EXERCISE 23: COMBINING EMOTIONS

Ask participants to combine the physicalization of two opposing emotional states. What happens when two emotional states are combined? Is it possible? Or must the emotions be physicalized in rapid succession?

EXERCISE 24: TRANSFORMING EMOTIONS

Ask students to transform from one emotional state to another . . . to another!

Final Neutral Mask Identification Exercises

In these final comprehensive exercises in the Neutral Mask, students are challenged to develop movement studies using all their insights into the properties, qualities, and dynamics of elements, substances, and textures, as well as their knowledge of dramatic structure—i.e., linear, epiphanic, cyclical, dialectical—that they have gained through the improvisational exercises and movement studies.

EXERCISE 25: THE ART GALLERY

Locate photographs or postcards, like those usually sold in art museum shops, of paintings or sculptural pieces. Ask the student to choose one that challenges him (e.g., Rodin's *The Thinker*). Using the pose established by the artist either as a beginning or ending position, the student should develop a movement piece based on his response to the work of art. But his response should first be conditioned by "getting inside" the work of art physically and letting that experience trigger his emotional and imaginative life.

EXERCISE 26: THE ART GALLERY REVISITED

Repeat the previous exercise with small groups of participants re-creating a famous work of art or sculpture. Wouldn't Rodin's sculptural group *The Burghers of Calais* be a challenging basis for a movement study?

EXERCISE 27: HAIKU IN MOVEMENT*

Haiku are lively, brief, poetic pieces used as a challenging capstone to the Neutral Mask identification exercises. Many haiku involve the poet's own recognition of an intimate identification with the world of nature.

A successive flow of images and/or movement in a haiku involves an emotional identification with nature and/or a transition, transformation, or metamorphosis. Such a metamorphosis can be a transformation from image to image; from objective to subjective points of view; from a "close-up" to a "long shot"; from images presented through a screen of human observer or narrator to images presented directly seemingly without human intervention: from obvious human emotional response and connection with nature to detached observation.

These transitions, transformations, and metamorphoses occur through the poetic devices of juxtaposition, correspondence, and analogy. The images in continuous transformation evoke a widening of metaphoric implication into a moment of insight, frequently called the "ah-ha!" experience. With your divided consciousness, be aware of your responses during your initial reading of the haiku for that little "electric shock" of discovery that signals your sudden realization of a new insight engendered by the poem.

OBJECTIVES

to unfold or release a potential metaphoric meaning through the images and the flow through the sequence of images as they transform and metamorphose into one another;

to avoid illustrating the haiku or presenting a personal interpretation that the haiku might have for you alone, so that you do not tell your observer what he must feel and think but rather invoke the observer's imagination to become involved in the creation;

to be as economical and evocative in movement as the original haiku is in words and images; and

to let the emotional atmosphere of the haiku color the movement qualities.

Since haiku do not present relationships in time and space as linear, you may want to pay particular attention to the collage structure, in which the meaning is conveyed by associative relationships among the images. In the collage structure there are a number of echoes, contrasts, and correspondences among the images as well as in the overall design. (On collage, see "Notes on Structure" in Appendix C.)

PARTICIPANTS: full group, working individually.

PREPARATION: Write a number of haiku on cards. Let the students choose their own haiku from the collection.[2]

INSTRUCTIONS: Students will need time to work on their presentations. The exercise will require more than one workshop session. After the observers comment on the content of the haiku, the haiku can be read.

PRESENTATIONS: See the movement study presentation guidelines in chapter 8.[3]

EXERCISE 28: MOVEMENT HAIKU

Allow the student to present his personal interpretation of the haiku through a series of original images that evoke the same "ah-ha!" response.

EXERCISE 29: HAIKU ENSEMBLES

Either of the previous two haiku exercises can also be improvised by a duet, trio, or an ensemble.

EXERCISE 30: RESONANCES*

This exercise is extremely challenging and needs a good deal of time outside the workshop for development.

In October 1993 I saw the Butoh master Kazuo Ohno's performance of his movement piece *Water Lilies* at the Walker Art Center in Minneapolis. He was accompanied by his son Yoshito Ohno. *Water Lilies* is a six-part movement collage inspired by Ohno's emotional identification with the aging artist Claude Monet and to Monet's struggle to capture multiple levels of perception in a series of paintings of water lilies during his final years. The movement collage incorporated images from Monet's own artworks, especially those produced during his later years at Giverny, as they "met" and interacted with Ohno's own life. The dance was a meditation on the "reality, appearance, and transparency" in nature and human life.[4]

It was an extraordinary performance by a eighty-seven-year-old dancer who held his audience entranced by his (re)experience and manifestation of a successive flow of compelling images. Ohno's performance demonstrated an important principle: As long as the dancer-actor lives fully in the constantly transforming and metamorphosing flow of images, he can take us with him on his journey.

The flow of images changed point of view and perspective from inner to outer; from object to subject; from male to female; from youth to age; from human to insect to plant (e.g., from woman with parasol crossing into the garden on stepping-stones to praying mantis in the garden to water lilies blooming in the pond); from the human to the spiritual world. One amazing moment occurred when this nearly nude old man metamorphosed into a baby and a youth. The series of images in continuous transformation took on meaning through "analogy and juxtaposition."[5] Movements and gestures flowed on a continuum between the mimetic and the abstract. Repeated movements and gestures took on new meanings within new contexts. Ohno's movements released a corresponding stream of associations, connotations, and reverberations in the observers, as the images played with and against each other, and with and against the evocative music.

As in Noh drama, the flow of images blurred time and space, subject and object, past and present. And the "logic" for this collage of images was maintained (and contained) by the continuing presence and successive flow of images embodied in the performer's moving body rather than projected by his mind, except as it listened and responded to his body's memory. The fragmented and fragmenting self/selves of the performer, and the audience, were held in suspension by the wholeness of the imagination of Ohno's bodymind.

OBJECTIVE: to create a movement collage from a personal metaphoric "ah-ha!" response to a collection of works of visual, aural, or verbal art by using the techniques of observation, identification, transformation, metamorphosis, analogy, association, and juxtaposition.

PARTICIPANTS: individual.

III

The Character Masks

The Beginning
Character Masks

You need states of being, presence. It is the state of being that justifies actions.
—*Ariane Mnouchkine*

Introduction

What do we mean when we use the words *character* and *characterization*? Why do these words refer both to human beings and to fictional creations? In order to answer these questions, it is necessary to look at some definitions of these and other words used in referring to "character" and "characterization":

Character: [fr. Gk *charakter,* fr. *charassein* to scratch, engrave] . . . 2a: one of the attributes or features that make up and distinguish an individual . . . c: the complex of mental and ethical traits marking and often individualizing a person, group, or nation . . . 7a: a person marked by notable or conspicuous traits . . . b: one of the persons of a drama or novel, c: the personality or part which an actor recreates.

Characterization: the act of characterizing; *esp:* the artistic representation (as in fiction or drama) of human character or motives.

Characterize: 1: to describe the character or quality of, 2: to be a characteristic of: distinguish <an cra *characterized* by greed>.

Persona: . . . 2a: an individual's social facade or front, b: the personality that a person . . . projects in public: image. . . .

Personality: 1a: the quality or state of being a person, b: personal existence . . . 3: the complex of characteristics that distinguishes an individual or a nation or group; *esp:* the totality of an individual's behavioral and emotional characteristics.[1]

From these definitions of words that we use to explain what we mean when we "characterize" the nature of our own or someone else's identity, it is obvious that what we are and who we are entail a matrix of meanings that is not easy to describe. At present there is a great debate raging over the question of whether we truly are a "one" or a "many," whether we have a single, essential, unified identity or one constantly in flux. As the critic Bert States explicates the dilemma, "Every person who interests us, literary or actual, is modified by character— that is, the property of a consciousness that behaves in a certain way, in one sense never precisely duplicating its behavior, in another always remaining itself, always in abeyance—always, in some part, held in reserve—yet always demonstrating a self-sameness and a principle of animation that lasts through time and transcends the process of its continual adjustment to the flux of the world."[2]

This question and the possible distinction between the fixity (permanence) and/or the fluidity (impermanence) of an actor's personality and a character's personality will become important as we investigate the various Character Masks. The

Student in Beginning Character Mask, American Theatre Association Workshop, Chicago. Photo by Andrew Tsubaki.

Student in Beginning Character Mask, American Theatre Association Workshop, Chicago. Photo by Andrew Tsubaki.

question will become even more important as we note what choices can be made in the interstices between the wearer and the mask. If one is to become the Other, as in Stanislavski's approach, then we want a merger to occur so that the observer's attention is focused only on the mask and not on the wearer. But if a more Brechtian separation is required, then a corresponding choice can be made as well. At this point in the mask improvisation training, we are seeking a union between the wearer and the mask.

The Beginning Character Masks

The Beginning Character Masks are basically two-dimensional masks made of heavy paper with bold but simple designs

printed on them (see templates in Appendix B). Those who have worked previously in the paper Neutral Mask will notice that these Beginning Character Masks use the Neutral Mask as a backing.

These masks were designed many years ago by a former student, Kathy Czar, who was inspired by a set of children's masks used in the "Creating Characterization" unit of *The Five Sense Store: The Aesthetic Education Program,* as well as by the nine permanent emotional states (*rasa*) of traditional Indian theatre.[3] Six of these designs show ways of expressing a particular emotion that have been recognized through empirical research as universal ways of expressing that emotion.[4]

This approach obviously flies in the face of the "received" notions of how to begin creating a character: "Not from emotion, but from action." Even though I was trained in the Stanislavskian approach (or at least the American version of it), it has always seemed to me that one of the first "handles" an actor has on a role is its state of being (emotional/mental content) and her empathetic response to it. So why not start with the physical side of that psychophysical response, instead of focusing on the head-centered, analytic "objectives"? This will be our "take" on Stanislavski's "method of physical actions"—his own explorations of an alternate method to his head-centered approach late in his life.

Our focus on an emotional-physical starting point is supported by Denis Salter in an article about Ariane Mnouchkine's production of *Les Atrides*. Salter makes an important observation about the value of having actors learn how to physicalize "the heightened expression of cardinal emotions." This method, he says,

> regrettably, fell into disrepute during the nineteenth century with the advent of naturalism and its insistence on intimate or domesticated acting conventions. When it is supported by an appropriate degree of "truthfulness," this style can still achieve an unparalleled combination of (seemingly disparate) things: perfectly grounded characterization, emotional amplitude, imaginative efficiency, and pictorial vividness. It is ideally suited to scenes of absolute stillness or evocative immobility—in which emotion is so completely self-contained that it conjures an autonomous world into existence—or to scenes of extraordinary physical speed and agility in which emotion seems to grow exponentially.[5]

As will be seen, it is impossible to physicalize the emotional state in one of these Beginning Character Masks for more than a few minutes before the physicalization evolves unconsciously into a more complete psychophysical characterization.

If the first law of mask improvisation and performance is *The mask is the reality,* then we now need to add the second law. That is, *The mask is the text.* In mask improvisation, just as in working with a playscript, all of the characterizations will flow from a meeting of the individual mask with the individual wearer. So even if we recognize that there are certain fixed or permanent character traits and qualities to a mask, there will always be an enormous variety of interpretations of that mask because of its encounter with the fixed and fluid character traits and qualities of the wearer.

Nine different Beginning Character Mask designs are provided in Appendix B, and at least two duplicate sets should be available so that all the students have access to a wide variety of masks.

These masks serve two important functions in the overall mask training: to initiate the student into the techniques and understandings for the bodymind identification with a wide range of characters; and to provide a further diagnostic look at the habitual choices each participant makes in physicalizing movement and behavior so she can be helped to develop the widest range of possibilities for herself.

Blocks to Creativity. In chapter 5 we identified the first major block to the flow of creativity in the actor as the critical voice. The second major block is habitual thinking and doing, as seen through unconscious habitual physical, psychological, and behavioral "choices." The actor's unconscious habitual behavior will become objectified in working with these masks and will assist the student (and teacher) in defining the Actor's Psychophysical Profile. These habits can then be used or set aside as needed in developing a characterization.

Mirrors. The work in the Beginning Character Masks requires mirrors. Mirrors give an added shock value to compel the actor into richer psychophysical realizations. What the student experiences in the first encounter of herself masked in a mirror is the image of the Other that she must become.[6]

Equipment/Preparation. Have a collection of various furniture pieces (chairs, tables, benches, etc.) available in the room for the exercises in the Beginning Character Masks. They provide further release for the characterizations that will be developed. Make sure these are sturdy, nonvaluable pieces, as they will most likely get rough treatment.

Brief Review of Ground Rules and Objectives. For a complete review, see chapter 6.

With the Beginning Character Masks, the time for contemplation and observation of them before putting them on should be very, very brief—no more than five seconds! If the students are spending more time here, they are already analyzing the mask. (In fact, once they have seen these masks, their imaginations will already have started to put them on.)

The participant's primary task is still the same as in the Neutral Mask: to bring her body into harmony with the mask. This means that the physicalization must be *appropriate* for the mask. There are many ways to physicalize each particular mask effectively, not just one way. The physicalization all depends upon the wearer's personal response to the mask.

After briefly contemplating the mask she has chosen, the participant goes to a mirror, stands before it, and moves into a neutral stance. She closes her eyes as she puts on the mask and focuses on her breathing to clear her mind. As she simultaneously opens her eyes and exhales, she sees the mask on her body in the mirror. She accepts the "shock" of the first encounter as an opening for reception of her intuitive impulses as she responds to the image in the mirror: the forming of the character's bodymind gestalt superimposed on her bodymind.

Trust the impulse! The participant must attend to her intuitive and spontaneous responses to the mask. She should not screen her impulses or let the critical voice intervene, telling her what to do or not do. She must follow where the mask leads without reservations.

As before, there is only one exception to following one's impulses in being led by the mask: violence toward oneself or others is not allowed!

Beginning Character Mask Exercises

EXERCISE 1: FREE-FOR-ALL*

OBJECTIVE: This is the first exposure to, and experience in, the Beginning Character Mask. It is a very different experience from the first encounter with the Neutral Mask in many ways, but in one way it is identical. The participants are asked to identify completely with the character they find in the mask.

PARTICIPANTS: half the group, or the full class.

INSTRUCTIONS

Go to the table and choose a mask that has caught your attention.

Contemplate it briefly. (Allow no more than five seconds.)

Then go to the mirror, take the neutral stance, and follow the procedures for assuming a mask.

When you open your eyes and see the reflection in the mirror, let the image of the mask lead and inspire you into your physicalization.

Transform your body to bring it into *harmony* with the mask. It may help if you move slightly toward and then away from the mirror, trying out a physicalization.

Once you've started a physicalization and an image of the character begins to form in your imagination, trust your impulses. Get away from the mirror and move off into the room, exploring your mask in movement. The mirror can become a terrible crutch, and it will activate your critical-analytic mind if you stand there observing yourself for too long a time.

Don't hold on to the image of the character with your mind, but let it flow into your whole bodymind.

Don't relate to others as yet. Work on yourself, for yourself.

Begin to explore the physicalization of your mask through the simple movement exercises, the same ones we examined earlier in the Neutral Mask: To Stand, To Sit, To Walk, Making an Appropriate and Necessary Gesture.

Remember: The mask is the reality! The mask is your text!

SIDECOACHING

(You will probably need to remind the participants of some of the exercise instructions during their improvisations in the Beginning Character Masks, especially the simple instructions for the exercise "To Stand.")

Explore the space. As you do so, be aware of how you walk.

Try sitting down. How do you sit?

Notice your breathing pattern.

What gestures seem most appropriate and necessary for you to make?

Continue to explore the room by moving to various locations.

Find a way to utilize the different pieces of furniture.

Stop exploring the room for a minute. Just stand and observe the others.

What is your response to each of the other people in the space with you? Does it differ with each one, or do you feel the same way about all of them?

(Time lapse) Begin to relate to others in the space with you, but do not get into conversations with them!

(Time lapse) Freeze! Close your eyes, relax, and come out of the mask.

Return your mask to the table.

Exercise 1a: Free-for-all Repeat

When the first half of the class has finished the first mask experience, the second group goes in and repeats the Free-for-all exercise. Alternate the two groups until each group has explored four different masks.

TEACHER OBSERVATION NOTES: Because of the bold designs on the Beginning Character Masks, they work quickly on the actors' imaginations, easily promoting an emotional and psychological identification. What needs to be observed closely is whether that emotional identification is carried into a physical identification or not. If the mask is filled by the imagination psychophysically, it will live. That means there will be no real awareness of actors wearing masks (a separation between wearers and masks). The body and the mask will appear to be one—a totally new figure.

Also watch for students who are blocking or screening this emotional and physical commitment to a mask and are merely "illustrating" it. They have analyzed what they believe to be an appropriate physicalization, but the masks do not live in or on their bodies. There can sometimes be a subtle difference here, but you become very aware of an actor wearing a mask. You know that the actor is doing all the work! This processing can occur if the student is taking too long before going to the mirror or observing herself in the mirror.

This is also a good time to observe each student's ability to create a range of different physicalizations. In the Free-for-all exercise, in which the students explore five different character masks in fairly rapid succession, any recurring habitual movement idiosyncracies or behaviors become objectified. Have you seen the actor create this particular physicalization before in any of her other performance work? If so, you want to make a special note of it. These recurring movement and behavior habits are not coming freely from the student's spontaneous creative imagination but from a habitual "compulsion tape" playing in her unconscious.

Along with these habitual movements and behaviors, you will discover that many students have already unconsciously typecast themselves. This self-typecasting may have had a significant negative influence on their auditions for productions. If this is so, this self-typecasting will become very evident as the Beginning Character Mask work proceeds. In addition, you may notice that each of the student's Beginning Character Mask characters falls into one of the following behavioral pattern categories: doer, joiner, fixer, manipulator, watcher, organizer, collector, builder, loner, depender, disrupter, attacker.

Ask each of the students to fill out a Personal Psychophysical Profile (see Appendix C), identifying any habitual movements or emotional behavior patterns that she has noticed at this point in her work. Now is an appropriate time for you to comment on your perceptions about any student's habitual movements and behavior patterns that you have noticed, but first make these remarks in response to the student's written comments in her journal, as you may be unmasking a part of the student's psyche here, treading on her persona. This kind of feedback should never be offered casually, as the persona is the shield that each of us has unconsciously constructed between ourself and the world for survival.

OBSERVATIONS/DISCUSSION: Once all the students have completed the exercise, ask them to respond to the following fundamental questions, either in class discussion or in their journals.

1. How are these masks different from the Neutral Mask? What additional demands do they make on you?

2. Did you find you were able to let the image of the mask take over and lead you into a physicalization?

3. Did you find that your physicalization developed into a definite pattern of behavior?

4. Did your physicalization and/or behavior reflect a definite emotional and mental state of being? An attitude about the world around you? About life?

5. How was your mental state or attitude about the world connected to the form of your physicalization?

6. How did your gestures express your mental and emotional state?

7. Did you discover a difference between contemplating the mask in your hands and seeing it on your face in the mirror?

If so, the student should always go with the image that she encounters in the mirror.

8. Did you have a strong need to relate to others in your masks? Why do you think this was so?

Here the participants realize that we frequently confirm who we are by others' reactions to us—by their acceptance or rejection. Others function as our mirrors too!

9. How strong was your need to talk to others?

We will continue to work in silence with this mask even though some students feel an overwhelming need to verbalize. It is important that we not allow this to happen as yet. We must channel that need into the physicalizations, so they will be strong and clear and not evaporate later with the release into the verbal.

10. What was the connection between your respiration and your physicalization in the different masks?

11. Did you avoid one or more of the masks? Why?

Before the exploration of Beginning Character Masks is over, each student should be challenged to explore any masks she has avoided.

12. Were you at all concerned about physicalizing a mask someone else had already done? Why?

This is not an uncommon response and reflects the need in our society to be unique and different—an individual. What students will realize, if they haven't already, is that the same mask on two different people looks somewhat different because the faces on which the mask is worn are shaped differently, the bodies underneath the mask are different, and each wearer fills the mask through different imaginative connections.

13. How easy or difficult was it for you to switch to a new mask? Was there still a residue of the old mask(s) within you? Is that still true even now, as we're discussing the exercise?

14. Thinking back on the experience, was an internal monologue or subtext taking place inside you while you physicalized each mask? If so, what was it? Was it stronger or weaker as you brought your body more in harmony with your mask? What does this experience tell you about how you might produce appropriate subtext in your other acting work?

The subtextual world develops in these masks without the wearer even thinking about it or trying consciously to manufacture it. This process often does not happen as easily in realistic acting training. In later exercises in the Beginning Character Masks, students will be sidecoached to talk to themselves in an inner monologue, to acknowledge this impulse and enrich their experience.

15. Were you aware at any time during the exercise of having a dual consciousness?

Actually, listening and responding to the sidecoaching requires operating from a dual consciousness, being both in and not in character simultaneously.

EXERCISE 2: CARRYING THE MASK*

OBJECTIVE: to discover the psychophysical lives of a number of Beginning Character Masks.

CARRYING THE MASK AND APPROPRIATE LEVEL: (See chapter 6 for further explanations of these terms.) Some students will only physicalize an identification with the emotional state or attitude found in the mask, rather than the sculptural qualities suggested by the design configurations on these two-dimensional masks. This is very likely to happen at the start in these Beginning Character Masks, because the designs for these masks were developed to capture different emotional states.

Students find it easy to develop "attitude" physicalizations for these emotional states, but they must come to understand that that is only an emotional-psychological exploration of the mask, not a psychophysical identification with it. Of course there must be a strong emotional connection with the mask, but students are asked to find a body that harmonizes with the mask—that harmonizes with the sculptural design features. As Shomit Mitter explains this approach, students should not try to feel the character's emotion so much as "physically inhabit a condition analogous to that required" by the mask.[7]

PARTICIPANTS: half the students at a time. The other half of the class is assigned as partners to the students participating in the exercise. The observers will watch their partners and give them notes on their work afterward. (See "Guidelines for Observers" at the end of this chapter.)

PREPARATION: Masks are placed on a table in the room.

INSTRUCTIONS: The instructions are the same as for the Free-for-all exercise, with the following additions:

Choose a new mask in which to improvise.

Follow the standard procedures for assuming the Beginning Character mask. When you observe yourself as the character in the mirror, try to find the body that "carries the mask."

Now work through the simple movement exercises: To Stand, To Sit, To Walk, Making an Appropriate and Necessary Gesture.

SIDECOACHING: (See Free-for-all exercise for the content and sequence of the sidecoaching. Additional sidecoaching:)

How does your body reflect and complement the expression on your face?

Freeze! In the freeze, expand and enlarge your movement and gestures to the maximum size and highest energy level of which they are capable. Fill this physicalization with the emotion required to sustain it. When you come out of the freeze, you will continue to explore your characterization in the space so that you are feeling and physicalizing more intensely the emotional state your mask has suggested to you. Ready? Go!

(Time lapse) Move an object from one place to another. How can moving an object express how you feel?

(Time lapse) Freeze! In the freeze, contract or shrink your physicalization to the smallest size and lowest energy level of which it is capable, while still maintaining the characterization.

Match your emotional level to this physicalization. When you come out of the freeze, you will continue exploring the space by moving objects from one place to another with this new size of physicalization and level of emotion. Ready? Go!

(Time lapse) Freeze! When you come out of the freeze, you will continue to explore this dynamic range in your mask. Connect your emotional life to the physical life of your mask. Find the external or internal triggers that compel you to enlarge or contract your psychophysicalization. Ready? Go!

(Time lapse) Freeze! Close your eyes, relax, and come out of the mask.

Meet with your observer-partner and talk about your effectiveness in "carrying the mask."

TEACHER OBSERVATION NOTES: Students may complain that this approach destroys their intuitive response to the masks and substitutes an analytic response. Why were they told to "trust their impulses" in physicalizing the mask the first time? They need to learn that for some of them their intuition and impulses need to be educated and that training begins here for the later, more complex work. Almost all students need to be coached into a bolder, clearer physicalization.

Unfortunately, we all too often do not "see" very clearly what we look at and tend to impose or project our own subjective agenda immediately onto the world around us without realizing it, shaping it to our purposes rather than molding ourselves to its purposes. Actors need to learn to "see" the masks with as transparent or neutral a personal "screen" as possible, in order to physicalize them effectively. Actors also do not realize that their bodies are not always physicalizing the mask when they think they are, or they believe that their physicalizations are very different when they are all very similar.

One of my former students chose the Beginning Character Mask with the most lines on it. It was clear that he had made an emotional-psychological connection with the mask, behaving with a definite attitude and intention, but he was not carrying the mask well physically. When I asked him during the evaluation session to tell me what he saw in the lines of the mask design, he said, "Tired." When I pressed him to describe the shape and configuration of the lines, he said they were sagging lines, broken lines, crumpled lines. I asked him to go back into the mask and find the sagging, broken, and crumpled body to match them. When he did so, he truly communicated "tired" to the rest of us, and his emotional-psychological connection with the character in the mask was even stronger.

The improvisations in the Beginning Character Masks ask an actor to make clear, strong choices in her work. Watch for an evolution into (or out of) a stronger physicalization, and comment on it.

Students may say that these Beginning Character Masks

seem too fixed, too limiting. It is a fairly common response to these masks. Ask the students to accept these limitations for the present. They will soon discover that there is more flexibility and subtlety in these masks than they ever imagined.

But it raises the interesting question of how characters are imagined and constructed. What do we mean when we say a character is two-dimensional or three-dimensional? It's the difference between our awareness of fixity and fluidity. These Beginning Character Masks suggest fairly fixed two-dimensional characters (one observer has described the improvisations in these masks as "watching a cartoon"). Characters that are "fixated" in a particular mental, emotional, and behavioral state have rigid personas (masks). Because of this fixity, it is difficult for them to change, to adapt, to develop. Characters with rigid personas are frequently the central figures in comedies, like Molière's *The Miser*. Interestingly enough, however, they are also the central figures in tragedy. King Lear's troubles also come because of his inflexibility.

Three-dimensional characters are just that: they have more dimension than their two-dimensional counterparts. They have more fluid and flexible personas; more facets, or sides, to their characters are revealed in addition to the persistent ones. They seem to adapt to the changing world around them. We call these characters "more complex." In these Beginning Character Masks, the actor is asked to create a character that has, or reverts to, a fixed response to every situation. So even if it wants to shout in anger, it has to laugh it off! The only change that can occur is that the response can become more or less intense.

The student must recognize, though, that both two-dimensional and three-dimensional characters are constructs by a playwright to serve her ends. Not all characters in plays are complex, especially many minor characters. One of the major difficulties for actors trained in realism in playing nonrealistic styles of theatre with many two-dimensional characters (as in Sophie Treadwell's *Machinal*) is that they do not understand the difference and keep trying to make all the characters three-dimensional.

Mask improvisation helps the student actor recognize and play the difference between the two types. She learns that she must construct the dimensions of her character guided by the playwright's parameters and purpose.

More complex character creation begins with the improvisations in the countermask exercises in the next chapter.

Exercise 2a: Carrying the Mask Continued

After meeting with their partners for a brief feedback session, the participants go back into their masks. Using their notes, they rediscover the body that harmonizes with the mask. They

should try to pick up the improvisation from the previous exercise where it left off, if possible.

The observer-partners now enter into the ongoing improvisation by moving among the actors. They sidecoach their partners to a more complete carrying of the mask. They may even sidecoach their partners to include parts of the body that seem to be left out of the identifications.

Continue into the next exercise.

Exercise 2b: Carrying the Mask Continued Still

After participants have moved back into their masks and are consciously working on their notes and/or are being sidecoached by their partners into a fuller realization of carrying the mask, suggest a theme for an improvisation or set up a situation and an action for the participants to complete.

One sample situation might be this: They are all in the holding tank of a police station waiting to be called in a lineup. One of the group is the guilty person. Without talking, the rest should try to identify which of their members is the guilty party and separate themselves from that person. (The group selects the guilty party, but usually one person willingly assumes this role in the improvisation.)

Or they are all in an emergency room at a local hospital, and there is a glitch in the computers so that all the patients, the doctors, and the nurses get mixed up.

As an alternative, set up a number of chairs in a semicircle in the center of the space and sidecoach the actors simply to sit in the chairs and observe each other.

After a time lapse, say, "Freeze! Close your eyes, relax, and come out of the mask."

Hold a brief follow-up discussion on whether the new work in the mask was more complete in carrying the mask. Note how effective it was simply to sit and observe. Actors frequently try to do too much in these masks.

After the discussion, the participants should go to their journals and quickly fill out a Character Psychophysical Profile on this mask (see Appendix C).

Exercise 2c: Carrying the Mask Repeat

Repeat the above sequence of exercises with the other half of the group.

TEACHER OBSERVATION NOTE: Watch for students who seem to be inhibited from doing anything in these masks—from making a clear psychological, emotional, intentional, or physical commitment. There is blockage here. Students may express this by saying they are feeling "trapped" in the mask. They need to talk this feeling out. Refer back to chapter 5.

Other students may remark that they do not find anything in a mask. They need to be told that they are not saying anything about the mask; they are saying something about themselves. They are not letting their spontaneous transforming imaginations engage in the process. They are not open and available to receive intuitive impulses coming from the mask.

At this point the students too will have observed whether a classmate is exhibiting the same or similar behavior in every mask; whether she is always choosing to physicalize the same parts of her body in the same way; whether she is choosing a mask in the same range as before; or whether she seems to be presenting herself (e.g., "The mask looked and acted like Andrea.") Actually what has happened is that the actor has unconsciously chosen to create a mask from her own habitual "compulsion tapes." You may allow the students to comment on this to each other, but they should be coached to do it respectfully.

It should be clear to such an actor that these personal habitual movements or behavior patterns are interfering with the development of her range. The mask's pattern of behavior should be distinctly different from the actor's. If the actor has already had personal movements and behavior habits identified, then little "red flags" may appear in her consciousness if she starts to physicalize or act in her habitual way. These "red flags" are extremely important for the actor to recognize and deal with, so that she can make choices that do not reflect this interference by her unconscious at work in the process.

When the "red flag" appears, the actor will have to choose consciously to do something different. That is fine for the time being, as new behavioral pathways need to be inscribed into the dark consciousness of the actor. But once the consciously chosen physicalization is developed, the actor needs to surrender herself to it.

This approach forces the actor to keep her attention first on the physical connection with the mask, not on the emotional or psychological connection. We are not looking for a mechanical type of physicalization, but this conscious working may result in a more caricatured or cartoonlike figure. Even so, the actor will have learned to let the mask dictate the bold, clear choices for her physicalization. These Beginning Character Masks are not subtle, and the choices in the mask should not be subtle either. Subtlety in mask work can be learned later. The danger in the work right now is that the actor will stop trusting her impulses and begin to analyze the appropriate physicalizations, thus manipulating her masks as lifeless puppets, not filling them with life from the inside. She will need comments on this improper alternate behavior too.

Exercise 2d: Carrying the Mask Repeated Again
Repeat the entire sequence with two more masks. It is important at this point to confirm the idea that the actor's bodymind must carry and support the dominant design features and level of the mask. At this time the teacher may wish to assign masks for the students rather than allowing them to continue to choose masks for themselves.

Investigating the State of Being and Pattern of Behavior

We are now going to work through a series of interconnected exercises focused on the relationship between different aspects of a characterization (emotional-physical states, intentions and objectives, relationships, patterns of behavior). These are, of course, not separate entities but inextricably entwined and layered in a character's personality. Its mental and emotional state is revealed through its physical behavior.

Once an actor has discovered the shape and pattern of body movement that harmonizes with her mask, it is important that she then become aware of the corresponding patterned (habitual) behavior this implies. A habitual way of moving and gesturing in space can reflect a habitual pattern of feeling and thinking.

This is an extended improvisation. Make sure you have allowed plenty of time for it before you begin.

EXERCISE 3: ESTABLISHING THE RHYTHMIC PATTERN*
OBJECTIVE: to discover the character's rhythmic pattern of movement as a way to uncover the inner life of the character.
PARTICIPANTS: full group.
PREPARATION: Place a number of furniture pieces around the room, and have a basket of small objects ready offstage.
INSTRUCTIONS: Take a new mask, contemplate it, and bring your body into harmony with the mask, discovering its shape and pattern of movement through the simple movement exercises.
SIDECOACHING

As you move through space, focus your attention on the rhythmic quality of your movement.

Heighten that rhythmic quality into a repetitive pattern of movement. Let it become a dance.

As you move, allow the rhythmic pattern to affect your thoughts and emotions. What images come? What stories? What needs?

(Time lapse) Freeze!—but keep the character's rhythmic movement alive in your imagination. When you start moving again, immediately move into the rhythmic pattern you have established for your character. Ready? Go!

(Repeat the instructions about stopping and starting more than once.)

(Time lapse) Keeping the rhythmic pattern of movement that you have found, vary the tempo of your movement through the space. (This can be combined with stopping and starting.)

(Sidecoach the participants to move faster and slower. This part of the exercise needs to continue until participants have moved through the "thinking about it" stage and the "tired of doing it" stage into the "automatic pilot" stage.)

(Continue into the next exercise.)

Exercise 3a: Essential Gesture*

OBJECTIVE: to discover the one, essential gesture that reinforces and defines the mask.

SIDECOACHING CONTINUED

(Time lapse) Freeze!—but keep your character's rhythmic movement alive in your imagination.

Discover a repetitive gesture, or set of gestures, that expresses your character.

(Time lapse) Get rid of that gesture and try another one.

(Time lapse) Enlarge this gesture until it is as big, powerful, and intense as possible. Let this behavior affect you emotionally and mentally.

(Time lapse) Make the gesture even bigger and more intense. Commit to it emotionally as well as physically. Talk to yourself in a silent inner dialogue as you gesture.

(Time lapse) As you continue to gesture, start moving though the space. Let your gesture support and feed the rhythmic movement you have discovered in your mask.

What need does this gesture express? Talk to yourself in a silent inner dialogue as you move.

(Continue into the next exercise.)

Exercise 3b: Finding the Need That Fits the Feeling*

OBJECTIVE: to extend the exercise into the discovery and promotion of an intention or objective prompted by an identification with the psychophysicalization in the mask. The actor must not continue to play the "being" state of the emotion that the mask immediately suggests. She should find the *need* that is being fulfilled or unfulfilled that prompts this emotional state and behavior.

SIDECOACHING CONTINUED

(Time lapse) Now shrink that gesture until it is as small and minuscule as possible but still present. Let this change in your behavior affect the rest of your body. How does this diminution of the gesture affect the intensity of your need?

(Time lapse) Explore the dynamic range possible between these two extremes. Find the trigger within yourself or within the environment that compels you to enlarge or contract your gesture.

(Time lapse. The teacher places objects in the space.)

Now move an object from one place to another in the room. Don't lose your rhythmic pattern or gesture, but let them feed the action. Find a need that fits the feeling you are already experiencing. Talk to yourself silently as you move.

(Time lapse) Move the same or another object from one place to another in the room.

(Time lapse) Move the same or other objects from one place to another. Let it become a pattern of behavior that is urgent and important to you.

(Time lapse) Increase the urgency of your need to move objects.

(Time lapse) Stop! Observe which objects you have moved and where you have moved them. Take one object that has become very important to you and examine it closely. Now either hold on to it or put it in a special place. Continue to talk to yourself in your inner dialogue about what you are thinking and feeling.

(Move immediately into the next exercise.)

Exercise 3c: Developing Relationships*

OBJECTIVE: to confirm and enrich the characterization through the establishment of relationships with other characters.

SIDECOACHING CONTINUED

If you have not already done so, become aware of the other people in the space with you. Don't make contact! Just be aware that they are there too.

What are your thoughts and feelings about these other people? Talk to yourself about them.

Are you aware of being observed by others in return?

Identify one of the group you would like to get to know. Find a way to establish and maintain contact, but do not get into a conversation!

TEACHER OBSERVATION NOTE: Always refer to previous observation notes to evaluate the students' psychophysical connection with the mask. Now that they will begin to relate to each other, watch and see that the physicalization of the mask is not lost because of the shift in focus to relationships. There may be some lessening or softening of it because of the interaction with others, but in fact the psychophysical connection should be reinforced and heightened by the interaction.

Watch for students who avoid contact or relate to all the others in exactly the same way, no matter what mask they are wearing. Their rigid, unaltering responses will not allow others to affect their behavior. As we have seen, the Beginning Character Masks suggest and promote this kind of behavior, but what you are looking for is another recurring pattern of behavior on the part of a student that signals something limiting in the student's choices and not just in this particular mask.

Also watch for those students who never develop a "doer" character but always depend on others to keep them involved.

Move immediately to the next exercise.

Exercise 3d: Discovering a Pattern of Behavior*

OBJECTIVE: to extend the discoveries to a realization of the connections between the psychological and the physical life in the habitual behavior of the character.

SIDECOACHING CONTINUED

Freeze! The life you have explored so far is a pattern of behavior for your character. When you come out of the freeze, explore and extend this pattern of behavior with others in the space. Ready? Go!

(If needed, provide a situation: for example, you are all in the emergency room of a hospital.)

(Time lapse) Freeze! Close your eyes, relax, and come out of the mask.

OBSERVATION/DISCUSSION: A lot of processing needs to be done following these exercises. If there is time, it can be done collectively in class; if not, make it a journal assignment.

1. How would you characterize the rhythmic pattern of movement you found in your mask?

2. How did the rhythmic pattern of movement affect you emotionally and mentally? What images appeared? What needs? Did this reinforce the image of or feeling for your character?

3. What did the stopping and starting part of the exercise do for you? How did this change you internally, if at all?

4. Did anything change in your awareness of the character when you varied the tempo of your movement?

5. What was the effect of the length of time you moved in the rhythmic pattern on your characterization?

6. What gesture or set of gestures did you discover for your character?

7. What happened when you enlarged that gesture? When you committed emotionally to it?

8. What did that gesture express about your character? Why was it essential to your character's self-expression?

9. What happened to you emotionally when you were side-coached to increase and decrease the intensity of your gesture?

10. Did you discover that you already had an emotional state inherent in and promoted by your gesture?

11. Which came first, do you believe, your gesture or your emotional state?

12. Did any of the objects you handled become a cherished possession, a precious object for you? Why?

13. Did you find a need that fit the feeling you were already exploring through your physicalization?

14. What does this tell you about the relationship between behavior, emotion, and intention? Where does emotion come from? Why does it happen?

15. According to Stanislavski-based training, should the actor really concentrate on emotion or intention in her work? Why?

16. Did you experience any external or internal conflict in the exercise? Why? What was the source of this conflict?

17. What did the ability to relate to others do to your own physicalization and characterization?

18. What personality traits did you discover in your mask? Which ones seemed more fixed and permanent? Which ones were fluid and adaptable?

19. What behavior pattern did you discover in your mask?

20. What prompted this pattern of behavior?

21. What recurring thoughts, if any, did you have in your mask?

22. Did you sense a connection between your behavioral pattern and your thought pattern? If so, what was it?

23. Did you have a strong subtext operating during this exercise? Was it stronger or weaker when you talked to yourself? Why? What can you say at this point about where subtext comes from and what releases it?

If the student is letting the compelling image of the mask lead her physicalization into a mental state and behavior that reflect both an intention and an emotional state within the context of the situation, she will not have to manufacture a subtext consciously. It will be present of its own accord.

24. Are you becoming more aware that you have a large cast of characters within you? What are your feelings about that now?

ASSIGNMENT: Complete a Character Psychophysical Profile on this mask.

Age

EXERCISE 4: THREE AGES*

OBJECTIVE: to explore how age affects the character's continuity of physicalization and its behavior pattern through time.

In most professional casting situations, people audition for a character as close to their own age as possible. In this class, the option is always the student's—or, more important, it will be dictated by the mask. But interestingly enough, that option frequently goes unnoticed.

PARTICIPANTS: full group.

INSTRUCTIONS: Choose a mask you have not worked in before. Go into your new mask and explore the physicalization and characterization through the simple movement exercises.

SIDECOACHING: (Sidecoach the students to discover simple intentions, to observe space, to move objects, to relate to each other, and so on).

Freeze! Consciously or unconsciously you have chosen an age for your character. How old are you now?

Now you are going to explore other ages for your character. These could fast-forward you into the future or rewind you into the past. In a moment I will announce a new age for your character. If you are already this age, or close to it, continue what you are doing.

While you are changing to a new age for your character, keep the continuity of all the permanent physical, psychological, and behavioral traits you have already found in your character. Only let them be modified by these age explorations. When I say "Go!" come out of the freeze, evolving into the new age announced and continue with the exercise.

When you come out of the freeze, you will be all be small children in a park playground. Ready? Go!

(Time lapse) Freeze! When you come out of the freeze, you will be all be elderly people spending the day in the same park. Ready? Go!

(Time lapse) Freeze! When you come out of the freeze, you can be either of the ages you just explored. Ready? Go!

(Time lapse) Freeze! Make the opposite choice. Ready? Go!

(Time lapse) Freeze! Relax and come out of the mask.

OBSERVATIONS/DISCUSSION

1. How did the different ages affect your physicalization?

2. How did the different ages affect your emotional and psychological state?

3. How did the different ages affect your behavior and attitude about the world? Your relationships with others?

4. Which physical or emotional traits did you discover that seemed to be fixed and permanent? Which were fluid and impermanent? Respond to this statement by the art critic E. H. Gombrich: "We model ourselves so much on the expectation of others that we assume the mask, or as the Jungians say, the *persona*, which life assigns to us, and we grow into our type till it molds all our behaviour, down to our gait and our facial expression."[8]

Exercise 4a: The Time Machine

PARTICIPANTS: half or full group.

INSTRUCTIONS: Repeat the Three Ages exercise, allowing the participants to choose three different age levels for their characters to "grow through" as they go into a new mask.

Choose one age level possibility from each of the following groups, in chronological sequence:

Group A: a baby, a toddler, a young child.

Group B: a teenager, a person in the twenties, a person between thirty-five and forty.

Group C: a middle-aged person, a person in the sixties, a very old person.

Participants are asked to "grow" their characters through time (either fast-forwarding from a young age to an old age or rewinding from old age back to babyhood). They should maintain all the permanent physical characteristics, emotional and mental behavior, that they discover in the beginning.

After some time elapses, the participants can present these character progressions to the rest of the class.

SIDECOACHING: (None. Each student can create her own locales and situations for her mask.)

OBSERVATION/DISCUSSION: What physical, emotional, and mental character traits continued as threads through this exercise? In the play *Victoria Regina* by Laurence Housman, the actress playing Queen Victoria is asked to create the role of Victoria over a long period of time. In the first act she is a young girl who learns that she is to be the queen. In the final act Victoria is a very old woman. How might this exercise help you play such a role?

Reconsideration of What Constitutes a Mask

Now that these exercises in the Beginning Character Masks have been completed, we can challenge our earlier definition of what a mask is. A mask is not just a literal covering that substitutes for the face of the actor but a metaphorical covering, revealing the whole bodymind and behavior of the character—a mask of dramatic action.

Therefore, one immediate benefit of mask improvisation training is the realization that all characters in plays not only wear masks but *are* masks. As Richard Schechner maintains, "A role is a theatrical entity, not a psychological being. Great errors are made because performers and directors think of characters as people rather than as *dramatis personae*, masks of dramatic action. A role conforms to the logic of theatre, not the logic of any other life system. To think of a role as a person is like picnicking on a landscape painting."[9]

Initially, we might resist this idea of considering characters in plays as masks—or masks of dramatic action. We misunderstand characters in plays of psychological realism as "real" and not as manifestations of a particular theatrical style, or a specific way of thinking about and constructing the characterizations, rooted in a definite belief system about the world we live in. As a consequence, it somehow doesn't feel right to think of them as masks. To see a character as a mask is, we may believe, devaluing its importance and complexity. It will lead to stereotyping. Through some irrational reasoning process, it also seems to diminish the value we place on the individual actor's unique creative involvement.

For now, though, let us accept the idea of the character as a construct—as a mask. We will start from this proposition and see what happens to our understanding of the acting process if we approach character creation from this point of view.

As we have been discovering, a mask informs the bodymind of the wearer, transforming it into the character by dictating a pattern of thoughts, emotions, and behaviors. Robert Benedetti, echoing Schechner's terminology, calls this the character's "mask of actions."

The principle of the mask must be understood in a very broad way: a mask, or the principle of maskness, is any mechanism or behavior which is designed to project a sense of the self.

Persona is the word for mask, and it's the word from which we derive the personality. Personality is a mask, a pattern of behavior whereby we present a sense of ourselves to our society. Theatre is, in fact, based upon this everyday life-principle. We, in real life, perform sets of actions which become a mask presented to others, upon which our social audience projects a sense of authentic "self" which they tend to credit to the person performing those actions. If I convince you that I am a certain way, it is not necessarily because I am that way, but because I have performed my mask of actions successfully.[10]

From our experience of mask improvisation, we need to add an important note to Benedetti's observation. To say that we know a person fully only by a mask of actions is not entirely accurate. We also know a person by her physical appearance, even though this may be greatly deceiving and we must be very careful about reading external qualities as an accurate reflection of the internal. But theatre operates by different laws in this respect. As we have discovered, a mask, besides having an effect on the character's actions, also affects the character's physical shape—its bodymind.

Evaluation

It is now time for the teacher to meet with each member of the workshop to evaluate her work in the Beginning Character Masks. What has the actor learned about her own movement and behavior habits? What range has she exhibited in her physicalizations of the different masks? The teacher has a record of the students' mask choices and notes on their physicalizations and behavior. Each student also has a record of her own work through the Personal and Character Psychophysical Profiles she has filled out. Has the student also come to a realization of her habitual physical and psychological choices?

In your meeting with each student, review the remaining masks, eliminating from the list any that will most likely elicit the same or similar physicalizations or behavior. Limit the choices to those that will challenge the student to stretch herself in new ways.

Guidelines for Observers

During the exercises, each student-observer will evaluate her partner's physicalization to see whether or not the physicalization fully carries the mask. Use the following questions to guide observations and comments:

1. Was the physicalization of the character complete from head to toe or localized in some part of the body?
2. Did the silhouette and configuration of the body reflect the sculptural design features of the mask?
3. Did the shape of the movement pattern in space reflect the sculptural design features of the mask?
4. Did the size and strength of movements and gestures reflect the design features of the mask?
5. Did the tempo and rhythm of movements and gestures reflect the design features of the mask?
6. Was the energy level appropriate for the design features of the mask?
7. Was the actor emotionally and psychically connected to the physicalization?
8. Was the student identifying with and illustrating an emotional state, an intention, or an attitude rather than physicalizing a character's state of being in action?
9. Did the physicalization evolve into a behavior pattern that revealed a mental state or attitude about the world?

11

The Countermask

The disguise that sticks is a map of the invisible.
—*Herbert Blau,* Take Up the Bodies

Introduction

In order to construct more complex characterizations, we are now going to investigate an additional way of working in a mask. Up to this point, in both the Neutral and the Beginning Character Masks, students have been asked to bring their bodies into harmony with the mask, so that the physical, emotional, and mental identifications reflect and carry the mask. We speak of that way of working in a mask as "playing *with* the mask." But there is also another way of working, and that is to play *against* the mask. What does this mean? The best way to understand the concept and techniques of the countermask is experientially.

Warning! Countermask training continues the learning experience that has occurred in the Beginning Character Masks, so that training must precede this work.

Masks for the countermask training as explained here are the same paper masks as those used in the exploration of the Beginning Character Masks. Sidecoaching for these beginning countermask exercises tends to utilize language that speaks to the actor more than to the character. At this point in the training process, this emphasis should not affect the participants significantly. It is interesting to observe how quickly the participants translate the instructions directed at them into instructions for their characters.

If you have been using music as part of your warm-up program, then you can now ask participants to explore moving against or in counterpoint to the music as well as in harmony with it.

Uncovering the Countermask

EXERCISE 1: THE NESTED MASKS APPROACH*

OBJECTIVE: to develop a more complex characterization.
PARTICIPANTS: half the class at a time. The other half acts as observers.
INSTRUCTIONS: (The teacher needs to demonstrate the mechanics.) Take a Beginning Character Mask and pair it with another mask that is quite opposite in personality. Decide which one of the two you want to be on top and which on the bottom. Observe both of them closely, fixing the images of the two masks, but especially the one you will put underneath, in your mind's eye. Nest the two masks. We will identify the one on top as the outside mask and the one underneath as the inside mask. In this exercise the observers will only see the outside mask no matter what you do.

Go to the mirror, assume the neutral stance, and then don your nested masks.

When you open your eyes, identify with the outside mask and begin to physicalize it. Start exploring the life of this mask through the simple movement exercises.

How do you stand, sit, walk, gesture? What attitude do you have toward the world?

(Time lapse) Freeze! When you come out of the freeze, you will identify with and physicalize the inside mask. Keep exploring the simple movement exercises. Ready? Go!

Now how do you stand, sit, walk, gesture? What attitude do you have toward the world?

(Time lapse) Freeze! When you come out of the freeze, you will switch your identification and physicalization back to the outside mask. Ready? Go!

(Time lapse) Start to observe and relate to others around you.

(Time lapse) Freeze! Switch to your inside mask.

(Shorter time lapse) Freeze! Switch to your outside mask.

(Very brief time lapse) Switch to your inside mask.

(Finally, as participants continue to work:) Switch back and forth between the inside and the outside masks as you will. Find an incident in what you are doing or how you are relating to others that triggers the switch from one mask to the other.

(Extended time lapse) Freeze! Close your eyes, relax, and come out of the mask.

OBSERVATIONS/DISCUSSION

1. (To participants:) What did you experience in switching to the countermask? (To observers:) What did you see?

2. (To participants:) In your own mind, were you switching to a new character or to a different aspect of your initial character? (To observers:) What did you see?

3. (To participants:) How would you characterize the personality, qualities, and behavior of your outside mask? Of your inside mask? (To observers:) What did you see?

4. (To participants:) What trigger did you find that made you switch from the mask to the countermask? Was it inside you or outside you? Or both? (To observers:) What did you see?

5. (To participants:) Did you at any point resist switching to the other mask? Why? How did the trigger make you respond differently then?

6. (To participants:) What happened as you were asked to switch faster and faster back and forth? Did any psychic connection begin to occur between the two characterizations? Did they in any way begin to merge? Or was there a mental, emotional, or physical part of you still caught in the other physicalization? (To observers:) What did you see?

7. (To participants and observers:) How might you justify the two physicalizations' being different aspects of the same character?

TEACHER OBSERVATION NOTES: Initially students can find this exercise to be a somewhat schizoid experience. What is very interesting is that if the actor fully commits to a physicalization of the *opposite* of his first physicalization that brought the mask to life, then the mask still lives! This discovery brings with it the potential for a more complex character creation. The face and body are in opposition, playing against one another. To paraphrase a line from an old song, "Your body tells me no, no, but there's yes, yes in your face." With the countermask we have now created ambiguity and the possibility for a private inner life separate from the one that appears to be in harmony with the outside mask. This situation is closer to our understanding of human behavior.

Sometimes when the teacher asks the actor to play in harmony with the mask, the actor actually plays a countermask. In a feedback session this needs to be pointed out, as the body is not "carrying the mask" as requested.

Exercise 1a: The Nested Masks Approach Repeat

Repeat the Nested Masks Approach exercise with the other half of the class.

The Nested Masks Approach exercise gives the students a compelling image of the concept of the countermask. But actual countermask work is done with only one mask. The countermask is then the actors' personal projections of the opposites of their originals.

EXERCISE 2: THE SINGLE MASK APPROACH*

OBJECTIVE: to deepen characterization by further exploration of the countermask.

PARTICIPANTS: half the class at a time. The other half acts as observers.

INSTRUCTIONS: Go into the mask and bring your bodymind into harmony with the mask. Now we will call this psychophysical identification "the visible mask." Start your work with the simple movement exercises, but incorporate the motivation and intention and relationship extensions also. At some point you will be asked to change to a countermask—the invisible (inside) mask—your imagined opposite to your external mask. Your countermask should be as strong and clear a choice as your original mask.

Choose your mask and establish the life of the visible mask.

SIDECOACHING

(When actors in masks are performing the simple movement exercises:) Freeze! When you come out of the freeze, switch to your countermask, your invisible mask. Find the physicalization and behavior that is appropriate for this inside mask. Ready? Go!

(Time lapse) Freeze! Switch to your visible mask.

(Time lapse. Sidecoach the participants back and forth between the two masks a few more times, constantly shrinking the time between the switches.)

Freeze! You have now discovered and developed both a visible mask and an invisible mask. When you come out of the freeze, develop a need to relate to others and to the space. Find the trigger in your relationship with others and/or that space that prompts you to reveal your invisible mask or tells you to put on your visible mask. Ready? Go!

(Time lapse) Freeze! Close your eyes, relax, and come out of the mask.

OBSERVATIONS/DISCUSSION: Repeat questions given for the Nested Masks Approach exercise. Some additional questions should also be asked:

1. Was it easier or harder to play the opposite of your initial mask when you weren't wearing an actual second mask?

2. What character traits remained the same in both masks? What character traits changed?

Exercise 2a: The Single Mask Approach Repeat

Repeat the Single Mask Approach exercise with the other half of the class.

ASSIGNMENT: Complete a Character Psychophysical Profile on this mask, incorporating realizations about the Character Mask and its countermask.

Application of Mask/Countermask

There are two major ways in which the concept and the techniques of mask/countermask can be understood and used in mask training and mask theatre. The actor can use the work in the countermask to develop different characterizations or a synthesized, single characterization.

Different Characterizations. One way to utilize the phenomenon of the countermask is to see the mask and countermask as two separate characterizations, both using the same mask. If students try this approach in the workshop, however, they will soon discover that the two characters will demand to be related to each other in some way—like Dr. Jekyll and Mr Hyde. Therefore, creating different characters in the same mask works best if the two are related.

Two possible types of relationships are ego/alter ego and different family members. Marsha Norman in her fascinating play *Getting Out* requires that two separate actors play the ego/alter

ego roles of Arlie/Arlene. But in a mask theatre presentation, one actor could create this type of ego-split character by playing with and against the mask. One of my former students explored family relationships by creating a father and son in a Complex Character Mask he had sculpted. The father was a brilliant but pedantic poetry teacher; the son was a dim-witted klutz. (See the Family Resemblances exercise in chapter 15.)

Brecht's characters Shen Te and Shui Ta in his play *The Good Person of Setzuan* are a good example of a pair of characters constructed on a dialectical model that could possibly use the same mask. With these two characters Brecht incorporates both the ego/alter ego concept and the family member concept.

The opportunity to create two different characters, fragments of one psyche, or a family of related characters in the same mask provides exciting opportunities for those interested in mask theatre.

A Single Complex Characterization. The actor who wants to create a complex characterization in a single mask needs to work from inside the mask to create not two different characters but a fusion, or synthesis, of the contrasting aspects he has discovered in his mask. If the mask is the text, then the countermask is a subtext. Dealing with these complementary or contradictory "faces" promotes a tension—both internal and external—for the character, for the audience, and for the actor as well. As Bert O. States observes in his intensive study of the concept of character, "We are miraculously able to fuse almost any visible or detectable combination of character qualities into a unity on a moment's notice, though the unity may change or become deeper on further exposure."[1] What happens for the observer in this use of the countermask technique is that the external, visible mask and the body of the actor provide a continuity of identity: all we ever see is the mask and the body, behaving both in an appropriate way and then in an apparently inappropriate or contrary fashion. This "persistence of vision" establishes one character for us, not two. Though what we as observers may initially experience is a seeming contradiction, our fertile imaginations will work at effecting a synthesis.

Mask/countermask is therefore a useful technique for creating characters based either on Stanislavski's psychological model or on Brecht's dialectical model. When creating a character on Stanislavski's psychological model, we tend to focus on the internal conflict between the character's persona and his "real Self." On the Brechtian model, we either focus on the dialectics of the character whose internal contradictions stem from conflicts rooted in the external social, economic, and political forces around him, or on the dialectic between the psycho-

Tom Luce as Pedantic Poetry Professor, Justin Morrill College, Michigan State University. Photo by Sears A. Eldredge.

Tom Luce as Poetry Professor's Vague Son, Justin Morrill College, Michigan State University. Photo by Sears A. Eldredge.

physical life of the mask (the character) and that of the actor playing the part. (Mask/countermask training can teach the actor how to perform these contradictions cleanly and clearly without dwelling on the transitions—just as Brecht wanted!)

With either model, the actor must determine which character traits remain constant and which are alterable.

Facets of the Countermask

Different Personality Traits and Emotional States. One application of the mask/countermask training is to emphasize different personality traits and emotional states in the same mask. Two excellent examples of mask/countermask—the switching back and forth between contrasting personality traits and emotional states—from the classical theatre are Oedipus's personality as both caring and arrogant (his emotional life oscillating between hope and despair) in Sophocles' *Oedipus Rex,* and the polarizing "heat" and "ice" of Phaedra's passion in Jean Racine's play.

EXERCISE 3: MOOD SWINGS*

OBJECTIVE: to deepen and extend a characterization through an exploration of opposite personality traits and emotional states of being.

PARTICIPANTS: full group, working individually.

INSTRUCTIONS: Take another Beginning Character Mask and find the body and life that harmonize with the mask.

SIDECOACHING: (Sidecoach as necessary to help establish the characters.)

Freeze! When you come out of the freeze, you will play the opposite emotional state of the one you have discovered in the mask. As you play the opposite emotional state, adjust your physicalization and your character's behavior so that they reflect this new emotional state. If the physicalization comes out as opposite to the one you originally discovered in the mask, don't try to question it. Just do it. Ready? Go!

(Time lapse) Freeze! Revert to the original emotional state. Let your body and behavior adapt to it. Talk to yourself in an interior monologue about your Self and the world around you.

(Time lapse) Freeze! Switch to the opposite emotional state and physicalization. Continue to talk to yourself.

(Time lapse) Freeze! Now change at will between these two emotional states. Develop a justification for the switch from one to the other. And discover the trigger that prompts the change. Continue to talk to yourself.

(Time lapse) Freeze! Consciously, or unconsciously, with your adjustment to two contrasting emotional states, you have been fulfilling an intention—a need—or, perhaps, two different intentions. Identify what need you have and what tactics you have been using to try and fulfill it. If you have been playing two intentions, then find how they are related. When you come out of the freeze, you will continue to play this objective, but find an opposite tactic to fulfill the same need. Relate each tactic to its corresponding emotional and physical state. Continue to talk to yourself about your experience. Ready? Go!

(Time lapse) Freeze! Revert to the original tactic.

(Time lapse) Freeze! Switch to the opposite tactic.

(Time lapse) Freeze! Change at will between these two tactics. Find the internal or external trigger that prompts the change in your relationship to others and the space. Continue to talk to yourself.

(Time lapse) Freeze! Close your eyes, relax, and come out of the mask.

OBSERVATIONS/DISCUSSION

1. Did your changing emotional states evolve into active or reactive behavior?

2. Did you find you could effect a merger between the personality traits and emotions in your mask and in your countermask? Which ones remained constant? Which changed?

Different Roles/Relationships. Another application of the countermask has to do with roles and relationships. Even though we may consider ourselves as one integrated and continuous personality, we know that we show different sides, or facets, of our personalities to different people at different times. This happens daily when we change emotionally or as circumstances change. It also happens daily as we perform various roles: student (to a teacher), lover (to a lover), adult (to a child), son or daughter (to a parent), and so on. Each of us in our ever-changing emotional states is also in the center of a matrix of different role relationships that compel us to behave differently because of the role we have assumed or has been projected onto us. And we behave differently according to the cultural, personal, social, political, and psychological values and expectations with which we identify. We could even call these values and expectations "societal and cultural masks," because they are strong forces shaping who we are.

EXERCISE 4: FLYING BLIND*

This exercise turns the process we have just been using on its head. Here participants are each given one of the Beginning Character Masks without knowing which mask it is. They must use all the hints, suggestions, and signals coming from others' reactions to them to identify which mask they are wearing. Then they must evolve the appropriate physicalization for it.

OBJECTIVE: to discover how much we rely on others to tell us who we are.

PARTICIPANTS: full group.

PREPARATION: Cover the mirrors, or turn them to the wall, so that they cannot be used at the beginning of the exercise.

INSTRUCTIONS: Stand in a row with your eyes tightly closed and your hands outstretched to receive your mask. Once the mask is in your hands, put it on and start to relate to others in the group. Respond to each other with an appropriate reaction suggested by your personal response to the different masks that others are wearing. (The teacher passes out the masks.)

SIDECOACHING

(Once masks have been assumed:) Start moving around the space, observing and responding to each other.

How are others responding to you? How does this help to show you who you are? Talk to yourself in an interior monologue about what you are thinking and feeling.

(Time lapse) Expand the physical manifestation of your character in consonance with any clues that you are picking up.

(Time lapse) Play the opposite of what you suspect is the emotional tone your face may be communicating. Continue to talk to yourself as you do this.

(Time lapse) Find a trigger that allows you to play these two sides—the mask and countermask—of your character.

(Time lapse) I am now going to uncover the mirrors so that you can see what mask you are actually wearing.

(The teacher uncovers the mirrors.) Adjust your characterization and physicalization to the mask you are actually wearing. Continue to talk to yourself while undergoing this adjustment.

(Time lapse) Play the opposite of this well-adjusted characterization.

(Time lapse) Freeze! Close your eyes, relax, and come out of the mask.

OBSERVATIONS/DISCUSSION

1. What clues did you pick up from others about who you were?

2. How much was your knowing mind sorting through the various masks to help you identify which one you might be as you reacted to others' reactions to you?

3. What conflict, if any, did you feel between how others were identifying you and how you identified yourself? Did talking to yourself in an inner monologue help you express these feelings?

4. What happened when you played the countermask? What kind of adjustment was this to the situation?

5. How did you adjust your behavior in response to seeing yourself in the mirror?

EXERCISE 5: MOVING PROJECTORS

OBJECTIVE: to investigate how character traits and behavior may relate to role-playing or projection.

INSTRUCTIONS: Repeat the instructions for the Flying Blind exercise. Only this time there will be a context, with definite role assignments made by the participants as they are in the exercise.

SIDECOACHING

(Time lapse) You are all at an important arbitration meeting to settle a disagreement between workers and management. Some of you are workers; some managers. Decide for yourself which category you fall into. Within that category, choose a specific role and rank for yourself. Make clear in how you relate to each other who you are, what your role or rank is, and who you believe the others are.

(Time lapse) Accept or reject the role that you find projected onto you by playing your own role or position more fully.

(Time lapse) Play an attitude or tactic that is opposite to the one you are presently using.

(Time lapse) Play the attitude or tactic that is opposite to the one you are presently using.

(Time lapse) Switch your attitudes or tactics at will.

(Time lapse) Freeze! Close your eyes, relax, and come out of the mask.

OBSERVATIONS/DISCUSSION

1. Did the role you chose for yourself and the role that was projected onto you coincide? If not, why not?

2. How much does a role assigned to us depend upon what we are consciously or unconsciously projecting?

The Private Face and the Public Face. The two aspects of mask/countermask described above are actually contained within this last and perhaps most productive way to employ the mask/countermask concept and techniques. For the countermask is best understood as a technique for helping performers discover and play the public face and the private face of their characters.

With the introduction of the countermask, an important ambiguity is introduced into the characterization: the possibility of a private inner life that is different from the face that registers harmony with the visible mask. This is a public face and a private face—as in life! In 1992 Glenn Frankel wrote in the *Minneapolis Star Tribune* about the British prime minister: "*On the surface,* John Major looks like a simple read: a warm, sincere, affable, mild-mannered perfectionist of a politician, more engaged by policy, details and statistics than by emotions or abstractions. Yet *just below the carefully constructed exterior* lies a different person, the one forged in Brixton: a passionate, even angry man who still carries the stigma of the British class system, hates being patronized and feels both a sense of disdain and a sense of inferiority about those who are better educated and more articulate." [2]

This recognition of the public face and the private face in an actual individual is really the recognition of the mask and countermask in everyday life. Most playwrights use the concept of public face versus private face in creating their characters because it is inherently dramatic. Internal and external contradictions and conflicts abound. The characters can now lie, have a secret, hide, be two-faced! And playwrights seem to delight in writing scenes in which the private face of a character is revealed behind his public face. This is the moment when "the mask slips," revealing the "true character" of the person. Many of the central characters in Molière's plays, for instance, experience just such an uncovering. In the case of the supposedly pious Tartuffe, for example, this slippage happens at least twice: once when he openly woos Elmire, Orgon's young wife, and again when he is confronted by Orgon, who has overheard his treachery. Of course, major characters in most realistic plays are not two-dimensional figures, and identifying the moments when their public and private faces are revealed is a very good place to start in constructing a more complex interpretation of them.

The Paradox of Mask/Countermask

It must not be assumed, however, that the public face is always the one in harmony with the mask and the private face is always playing against the mask. Interestingly enough, sometimes an actor will decide that the countermask *is* his public face—the face he will present to the world around him—and the figure in harmony with the mask is his private face—the vulnerable face he will reveal only in rare moments or when he is forced to do so. With either of these choices, the actor can incorporate into his work an even more complex and dramatic understanding of characterization.

By employing Michael Chekhov's technique of "inner/outer tempo," the private face of a character can also be nested within his public face so that the two are experienced and played concurrently. This method is useful for a character who has to maintain an outer tempo because of the context in which he finds himself but whose inner state or tempo is quite different.[3]

EXERCISE 6: BRIEF ENCOUNTERS*

OBJECTIVE: In this full group improvisation, participants review what has been learned about the Beginning Character Masks and countermasks to this point.

PARTICIPANTS: full group, working independently at first.

PREPARATION: Set up some benches or chairs in the center of the space.

INSTRUCTIONS: You can choose a new Beginning Character Mask or work with one you have used previously.

The space is a waiting area in an airport terminal. Each of the characters has come to the airport for a particular reason. Some are departing on a plane, others are waiting for someone, some work there, some are looking for a lost item, and so on. Decide on a personal reason for coming to the airport. Make it important and urgent.

While you are there you will encounter other people in the airport. Make sure you find a way to use your public face and your private face during the time you are in the airport. Talk your subtext to yourself in an interior monologue as you go.

Now find the psychophysical life within your first mask, including its public face and its private face. Do not relate to each other yet! Work only on yourself and for yourself.

SIDECOACHING: (After the participants have had a chance to find the public face of their characters, sidecoach them into the discovery of the private face.)

(Time lapse) Find the trigger that switches you from your public face to your private face. Talk to yourself in an interior monologue about others and the world around you as you work.

Please move to the sides of the space so that we can have the center free.

Person A, go into the waiting area. Work on fulfilling your need. Talk to yourself about it.

Person B, go into the waiting area to fulfill your need and encounter the first person.

Person C, go into the waiting area.

(Time lapse) You may decide to leave the waiting area at any time that it becomes necessary for you to do so. You may also decide to reenter the area if you still need to complete your objective.

Person D, go into the waiting area.

(Time lapse. Interrupt at any time during the improvisation with additional complications, such as:)

(a) There's a policeman watching you at this very moment. Are you doing something you shouldn't?

(b) There is somebody possibly stalking you. What will you do about it?

(c) The flight you have been waiting for has been canceled. What will you do?

(Continue the exercise until everyone has completed it.)

OBSERVATIONS/DISCUSSION

1. How well were you able to use your public and private faces in the exercise?

2. Which physical and personality traits remained constant throughout? Which ones changed?

3. Did you find that the ability to talk to yourself helped you create your character in any way? How? Was the interior monologue a reflection of your public face or your private face?

4. Did you allow the encounters with others to affect your behavior in any way? How?

TEACHER OBSERVATION NOTES: Did each student allow himself to work from his spontaneous imagination in the encounters, or did you see a "script" being performed?

ASSIGNMENT: Examine a major work of dramatic literature. Has the playwright created characters with private and public faces? If so, does the play include at least one unmasking scene?

Conclusion

The concept and techniques of mask and countermask are fundamental creative principles and techniques for the actor to use in analyzing and developing characterizations with or without masks. An actor should always look for the countermask—the opposites—those conflicts and contradictions between what his character is and what his character does in every scene and in the whole play.

Learning to discover and play the mask and countermask can also be applied to the technique of playing with and against the text. In nonmasked theatre, playing against the text is an invaluable technique for the actor to use, especially with such highly ambiguous scripts and characters as are found, for example, in Shakespeare's *Measure for Measure* or *Troilus and Cressida*.

Students will use and explore the concept and techniques of mask/countermask, public face and private face, extensively during the rest of this course.

The Life Masks

*From the first shock of the contemplation of a face depends
the principal sensation which guides me constantly
throughout the entire execution of a portrait.*
—*Henri Matisse*

Introduction

Now the class will work with three-dimensional Character Masks. They are Life Masks of the participants' own faces! (For instructions on making these masks, see Appendix A.)

Many students find physicalizing these three-dimensional masks more liberating—and more demanding—than physicalizing the Beginning Character Masks. Students also feel some apprehension because the masks are of themselves. This apprehension increases when the students discover that they will never improvise in their own Life Masks. They will only improvise in each other's Life Masks. This strategy prevents a highly subjective interpretation of one's Self from being presented in front of the group; this is a therapeutic application of mask improvisation, and such is not our intent. (The goal for the wearers is not to try to imitate the actual owners either, as we shall see.)

Asking students to improvise in each other's Life Masks raises a fascinating, yet troubling, issue that has absorbed the attention of writers, artists, social scientists, and performers East and West for a long time. That is the question of physiognomy: How much do a person's facial features act as a guide to her character? A standard dictionary defines *physiognomy* as

> 1: the art of discovering temperament and character from outward appearance, 2: the facial features held to show qualities of mind or character by their configuration or expression, 3: external aspect; *also:* inner character or quality revealed outwardly.[1]

Although scientists have offered no proof that there is any connection between the architecture of a person's facial features and her personality traits, we seem to be conditioned by our social and cultural contexts to make such stereotyped judgments. "In everyday interpersonal relations," writes psychologist Thomas R. Alley, "judgments of other persons can be continually corrected and adjusted in light of their behavior. Hence, facial stereotypes are likely to have their greatest impact in our dealings with strangers and in the formation of first impressions, particularly when little information about them is available (e.g., when simply shown in a photograph). Likewise, physiognomy seems unlikely to dominate our judgments of those with whom we are well acquainted."[2]

Unfortunately, many of our casting procedures in film and television, and even in theatre, rely upon such physiognomic stereotyping, as a glance at any agent's casting books will tell you. Paradoxically, the most exciting theatre and film have involved prominent actors cast against their "type."

Physiognomic stereotypes are culturally specific, although

Seth Nesbitt in a Woman's Life Mask, Macalester College. Photo by Sears A. Eldredge.

Kelli McCue in a Man's Life Mask, Macalester College. Photo by Sears A. Eldredge.

researchers have found some to be cross-cultural. Physiognomic stereotyping involves attributing personality traits to certain dominant features found in the face and/or surrounding regions. These include our cultural associations with the amount and arrangement of head and facial hair; the size and shape of the forehead, the eyes, the nose, the cheekbones, and the mouth, lips, and teeth; and the presence of a protruding or a recessive chin.[3]

Students improvising in each other's Life Masks may be uncomfortable engaging in such physiognomic stereotyping, but they will quickly come to realize how inaccurate such an activity would be for determining the real personality traits of their classmates. Yet at the same time, students in training for performance onstage or in the media can learn from watching their Life Masks being identified by dominant sculptural qualities. They need to be aware of what impressions their facial features alone may create in others and how these can be highlighted or downplayed in developing a résumé head shot or a character onstage.

Beginning Life Mask Improvisations

EXERCISE 1: THE LINEUP*

OBJECTIVE: to initiate students into the effect of the three-dimensional Life Masks on their perception of the human body supporting it, and to explore the sculpted effects of the human body on their perception of the "life" in the Life Masks.

PARTICIPANTS: half the class at a time. The other half of the class serves as observers.

INSTRUCTIONS: The participants stand in a lineup in front of the observers. The teacher gathers the Life Masks of the participants and sets them down at one end of the line, corresponding to the order of the people in the lineup. The mask of the last person in the lineup is used first.

The students do nothing in the lineup except stand as themselves. The first person in the lineup puts on the first mask, the class observes her for a few moments, and then she takes off the mask and passes it to the next person in line, who dons the mask, is observed, and passes the mask along. This procedure is repeated until each person in the lineup has worn each mask.

TEACHER OBSERVATION NOTES: You may find that it is virtually impossible for the participants not to respond physically to the excited comments being made by the observers—to play into the observations. This is fine, but it should be kept within strict bounds, so that the main point of the exercise is not lost. It is interesting, though, how easily this projection happens and how easily the actor responds to it.

QUESTIONS FOR OBSERVERS

1. Whom do you see when an actor puts on someone else's Life Mask, the actual person represented by the mask or someone else?

Ninety-nine percent of the time the answer is "someone else." In this way the participants realize again what they may have perceived earlier, that the same mask on different bodies looks different. So they have nothing to fear when other members of the class wear their Life Masks, since the masks are no longer them!

2. What conclusions can you draw about the relationship between the size of the mask and the size of the body underneath it?

When there is great incongruity between the size of the mask and the size of the face or body of the wearer, an unusual effect occurs. Large masks on small faces and bodies seem to shrink the height, size, and weight of the actor. Small masks on large faces and bodies appear to increase the height, size, and weight of the wearer.

3. Does your perception of the dominant physiognomic features of the mask change depending upon who is wearing it or how the mask sits on the wearer's face?

4. What do you perceive about the relationship of the Life Mask to the body of the owner when she dons it?

Exercise 1a: The Lineup Repeat

Repeat the Lineup exercise with the other half of the class.
NOTE: Doing the whole group in this fashion takes a long time, and you may decide that you do not want to spend so much time on this exercise. If so, select a variety of head sizes and facial types—of Life Masks and participants—to fulfill the exercise.

When the Lineup exercise is completed, the class is ready to begin improvisations in these Life Masks. But before improvising, remind the students of one additional ground rule and four reminders to heed in working with Life Masks. The ground rule is this: *Do not image or try to imitate the movement or behavior of the person whose life mask you are using.* Clear your mind of the image of the person whose Life Mask you have. See the mask as a set of sculpted design features that you are asked to identify with and physicalize, just as you did with the Beginning Character Masks. As the Lineup exercise has demonstrated, another person's Life Mask on your body is a new character creation, so trying to imitate the actual person will be not only inappropriate but also ineffective.

The four reminders are these:

1. *Take time to observe and watch your mask.* You will find these masks more subtle than the Beginning Character Masks. It is now time to take note of the thoughts of the mask improviser Ron Jenkins on the importance of the contemplation phase: "When an actor does not take the time to sit motionless and study the facial lines of a mask as carefully as he studies the lines of a script, it is no wonder that the audience sees little more than the shell of the sculpted face's full expressive quality."[4]

Squint your eyes when contemplating the mask, to shut out the peripheral field. Hold the mask away from you at arm's length, turning and tilting it slowly in the light so that you can let the light and shadows play over the sculptured features of the mask.

Be aware of the impulses and suggestions of personality traits, emotional states, movement characteristics, and behavioral possibilities coming from the mask as it moves through the light and shadows. Some of these may be conflicting impressions. Remember that these are only initial impulses and suggestions. As you already know, the mask on your face supported by your body might look quite different from the mask in your hand. So you should not attempt to fix any interpretation of the character or personality of the mask from these observations. Do not rush this contemplation of the mask.

Close your eyes and explore the sculptural features of the mask with your fingers.

Stand before the mirror, holding your mask in front of your body, observing it as you turn and tilt it in the light.

If you are having difficulty divorcing your contemplation of the mask from your knowledge of the person whose face the mask represents, then go to the mirror and put the mask on. Discover the potentials for the character there.

Do not analyze! Just watch and notice. Concentrate on the visual, tactile, and kinesthetic sensations being given to you by the mask.

2. *Let the mask decide when it is ready to wear you.* Follow the standard procedures for donning the mask (see chapter 6).

3. *Always work from the image that comes back at you from the shock of the first encounter in the mirror.* Follow your impulses at this point even if they are very different from your impressions of the mask as you contemplated it in your hands. Later you can try to incorporate the suggestions, impulses, and images that came to you in your contemplation of the mask.

4. *Find the body that harmonizes with and carries the mask.*

TEACHER OBSERVATION NOTES: The time needed to contemplate a mask will be different for each person—and for each mask, perhaps. There is no set period that is the right amount of contemplation time for everyone. For one person, a particular mask may work quickly. For another, the same mask may take longer.

If you find that you have a student who is spending an inordinate amount of time contemplating the mask before putting it on, or at the mirror after donning it, you know that that person is analyzing the mask, trying to decide how to "do it right." This person, too, needs to be told to choose a mask and immediately put it on.

EXERCISE 2: ROUND ROBIN*

This is an exercise, like the Free-for-All exercise in chapter 10, in which participants get a chance to explore a number of masks in a relatively short time. In this case they are auditioning the masks for future reference—or should we say that the masks are auditioning them? At some point each participant will be asked to choose Life Masks with which she would like to work more extensively. In order that the students not be disappointed in their choices (since more than one person cannot have the same mask), it is wise for each participant to select three or four masks that she would like to explore further.

OBJECTIVE: to allow the class to try on, or audition, all the masks (even though each participant will not try on all the masks).

PARTICIPANTS: half the group, working individually.

PREPARATION: Place a table at one end of the room. Place all the Life Masks on the table.

INSTRUCTIONS: Choose a mask. Take time to contemplate it before going to the mirror.

Then go to the mirror and discover the physicalization that is appropriate for the mask. Bring your body into harmony with the mask.

Explore the physicalization and characterization by completing the simple movement exercises: To Stand, To Sit, To Walk, Making an Appropriate and Necessary Gesture. Also work on moving an object from one place to another in the space.

SIDECOACHING

Be aware of any pulse, tempo, rhythm, or movement or behavior pattern that may be developing in your mask. Explore it. Go with it. Let it feed the physical, psychological, emotional, and mental needs of your character.

(Time lapse) Find a place to be by yourself, either standing or sitting.

Observe the others in the space with you.

Leave your private space and try to observe more closely a person who interests you without that person knowing it.

(Time lapse) Start to make contact with that person, but do not get into pantomimic dialogue.

(Time lapse) Freeze! Close your eyes, relax, and come out of the mask.

Exercise 2a: Round Robin Repeat

Repeat the Round Robin exercise with the other half of the class.

Exercise 2b: Round Robin Repeated Again

Repeat the Round Robin exercise as many times as necessary, alternating groups. Make sure that each of the participants tries three or four of the masks and that everyone's Life Mask has been explored.

TEACHER OBSERVATION NOTES: Take notes on the psychophysical identifications that reveal the intentional, emotional, and behavioral choices that the actors are making.

This is another good exercise in which all can learn more about their ability to make choices. With these Life Masks, be on the lookout for startlingly new physicalization breakthroughs by any members of the class and comment on those. Also notice and comment on the appearance of any repetitive physicalizations or behaviors.

Did the students let the masks wear them? Did they release into their masks and truly connect physically, emotionally, and mentally with their choices, or did they keep themselves distanced from the commitment?

Did they discover bodies that harmonize with and carry their masks? Because of their prior work in the Beginning Character Masks, students frequently overphysicalize these masks, so that the scale and size of their physicalization are pushed larger and broader than these masks require. They need to learn that human-scale Life Masks need human-scale physicalizations. Their impulse for appropriate physicalizations are probably effective, but they need to pull them back, simplify them.

OBSERVATIONS/DISCUSSION

1. How does improvising in these Life Masks compare with

improvising in the Beginning Character Masks? Do you find that these masks give you more impulses and suggestions?

2. Does that mean you have more freedom of interpretation? Why? Why not? What character traits will become fixed and constant? Which ones will remain fluid?

3. How do these masks differ from the Beginning Character Masks in the scale and size of the physicalization required to carry them?

4. Did you discover your character by simply sitting and observing?

One important thing this part of the exercise is trying to teach you is how to be still onstage. Let the mask do the work. Simplify! Less is more! It is an important lesson to learn in mask improvisation, and in acting generally. But this ability to let the mask do the work means, of course, that you have to live into the mask more completely. You have to surrender yourself fully to the life in the mask.

5. What physiognomic facial features were dominant for you in each of your different masks?

6. What personality traits did you attribute to these dominant features?

7. Did the ability to create an interior monologue give you more release into the character? Into its thoughts and feelings?

8. Did the observers' reactions affect your work in the improvisation?

Life Masks and Counter-Life Masks

EXERCISE 3: IT'S YOU!*
It is important to move the participants beyond what has most likely been their initial stereotypical response to the dominant physiognomic features of their Life Masks. This exercise helps them do that.

OBJECTIVE: to explore the potential countermask(s) that a Life Mask may have.

PARTICIPANTS: full group.

INSTRUCTIONS: Choose one of the Life Masks for the improvisation. It should not be one you have worked in previously. Discover the body that harmonizes with the mask by completing the simple movement exercises.

SIDECOACHING

(Time lapse) Freeze! Identify your character's dominant physical, behavioral, emotional, and personality traits. What needs does your character have? When you come out of the freeze, you will physicalize the same body, but you will explore the opposite behavioral and emotional personality traits and attitudes about the world you live in. Ready? Go!

(Time lapse) Explore these new personality traits and be-

haviors. Let them make adjustments to your physicalization if that seems appropriate. What additional needs does this character have now, if any?

(Time lapse) Freeze! Revert to the original physicalization and personality.

(Time lapse) Switch to the countermask.

(Time lapse) Revert to the original mask.

(Time lapse) As you continue to work, change at will between the original and countermask physicalizations and personalities. Find the triggers that prompt the changes. Explore any conflict between the two personalities created by these changes.

Decide which of these two manifestations is your public face and which is your private face.

(Time lapse) Freeze! Close your eyes, relax, and come out of the mask.

OBSERVATIONS/DISCUSSION

1. What dominant physiognomic features did you identify in your Life Mask? What personality traits did you associate with these features?

2. Given your establishment of this first characterization, what differences in personality traits, emotional states, and behavior were you then required to project onto your countermask? Did any character traits remain constant?

3. How do the countermasks in the Life Masks differ from the countermasks in the Beginning Character Masks? Which were easier to perform?

4. Which was the public face of your character? The mask or the countermask? Why? Why was the other the countermask?

5. Did you feel that there was more than one possible public face to show to the world? Did you feel that there was more than one possible private face to hide from the world?

Beginning Life History Investigations

EXERCISE 4: WISHES, MEMORIES, LIES, AND DREAMS*
OBJECTIVE: to deepen and extend the characterization in a Life Mask by further exploration of its mask/countermask. This exercise will also allow students to consolidate what they have learned in the class up to this point.

PARTICIPANTS: full group, working individually.

PREPARATION: Have a clothes basket filled with a collection of interesting and evocative hand props available for this exercise. Costume pieces can also be available for the participants' use.

INSTRUCTIONS: Each participant has a choice of taking a new Life Mask or continuing in her present one. She is to assume the mask and find the body that harmonizes with it, utilizing the simple movement exercises and the exploration of the mask and countermask (or public face versus private face).

SIDECOACHING

(Once the participants are working in the masks:) Stop for a moment and remember the funniest thing that ever happened to you, or the happiest moment in your life.

(Time lapse) Continue on with your life.

(Time lapse) Stop for a moment and remember the most painful thing that ever happened to you.

(Time lapse) Continue on with your life.

(Time lapse) Stop for a moment and think about your deepest longing. What have you wanted to be or do or have more than anything else in the world?

(Time lapse. Place the basket of hand props in the center of the space.) One at a time, go to the basket and locate an object that is personally meaningful to you.

Where did you acquire this object? Who gave it to you? Why is it so important to you? Remember the exact event in which you acquired this object.

Notice the others in the space with you. Find one other person whom you would like to get to know better, someone with whom you would like to share the meaning of your precious object.

Give that other person your precious object as a gift.

Freeze! Close your eyes, relax, and come out of the mask.[5]

ASSIGNMENT: Complete a Character Psychophysical Profile on the Life Mask used in the Wishes, Memories, Lies, and Dreams exercise.

EXERCISE 5: WINDOWS, MIRRORS, DOORS*

In this exercise students work with a highly evocative archetypal image (a form without content) as the setting for a character movement study.

The task is now to develop a private moment of awareness in this character's life that reveals a secret wish, memory, lie, or dream/fantasy. Participants should choose a moment when a change occurs (internally and/or externally) that alters the character's perception of herself and/or her situation (and therefore our perception of the character). The change may be temporary or permanent. This "moment of awareness" could also involve a change in mood and/or personality traits. Students should consider how a costume piece or prop can be an essential part of this moment of awareness.

This exercise is in three parts. First, students work on discovering their characters and the possibilities for the "moment of awareness" by improvising with the group. Through improvisation with the rest of the group they uncover the life of their masks—their public faces and their private faces. Next, they work by themselves, developing their moments of awareness. Finally they show their moments of awareness to the rest of the group for comments.

Each study should be very brief—three minutes at most. No attempt to present *War and Peace,* please!

OBJECTIVE: to reveal the public face and the private face of the character.

Remember that there is no necessary correlation between the mask and the public face and the countermask and the private face. It could very well be that the countermask is the public face and the mask is the private face. That choice is up to the wearer—or rather, it is up to the mask to inform the wearer which is which.

PREPARATION: Have chairs available to establish the boundaries, or frame, of the archetypal image.

INSTRUCTIONS: Take a new Life Mask and find the psychophysical character in it. You may notice and interact with other characters to help you in your character discovery. Then develop a movement study that reveals the mask and countermask, the public face and the private face, of the character.

Choose one of these archetypal images as a basis for improvisation: a window, a mirror, or a door. Use two chairs to establish the boundaries, or frame, of your window, mirror, or door. Window and mirror frames should be placed so that the actor is facing the viewers directly. Door frames should be placed on an oblique angle at the viewers' right. After establishing the frames, repeat the following pattern of movement, providing the context and motivation from the external and internal life of the character you have discovered in your mask.

If you have chosen the window, start at the side of the room and approach the window, motivated by some reason that you determine. Look out the window and see something you did not expect to see. React to what you see. Then move away from the window and go to the side of the room. You can return to the side where you entered or move to the opposite side.

If you have chosen the mirror as your image, use the same sequence and structure of movement. In this case, the character sees something in the mirror that she has not noticed before.

If you have chosen the door, the basic pattern of movement alters at two points. First, the character approaches and confronts the door, focusing on what may be on the other side. Second, in the last movement the character either goes through the door or away from it.

Remember that it is the actor's job to flesh out the context and moment-to-moment awareness through which this movement study takes place.

PRESENTATION: When all students are ready, begin the presentation of the moments of awareness. Provide a copy of the Observations/Discussion questions to the observers so that they will know what to watch for in the presentations.

OBSERVATIONS/DISCUSSION

1. What story did you see told in this movement study?
2. What parts of the study were most effective?
3. At what points was it confusing to you, if at all?
4. Where did you see the private face revealed?
5. What did you learn about the private face of the character?
6. What public face did the character present to the world?
7. Was the public face the mask or the countermask?

Exercise 5a: Windows, Mirrors, Doors Repeat

Repeat the Windows, Mirrors, Doors exercise, with each student choosing a different image.

TEACHER OBSERVATION NOTES: In this exercise the actor discovers, if she hasn't already, that every moment demands clarity. For that to occur a very important lesson must be learned: every change of thought needs to be physicalized. This is not to ask for an exaggerated "pointing" of every thought change, but the realization that every new thought is a discovery that needs to register physically in performance—as it does in life.

Unlike film or video, theatre is not about the geography of the face but about the landscape of the three-dimensional body in space. The camera can catch the subtle shifts in an eye and magnify it thousands of times; this is not possible on the stage. So thought changes need corresponding shifts in the physicalization of the actor to communicate to an audience who may be distant from the stage, or even behind the actor in a thrust or arena staging.

Many times, of course, this shift can and should be minute and subtle. It all depends on whether the thought change is minute and subtle and on whether the actor is trying to create a characterization based on a realistic or a nonrealistic style.

If the actor is working from a realistic model of character creation, then you want to watch to see that the actor does not "jump" discoveries but that every moment is filled in, lived through, and connected to the next moment (always allowing for abrupt changes in thought). If the actor is living every moment completely, this minute change in physicalization will normally happen of its own accord. If not, the observer will discover "gaps" or "blurs" in the internal logic of the sequence of units that make up the moment. These need to be brought to the actor's attention.

If the actor is working from a dialectical model of character creation, then the switch can be a sudden, nonpsychologically justified reversal in order to reveal a contradictory aspect of the character determined by an adjustment to an external stimulus.

Actors need to understand that there can be a difference between what they think they are communicating and what is perceived, especially if the thought change is not physicalized.

Students invariably do too much in this exercise. They need to learn the important lesson of economy—that less *is* more! With either the realistic or the nonrealistic style, no extraneous or unnecessary material or moments should clutter up the work. Every movement has to receive its essential value and only that. As many great actors have testified, the final task for the actor is to simplify her work, cutting away material, not adding to it. Less is more!

You will need to watch closely and note the difference between the student "presenting" her piece and "living" her piece, so that a nonrealistic approach to the moment can be identified as different from a realistic approach.

For an interesting variation, ask the participant to present her moment of awareness facing upstage away from the observers. Is the moment of awareness still communicated?

ASSIGNMENT: Complete a Character Psychophysical Profile on the Life Mask used in the Windows, Mirrors, Doors exercise.

Life History Lessons: Extended Improvisations

EXERCISE 6: THE REFUGEES*

Participants are asked to go into the masks and begin developing their characters as refugees. Sidecoaching will be given to help them explore the refugee theme and deepen their characterizations. If they wish, they may establish nonverbal relationships with other persons in the group before they begin to improvise.

OBJECTIVE: to develop a character who lives through an extended improvisational situation with a serious or tragic atmosphere, incorporating and combining elements learned earlier in the workshop: fixed or fluid mental and emotional states, intentions, relationships, public face versus private face. Now the participants are asked to develop a more complete life history. This improvisation can get quite intense.

PARTICIPANTS: full group.

INSTRUCTIONS: Ask the participants to choose another one of the Life Masks and begin to discover the physicalization and behavior of the mask and countermask of their characters through the simple movement and relationship exercises.

Give the participants workshop time to work on this. When most are ready to continue, begin the sidecoaching.

SIDECOACHING

The space is a refugee camp. The center of the refugee camp is reserved as an assembly area. No one is permitted to stay there without permission.

The refugee camp is overcrowded. Before you go through processing, you need to find and establish your own living quarters in the camp.

(Time lapse) Night is coming on. You need to find food and water before you go to bed.

(Time lapse) It is night. Stay in your shelter and think about how this happened to you. What memory from the past do you particularly cherish now?

What do you fear might happen to you next?

(Time lapse) Sleep. In your sleep you dream.

(Time lapse) You are beginning to wake up. It is now sunrise. When you are ready, go and find food. Leave your private space, put on your public face if you need to. Enter the public space and work to establish a relationship with at least one other person in order to fulfill your urgent need.

Let your behavior and emotional state be conditioned by the changing nature of your relationships with others.

In a few moments you will be called for processing. At that time you will be asked questions about your background. Will you answer all questions truthfully? In order to prepare yourself for this interrogation, you mentally rehearse the following questions and your answers:

What is your name?

How old are you?

Where were you born?

What do you do for a living?

Are you married? or Have you ever been married?

What is your spouse's name?

Where is your spouse now?

Do you have any children? What are their names? Their ages? Where are they now?

Are there any reasons that you should be given special consideration or treatment?

While you are waiting for processing, simply observe others and the space. What do you observe? What do you think or feel about each of the others and the space? Talk to yourself in an interior monologue about your thoughts and feelings.

(Time lapse) This is an announcement! Your processing will not take place here at this camp as previously announced but will occur at your next destination. You will be leaving momentarily. The buses are pulling up to the gates, and you will board either the A bus on the right or the B bus on the left. I am told that the buses are headed for two different destinations but have been given no word about what those destinations are.

Please gather your things together and line up in the assembly area to get ready to board your bus.

(Place two chairs to serve as gateways downstage right and downstage left in the space.)

(When all are assembled:) You must choose to board one of the buses—either the one at Gate A on your right or the one at Gate B on your left. Make sure you take everything with you. Do not, repeat, *do not* leave anything behind.

The buses are here. Make your choice now and proceed through Gate A or Gate B to your bus.

(Time lapse) Freeze! Close your eyes, relax, and come out of the mask.

OBSERVATIONS/DISCUSSION

1. What demands does an extended improvisation with tragic overtones make on you as you improvise?

2. At what points did you use or explore your private face and your public face? Was this ability to have a public face and a private face useful to you? How did your private face and public face and your mask and countermask equate?

3. What intention or objective became the dominant motivation for your behavior?

4. How did your relationships with others affect your behavior? Your need? Your emotional state?

5. Did you discover a more complete life history subtext that was there ready to flow in answer to the supposed processing questions?

6. Was there a difference between the real facts and what you would have told the interviewer?

In a remarkable number of cases, a life history can be prompted by the mask and will flow easily in an interview situation. This can be a mysterious, and sometimes unsettling, experience for students (remember the "Jake" interview in the Prologue). What they need to learn from it is this: If they are truly engaged by the mask (character) and have released into it, living totally in the here and now, the subtext will flow of its own accord. It does not have to be manufactured but will be generated spontaneously, consistent with the character in the situation. In working without masks, this same kind of subtextual flow is most apt to happen during an intense rehearsal period when the image of the character has become very vivid and lives a separate existence in the actor's bodymind and consciousness.

ASSIGNMENT: Complete a Character Psychophysical Profile. Then write in your journal about your experience in this extended improvisation in two different ways: first, from the point of view of the character who underwent the experience; and second, from the point of view of the actor who lived this character and the character's life history.

EXERCISE 7: THE CIRCUS*

OBJECTIVE: to explore the life history of another character through an extended improvisation—this time one with a comic or farcical atmosphere.

PARTICIPANTS: full group, working individually or in pairs.

INSTRUCTIONS: Take another mask for this extended improvisation. The context for this improvisation is the circus. You are all circus performers auditioning for a place in the new Barnum and Bailey world tour. Go into your mask and establish the mask and countermask (public face and private face) of your circus character by employing the simple movement and relationship exercises. Then work on the development of your circus routine. At some point add some sort of surprising complication to create interest, risk, or the possibility of heightened tension in your act. You may team up with another character, if this is appropriate. When your routine is ready, come out of your mask.

SIDECOACHING

(After all participants are working on developing their circus routines in their masks:) Stop a moment and observe the others in the group. What do you think or feel about each of the other circus performers? Which ones do you like? Which ones do you not like? How good is your circus routine? How competitive are you? When do you need your public face? When do you need your private face?

(Allow time for participants to finish developing their routines. When most are ready and have removed their masks, ask for titles for the acts. Make a list of the act titles and then proceed with the rest of the exercise. Instruct all participants to go into their masks and reestablish their characters.)

As you know, times have been tough in the circus world. There aren't many jobs available anymore. You are all anxious to be chosen by Ringling Brothers, Barnum and Bailey, to be part of their international tour. Word has been received that only one act will be chosen from this audition to be in the tour show. So if you want to make sure you are part of the tour, then your routine must be exciting, original, and skillfully performed!

The audition time has now arrived. Can we please clear the center ring? Please stand downstage on either side so you will be ready to go into the ring to present your act. First we shall see [give the title of an act].

(Clap as you feel you should for each routine. When each routine is finished:) Thank you very much. Next we shall have [give the title of another act].

(Continue until each person has performed a routine. Be prepared as announcer and ringmaster to pick up on and exploit shamelessly any events or relationships that develop. And finally:) We want to thank you all for your participation in these auditions. The names of the successful candidate will be announced later.

Freeze! Close your eyes, relax, and come out of the mask.

OBSERVATION/DISCUSSION: Adapt questions from the

Refugees exercise as appropriate. Some additional questions that can be asked include:

1. What particular demands does developing an extended comedic or farcical improvisation have in contrast to a serious or tragic improvisation?

2. What are the differences in scale between this exercise and the previous one?

ASSIGNMENT: Complete a Character Psychophysical Profile. Then write in your journal about your experience, both from the point of view of the character who underwent the experience and from the point of view of the actor who lived the character.

EXERCISE 8: THREE AGES REVISITED

Using the Life Masks, repeat the Three Ages exercise from chapter 10.

EXERCISE 9: THE TIME MACHINE REVISITED

Using the Life Masks, repeat the Time Machine exercise from chapter 10.

EXERCISE 10: BRIEF ENCOUNTERS REVISITED

Look at the Brief Encounters exercise in chapter 11. Repeat that exercise with the Life Masks in a new setting or context. The setting is a public space, such as a bus station, a restaurant, or a theatre lobby.

Life Mask Transfer Exercises

EXERCISE 11: THE PORTRAIT GALLERY

OBJECTIVE: to transfer the lessons learned in the Life Masks to nonmasked acting.

PARTICIPANTS: full group, working individually without masks.

PREPARATION: Collect a variety of close-up photographs of people of all ages, group them together, and display them in the room. Postcards of famous personalities are not useful for this exercise because students may mimic the well-known physical and behavioral traits of such personalities.

INSTRUCTIONS: Choose a photograph from the portrait gallery. Contemplate the image of the person in the photograph and then imaginatively put that face on as a mask. Move into the space and take a neutral stance. Close your eyes and visualize the face, letting it inform your whole bodymind. When the image is strong, open your eyes and explore the simple movement exercises.

Move around the space, experiencing this character's psychophysical being.

(Time lapse) Relate to each other physically but not verbally.

(Time lapse) Now start relating to each other verbally. Keep the contact simple. Don't start writing plays.

(Time lapse) Freeze! Close your eyes, relax, and come out of the character.

EXERCISE 12: PORTRAIT MONOLOGUE

PARTICIPANTS: full group, working individually without masks.

INSTRUCTIONS: Each student creates a monologue for her character about a significant moment in the character's life and presents it to the class. Class time is used to conduct the beginning discovery of the character, but this monologue must be worked on outside of class, incorporating the use of mental rehearsal techniques.

ASSIGNMENT: Make a character collage. Construct a character from a variety of different sources, such as paintings, drawings, commercial art, and photographs. Then find the psychophysical life of the character you have created and present it to the rest of class for comments.

The Totem Masks

In the very earliest time,
when both people and animals lived on earth,
a person could become an animal if he wanted to
and an animal could become a human being.
Sometimes they were people
and sometimes animals
and there was no difference.
All spoke the same language.
That was the time when words were like magic.
The human mind had mysterious powers.
A word spoken by chance
might have strange consequences.
It would suddenly come alive
and what people wanted to happen could happen—
all you had to do was say it.
Nobody could explain this:
That's the way it was.
— "Magic Words," after Nalungiq (Inuit)

Introduction

The exercises in this chapter involve improvising with Totem Masks. A *totem* is defined as "an object (as an animal or plant) serving as the emblem of a family or clan and often as a reminder of its ancestry."[1] In these exercises we will only concern ourselves with animal totems. (Here I use the term *animal* rather loosely, to mean a nonhuman living creature.) The Totem Masks I now use are one-half and three-quarter leather masks created by the brilliant Uruguayan mask-maker Jorge Añón, but I have also successfully used papier-mâché masks sculpted by a talented student or by the participants themselves. These Totem Masks suggest a range of different animal types. With the Totem Masks we will explore two aspects of the mask: the animal and the human. We will explore each of these aspects separately, and then we will combine them.

There is a new ground rule for working in these Totem Masks: *Find the mouth or jaw that completes the mask.* Since the Totem Masks are one-half or three-quarter masks, the wearer's own jaw, chin, and lower lip will be visible. After assuming the mask, the student should first look in the mirror to see how the lower part of his face completes the mask. Standing in front of the mirror, the student moves his lower lip and jaw around until he discovers the facial positions that complete the sculpture of the mask. Participants should not rush this exploration. They need to make exaggerated and contrasting facial expressions. For each mask, more than one mouth and jaw alignment may be very appropriate.

Students will also be vocalizing and verbalizing! Each animal has a whole vocabulary of sounds, so students should not be shy about exploring them when sidecoached to do so.

Because of the physical demands of improvising animals in the Totem Masks, students will need longer, more demanding warm-ups before starting the work. Also, knee pads and elbow pads should be available for use in the improvisations. These devices give the students more flexibility to use their bodies with confidence and to risk unusual movements with less fear of injury. Tumbling mats or wrestling mats would also be helpful.

Bring all kinds of staging pieces (boxes, platforms, etc.) or old but sturdy furniture into the room for the students to use during these improvisations—anything that can imaginatively become dens or perches for the animals. These staging pieces or furniture will also be useful for the animal-into-human improvisations later on. Portable scaffolding is also a wonderful addition to the resources for these classes.

Tom Lommel in papier mâché "Fly" Totem Mask made by Lars Myers, Macalester College. Photo by Tom Barrett.

Exploring the Animal in the Totem Mask

Physicalizing the animal in the Totem Mask can be difficult, because the human body does not easily perform many of the physicalizations that are required. Some students will find it very hard to mold their bodies fully into a physicalization of their totem animals. They should capture as much of the overall shape of the animal as possible. The goal is to capture the essence of the creature, creating an illusion of the whole, even though it cannot be completely represented. The great Japanese Butoh dancer Ojima Ichiro, in an interview about the value of animal identifications to his training techniques, stated, "I began by studying a rooster for many days. The idea was to push out all of the human insides and let the bird take its place. You may start by imitating, but imitation is not your final goal; when you believe you are thinking completely like a chicken you have succeeded."[2] Students must work to reproduce the typical traits that can be physicalized and suggest those that cannot: shape, size, weight, center, movement qualities, rhythms.

We can never fully know what animals think and feel about themselves and the world around them. We only gather clues from observing their behavior, body language, and sounds—and from observing their brain activity in scientific tests. We all anthropomorphize animals by projecting our own human thoughts, feelings, and needs onto these creatures. As students begin their explorations, they should start with the neutral innocent mind, clearing their mind of preconceptions and pro-

Tom Lommel in leather "Vulture" Totem Mask made by Jorge Añón, Macalester College. Photo by Tom Barrett.

jections. Can they look out of the eyes of their masks as the animals might?

EXERCISE 1: THE PEACEABLE KINGDOM*

OBJECTIVE: to discover how to suggest the physicalizations and essences and live in the minds of different animals.

You may not have time to allow all the students to improvise in all the different masks. You do want to allow each person to improvise each type of animal: mammal, fish, bird, insect.

The goal in this beginning work in the Totem Masks is a deep identification and connection with the creature.

PARTICIPANTS: full group, working individually.

INSTRUCTIONS: Choose a mask that interests you. The world you will first enter in your animal mask is an imagined world that does not exist. It is a world of peacefulness represented in the early American painting *The Peaceable Kingdom*. Animals in this world are not territorial and do not recognize each other as part of their food chain, even though they are immensely curious about each other.

It is also a fantasy world, in which different types of environments exist at the same time and in the same space. So a fish might be swimming though someone else's jungle.

Go to the mirror and assume your mask. Discover how your mouth and jaw can complete the mask. Find your physical identification with your animal.

Do not relate to the other animals at first. Work only on yourself and for yourself, discovering the physicalization until you are sidecoached to relate to others. How will you suggest the animal's shape, size, and weight? Where is the animal's movement center?

When you find something, move away from the mirror and explore the movement of your animal in the room. How does your animal stand? Move through space? Sit or lie down?

SIDECOACHING

(Time lapse) Continue the investigation of your movement as you explore your environment. This is the environment in which you live, so you know every inch of it. See the environment through your animal's eyes.

(Time lapse) Explore the range of movement and behavior possibilities that you have. When and how do you move slowly? When and how do you move quickly? What senses do you most rely on?

(Time lapse) Notice and begin to relate to the other animals in the space with you. Remember, though, that at this point you all live in the Peaceable Kingdom.

(Time lapse) What sounds does your animal make? Explore the range of sound possibilities. Connect the sound possibilities with your physical, mental, and emotional explorations. Let the sound come out of and support the movement. Let the movement come out of and support the sound.

(Watch the participants and move among them, commenting to each, if necessary, on something that needs to be adjusted. For example, "Your hands or fingers need to complete the mask," "Your neck can be brought more into play to complete the head movements of your animal.")

(Time lapse) What range of mental activity does your animal have? How does this affect its movement?

What range of emotional states does your animal have? How might these affect its behavior?

Where are your food and water located in this environment?

(Time lapse) Where is your shelter—your perch, nest, den, cave, hole, or whatever else?

(Time lapse) Freeze! Close your eyes, relax, and come out of the mask.

OBSERVATIONS/DISCUSSION

1. What are the challenges in finding the physicalizations for these masks?

2. What is the nature of this environment for you?

3. Did you experience a mental, emotional, and motivational life in the animal mask?

4. How did you relate to the other animals in the space with you?

5. Did the ability to vocalize increase your identification with the animal?

6. What range of sound possibilities did you discover for your animal? When, and why, did your animal make sounds?

7. How did you identify your food and shelter?

Exercise 1a: The Peaceable Kingdom Repeat

Repeat the Peaceable Kingdom exercise three times, each time with each participant in a different type of Totem Mask.

TEACHER OBSERVATION NOTES: For most students this identification with the animal is very liberating. It seems a safer way to release the physical and vocal in a bold, assertive way without the fear of physical exaggeration or verbalization.

Watch for those students who are genuinely released for the first time and, of course, also for those students who shy away from being animals because it may be beneath their dignity. Both types need to hear your comments on their behavior. You will also want to make notes for later use about who has created a less active and assertive animal (and vice versa), so that you will be able to assign the opposite to those students in a later exercise.

EXERCISE 2: IT'S A JUNGLE OUT THERE!*

OBJECTIVE: to deepen the vocal and psychophysical explorations of the animal in the Totem Mask.

PARTICIPANTS: half the group at a time. Each participant is paired with an observer.

INSTRUCTIONS: Inform the participants which, if any, of the animal types they have not yet explored. It is important that each student investigate each type before being assigned two for the more challenging exercises that follow.

SIDECOACHING

Go into your mask and explore the appropriate movement for your animal in the environment. (Use sidecoaching instructions from the Peaceable Kingdom exercise.)

(Time lapse) Freeze! When you come out of the freeze, you are no longer in the Peaceable Kingdom. You are now in the animal world as it actually exists. You are hungry. Find food. Use your vocalizations to express your need and to get what you want. Ready? Go!

(Time lapse) Freeze! Close your eyes, relax, and come out of the mask. Meet with your observer to consult about your work.

(Give the pairs time to discuss.) Now go back into your animal mask. Working with the notes you received, continue the improvisation.

(Time lapse.) Freeze! Close your eyes, relax, and come out of the mask. Meet with your observer for a brief follow-up session. TEACHER OBSERVATION NOTE: Remarkable changes usually occur in the participants' vocal and physical behavior following their consultations with their observers.

Exercise 2a: It's a Jungle Out There! Repeat

Repeat the It's a Jungle exercise with the other half of the class. Then, if there is time, repeat the exercise for both groups again, with a second mask for each person.

Assigning the Animal Masks

When the students have improvised in each type of animal mask, consult with each student individually to ascertain which of the animal masks will require the student to stretch in ways that he needs to go. Then assign each student a pair of highly contrasting masks for use in the following exercises. (If there is not time enough, assign each student only one mask.)

RESEARCH ASSIGNMENT: It is now time for some research to be conducted on the animal (or the two contrasting animals) before any further progress can be made in the Totem Mask work. You have been improvising your animals from remembered images. These are too general. Specificity is needed now, and that can only come from further knowledge based on observation and secondary sources. The art critic E. H. Gombrich, in his study of masks and faces, said that "our reaction to our fellow creatures is closely linked with our own body image." He remarked, "Unless introspection deceives me, I believe that when I visit a zoo my muscular response changes as I move from the hippopotamus house to the cage of the weasels."[3]

If there is a local zoo, then make a field trip to the zoo and observe your animals—or ones as much like them as possible. Sketch the animals as part of the observation. Also locate articles and books in the library. Find photographs. See whether videotapes of the animals are available at the library or at a video store. Use the Totem Mask Research/Field Trip Log provided in Appendix C as a guide.

Bring your sketches, photographs, and notes to the next workshop session.

EXERCISE 3: VARIABLE SEASON

Now that students have had a chance to research their animals' physical and social behavior, they can again work on the physicalization of the animals. Note how the research gives more specificity to the physicalizations, especially by adding the details that give the physicalizations richness and depth. Specificity in the physicalizations suggests more about the movement and "inner life" of the animals. A still photograph captures a freeze-frame moment out of a movement sequence. In this exercise students will try to recover the rest of the sequence.

OBJECTIVE: to discover the movement and inner life of the animal through analysis of still photographs.
PARTICIPANTS: full group, working in pairs.
INSTRUCTIONS: Using one of your photographs of your animal, take the position of the animal in the photo. You will need your partner to observe and coach you into the correct position here.

Then ask yourself to imagine and move into the physicalization of the moment before the photo was taken. Then the moment before that one. Then the moment before that one. And so on.

Also ask yourself to imagine and move into the physicalization of the moment after the photo was taken. Then the moment after that one. Then the moment after that one. And so on.

By imaginatively stretching out the still photograph into these before and after moments, you can begin to get a sense of a "moving picture" of your creature.

(Continue into the next exercise.)

Exercise 3a: Just Be!*

INSTRUCTIONS: Explore sitting, standing, lying down, and just being. Have your creature observe the world around it quietly. It is not actively doing anything. It is not looking for food or listening for danger. It lives totally in the present moment. Let yourself "just be," living and breathing as your animal.

(Continue into the next exercise.)

Exercise 3b: Exploring the Environment

INSTRUCTIONS: Accept the space as your environment, even though that might mean that fish will be swimming in the same space that has been identified as another animal's jungle.

Explore this entire space as if it were your natural habitat, but do not relate yet to other creatures in it.

Explore the physical features of your environment. Map out the area for yourself and establish it as your territory.

What primary senses do you use in mapping out your environment?

Locate and/or make your shelter.

(After a time lapse, continue into the next exercise.)

Exercise 3c: Exploring Relationships

INSTRUCTIONS: Find a safe vantage point. Stay there quietly, observing the other creatures. What unique sensing devices do you have that you use to hunt or for protection?

(Time lapse) When you are ready, move into the area and start to relate to the other creatures. What compels you to move? When do you make sounds? Why?

Discover which animals you should avoid. How do you recognize and respond to danger? What do you do for protection?

You have not eaten for a while, and you are very hungry. Go on a hunt for food. If you are a predatory animal, you may only stalk your food source. You may not actually catch it!

Respond to any sounds, sights, smells, and shadows occurring in the environment as your animal would.

(Time lapse. End the exercise and bring the students out of their masks. Students should immediately fill out a Totem Mask Information Sheet [see Appendix C].)

EXERCISE 4: A DAY IN THE LIFE OF YOUR ANIMAL*

OBJECTIVE: to take the bodymind knowledge from the previous exercises and extend them through a day in the life of an animal.

PARTICIPANTS: full group.

PREPARATION: Use recorded environmental music as background for this exercise, if you wish.

INSTRUCTIONS: In this exercise time is compressed, as in time-lapse photography. You will be sidecoached to move from one time of day to the next.

Assume your masks and reestablish the physicalization and vocalization of your animal. When do you rest or sleep? When do you move about? When do you find food? When you want to, or need to, add vocalizations. When all participants are in their masks and rediscovering the physicalizations, the exercise will begin.

SIDECOACHING

It's 3:00 A.M. Where are you and what are you doing?
It's 6:00 A.M. Where are you and what are you doing?
It's 9:00 A.M. Where are you and what are you doing?
It's noon. Where are you and what are you doing?
It's 3:00 P.M. Where are you and what are you doing?
It's 6:00 P.M. Where are you and what are you doing?
It's 9:00 P.M. Where are you and what are you doing?
It's midnight. Where are you and what are you doing?
Freeze! Close your eyes, relax, and come out of the mask.

OBSERVATIONS/DISCUSSION

1. How did your animal spend its day?
2. Did you discover anything about the life and behavior of your animal that you didn't know before?
3. When did you need to use your creature's voice?

4. How well were you able to experience the world as your creature and not as yourself? What sensations, thought processes, and emotions did you experience?

EXERCISE 5: LIFE CYCLES

This exercise is good for exploring age levels and the corresponding changes and evolution in physical behavior.

OBJECTIVE: to explore the life cycle of the animal.

PARTICIPANTS: full group.

INSTRUCTIONS: Again we use the technique of time-lapse photography to move through the life cycles of the animals. You will transform into the next stage of growth during these periods.

Go into your masks and reestablish the physical and vocal life of your animal.

SIDECOACHING

We are going to move backward in time to the moments just after your birth. Take the position you believe you would be in at this time.

You grow to five days old.
There is danger, suddenly. What do you do?
You grow to a month old.
You grow to six months old.
You grow to a year old.
You become a full-grown adult. Explore your basic survival needs.
You are becoming quite old.
Freeze! Close your eyes, relax, and come out of the mask.

OBSERVATIONS/DISCUSSION

1. What physiological changes did you experience in the maturation of the animal?
2. How well were you able to live in the animal's senses, mind, and emotions?
3. How did it feel to be a month old?
4. How did you know what danger was and what to do about it?
5. How did it feel to become old?

EXERCISE 6: ANIMAL ENCOUNTERS*

PARTICIPANTS: full group, in pairs or trios.

INSTRUCTIONS: Form pairs or trios of different animals. Work on exploring the relationships between these animals.

Present these explorations to the class for comments about physicalizations and relationships.

EXERCISE 7: EXPLORING THE ANIMAL MASK REPEAT

Repeat exercises 3–6, with each student in his second animal mask.

EXERCISE 8: MORPHING I*

INSTRUCTIONS: After the participants have explored each of their two contrasting animal masks, try the following variations with each mask:

1. One animal's physicalization, movement, and behavior are in harmony with the mask, but the actor uses the vocal qualities of the other animal mask.
2. The physicalization, movement, and behavior of the other animal are used, but the vocal qualities are in harmony with the mask.

Exercise 8a: Morphing I Repeat

Repeat the Morphing I exercise with another animal mask.

OBSERVATIONS/DISCUSSION

1. What discoveries did you make about the relationship of the physical and behavioral qualities and the vocal qualities of your animal in fulfilling this exercise?

2. What imaginative process did you use when you had to switch the physical and behavioral qualities and/or the vocal qualities?

3. What possibilities exist for making creative use of these contrasting qualities when you embrace contradictions rather than resisting them?

Discovering the Human in the Totem Mask

Antony Sher wrote, "You can find any character by watching animals."[4] Throughout history humankind has been fascinated by the connections between humans and animals. Myths, fairy tales, and legends abound with such connections. Certain peoples, like the Kwakiutl Indians of the Canadian Pacific Coast, who have adopted animal crests and totems for their families or groups, have felt a special and jealously guarded connection with their animals. When they portray their totem masks and their unique dances for celebrations, they usually portray the transformation of the animals into humans or vice versa. The Kwakiutl believe that their mythic ancestors transformed into animals to visit the human world.

In physicalizing the human in the totem mask, the goal is to retain qualities of movement and vocalization that have been learned in discovering the animal in the Totem Mask and to incorporate them into a human characterization. Performers may rarely be called upon in their careers to portray animals, although the world of theatre and dance is filled with plays and ballets in which that is a necessity. You could be cast in André Obey's *Noah*, George Orwell's *Animal Farm*, or Karel Čapek's *The Insect Play*. You could dance in Igor Stravinsky's *The Firebird* or Gian Carlo Menotti's *The Unicorn, the Gorgon, and the Manticore*. And think of the many Christmas children's shows, such as *Toad of Toad Hall* and *Beatrix Potter's Christmas*!

Using animal imagery to help an actor develop a characterization is a time-honored tradition. In his fascinating book *Year of the King*, Antony Sher writes about developing the physicalization of his highly praised characterization of Richard III by incorporating different animal images. In one place he writes, "An image of massive shoulders like a bull or ape. The head literally trapped inside his deformity, peering out. Perhaps a whole false body could be built, not just the hump, to avoid having to contort myself and the strain or risk of injury that would entail." Then later, "Also, Margaret calls him a 'bottled spider'—a striking image. . . . The crutches could help to create the spider image." Again he considers the bull: "Watching the fighting bulls today, I realise they have many of the qualities that I've been thinking about for Richard. Sketching them. . . . Look at the head closely and it has a primeval, reptilian quality; heavily wrinkled, a stupid brutal face, slightly sad." He also returns to the spider: "Sketch the bottled spider. Very pleased by this."[5]

EXERCISE 9: NAME-CALLING

OBJECTIVE: to increase awareness of how frequently we use animal images to refer to human beings or their behavior in our daily life.

PARTICIPANTS: full group.

INSTRUCTIONS: Animals have frequently been used to describe human physical qualities and behavior—usually in a pejorative sense. Make a list of as many of these animal similes and metaphors as possible. Here are some for starters: proud as a peacock, stubborn as a mule, eats like a bird, pig-headed, monkeying around, pigeon-toed, horse-faced, eagle-eyed.

What connections, if any, do you see between the animal's shape and/or behavior and the human's shape and/or behavior suggested by these metaphors?

EXERCISE 10: DEVELOPING HUMAN PERSONALITY AND BEHAVIOR*

E. H. Gombrich wrote, "A recognisable human face can look strikingly 'like' a recognisable cow."[6]

OBJECTIVE: to take the facial or head shape, movement, behavior, and vocal characteristics of the animal and transform them into human ones.

INSTRUCTIONS: Think back on one of the animals you have identified with and explored in the previous exercises. What human qualities does the facial or head shape suggest? What habits, "personality" traits, movement and vocal qualities, emotional and behavioral characteristics, can be applied to the development of a human characterization?

One student of mine developed a wonderful turtle in her mask and physicalized it crawling around the territory during the earlier exercises. At any sign of danger, the turtle would stop and pull into its shell until the danger passed. Then it would reemerge and slowly move on. When asked later what personality traits the turtle had, the student said, "Patience." When she worked on the human side of her Totem Mask, she explored this quality as well as the ability to "pull into her shell" at uncomfortable physical or emotional moments.

Verbalizing: Freeing the Character to Speak

Participants will speak in these exercises for the first time. They take the vocalizations found in their animals and first transfer the vocal qualities to human ones. Then they build the language from that foundation. As Peter Brook has said, "A word does not start as a word—it is an end product which begins as an impulse, stimulated by attitude and behavior which dictates the need for expression."[7]

EXERCISE 11: VOCALIZING AND VERBALIZING*
PARTICIPANTS: full group.
INSTRUCTIONS: Take your Totem Mask and rediscover the physicalization of the animal, including the range of sounds that your animal makes.
SIDECOACHING
(After all participants are working in their masks:) Freeze! When you come out of the freeze, you will transform into a human being that still carries the physical, vocal, and behavioral traits of your animal mask. Start your transformation with the physical or the vocal and then incorporate the other aspects. You can transform gradually or quickly. Ready? Go!

(Time lapse) Continue your physical exploration with the simple movement exercises until you know how your new character moves through space, stands, and sits. Explore the human sounds.

See the space as a room and the objects in the space as furniture. Keeping the appropriate vocal qualities, let the sounds evolve into words. Mumble to yourself, describing your feelings about the space and the objects.

Observe the others in the space with you. Mumble to yourself, describing your thoughts and feelings about these people.

Relate to others in language but avoid writing plays.
TEACHER OBSERVATION NOTES: The participants' transformation of the vocal qualities of the animal into human ones can open up all sorts of new vocal and verbal experiences. At times there can be a loss in the corresponding physicalization. If this happens, sidecoach the students back into the animal

mask and remind them to keep the physicalization and behavior strong at the same time that they are vocalizing and verbalizing the human in the animal mask.
OBSERVATIONS/DISCUSSION
1. How did the animal imagery enrich characterization? Was the facial shape or the behavior of the animal most helpful?

In Jonathan Miller's production of Aeschylus's *Prometheus Bound* at Yale University in 1967, Irene Worth played the character of Io. Io is a human whom Zeus transforms into a heifer because of her refusal to allow him to make love to her in human form. When Io appears in the play, she is in the early stages of this transformation. In Worth's remarkable interpretation of this role, her braided hairdo suggested horns beginning to form out of her head, and she used one slippered foot, appearing from under her long skirt, to suggest pawing the ground. She also manipulated her upper torso and tossed her head in movements reminiscent of those of a heifer's head and neck movements.

In the film *Turtle Diary*, scripted by Harold Pinter, two top British actors, Glenda Jackson and Ben Kingsley, work with turtle images as a basis for the movement and behavior of their characters.

2. What relationship(s) did you discover between your animal physicalization and your human physicalization?

3. What relationship(s) did you discover between your animal behavior and your human behavior? What additional possibilities for behavior and relationships did you find in your human manifestations?

4. What relationship(s) did you discover between your animal sounds and your human vocal qualities? Did you let the animal's vocal qualities also suggest words, phrases, dynamics?

EXERCISE 12: METAMORPHOSIS: ANIMAL AND HUMAN*
OBJECTIVE: to explore the animal and the human figures as countermasks to each other. The physical and vocal will always stay joined.
PARTICIPANTS: full group.
INSTRUCTIONS: Begin by physicalizing the animal in the Totem Mask.
SIDECOACHING
(Time lapse) Freeze! When you come out of the freeze, switch to the physicalization and vocalization of your human character. But retain the vestiges of physical and vocal qualities found in the animal. Ready? Go!

(Time lapse) Freeze! When you come out of the freeze, switch to the physicalization and vocalization of your animal characterization. Ready? Go!

(Repeat the sequence.)

(Time lapse) Continue the exploration by changing your

physicalization and vocalization to either of the characters at your own will. Find the trigger in events or relationships that effects the change from animal to human and back again.

(Continue into the next exercise.)

Exercise 12a: Morphing II*

OBJECTIVE: to create an even more complex characterization by exploring the variety of different physical and vocal countermasks possible with the Totem Masks.

SIDECOACHING

(Time lapse) Freeze! When you come out of the freeze, you will switch to the appropriate human physicalization that is in harmony with the mask but will continue the animal vocalizations.

(Time lapse) Now allow your animal vocalizations to transform into human sounds, including words and phrases.

(Time lapse) Continue to relate to each other and start talking. Talk about anything, but keep talking until told to stop.

(Time lapse) Freeze! When you come out of the freeze, you will transform back into the appropriate animal physicalization. But keep the human vocal quality and verbal skills you just evolved.

(Time lapse) Keep relating to each other and the space.

(After a time lapse, repeat the transformations and explorations of the animal and human sides of the mask and its countermask.)

Now explore the various physical and vocal countermasks at your will. Find the trigger or triggers that change you from one to another.

(Time lapse) Freeze! Close your eyes, relax, and come out of the mask.

TEACHER OBSERVATION NOTES: This was not an exercise to induce schizophrenia, but to teach the students that they have a tremendous number of options in creating any characterization. There are not only physical countermasks to explore but vocal ones as well.

A performer can play the physical and vocal in consonance with the mask or against the mask; or the physical against the mask (standard countermask); or the physical with the mask and the vocal against the mask (vocal countermask); or the vocal with the mask and the physical against the mask (physical countermask).

OBSERVATIONS/DISCUSSION

1. What did you find to be the more interesting combinations of the physical and the vocal?

2. How difficult did you find it to play the vocal against the physical?

In the movie *Singing in the Rain,* a silent film star's popularity is destroyed at the premiere of a new "talkie," because her vocal qualities on the sound track do not match her silent screen image (her mask!). Worse yet, the vocal qualities get out of sync with her image. What is the effect of this incongruity on the audience at the premiere? On you as you watch the film?

When you see a Laurel and Hardy movie, notice that Ollie's vocal qualities do not match what you are led to expect by his physical image. Lou Costello of the comedy team Abbott and Costello also played with a similar vocal countermask.

These are further examples of utilizing vocal countermasks to create characterizations.

3. What types of roles are normally played by the vocal and physical qualities in harmony with the mask of the character? Name some examples from your experience.

4. What types of roles are normally played with either the physical or vocal qualities as countermasks to each other? Name some examples from your experience.

None of the vocal and physical options available for creating a characterization should be chosen for superficial or gimmicky reasons. They should be made consciously as well as intuitively, through a deep identification with the character, the script, and the style and concept of the production.

Totem Mask Transfer Exercises

In the following exercises we will explore the transfer of the Totem Mask explorations to nonmasked acting in two ways: in three improvisations that ask the actor to be both masked and unmasked, and in one final improvisation that requires only the unmasked actor.

EXERCISE 13: TOTEM TRANSFORMATION MYTH*

OBJECTIVE: Each student creates an extended moment employing the mask and its countermask(s).

PARTICIPANTS: full group, working individually. (This exercise could also be done in pairs or trios, with narration.)

INSTRUCTIONS: Herbert Blau wrote that "the voice coming out of the mask is always an ancestral voice."[8] Taking this quote or the "magic words" at the opening of this chapter for inspiration, each student creates a brief but imaginative sound and movement piece in his Totem Mask that tells a legend about how the animal became a human being or, conversely, how the human being became an animal. Students need to pay particular attention to the moments of transformation. Their original pieces may be based on research into myths and fairy tales.

EXERCISE 14: METAMORPHOSIS REVISITED*

INSTRUCTIONS: Adapt the Metamorphosis exercise in chapter 9 for use with the Totem Masks.

EXERCISE 15: LEGEND OF THE ENCHANTED VILLAGE

Many fairy tales incorporate a human being trapped inside an animal because of a curse (e.g., "The Frog Prince," "Snow-White and Rose-Red"). This extended improvisation explores that cultural heritage.

OBJECTIVE: to explore through an extended improvisation the student's ability to transform from animal to human.

PARTICIPANTS: full group.

PREPARATION: Set up the furniture used in previous exercises. Provide a small jewel.

THE STORY: Once upon a time in Central Europe, a whole village suddenly and mysteriously fell under a spell. Everyone in the village was transformed into an animal. Appropriately enough, every person was changed into the very animal whose behavior he or she had most resembled in life. The village itself was also transformed into a dark and forbidding forest.

On only one night in a hundred years, during the summer solstice when the moon was full, the villagers were temporarily released from this spell and transformed back into their human shapes. During this brief time they desperately tried to discover why this spell had been cast on them. They knew that if they could find that answer, they would forever be set free and would be permanently restored to their human shapes.

A hundred years ago, during the previous release, the villagers discovered part of the answer they were seeking. It seems that one among them had stolen the jewel from the crown of the Madonna in the sacred icon in the village church.

Another hundred years have passed, and it is time for another release from the spell. During this release, the villagers hope to discover the identity of the thief.

INSTRUCTIONS: Choose a new Totem Mask. Assume the mask, and start improvising. When appropriate, you will come out of the mask. Depending upon how the improvisation develops, you may later have to return to the mask.

Stand in a circle, facing out, with your eyes shut and your hands behind your back. The teacher will pass around the inside of the circle while giving the beginning instructions. The teacher will also give the stolen jewel to one member of the group, who will conceal it on his body.

You will be sidecoached through the events in the legend. Let the animal movement, vocalizations, and behavior determine your human characterization.

Open your eyes and discover the physicalization of your animal through the beginning movement and vocal exercises.

SIDECOACHING

(Time lapse) Go to the mirror. Find the appropriate animal vocalization and physicalization for your mask.

Move away from the mirror and explore the space as your animal.

(Time lapse) Return to the mirror. This time when you observe yourself in the mirror, you see a human being trapped inside an animal exterior. Who were you in the village before you were transformed? Move away from the mirror and continue your physical and vocal explorations.

(Time lapse) It is now dusk on the only night in one hundred years that you are released from your animal body. The full moon has appeared on the horizon, so you can start to emerge from your animal body, slowly transforming back to your human shape. But you are not fully restored until the moon is at its zenith overhead, so you must keep animal movement, behavior, and vocal qualities alive in your characterization until then.

(Time lapse) The moon is getting nearer its zenith. You are almost fully released from your animal body.

(Time lapse) The moon is now at its zenith. You are fully released from your animal's head and body. But remember: you were transformed into the animal you most resembled in life.

(Time lapse) Try and discover who was guilty of stealing the jewel from the sacred icon. This was the reason you were all transformed into animals. If you don't find the thief before the moon goes behind the horizon, you will be transformed back into animals again for another hundred years.

(If the villagers discover the thief, the teacher, through sidecoaching, can tell them that they are permanently restored, and the villagers can celebrate. If they do not discover the thief in the time allotted, then the instructor must transform them in stages back into their animals.)

TEACHER OBSERVATION NOTES: Watch to see which students can find the transitional points when their character is part animal, part human.

Which students retained and which students lost their animal likeness in their human characterization?

Did the students use their animals as a basis for movement, vocal quality, and behavior?

EXERCISE 16: ANIMAL HOUSE

OBJECTIVE: to have students confirm their understanding of vocal and physical countermasks in creating characters during an extended improvisation.

PARTICIPANTS: full group, without masks.

INSTRUCTIONS: Students are to develop human characters using animal images as a basis for their characterizations. At the same time, they need to explore the techniques of physical and vocal countermask.

Decide which students will be hosting this party at a fraternity house. All the rest will be invited guests, except three, who will try to crash the party.

The hosts should plan two events that will take place during the party.

Each student should decide on his character's motivations for attending the party.

Because of time constraints, the teacher will sidecoach the passage through the various stages of the improvisation. The participant's job is to incorporate the sidecoaching into the action.

SIDECOACHING: (Using what you see happening, try to sidecoach complications into the characters' actions and relationships. Also add urgency by announcing the passage of time.)

OBSERVATIONS/DISCUSSION: When the exercise is over, evaluate the students' abilities to fulfill the objectives of the exercise.

Progress Report: Evaluation

The conclusion of the Totem Mask improvisations is another important time to conduct an evaluation of the students' progress to date. These masks have stretched the participants in unique and valuable ways. As you look back over the work, what have you observed—and what have they learned—about the type and pattern of their mental, physical, and emotional behavior in the workshop? Students should now have a profound understanding of how the mask conceals in order to reveal. But what do they need to do at this point, either to build on or to change their work, as they proceed to their final masks—the Found Object Mask and the Complex Character Mask?[9]

14

The Found Object Masks

Introduction

For Renée Marcousé, "How we look, what we see, how we react to the same object is intensely varied and personal. Factual, objective information such as length, height, width, names, dates is accepted without query, but our response to the subjective element in ideas of colour, in shape or texture is personal and individual and is influenced by our associations and previous experiences. This personal response is inherent in visual awareness. It has to be recognized and carefully nurtured for it contains the germ of original creative thought and expression."[1]

The Found Object Masks are meant to "shake up" the experience and expectations of the workshop participants. They offer an experiment in object transformation. The actor takes a found object, contemplates it with her transforming imagination, and then manipulates it in such a way as to transform it into what it is not—a mask, or a partial mask. Now the mask should be understood as a substitute not just for the face but for any appropriate part of the body. The performer's job is to let this Found Object Mask transform her body, or a specific part of her body, into a unique character creation. If only part of the body is being transformed, then the actor can perform in such a way that implies that she is divorced from the transformation happening in that part of her body and can thus comment on it.

The objectives of the exploration of the Found Object Masks are threefold. These improvisations aim to open up the transformative imagination of the participant so that she can see inanimate objects as potential masks; to enhance the performer's sensibilities to shape, texture, weight, plasticity; and to expand the actor's exploration of her movement and vocal qualities. The Found Object Mask improvisations combine the work in the Neutral and Character Masks, incorporating understandings gained earlier to challenge the participants' psychophysical imaginations in new ways.

In these improvisations, mirrors are not used! The space should be empty of furniture. Pieces of elastic bands in different lengths and widths, with clips attached, need to be available.

Either the teacher or the students bring found objects to class to function as masks. The objects must be used as they are found. They should not be altered in any way (except to add tiny eye holes if absolutely necessary). The integrity of the original found object is important! All the found objects are placed on a table in the work space.

In the found object exercises we want the actor to stretch her imagination even further so she can see the inanimate world around her as a rich resource for creative performance possibilities. This means that she must improvise based on the

Lars Myers in "Hole Punch" Found Object Mask, Macalester College. Photo by Sears A. Eldredge.

Judith Howard in "Acoustical Foam" Found Object Mask, Macalester College. Photo by Sears A. Eldredge.

found object's dominant physical properties and qualities and by physicalizing its potential dynamic movement and sound possibilities. The following procedures are employed:

1. First impressions of the found object are quickly noted.
2. The found object is briefly observed and manipulated, to stimulate sensory responses and to awaken the transforming imagination.
3. The transformed found object is assumed, worn, or used by the actor to reveal its transformed state as a mask. In some cases the performer, or part of the performer, may be released by the found object into a creature or character that has a life of its own.

Some of the beginning explorations will prove rewarding; others, a dead end. So the participant must learn to select the most potentially transformable from the variety of possibilities uncovered. She should always begin by acknowledging and using the first impressions and expectations that the object signals to her and others. Then she should take her audience somewhere unexpected through the powers of her transforming imagination.

In their book *Nonverbal Communication*, Jurgen Ruesch and Weldon Kees investigate the effect that objects exert upon us. They write, "The effects that objects achieve in terms of their communicative value are dependent not only upon arrangement but also upon variations of material, shape, and surface. Any material evokes tactile and thermal images—

of smoothness, roughness, hardness, softness, coldness, and warmth. . . . all set up 'chords' of tactile images that often produce sharp and immediate physical and emotional reactions." [2]

Found Object Exercises

EXERCISE 1: FIRST IMPRESSIONS*

It is important that the actor first see the object for what it is before attempting to transform it into what it is not.

OBJECTIVE: to take note of the first impressions and expectations the object signals.

PARTICIPANTS: full group, working independently.

INSTRUCTIONS: Choose a found object that provokes your imagination and go to a private work space in the room. Place the object on a table or chair and observe it from all sides. Do not handle the found object in this observation phase. Quickly jot down answers to the following questions in your journal about your first impressions of the object:

1. Which of the following is the immediate *dominant* first impression? Choose only one: overall shape/structure, color, size, texture, weight, movement, sound.

2. What are the secondary impressions? Place them in priority order.

3. What other properties and qualities are important? (See the Found Object Mask Properties/Qualities Checklist in Appendix C.)

4. What expectations for movement, change, and alteration are inherent in the object or suggested to the observer because of what the object is?

5. What allusions or metaphorical associations does the found object suggest to you? What associations would most likely be suggested to your observers? These may prove useful later.

Continue on into the next exercise.

Exercise 1a: Contemplating the Found Object*

OBJECTIVE: to observe the found object with the active transforming imagination.

INSTRUCTIONS: Take no more than three minutes to contemplate the found object with your transforming imagination. You now need to see the object not for what it is but for what it can become. See the object with your innocent neutral mind. Do not impose something on the object that isn't there.

Continue on into the next exercise.

Exercise 1b: Manipulating the Found Object*

INSTRUCTIONS: As you continue to contemplate your found object, take it in your hands. Let your tactile experience of the object also awaken your transforming imagination. What side of the object do you identify as its "face," or the part that will be "facing" the observer?

If you see the object as a face mask, or a partial face mask, then hold the object in one hand at arm's length with its "face" toward you. Manipulate the object with your wrist so that you try out a sequence of potential head movements (tilts and rotations) that you have learned in the previous mask work. In this way you can see what effect these movements have on the possible "facial expression" of the object. You are beginning to discover the latent character living in the object.

If the object will mask another part of your anatomy, then move on to the next exercise.

After any necessary manipulation of the found object, continue on into the next group of exercises.

EXAMPLE: The found object is a slipcase for a folding umbrella. The dominant impression is of its color: hot pink.

The secondary impressions are of texture (silky), overall shape (cylindrical), size (compact, small), weight (light), and movement (flexible). The hot pink color demands a vibrant, high-energy physicalization; it suggests an intense emotional state. The observer expects that sometime during the improvisation the object will be inflated and/or deflated. Associatively, the object suggests a Pinocchio-like nose that inflates and collapses according to the way the actor inhales or exhales. It also suggests a oversized condom; tucked into a belt at the waist, it could represent a phallus.

EXERCISE 2: ASSUMING THE FOUND OBJECT*

INSTRUCTIONS: When ready, attach elastic and any padding necessary so that the mask is held securely and firmly to your face or other part of your body.

Now assume the object and begin your improvisational exploration.

Continue on into the next exercise.

Exercise 2a: Physicalizing the Found Object*

In transforming the found object into a character mask, your body must become subordinate to the dominant image of the object and a complement to or extension of it.

INSTRUCTIONS: If the found object is placed on the face, identify with the object, or with what it suggests, and let it begin to transform you.

If the found object is placed elsewhere on the body, let it influence and transform either the rest of the body or a specific part of the body.

Discover the body and movement that support or complete the mask. As in your earlier work, the physicalization must "carry the form."

Discover the range of the mask, its properties, qualities, and mental and emotional states.

Explore the countermask possibilities. Work against the properties, qualities, and states that you have identified. Discover the possibilities for conflict, contradictions, and inconsistencies either inherent in the object, existing between the rest of the body and the part the object masks, or existing between your transformative vision of the object and your viewer's expectations.

Continue on into the next exercise.

Exercise 2b: Dance of the Found Object

Art critic E. H. Gombrich wrote: "It is not only the perception of music which makes us dance inwardly, but also the perception of shapes."[3]

OBJECTIVE: to explore the physicalization of the found object fully.

INSTRUCTIONS: Develop your physicalization into a brief dance or sound and movement study inspired by the found object.

At some point in this exploration, the participants can ask for feedback on their work in progress.

EXERCISE 3: FOUND OBJECT MONOLOGUE

Your Found Object Mask, like other masks, will suggest potential sound and vocal qualities. These will depend on how you image, transform, and physicalize the object or how it transforms you. What potential sounds might it have? The actual inanimate object may not make any sound of its own unless it is jiggled, tapped, struck, scraped, or squeezed by something else.

INSTRUCTIONS: Investigate your found object to discover its sound potentials. Choose one sound quality that best captures the essence of your Found Object Mask and use the other sounds as variations or punctuation marks within that constant sound. What sound expectations does the object suggest to an observer?

SIDECOACHING

Begin releasing sounds that you believe are appropriate for the mask as you are transforming it into a character, or it is transforming you.

· Let those sounds develop into a flow of gibberish.

How does the sound relate to the movement you have discovered?

Transform the gibberish into words and sentences. Let it vocalize and verbalize its inner thoughts. How does it feel about itself? About others? About the world?

Try countermask sounds! These could be very interesting.

(See the Found Object Mask Properties/Qualities Checklist for further information.)

EXERCISE 4: FOUND OBJECT PERFORMANCE PIECE

OBJECTIVE: to create a performance piece based on the ability to transform found objects into other objects and/or characters.

PARTICIPANTS: full group, working individually.

INSTRUCTIONS: Allow at least one full workshop session for this exploration.

The performance piece should explore either the actor's ability to transform the found object into other objects by the ways in which she uses it, or the actor's transformation of the found object into a mask characterization. Or both!

If the actor is exploring only the transformation of the object into a mask characterization, then playing with the mask and playing against the mask (the countermask) should be incorporated into the performance. The piece should also exhibit the physical, inherent movement, emotional, and associative properties of the found object.

If the actor is creating a combined performance piece, then eventually she will not be a human being wearing the object but a new creature.

Whatever the approach, the performance piece must be arranged and presented in a sequence or storyline. So selecting and arranging the parts into a whole composition is important. As usual, it is also a good practice to have each student present a work in progress for the class to critique.

EXAMPLE: The found object is a roll of masking tape. The dominant first impression is of its round shape. Secondary impressions are of its sticky sides and its layers. Associatively, it suggests a hole or window. The observer expects to look through the hole or to stick something through the hole.

The actor attaches elastic bands and places the roll of masking tape on her face. As she covers her nose and eyes, the actor spontaneously images the roll of masking tape as a scuba diver's mask. Following this image, the actor "jumps into the ocean" and takes us into an undersea world. She swims along, enjoying the sights.

Then her behavior signals that she sees something huge and frightening coming toward her. By turning around and adjusting the mask slightly, covering one eye in the process, she is no longer the scuba diver. We see the eye of a giant sea creature swimming toward the diver. By lowering her head and making another slight adjustment of the mask, now over her mouth, she shows us the gaping mouth of the giant sea creature opening and closing. Turning and adjusting the mask back to cover her nose and forehead, the actor becomes the diver again. We see the diver's panic and flailing as she is attacked by the giant sea creature. As her eyes roll back, the diver turns away from us.

In the turn, the actor again adjusts the mask, this time to her forehead, so that when she completes the turn she is transformed into the doctor examining the diver, who is now an injured patient.

LENGTH AND STRUCTURE OF THE PERFORMANCE PIECE

1. The performance piece should be brief, no more than a minute long.

2. You should create a movement composition or choreography for your mask that has shape and development (see "Notes on Structure" in Appendix C).

3. Corresponding to the structure of the movement, you can create a mime piece or monologues relating a story that reveal situation, character, and a "journey" of some sort.

4. You will need to explore ways of transforming from one state of being to another. The transformation should have an "internal logic" of its own and lead the observer to the next moment.

Exercise 4a: Found Object Performance Piece Presentation

OBJECTIVE: to polish and present a found object performance piece for evaluation by the rest of the group.

PARTICIPANTS: full group, one at a time.

INSTRUCTIONS: Allow time for the students to polish their found object performance pieces, and then have them present the pieces one at a time. The full group evaluates the presentation for its effectiveness.

OBSERVATIONS/DISCUSSION

1. Did the found object come to life as a mask in its own right, or was it transformed into a mask that transformed the wearer in a new way? If not, why not?

2. Did the student explore all the shapes, designs, and properties of the found object? If not, what was left out?

3. Were the physicalization, sounds, language, and movements appropriate for the mask?

4. Did the movement composition have an appropriate overall shape? Was there a story?

5. Did the mime or monologue reveal character and situation and take the audience on a journey of some sort?

6. Did the performer work with any images, allusions, or associations suggested by the found object?

EXERCISE 5: DIALOGUE OF THE FOUND OBJECTS

OBJECTIVE: to extend the exploration of the Found Object Mask through a dialogue (silent or verbal) with another Found Object Mask character.

PARTICIPANTS: full group, working in pairs.

INSTRUCTIONS: Find a partner with a Found Object Mask that is a good contrast to your own. Assume your Found Object Masks and start to develop a physical, and perhaps a verbal, relationship with each other.

SIDECOACHING

As you continue to develop your relationship, begin to have a strong emotional reaction to your partner's Found Object Mask and presence.

Let this deepening relationship become very intense.

Now find a way to change the relationship and develop the opposite emotional response.

(Time lapse) If you have ended up disliking each other and fighting, then find a way to make up. If you have ended up falling in love with each other, find a way to break off the relationship.

(Time lapse) Freeze! Close your eyes, relax, and come out of the mask.

VARIATION: Have students develop a relationship, both wearing identical Found Object Masks.

EXERCISE 6: INSTANT PUDDING*

OBJECTIVE: to test the students' abilities to transform found objects into characters.

PARTICIPANTS: full group, working one at a time.

PREPARATION: Before the class, the teacher collects a number of found objects for use in the improvisation. They must be kept out of sight, because the moment they are revealed, the participants will be trying to improvise with them or put them on imaginatively.

Do not use mirrors. Elastic bands with clips attached to them need to be available for the students to use.

INSTRUCTIONS: One participant at a time goes up in front of the class and is handed one of three objects chosen by the group. She is given fifteen seconds to contemplate the object. Then she must put it on and bring the object to life. After she has presented one object, she is handed another one.

SIDECOACHING

Find and present the physical and vocal life in your found object.

(Time lapse) Freeze! Close your eyes, relax, and come out of the mask.

(Repeat the sequence twice.)

Exercise 6a: Instant Pudding Repeat

Repeat the Instant Pudding exercise until all of the students have participated.

EXERCISE 7: STREET THEATRE ROUTINE*

This is an extension of the found object exercises into a street theatre performance.

OBJECTIVE: to create a street theatre routine.

PARTICIPANTS: one person at a time. The rest of the group serves as the street audience.

INSTRUCTIONS: The performer brings her own small collection of unusual objects with which she will improvise. These are not new objects but ones she has previously explored, discovering their transformational uses and/or characterizations. The actor begins her performance with her own collection of unusual objects. As an audience gathers, she can challenge the audience to supply her with new objects for improvisation.

This performance can be transferred to an actual street corner. Always have a hat or some other container ready for donations!

15

The Complex Character Masks

Introduction

The work in the Complex Character Masks is the culmination of the explorations in Character Masks. Complex Character Masks are one-half or three-quarter masks of human faces in which the bottom lip and jaw are intentionally left out.[1] In these masks, as in the Totem Masks, the actor must complete the missing parts of the mask with his own face. If participants have not improvised in the Totem Masks before beginning the exercises given here, then they should review the special instructions for assuming the half and three-quarter masks noted in the introduction to chapter 13. The masks used here are called *complex* because they have an ambiguity sculpted into them that allows the improviser to create a variety of interpretations and a range of emotions. Complex characters are those that reveal more sides, facets, and layers to their fictional personalities than simple characters. These multiple facets are often contradictory.

As always in theatre, the human actor, whether masked or unmasked, augments and heightens the impression of complexity just by the addition of his living presence. Even so, we do not experience the fullness of the human being that is the actor, because the template of the mask allows only certain aspects of that actor's own human personality to shine through it.

The challenge for the participants in the Complex Character Mask improvisations is to create characters that have as many layers as possible. In other words, the actors should create characters whose "fixed" aspects—physicality, dominant personality traits, and temperament—do not prohibit them from developing, adapting, and functioning in a wide variety of changing circumstances and emotional states.

Two Approaches to Complex Character Mask Improvisations

There are two major approaches to working with the Complex Character Masks. First, the students can work with the masks to create characters out of their own imaginations. With this approach, it is important to establish some context that all the characters share. For example, all of the characters might be placed in the same locale, in the same situation, or in the same age range. Second, the masks can embody characters from a preselected piece of fiction (including plays), a sociological study, or an ethnography on which the improvisations will be based.[2]

If you are going to use the first approach, then the exercises can be applied as they given here. The benefit of this approach

Jeff Nelsen, Josh Schultz, and Megan Odel in Complex Character Masks, Macalester College. Photo by Tom Nelson.

is that students are fully the creators as well as the performers, and the originality of the actor-as-playwright or performer can thus be developed and celebrated.

One of the most effective ways that I have found to help the students create original characters and not be inhibited by being on their own is to designate their Complex Character Masks as members of an extended family. This means that when you decide what type of character will be a challenge for each individual in class, you need to have in mind the eventual creation of an extended family. The group can "grow" a family tree, with grandparents, mothers, fathers, children, aunts, uncles, and so on. The students can thus develop complex relationships, personal and collective memories, and life histories. There can even be family secrets that some members of the family don't know about. The possibilities are endless. But a decision to follow this method should be made early and should be kept in mind as the exercises in this chapter are explored.

If you are going to use the second approach, then you need to adapt the exercises in this chapter to fit the specifics of the text you are using. Identify the characters for the later improvisations early so that the masks can be sculpted to capture those fictional personalities. You will also need to base the topics for improvisation—such as the environment, status, roles and occupations, gender and age relationships, and the intentions and throughline of action—firmly on the text you are using, but do not limit them to the events of the text. The text of a novel or short story, for example, should not be thought of as a script, but as a *pre-text* for the improvisations. The best texts to choose for this work focus on a small group of people in an isolated setting or a confined situation. In this type of scenario, the original author has forced his characters to relate to each other and to deal with the central events individually and collectively.

The benefits of the second approach are that the students have a solid basis for their characterizations within a given situation that also provides them with a common context for a variety of individual, small group, and ensemble scenarios

Jeff Nelsen and Megan Odel in Complex Character Masks during a Field Trip exercise, Macalester College. Photo by Sears A. Eldredge.

for improvisation. This approach also teaches the students to comb a text for clues to their characters' physical, psychological, emotional, and intellectual lives and behavior within a given situation. These skills will greatly benefit the students later in their work with playscripts.

If students are going to sculpt their own Complex Character Masks (see Appendix A), then they need to read the piece of fiction early on, identify the character that each participant will create, and make notes on the characters' physical, emotional, and intellectual lives and habits before they start to sculpt. If, instead, the masks are already available, then students need to read the text as preparation for the first session with the masks. It is also possible for the teacher, knowing both the text and the students, to preselect a mask for each of the participants.

Either approach can be exciting and rewarding. But whatever the approach, students should be creating characterizations that stretch their abilities, not simply confirm their habitual choices and self-typecasting. At this point they should know a great deal about their habitual choices, but those old images are amazingly tenacious and demanding on the stu-

dents' psyches. And of course, masks offer the potential for cross-dressing, so a male can play a female character and a female can play a male character, if that is what will be most challenging to the individual.

Selecting and Assigning the Complex Character Masks

If you are working with a given set of Complex Character Masks, more than one person in the group may wish to use the same mask. Use a Round Robin exercise (see chapter 12) to help you determine which actor should wear which mask. By the end of that exercise, each of the participants should have a list of three or four masks in which they would like to improvise for the rest of the work in the Complex Character Masks. The teacher also should have generated a list of possible masks for each student from observations and from his knowledge of the needs of each participant. If time allows, meet with each student to discuss which of the masks would challenge him to stretch in a way he needs to go at this point in his work. After discussing the choices with each student, assign the masks.

If the students are sculpting their own Complex Character Masks, then discuss with them what character types or traits will challenge them. This discussion should suggest to the student a clear direction—definite physicalization and behavior qualities (e.g., the Social Climber, the Nerd, the Jock, the Actor, the Wanna-be). Each student needs to be challenged to create a character that will totally mislead observers about the identity of the person under the mask. Ask the student to find photographs of the character type or to create a collage from different sources to use as models for his sculpture.

Roles and Functions of the Observer-Teacher

In the work with the Complex Character Masks, the observer-teacher has various roles and functions. You act as the informed observer, giving sidecoaching instructions. You also serve as a participant, fulfilling a role within the improvisation. It is important to assist the students in stretching and confirming their characterizations in these masks. To be most effective, the teacher must also role-play in the improvisations. Step into the improvisation among the students while they are exploring their characters, speaking to each of them in character and asking them questions. You are not trying to break the students out of their characterizations but helping to confirm and validate them. Pick up clues on who to be or what to say to the characters from your observations of who they seem to be and what they are doing. In other words, lead them in the way they are already going. You might act as a facilitator: as an interviewer, a bartender, or a waiter, for example, you can elicit life history information. Or you might act as an alter ego: as a countermask inner voice, you can encourage a character to a certain behavior or action. The latter approach is useful for nudging a student into an area not being properly explored.

It is also possible to conduct the exercises with half the class in character at a time, using the other half to assist in the observation and role-playing.

The teacher performs in these exercises to help develop and complicate the improvisation so that it becomes more urgent and important. Students should also understand that they can be interrupted at any time in an exercise for a life history interview. This strategy should serve to deepen the characterizations by challenging the students to "go with the flow," to allow the mask to lead in providing the text and subtext for the moment.

As the students work through these improvisations in the Complex Character Masks, the teacher should watch to see that they are developing characterizations that are not so fixed that they cannot adapt to changing circumstances. If a student says that his mask will not do a certain exercise, tell him to find a justification that allows his character to participate in the exercise. Given the right circumstances, physical and/or psychological, we will all do almost anything! Also, if a student says that his mask does not talk, then tell that student that he may very well feel that his mask doesn't want to talk much, but that all of us must talk and relate to others at times, even when we don't want to. This is one of those times. Ask the student to find one or more confidants in the group to whom he can pour out his heart. Both of these behaviors may be conscious or unconscious ways to avoid aspects of the work with which the actors are not comfortable. They are still trying to control their characters rather than trusting to let their characters control them.

Also watch to see that the characters keep pursuing clear choices for their objectives and do not just settle into conversations, passing the time with each other. Getting into dialogue with others can fulfill a purpose, but some students will want to keep all their work at this verbal, nondemanding, nonthreatening "chatty" and reactive level. They must be encouraged to pursue an action physically—and to take risks. They also need to be challenged to make emotional investments with these characterizations, exploring a variety of different emotional states.

The question that always needs to be asked and answered is this: Is the student discovering and exploring all the rich potential of the mask, or has the student retreated to safer, less

risky choices? The mask is always capable of more; therefore, the student should be challenged to extend his discoveries also.

Finding and Developing the Vocabulary of the Mask I: The Complex Mask

The vocabulary of a mask is a listing of all the physical, emotional, and mental possibilities one has found in a particular mask. Finding and developing the vocabulary of a mask require that the participants create a synthesis of two perspectives: objective/external and subjective/internal. Even though it is impossible to separate these two perspectives into discrete and disparate learning experiences, we still need to foreground one approach to see what benefits it gives us before we employ the other. By alternating the perspectives through the exploratory exercises in the Complex Character Mask, the participants will discover the rich potentialities in the mask before they have to make the final decisions concerning the character they wish to create. These exercises should be revised, abridged, and/or consolidated as seems most appropriate to fit the needs of the group.

The assumption behind the following exercises is that students will be working almost exclusively in their own Complex Character Masks (whether self-created or provided for them). The exercises will ask that the students go in and out of their masks/characters. At some point it will not be necessary for the students to return to the mirror to get confirmation of what or who their characters are because the image of their characters will be so potent inside them. But if you find that students are having difficulty rediscovering their characters, then sidecoach them to check themselves in the mirror from across the room and let that reflected image compel them to reconnect with their characters.

EXERCISE 1: WATCHING THE MASK*

OBJECTIVE: to give the students time to observe their masks outside themselves, without the pressure to live in them immediately.

PARTICIPANTS: full group, working individually.

INSTRUCTIONS: If students have not sculpted their own masks, they should not actually don the masks until the next workshop session. In this way they can allow the images of the masks to take root in their imaginations. They should take time during the interval between workshop sessions to visualize their masks with their minds' eyes. If the students have sculpted their own Complex Character Masks, then the time for this exercise should be greatly reduced, as the students have spent a lot of time contemplating their masks in the sculpting process.

SIDECOACHING

Take time to contemplate your mask. Remember: The mask is your text!

Place the mask on a chair. With your eyes in the same plane as the mask, examine its sculptural qualities from full front and then from each side. Does each perspective suggest different aspects of the mask's total personality?

Hold your mask in one hand at arm's length, turning the mask in the light to capture its personality. Try turning it slowly from side to side. Now try quick turns and sudden stops. Tilt it slowly up and down. Tilt it quickly with sudden stops. During this exploration, try to live into the potential life in the mask. If you see a suggestion of an emotional state in the mask, try to manipulate it so that state increases in intensity.

Does the mask notice and look at things?

Can it react to things happening in its head or in the room?

Can it make eye contact with you, or does it have to keep looking away?

Try to experience the mask's breath, its energy, its physicality, its emotional states, its thoughts.

Standing in front of the mirror, hold the mask in front of you, and watch the mask in the mirror as you manipulate it. What is the mask's age? gender? health? social status?

Make notes in your journal about what you have discovered.

(Continue on into the next exercise.)

Exercise 1a: Watching the Mask with a Partner

PARTICIPANTS: full group, working in pairs.

INSTRUCTIONS: Participants switch masks with a partner. Each partner now manipulates his new mask for the original owner to observe.

EXERCISE 2: JUST BECOMING!*

OBJECTIVE: to begin the individual exploration of the physicalization of the Complex Character Mask in order to discover the character's bodymind (its physical, emotional, and intellectual behavior), including those dominant attitudes and feelings about life that pervade the character's relationship to others and the world.

PARTICIPANTS: full group.

PREPARATION: Have a variety of pieces of furniture available in the room for the improvisations.

INSTRUCTIONS: If the students have sculpted their own Complex Character Masks, then now is the moment of truth. Whatever personality traits they may have attempted to sculpt into the mask, they must finally follow what comes back at them from the mirror. At first they should try out the physicalization, personality traits, and behavior of the character they tried to sculpt. But if that doesn't work, then they must abandon those attempts and work with what is there in the mask.

In this exercise and those that follow in the series, the participants should only explore playing with the mask, not against it.

SIDECOACHING

Explore only those aspects of your mask that are in harmony with the mask. We will explore countermask possibilities at a later time.

Do not explore the vocalization and verbalization of your character yet, even though you may have strong impulses to do so.

Do not relate to each other until you are sidecoached to do so.

Assume your mask and work in front of the mirrors to begin your discovery of your complex character.

Explore how your mouth and lower jaw complete the mask.

Explore a physicalization that is appropriate for the mask. When you have discovered something, move away from the mirrors. Use the simple movement exercises—To Stand, To Sit, To Walk, Making an Appropriate and Necessary Gesture—to explore the physicalization of your character in space.

Explore the room. How do you respond to this room?

Move an object from one place to another in the room. Why do you need to do this?

Do you recognize a pattern developing in your behavior in the space? If so, explore and extend it further.

How does this pattern of behavior reflect your needs, thoughts, or attitudes?

(Continue on into the next exercise.)

Exercise 2a: Discovering the Vocal*

SIDECOACHING CONTINUED

Now let your physicalization and behavior prompt your vocalization. Let your physicalization lead you to explore sounds or vocal qualities. If words or sentences want to happen, let them happen.

(Time lapse) Take your sound or vocal quality and let it evolve into gibberish.

(Time lapse) Let your gibberish become a word.

(Time lapse) Explore using your word in different ways to communicate different meanings. Let your physicalization adapt to the vocal changes, and let the vocal changes adapt to your physicalization.

(Time lapse) Extend your word into a phrase or sentence.

Explore using the phrase or sentence in different ways to communicate different meanings.

(After a time lapse, continue on into the next exercise.)

Exercise 2b: Exploring Attitudes and Emotional States*

SIDECOACHING CONTINUED

Your character has already developed feelings about the world it inhabits. Find a place to be by yourself, either standing or sitting. Be aware of others in the space with you. From your private vantage point, observe these other people and the world around you.

Mumble to yourself out loud, in a continuous monologue, telling yourself what you feel about these other people and the world around you. You do not hear the others talking to themselves.

Verbalize what attitude or emotional state seems to dominate your life.

Find as specific and unique a phrase as possible to describe your outlook on life. Keep repeating this phrase.

Why do you have this attitude or emotional state?

Play this attitude or emotional state constantly and consistently as you begin to relate to others in the space.

(Continue on into the next exercise.)

Exercise 2c: Discovering Needs and Relationships*

SIDECOACHING CONTINUED

While you are sitting or standing in your private place, answer the following questions to yourself in an interior monologue: What goal do you have in life? What need do you have right now? How will you go about fulfilling this need or goal? How do you plan to become involved with the others to help you fulfill your need or goal?

Now leave the security of your private space and begin to relate to others, finding opportunities to explore the need or goal you have just identified.

(Time lapse) Expand what you are doing—your physicalization, behavior, attitude, and emotional state of mind—so that it is very obvious to others. Match the volume of your voice to the size of your physicalization as you expand. Commit emotionally to what you are doing.

Keep relating to others. Don't lose contact with your body in concentrating on the verbal.

(Time lapse) Contract what you are doing—your physicalization, behavior, attitude, and emotional state of mind—so that it is barely perceptible in your relationship with others and the space. Match the volume of your voice to the size of your physical being as you contract. Justify emotionally what you are doing.

(Time lapse) Freeze! Close your eyes, relax, and come out of the mask.

ASSIGNMENT: Complete a Character Psychophysical Profile on your mask. Start to develop the parameters for your Complex Mask characterization by identifying the attributes of your character that may become "fixed" and those that might be considered "fluid" or changeable, depending upon the circumstances. You are searching for the ongoing, engendering pulse and core of the character.

1. What did you discover about the physical, attitudinal, behavioral, and emotional life of your character? Which of these attributes are "fixed" and which are "fluid"?

2. What did you discover about your vocal qualities and diction? Which of these qualities are "fixed" and which are "fluid"?

3. What did you learn from expanding and contracting the physical, emotional, and vocal aspects of the character?

Create a chart in your journal that separates your discoveries about the mask into two major categories: fixed aspects and fluid aspects. Consider physical, vocal, mental, emotional, and behavioral qualities.

Finding and Developing the Vocabulary of the Mask II: The Complex Countermask

EXERCISE 3: EXPLORING A PHYSICAL COUNTERMASK*

OBJECTIVE: to extend the exploration in the Complex Character Masks into areas that may enrich the final characterizations through the use of physical countermasks.

PARTICIPANTS: full group, working individually.

INSTRUCTIONS: Assume your Complex Character Mask and recover the physicalization and vocalization that you have already found. Rediscover how your character sits, stands, walks, and talks. Rediscover your character's needs and behavior. You can relate to others, getting into dialogues to fulfill your needs.

SIDECOACHING

(Time lapse) Freeze! When you come out of the freeze, you will physicalize the opposite of what you are presently doing, to create a countermask. Do not relate to others as yet, as you explore this new physicalization. Ready? Go!

(Time lapse) Where is your center now, in this countermask? Is your head and neck placement different? Is your spine, chest, and pelvis placement different? Are your feet, legs, arms, and hands placed differently? Glance in the mirror to receive the impression of this physicalization in the mask. Explore how you stand, sit, and walk with this body.

(Continue on into the next exercise.)

Exercise 3a: Exploring a Vocal Countermask*

SIDECOACHING CONTINUED

(Time lapse) Now find the vocal quality and diction that seem appropriate for this new body. Let the physicalization produce a sound that seems appropriate for it.

(Time lapse) Let the sound become gibberish.

(Time lapse) Let the gibberish evolve into a word or phrase.

(Time lapse) Let the word or phrase develop into a sentence.

(Continue on into the next exercise.)

Exercise 3b: Exploring Emotional Range*

SIDECOACHING CONTINUED

(Time lapse) Mumble to yourself, describing your emotional state at the moment. What is your attitude about the world and other people in it? Start relating to others in the group and talk to them about these things.

(Time lapse) As you continue to relate to others and the space, increase the urgency of your need to share your state of mind and point of view. Increase the urgency of your need to the most intense level you can manage, physically and vocally. Match the vocal and the physical to the emotional.

(Time lapse) Now contract your attitude and emotional state of mind so that it is barely perceived by others but still present. Again, match the vocal and physical to the emotional.

(Continue on into the next exercise.)

Exercise 3c: Mixing It Up*

SIDECOACHING CONTINUED

(Time lapse) Freeze! When you come out of the freeze, you will restore the physicalization and vocalization, and the behavioral life, that you found in your original visible mask. Ready? Go!

(Time lapse) Freeze! When you come out of the freeze, you will revert to the physicalization and vocalization, and the behavioral life, you found in the countermask. Ready? Go!

(Time lapse) As you continue to improvise, find the trigger that allows you to switch from your mask to your countermask. Explore different attitudes and emotions appropriate for your mask and countermask. Expand and contract their size and volume.

(Time lapse) Freeze! When you come out of the freeze, you will continue to physicalize the countermask, but you will switch your vocal qualities to those for the original physicalization. Ready? Go!

(Time lapse) Switch your physicalization to your original one and your vocal qualities to those for your countermask.

(Time lapse) Switch your vocalization back to the original one.

(Repeat this exercise.)

(Time lapse) Freeze! Close your eyes, relax, and come out of the mask.

OBSERVATIONS/DISCUSSION: Now is the moment of decision. Before continuing any further into the Complex Character Mask extension and confirmation exercises, students must decide about the parameters of their Complex Character Mask characterizations, especially which attributes or qualities compose its public face and which attributes or qualities make up its private face. Students should now be able to sense the growing formation of their "true" complex characters in their body-minds and therefore make informed decisions about the physical, mental, emotional, and behavioral core of their characters. We are looking for characterizations that have both fixed and fluid attributes and are able to adjust to, and live in, a variety of changing situations.

The previous series of exercises led the students to explore a wide variety of possible countermask choices. Not all of them will be useful in the final formation of the public face and private face of the characters. The students should consider the following questions:

1. Which physicalization did you discover was most appropriate for your mask to use for its public face? Is it possible to incorporate the other physicalization into the life of your character? As the body of the private face? As an ideal? As a negative self-image?

2. Which vocal qualities and language did you discover were most appropriate for your mask to use for its public face? Is it possible to incorporate the other vocal qualities and diction for its private face?

3. Which emotions and attitudes most reflected your public face? Is it possible for your character to experience and express a whole range of emotions even though one may dominate?

4. What did you discover about the possibilities for a richer, more complex characterization through mixing and switching the physical and vocal countermasks with the originals?

ASSIGNMENT: Return to your Complex Character Mask Psychophysical Profile and make additional notes. After exploring the countermask, what can you say about the fixed and fluid aspects of your character? What possibilities now exist for a public face and a private face in your mask?

Extending the Characterization

These exercises should not be undertaken until the students have decided on the public and private faces of their Complex Character Masks.

EXERCISE 4: COSTUME*

Clothing that a character wears is an extension of that character's personality, at least the public face of the character. So clothes should be chosen by the actor to enrich the characterization.

In this exercise the students function as their own costume designers, and having the responsibility for choosing their characters' clothes greatly enriches the characterizations. The costume selected should be consistent with the public face of the character that is being developed. We are not dressing up the characters for a masquerade party!

OBJECTIVE: to discover the appropriate costume for the character.

PARTICIPANTS: full group.

PREPARATION: If you are in an educational theatre situation, ask permission for the students to choose their own costumes from the costume shop. Otherwise, try any secondhand clothing store, or have the students ask help from friends and relatives.

INSTRUCTIONS: Find the appropriate costume for the public face of your character, including shoes and a hat or scarf if needed. If you have worked through the explorations in the Neutral Mask, you should know how to think about questions of texture, color, and style and design that are appropriate for your character's costume. Let the mask choose its own costume through you!

Ask yourself these questions while you are selecting the costume pieces: In what ways are the clothing choices appropriate or inappropriate for the character? In color? fabric type? texture? design? expense level? size? type of item? How does the costume extend, enrich, and clarify the characterization?

EXERCISE 5: HATS AND HAIRSTYLE*

A character's hairstyle can be very revealing about its personality. How can you arrange your hair to create your character's hairstyle? You may want to think about a hat for your character to help you create the best illusion. Or you may want to consider a wig to complete your characterization. Make sure you receive special permission from the costumer if you want to borrow a wig, as costumers are rightly protective of these expensive items. (If a wig is mandatory and not available from the costume shop, you could always buy a cheap one from a local store.)

IMPORTANT FOLLOW-UP: Be sure to sign out your costume choices properly with the costumer, friend, or relative. Return any extra costumes you have borrowed to the costume shop, friend, or relative. Bring your costume to class with you so you can change into it after the warm-up session. All subsequent improvisations will be conducted with the characters fully in costume—even down to their underwear!

EXERCISE 6: HAND PROP AND/OR ACCESSORY*

When the script of a play calls for a character to use or be associated with an object (a hand prop), such as a cigar or an umbrella, or an accessory, such as a piece of jewelry, the playwright sees that object as a significant extension of the character. It tells us something about the prior life or psychological makeup of the character that may not be known in any other way. That hand prop is necessary for the character's identity and well-being. It is a projection or extension of the way the character is or wishes to be seen. But interestingly enough, the prop or accessory usually signifies the private face of the character. This is an important lesson for acting students and performers to learn.

Ask the students to name characters from plays that are associated with specific objects. Some examples include Laura in *The Glass Menagerie* with her glass unicorn, Captain Quiqq in *The Caine Mutiny Court Martial* with his ball bearings, Hedda Gabler with her guns, Mary Poppins with her umbrella, and Gayev with his remembered pool cue. Ask: Why do you think the playwright has given these objects to the characters? Do they point to the public or the private face of the characters?

OBJECTIVE: to extend and clarify the characterization through the discovery and use of a hand prop and/or an accessory that is necessary to the characterization. It is a "precious object" to the character because of the memories associated with it, not because it necessarily has a high monetary value.

INSTRUCTIONS: Find an appropriate and necessary hand prop and/or accessory for your character. Bring it to class and always have it available for your character to use. Does it reveal the public face or the private face of your character?

EXERCISE 7: LOST AND FOUND

This is not a necessary exercise, but one that is effective if time allows.

PARTICIPANTS: half the group at a time. The other half of the class serves as observers.

PREPARATION: Collect all the hand props from the students and set up a Lost and Found Department of a large department store. Make sure that you also have available other props similar to those chosen by the students for their characters. Also make sure that these props are not visible to the characters as they come to recover their lost articles.

INSTRUCTIONS: One student from the observer group volunteers to be the clerk at the Lost and Found (this role could be played in mask also). The clerk should decide which items are to be found and which are to remain permanently lost.

Students in their costumes assume their masks and rediscover their characters.

SIDECOACHING

Discover that your important personal item is lost.

Go to the Lost and Found and try to recover it.

Tell the clerk about what your personal item means to you.

Exercise 7a: Lost and Found Repeat

Repeat the Lost and Found exercise with the other half of the class.

OBSERVATIONS/DISCUSSION

For observers:

1. Did the character invest the lost personal item with enough personal and emotional value?

2. Was the student taken by the improvisation beyond any preparation he could have made?

3. What emotional response occurred when the item was restored? When it was not restored?

For participants: Write your discoveries and responses in your journal.

Confirming the Complex Mask Characterization

EXERCISE 8: THE INTERVIEW*

This exercise can be used at any time in the work with the Complex Character Masks. The interview with "Jake" described in the Prologue to this text demonstrates the powerful results this interview exercise can produce.

OBJECTIVE: to help the actors confirm their characterizations by undergoing individual and/or group interviews.

The Interview exercise helps the actors further their characterizations by inquiring about their personal life histories. The goal here should be to get the actors to release into the subtextual lives of their characters, trusting the mask to lead, by asking questions that the students could not have prepared in advance.

PARTICIPANTS: one student at a time. (This exercise can also be done as a series of small group interviews, with three or four students at a time.) The teacher and others role-play the interviewers.

If you must do three or more interviews at a time, start the actual interviewing with one person in the group but let the interviews spread to other characters if what is happening

warrants it. Frequently characters start relating to each other during these interviews. Be careful that one character does not dominate; be sure to elicit the necessary information from each one.

PREPARATION: Set up the requisite number of chairs in front of the group.

INSTRUCTIONS: The interviewees should live fully in the moment and let the masks lead them in their response to the questions. They should "go with the flow" and discover where their impulses will lead. They should not be concerned if impulses for their answers seem illogical.

The interviewers should try to follow leads given by the character in his answers to the questions; they should work to get the actor to be specific in his responses. Interviewers should use follow-up questions to probe for family history, life experiences, memories, and so on. Trick questions should not be asked, and attempts should not be made to break the actor from his involvement in the character.

Ask the students to assume their masks and rediscover their characters.

SIDECOACHING

Are you the person who is waiting to be interviewed?

Thank you for coming to the workshop today. Thank you for being willing to be interviewed. Would you please sit in the chair provided?

Are you comfortable?

Before we begin, would you please tell us your name and where you are from?

(Follow with interview. Some possible topics include a personal life history; family; occupation; values and beliefs; wishes, lies, and dreams; the happiest day of your life; the saddest day of your life; a favorite story or joke; feelings about being interviewed; clothing choices; prop and/or accessory; and hat or hairstyle.)

(When finished interviewing a character:) Thank you for sharing your life with us. You may go now.

Freeze! Close your eyes, relax, and come out of the mask.

OBSERVATIONS/DISCUSSION

For participants:

1. Where did your information to answer the interview questions come from?

2. Did you experience the character flowing through you?

For observers:

1. Did you sense that the actor truly allowed the mask to lead in the interview? If resistance was evident, was it the character's resistance to being interviewed, or the actor's resistance to trusting the mask and letting it take over?

2. Were the answers consistent in thought, language, and diction with the characterization?

3. Was the physicalization and behavior appropriate for the characterization?

4. Was a private face revealed, or did you only see a public face?

Exercise 8a: The Interview Repeat*

Repeat the Interview exercise until everyone has participated. Be aware that after the first interview, the other actors will be prepared for the questions asked, so always find a way to challenge them into the release beyond the planned.

EXERCISE 9: CHARACTER MONOLOGUE*

This exercise can be an alternative to the Interview exercise or can be done in addition to it.

OBJECTIVE: to allow each student to present a monologue that reveals his character in depth.

PARTICIPANTS: full group, one at a time.

INSTRUCTIONS: On your own, develop a two- or three-minute monologue for your character to present to the class for evaluation.

This monologue will allow you to present your complex characterization in its final form. This does not mean that you can present all the sides of your understanding of the character in one monologue. You must choose what is most important about your character that you want to share with us. Your character must have some need to share his or her thoughts with us. Your monologue must present the character's public and private faces.

You should rehearse and develop your monologue so that it takes us, your observers, on a "journey" that includes discoveries for us in it. Your character could even reflect on old material and make discoveries as you relate it. Remember, countermask techniques are a good way to add character enrichment.

Involve different emotional states and attitudes in as organic a manner as possible.

Present your monologue in front of the group for response and evaluation.

OBSERVATIONS/DISCUSSION

For observers:

1. Describe the personality type of the public face that you just experienced in front of you.
2. Did the actor find an appropriate physicalization for the physiognomy of the mask? Or did you experience a countermask physicalization?
3. Did the actor discover an appropriate pattern of behavior for the character?
4. Did the actor find an appropriate vocalization or verbalization for the character?

5. Was the diction level of the dialogue consistent with the rest of the characterization?
6. What character or personality traits did you not see as part of the characterization presented but that seemed to be present in the mask as you observed it?
7. How did the actor reveal the private face of the character?

EXERCISE 10: THE BLIND DATE*

OBJECTIVE: to extend and confirm characterization.

PARTICIPANTS: full group, working individually at first and then in pairs. The teacher role-plays as the representative of a computer-dating organization.

PREPARATION: Have a tape player ready, with a wide variety of dance music available. Each member of the group writes a note on a slip of paper, describing how he will be recognized by his blind date. Clear the center of the workshop space for dancing. Arrange tables and chairs around the perimeter.

INSTRUCTIONS: Before beginning the improvisation, explain the situation and the location. The setting is the Stardust Ballroom. Ask the participants to assume their masks and rediscover their characters. Turn on the tape player.

SIDECOACHING

Tonight is an exciting Saturday night here at the Stardust Ballroom. And it's very special for all of you assembled, because tonight you're going to meet your blind date that has been arranged by our amazing computer-dating service. I know you have all been waiting anxiously all week for this, so let's get going!

I will now pass out the slips that tell you how you will recognize your blind date.

(Hand out the slips to the group, making sure that there are interesting combinations and obvious mismatches.)

Check the information on your computer-dating slip, locate your blind date, and start to get acquainted. If you have any problems, please see me.

(Time lapse) If you do not like the person with whom you are presently matched, find a way to disengage from that person and see if you can find a better match at the dance.

(Time lapse) Freeze! Close your eyes, relax, and come out of the mask.

OBSERVATION/DISCUSSION: How well did the students remain in character and develop behavior consistent with their characters?

EXERCISE 11: THE FIELD TRIP*

This exercise can be one of the most exciting and challenging experiences of the course. It takes a whole workshop session but is well worth it. The participants are asked to be in character for an extended period of time outside the safe workshop space.

OBJECTIVE: to confirm characterization outside the safety of the classroom, forcing the actors to work spontaneously from their understanding of the characters' lives, belief systems, and attitudes about the world.

PARTICIPANTS: full group. The teacher goes with the group, stepping in when needed to facilitate the improvisation. The teacher also watches the clock, in order to bring the group back to the classroom when the allotted time is up. Allow plenty of time for this exercise.

PREPARATION: Set up a field trip experience for the group. Talk with the staff at a cafeteria on campus or a local restaurant to get their permission to do this exercise in their establishment. Assure them that nothing harmful will happen to the place or its customers.

During the exercise, staff and customers in the cafeteria will usually go along with this exercise if it is approached in the right way. And that depends most upon the attitude of the characters toward the nonmasked people. It is necessary to create an atmosphere that allows those new to the masked figures to play into the characterizations, thereby helping the actors confirm their characterizations, not unmasking them. (It is wise to spend a few minutes talking with the actors about what behavior might elicit negative responses to the exercise. If the actors meet people who seem to be threatened by them as masked figures, they should move on to other possibilities, not confront them.)

If possible, videotape this exercise to aid in evaluation.

INSTRUCTIONS: In full costume and with your hand prop and/or accessory, you will make a field trip to the cafeteria for lunch—or for a snack.

You must bring enough money to buy something that your character wants to eat and/or drink.

You must remain in character the whole time you are on the field trip.

You should determine a simple achievable objective and possible tactics for achieving that objective before you go.

Once in the cafeteria you should not go off by yourself or remain in a protective group. You should seek ways to meet and mingle with other people and relate to them.

Once you have returned to the workshop space at the end of the improvisation, we will have a short debriefing session.

Exercise 11a: Field Trip Evaluation

This is a time set aside when the videotape of the field trip is shown and the students get a chance to observe their work and comment on their ability to remain in character.

EXERCISE 12: THE BLIND DATE REVISITED

This can be an alternative exercise to the Field Trip exercise, especially if you plan an open class presentation at the end of the workshop. Get the students working as in the Blind Date exercise. Then sidecoach them to decide that there is a better possibility for their date if they choose someone in the audience. They need to try to get that person to do something for them or with them.

Final Projects: Solo Performances of Multiple Characters

These final projects require extensive time for research and development, but they are excellent summations of the lessons learned in the workshop. The performer is to generate a series of characterizations that clearly demonstrate his ability to create multiple characters in the telling of a story, the investigation of a theme, or the exploration of a situation.

Each character is to have its own monologue within the overall structure of the piece. Not all monologues should be the same length, and one or two might be broken up and dispersed throughout the performance.

Each character should have its own costume and prop.

The characters should exhibit variety in age, gender, and physical types. They should have differing qualities and personality traits. How do they differ from each other in attitude and point of view?

The subject matter for the series of monologues should focus on a central issue, situation, event, or personality that all the characters have in common. The discovery and development of the story, theme, or situation, however, should flow from the students' discovery of the characters and their lives in the masks, not from some imposition on the masks.

Staging—furniture, props, costume pieces, and so on—should be used minimally. Part of the delight of these pieces is to see how inanimate objects also can be transformed by the actor's and the audience's imagination.

The arrangement of the separate monologues can follow a linear, circular, or collage structure, or combinations of these. The arrangement is important, as each different arrangement of the monologues will create a different experience and provoke a different meaning for the audience. At the same time, the piece should not tell the audience what it should think or feel—even though characters may—but should set up a condition or situation in which the audience learns, or becomes aware of, a truth beyond what the characters say. Students should investigate the use of dramatic irony, where the audience knows something that one or more of the characters do not. The chosen structure should allow the audience to make discoveries and give them the longest "learning curve," as this strategy offers the most engaging and enjoyable experience for the audience.

The focus of the piece should be introduced very early on. If it is not clear from the first monologue, then it should become evident to the audience by the second monologue. Where is the tension or conflict located in the presentation? Is the conflict only one-dimensional? What are the characters' vulnerabilities, and how are they revealed? Directly or indirectly?

Students need to plan how they will move from one character to the next. Do they want to use themselves or one of their characters as narrators linking the monologues? Do they want to find a way to "morph" directly from one character to the next? How might a change in movement, in a gesture, in an activity, help to effect the transition or transformation?

Performers also need to decide how their characters will acknowledge and relate to their audience. All of the monologues should be played front, toward the audience. Most of the characters need to speak to the audience directly; others may evoke other characters who may be offstage, but these offstage personalities must be oriented toward the audience.

The presentation should be well rehearsed, always leaving room for improvisational moments in front of an audience. If time allows, a work-in-progress presentation before the group, requesting feedback, would be valuable. Each finished presentation should last approximately fifteen minutes.

EXERCISE 13: FAMILY RESEMBLANCES

OBJECTIVE: to create a range of possible characters from the student's research in a Complex Character Mask.
PARTICIPANTS: individuals.
INSTRUCTIONS: In this exercise the participants are asked to develop a solo performance piece presenting the primary characters they have created in their Complex Character Masks as

well as other personality formations that have been set aside because they did not assimilate into the mask/countermask of the major character discovered. These additional personalities are understood to be relatives of the major character because of the strong continuity of "family resemblances" provided by the mask.

Ask the student to find at least three other characters possible in his Complex Character Mask and create a story that introduces each character and its relationship to the main character.

EXERCISE 14: SUITCASE*

Either the participant or the teacher chooses five masks for the student to work with in developing a solo performance piece. All the masks, costume pieces, and props are kept in an old suitcase, which the actor brings onstage. Then he proceeds to unpack the suitcase while he transforms into the various characters to tell his story.

EXERCISE 15: SCENE STUDIES

OBJECTIVE: to develop an extended, repeatable improvisation that will function as a summary of each participant's work in the Complex Character Mask.
PARTICIPANTS: full group, working in groups of two or three with a variety of masks of their own choosing.
INSTRUCTIONS: Work with one or two partners and develop a repeatable scenario. Rehearse and polish this scenario for presentation to the rest of the group. Each actor should create at least three different characters in the playing of the scene.

This completes the work in the Complex Character Mask and in the series of Character Mask explorations. Further investigations should now focus either on the application of the mask training to nonmasked acting (chapter 16) or the possibilities of extending or adapting this training into mask theatre (chapter 17).

IV

The Application of Mask Improvisation Training

Masks and Faces

A human being can be represented in the theater only by a set of masks, one inside the other, all of them worn by an invisible presence.

—*Tom Driver,* Romantic Quest and Modern Query

Thus a characterization is the mask which hides the actor-individual. Protected by it he can lay bare his soul down to the last intimate detail. This is an important attribute or feature of characterization.

—*Konstantin Stanislavski,* Building a Character

. . . if Stanislavski had previously undergone the mask training, he would have brought to the stage a submissive body in the interpretation of his first role.

—*Léon Chancerel, "Notes personnelles"*

Introduction

Mask improvisation training gives actors concepts, principles, guidelines, and techniques for performing masked and unmasked. In this chapter we will focus on the application of the training to nonmasked acting—the purpose emphasized in most schools where mask improvisation is taught. Chapter 17 will address the application of the training to mask theatre.

If one of the major goals of mask improvisation training is, paradoxically, to teach actors how to perform more effectively unmasked, then how is mask characterization applied to nonmasked acting? It seems more readily transferable to non-realistic acting styles. How does it apply to the dominant form of the realistic style in performance? It is true that the style of acting that masks evoke is not the same as in realism. Masks elicit a more heightened, more schematic performance. What is needed, then, is not a direct transfer, but a translation. And not from one language to another, but from one dialect to another—from the dialect of the mask to the dialect of realistic acting.

The understandings revealed by mask training about the Self, the persona, characterization, and mask of actions can be readily applied to nonmasked performance. Students in this workshop should be able to detail a number of ways in which mask improvisation training has application to nonmasked acting, having participated in a number of transfer exercises that make connections between performing masked and performing unmasked.

Here, then, we will review the general lessons about acting that mask improvisation teaches, and then we will focus on the specific lessons taught by the Neutral Mask and the various Character Masks. And as we come to the close of this training process, we will reflect further on the nature of acting itself.

Lessons Learned from Mask Improvisation Training

Mask improvisation training teaches participants many things about the process of performance. Some of these lessons appear to be contradictory, but actually they emphasize how different facets of the experience of masks and masking can serve a variety of needs and performance styles. In this workshop, students have learned several important general lessons about masks:

1. The mask is the reality.

2. The actor's body, not her face or her voice, is her main means of communicating onstage.

3. Visualization is a powerful tool for affecting the psychophysical being of the actor.

4. The physical can awaken the corresponding psychological and emotional realms.

5. The character's emotional state of being can be used as a starting place in the search for the character's motivation and behavior.

6. The actor must be aware of her divided consciousness in rehearsal and performance. For training and performance in psychological realism, the conscious awareness and use of the divided consciousness are discouraged; in Brechtian theatre, they are encouraged.

7. Acting involves an actor in objective and subjective processes concurrently. The actor, possessed by the character, lets the character take over her bodymind. Therefore she knows when she is living in the moment—in flow—and when she is not.

8. The actor learns of her personal psychophysical habits so that she can set them aside, if necessary, and not impose a personal agenda on the material.

9. The mask is both a mirror to catch one's own reflection and a frame through which to see into another world.

10. Playwrights construct characters of different complexities. Some are meant to be two-dimensional, some three—depending upon the type of play and the playwright's "sculpting" of the characters' masks.

11. The actor learns techniques for constructing and performing the character according to the "dimensions," "scale," and "level" of the mask.

12. The actor learns the concepts and techniques of mask and countermask: family resemblances, public face and private face, playing with the text and against the text.

13. Dramatic moments are constructed through the forming and shaping of experience.

Pierre Lefèvre writes that "the masks are a catalyst. They release or liberate the actor's breathing, presence, physicality and imagination, particularly in training. They are an instrument of concentration. When you wear the mask, you are left alone with yourself. You must tap the inner region of your existence. You become very aware of your body and aware that it is being observed. It is like a magnifying glass for the actor. An unforgettable experience. Suddenly, he is aware that he is his own source of inspiration. He must do something that can be shared."[1]

Starting from Zero: Lessons from the Neutral Mask

From their own experiences in the Neutral Mask, students understand how to conceive of a character as other-than-neutral and other-than-themselves. Now they need to consider the transference of that understanding—starting from neutral—to the development of characterizations for nonmasked acting. The strategy is not irrelevant. Charles Janasz has said: "I went into [the rehearsal process] trying to make myself absolutely neutral: idling, waiting for the stimulus I'd get from rehearsals, from [director] Garland Wright, from other actors, dramaturgs, designers. I got all kinds of stimuli."[2]

Neutral Mask training teaches an actor how to approach each new role with an innocent bodymind or, in Stanislavski's famous phrase, "as if for the first time." In this way, as Janasz points out, the actor will be open to receive stimuli not only from the text but from all aspects of the production. Brecht, even though he, like Stanislavski, did not use the term *neutral*, recognized the concept of neutral when he declared that "the right starting point" for the actor, as for the designer, is "point zero."[3]

Besides seeing her character as Other and from a neutral perspective, the actor can apply her experience in the Neutral Mask to heighten her awareness of

1. the presence and stillness at the center of her character in its "being state."

2. the economy of gesture and movement that is most essential and appropriate for the character (or, put another way, she can eliminate all that is nonessential).

3. the appropriate levels of energy (as well as their intensity and dynamics) and scale of the gesture and movement required by the character's changing emotional, psychological, and social needs within the situation.

4. her character's identification with various images from nature—the four elements, substances, colors, sounds, vegetation, living creatures, and so on—so that her psychophysical imagination can be provided with a rich library of resources to facilitate characterization.

5. the intimate interrelationships between the physical, the mental, and the emotional aspects of her Self and her character.

Starting from zero also means that the actor has learned enough about herself in the Neutral Mask, her own habitual physical and psychological choices, so that she will not begin the process of characterization by immediately projecting onto the character or the situation material from her own past experience. Anthony Heald says, "When I stop performing one role and go on to another, I try to lose the old role as much as possible. It's much better to start with a blank slate. Every character has a signature. That signature may express itself in both vocal and physical ways."[4] The idea of starting from a blank slate—in other words, the concept of an innocent, neutral bodymind—should already have proved a valuable concept for members of this workshop.

Applying the Concept of Neutral

For the following exercises, the student should take a monologue or speech by any character she has performed in the past (or is presently performing) as the basis for the improvisation.

EXERCISE 1: IDENTIFICATIONS*

OBJECTIVE: to root the characterization in each of the Neutral Mask identification areas.

PARTICIPANTS: full group, working individually.

INSTRUCTIONS: Start from the neutral stance. Decide which of the four elements, or combination of elements, best identifies your character's temperament. Then rehearse your monologue, physicalizing that identification.

Decide what substances, combination of substances, or change in chemistry best captures some aspect of your character and/or its behavior. Then rehearse your character with those identifications.

Rehearse your character as a particular color, sound, texture, type of vegetation, and animal.

OBSERVATIONS/DISCUSSION: Which of these identifications, or combination of identifications, provides the best stimulus for capturing important aspects of your character?

EXERCISE 2: SOUND QUALITIES

OBJECTIVE: to discover the sound of a character's words as other-than-neutral.

PARTICIPANTS: full group, working individually.

INSTRUCTIONS: Take a key word or phrase that your character uses repeatedly in the play. Memorize it, and then explore its sound qualities by repeating it over and over, identifying with and physicalizing the sound qualities.

Create a dance with the word or phrase.

Move from your physicalization of the key word or phrase to neutral and back again several times.

OBSERVATIONS/DISCUSSION

1. Does the character affect you most psychophysically with its vowels or its consonants?

2. How is the word or the phrase other-than-neutral? Does your character love certain sounds, such as *m*'s or *l*'s? What is an *m* person like? What is an *l* person like? What is a *k* person like?

3. What does this exercise tell you about the possible subconscious connection between the sounds of your character's diction and your character's mental, emotional, and physical qualities?

EXERCISE 3: LETTING THE WORDS ACT YOU!*

Anna Deavere Smith's provocative performances in *Fires in the Mirror* and *Twilight, Los Angeles* demonstrate the awareness that the language a person speaks embodies her character. In speaking about her process of characterization, Smith says, "If you say a word often enough, it *becomes* you."[5] She sees the character's words as part of a whole, as aspects of the character's physical mask that can affect her total psychophysical being. "*I had not controlled the words. I had presented myself as an empty vessel, a repeater, and they had shown their power. I was soon to learn about the power of rhythm and imagery to evoke the spirit of a character, of a play, of a time.*" She continues: "The body has a memory just as the mind does. The heart has a memory, just as the mind does. The act of speech is a physical act. It is powerful enough that it can create, with the rest of the body, a kind of cooperative dance. That dance is a sketch of something that is inside a person and not fully revealed by the words alone. I came to realize that if I were able to record part of the dance—that is, the spoken part—and reenact it, the rest of the body would follow."[6]

OBJECTIVE: to let the words of a text act you.

PARTICIPANTS: full group, working individually.

PREPARATION: Collect a number of monologues from a wide variety of dramatic sources.

INSTRUCTIONS: Choose a text to work on by yourself. Stand in neutral. Read the text to yourself over and over, letting the body be affected by the words and rhythm of the speech. Then memorize the monologue and let the act of memorization also affect you physically. Repeat the speech out loud to yourself many times, starting from neutral. As you speak the text, hear the words with your imagination, feel the rhythm in your body. Let the words change your consciousness and physicalization.

OBSERVATIONS/DISCUSSION

1. What muscular and emotional response did you have to the text?

2. What images affected you?

3. How did the sound and rhythm of the words affect you?

4. What does this exercise show you about the possible conscious and unconscious interconnections between your character's verbal, mental, emotional, and physical qualities?

I have heard a number of language teachers remark that when they speak in a foreign language, they take on a different personality. They experience a psychophysical change; they think and feel differently. What a great sensitivity for the actor to gain!

EXERCISE 4: PHYSICALIZING INTENTIONS

OBJECTIVE: to explore the character's primary and secondary motivations in a physical way, discovering how they are other-than-neutral.

PARTICIPANTS: full group, working individually.

INSTRUCTIONS: Follow the same procedures as for the Sound

Qualities exercise above, but this time physicalize a stated intention for the scene and/or the throughline of the character.

Continue on into the next exercise.

Exercise 4a: Physicalizing the Opposite Intentions

INSTRUCTIONS: Follow the same procedures as for the previous exercise, but this time physicalize the opposite of your stated intention for the scene and/or the throughline of the character.

Continue on into the next exercise.

Exercise 4b: Intensification of the Physicalizations

INSTRUCTIONS: Enlarge or shrink the scale of the physicalization of the verbs you used in stating the intention or the throughline and their opposites.

Exercise 4c: Combinations of Physicalizations

OBJECTIVE: (for psychological realism) to physicalize the major internal-external conflict that dominates the character's life in a play; (for the Brechtian approach) to explore what other options the character might have chosen but did not or to explore stepping aside to comment on the character created.

OBSERVATIONS/DISCUSSION: See questions for the Sound Qualities and Letting the Words Act You! exercises above.

EXERCISE 5: QUALITY TIME

OBJECTIVE: to physicalize the character's unique traits, qualities, and temperament as a way to discover how the character is other-than-neutral.

OBSERVATIONS/DISCUSSION

1. What are the most important qualities your character exhibits? How are these qualities other-than-neutral?

2. Which ones are fixed? Which are fluid?

Antony Sher suggests an additional wrinkle to the application of the concept of neutral to characterization when he wonders what "basic neutrality" his Richard III needs to have "so that he can slip into his various acts without arousing disbelief from the other characters."[7]

These explorations in the applicability of the Neutral Mask allow the performer to see how her character is other-than-herself. At the same time, they throw into sharper relief the character's unique and idiosyncratic attributes.

The Neutral Mask in Rehearsal

If an actor is having difficulty finding an appropriate physicalization for her character, then use the Neutral Mask and put the actor through an Individual Movement Analysis (see chapter 7). In this way you can determine her idiosyncratic physicalization and movement patterns that are other-than-neutral. Then, while she is still in the Neutral Mask, explore the physicalization and movements that you want to test as possibilities for the character. Where is the character's movement center? What is the relationship between the character's head and neck, chest, and pelvic placements? How are these centers other than the actor's?

The Character as Mask: Lessons from the Character Masks

Peter Brook states that "an actor's motivation doesn't come from a sort of technical understanding of his body; it comes from his capacity to create an incredibly powerful image in himself that he's convinced by."[8] It should be evident from the experience of mask improvisation that the compelling image Brook is talking about, the "incredibly powerful image" that not only affects the physical being of the actor but also her whole psychophysical being, is a mask. As Stanislavski himself said, "If you do not use your body, your voice, a manner of speaking, walking, moving, if you do not find a form of characterization which corresponds to the image, you probably cannot convey to others its inner, living spirit."[9]

Reconstructing the Mask of the Character from the Text

To discover the character's mask in the text, we need to reverse the process we have been employing in this course—the mask is the text—and adapt it to a new set of circumstances. With a playscript, the character's dialogue and the playwright's descriptions and stage directions are themselves the most evident external, physical manifestation of the role (the character's mask). Now the text suggests the mask! Brook writes, "A role is a meeting, a meeting between an actor as a mass of potentialities—and a catalyst. Because a role [mask] is a form of catalyst, from outside, it makes a demand and draws into form the unformed potentiality of the actor. That is why a meeting between an actor and a role always produces a different result."[10]

We can begin to reconstruct the mask of a character by building up a composite picture from the fragments available to us in the text. These fragments constitute the vocabulary of the mask. In every fragment, as in a hologram, the whole is represented. Potential fragments found in a text would therefore include tangible, external fragments and intangible, internal fragments. The tangible, external fragments comprise the character's physical appearance, including clothing; the character's movement and gestures; the character's speech patterns, rhythms, and diction; and comments about the character by other characters. The intangible, internal fragments include the character's motivations perceived through its words and actions; the character's behavior and relationship(s) with others and the world; the character's thoughts as revealed in dialogue; the changing intensities of the character's emotional life; and the character's qualities and traits (e.g., "brave," "resourceful").

During the rehearsal period, the actor needs to be consciously (and unconsciously) constructing from these tangible and intangible fragments a compelling image of the character. Eventually, as in a photographic process, the character's mask materializes on the sensitized plate of the actor's bodymind imagination. To do this, Brook counsels, "an actor has to forget 'fabricating,' he has to forget 'making effects,' he has to get away from the idea that he is there as a showpiece. And in its place he has to put another notion, that of being the servant of an image that will always be greater than himself. Any actor who plays a part and sees the part as being smaller than himself will give a bad performance. An actor must recognize that whatever part he is playing, the character is more intense than himself." [11]

In addition to the exercises described above on the potential uses of the Neutral Mask for nonmasked acting, the following exercises will help the actor discover the unique vocabulary of the individual character's mask in the text. We will begin by employing the techniques of imaging or visualization.

Students need to examine the playwright's notes in a script very carefully. They are prone to pass over descriptions and stage directions as inconsequential. (You must be certain, of course, that you are dealing with the playwright's own notes and not those from an acting version of the play that describe the decisions reached by a particular director with a particular set of actors and designers. In the case of classical texts, such notes often represent an editor's or translator's imaginative amplification.)

Many modern playwrights know that dialogue is only one of the many theatrical languages they can use to communicate to an audience. So their notes on setting, lighting, costuming, and so on are important to an understanding of how they visualized plays while writing them. This does not mean that a director, designers, and actors must follow such notes as prescriptive, but neither should they totally ignore the playwright's intentions. Frequently these notes are ignored at the peril of the production. One should consider the playwright's description of the characters as a serious attempt to communicate to readers her compelling images—her characters' masks.

In the following exercises we will explore visualizations of characters from Henrik Ibsen's *Hedda Gabler* and Samuel Beckett's *Endgame*.

EXERCISE 6: VISUALIZING HEDDA GABLER'S MASK*

Hedda has just returned home from her honeymoon the previous evening and will meet her husband's aunt Julianna first thing this morning. Aunt Julianna and her sister raised Hedda's husband from boyhood. Here is Ibsen's description of Hedda's first entrance: "Hedda enters from the left through the inner room. She is a woman of twenty-nine. Her face and figure show breeding and distinction; her complexion is pallid and opaque. Her steel gray eyes express a cool, unruffled calm. Her hair is an attractive medium brown, but not particularly abundant. She wears a tasteful, rather loose-fitting gown." [12]

OBJECTIVE: to visualize Ibsen's description of his characters in detail, to see how he has imagined the characters' masks.

PARTICIPANTS: half the class, working individually. The other half of the class serves as observers-coaches.

INSTRUCTIONS: Stand in the neutral position. Close your eyes and clear your mind by concentrating on your breathing. You will visualize the images suggested by the teacher as specifically as possible. Combine and superimpose images if necessary to create a vivid composite picture of the figure.

SIDECOACHING

You are a twenty-nine-year-old woman and have just returned home from your honeymoon in Italy.

Your figure and features betoken a person of "breeding" and "distinction."

Find a physicalization that epitomizes the word *breeding* or *dignity*.

Superimpose an image of the quality "distinction" on top of your physicalization of the word *dignity*. This is the public face you want the world to see.

When you open your eyes, you will be alone in your dressing room, looking at yourself in a full-length mirror. You are preparing to meet your husband's aunt Julianna for the first time since the honeymoon. Remember, Aunt Julianna reared your husband.

Open your eyes and observe yourself in the mirror. Do you see a woman of dignity and distinction? What impression do you hope to make on your husband's aunt?

Move closer to the mirror and observe your eyes. Their color is steel gray.

What do you feel about your eyes being that color?

Do you believe that the color of your eyes affects other people's response to you? Do you like that response?

Now observe your face in the mirror.

Feel the skin on your face. People have said that your skin is "pallid" and "opaque."

What do those terms mean to you? What do you feel about your skin?

Observe your hair. It is medium brown in color, but it is not particularly thick.

What do you do to make it appear more thick and luxuriant?

Observe the morning gown you have put on.

What color is it? Feel the fabric against your skin. How does it feel? How does the color complement your hair color and skin tone?

Why did you choose to put on this particular "loose-fitting" gown this morning? Are you trying to impress Aunt Julianna? Are you trying to conceal or reveal something to her inquisitive eyes?

Move about the space in front of the mirror, observing yourself in the mirror. Does the gown create the effect you want?

How does the gown affect your attitude about yourself and how you move?

Now put on your public face, leave your dressing room, and go downstairs to meet Aunt Julianna.

(Time lapse) Freeze! Close your eyes, relax, and come out of the character.

OBSERVATIONS/DISCUSSION: This exercise focuses primarily on Hedda's private face in an imagined offstage moment before her first appearance. But note that she is readying herself for a public moment. Her words and behavior in front of other characters in the play will establish her public face, which will combine with the private face revealed at certain moments to establish the character Hedda Gabler in front of us. Participants should compare notes on their responses, reconsidering the sidecoaching questions.

1. What differing interpretations do different members of the class produce? Differences in interpretation illustrate Brook's point that a characterization is always a "meeting" between the character in the text and the personality of the actor playing the role.
2. What similarities do different actors produce?
3. What do you perceive about Hedda's personality and character traits from your physicalization of her age, her appearance, and her qualities? What does this tell you about her mental and emotional state? How does she perceive herself and the world around her?
4. Did this exercise help you begin to develop a composite picture of Hedda? What insights did it give you as a starting point for exploring her character further?

Exercise 6a: Visualizing Aunt Julianna's Mask*

PARTICIPANTS: half the class, working individually. The other half of the class serves as observers-coaches.

INSTRUCTIONS: Repeat the previous exercise, but this time focus on Ibsen's description of Aunt Julianna in her first appearance. Imagine her possible offstage preparation for meeting her new niece, Hedda.

Exercise 6b: Interactions of Hedda Gabler and Aunt Julianna*

INSTRUCTIONS: Ask two actors (one as Hedda and one as Aunt Julianna) and two coaches to repeat the visualization exercises separately but simultaneously. Then sidecoach the two to improvise their first meeting. Afterward, compare the improvisation with the actual text of the scene. (An alternative method would be to have the two actors memorize and use the actual text after completing their visualizations.)

EXERCISE 7: VISUALIZING HAMM'S MASK*

Here is Samuel Beckett's description of the character Hamm at the opening of *Endgame:* "Center, in an armchair on casters, covered with an old sheet, Hamm . . . [i]n a dressing-gown, a stiff toque on his head, a large blood-stained handkerchief over his face, a whistle hanging from his neck, a rug over his knees, thick socks on his feet, Hamm seems to be asleep. . . . Pause. Hamm stirs. He yawns under the handkerchief. He removes the handkerchief from his face. Very red face. Black glasses." [13]

PARTICIPANTS: half the class, working individually. The other half of the class serves as observers-coaches.

PREPARATION: Each participant will need a chair with arms. Explain any terms or objects (like "rug").

INSTRUCTIONS: Sit in a chair with arms in a neutral position. Your back must not be resting against the back of the chair. Let your hands rest on your thighs, not on the arms. Close your eyes and clear your mind by concentrating on your breathing. Visualize the images as they are given to you, making any adjustments necessary in your physicalization. Try to see the images in your mind's eye as vividly and specifically as possible.

SIDECOACHING

Image yourself sitting in an old armchair.

How does it fit your body? What kind of padding does the chair have?

Move around in the armchair until you are comfortable.

Place your arms so that they rest on the arms of the chair. Your fingers are curved down over the ends of the arms.

What kind of fabric is covering the chair? Feel the fabric. What's the texture like?

You have been in this chair a long time. How does it feel to know you are probably confined to this chair for the rest of your life?

You are wearing a stiff toque on your head.

Why do you like this type of hat on your head?

You are wearing dark glasses over your eyes.

Why do you have to wear dark glasses?

Someone has put casters on your chair.

Who could have done that? Why?

There's a whistle around your neck.

How did you get this whistle?

How does it sound when you blow it?

When do you blow it?

You have thick socks on your feet.

Feel the texture of these thick socks with your toes and the skin of your feet. How do they feel?

Why are you wearing thick socks on your feet?

There's a handkerchief in your lap. Pick it up.

What does the fabric of the handkerchief feel like?

Notice that there is a stiff section of the fabric.

How does it feel? How does it smell?

It's blood. How did the blood get on the handkerchief?

Now find a reason to cover your face with this handkerchief.

How does it feel to sit there with your face covered by this handkerchief?

Your knees and legs are covered with a rug.

Feel the weight of this rug on your thighs, knees, and legs. How heavy is this rug?

Feel the rug's texture with your fingers. How does it feel?

Where did the rug come from? Who put it over your knees?

Why do you want or need a rug over your knees and legs?

Now someone is covering you and the armchair you are sitting in with an old sheet.

Why are you being covered with a sheet?

Who is putting this sheet over you? What do you feel about this person?

Feel the texture and weight of the sheet on your face and hands.

How does it feel to sit there covered with a sheet?

Freeze! Relax, and come out of the character.

OBSERVATIONS/DISCUSSION: This visualization, even more than the previous ones with *Hedda Gabler,* appears to focus on the character's "state of being" more than its "doing." But it is this "being" out of which the "doing" of the character, his words and actions, will come. The participants in this visualization should be able to suggest not only what kinds of things the character will say and do but how he will say and do them. They should also be reminded that "to sit" is an action that can be played in a variety of ways. If they previously experienced the Neutral Mask exercise To Sit, then they can understand Hamm's sitting as an action that is other-than-neutral.

See the questions above for the exercise Visualizing Hedda Gabler's Mask.

Exercise 7a: Visualizing Clov's Mask*

PARTICIPANTS: half the class, working individually. The other half of the class serves as observers-coaches.

INSTRUCTIONS: Now take the character of Clov from *Endgame* and follow through an extended visualization, using Beckett's description of him on his first entrance.

Exercise 7b: Interactions of Hamm and Clov*

INSTRUCTIONS: Using two actors to demonstrate Hamm and Clov and two observers to coach, take the two actors simultaneously through their visualizations. Then bring them together to improvise an interaction. Check their improvisation against the actual text.

In 1984 Peter Evans played the character of Clov for Alvin Epstein's production of *Endgame.* He had great difficulty in finding the appropriate characterization. He first struggled to create the character through the principles and techniques of psychological realism, but he quickly found that that approach did not serve him well in this instance.

> It became clear after a while that [the psychological acting approach] wasn't working for the play, and I had to make some kind of leap. . . . I mean, I always thought that those kind of external things were dangerous. But in *Endgame* . . . as soon as I made up that crazy voice and the extreme physicalness of it, it freed me to make choices that before I couldn't make, because I was locked into my own given physical self. . . . It's funny, imposing this leap of faith. When you create a character not just through intellectual means but through real physical things, it opens up all kinds of doors that you could never have foreseen.[14]

If Evans had undergone mask improvisation training in addition to his training in psychological realism, then he would have had the resources readily available to choose the best approach for his creation of the character of Clov. It is amazing how much the mask of a character can be "sculpted" by examining and physicalizing the visual and kinesthetic images—the vocabulary of the mask—embedded in the text.

Visualizing the Imaginary Body

Visualizing an imaginary body for the character is not a new idea. It was one of the major techniques that the great actor-teacher Michael Chekhov taught his students. He had been trained by Stanislavski to appreciate the value of living "in the image."[15] In his text *To the Actor,* Chekhov describes his technique for visualizing the character's body in language reminiscent of mask improvisation.

You are going to imagine that in the same space you occupy with your own real body there exists another body —the imaginary body of your character, which you have created in your mind.

You clothe yourself, as it were, with this body; you put it on like a garment. What will be the result of this "masquerade"? After a while (or perhaps in a flash!) you will begin to feel and think of yourself as another person. This experience is very similar to that of a real masquerade. . . . But "wearing another's body" is more than any raiment or costume. This assumption of the character's imaginary physical form influences your psychology ten times more strongly than any garment!

The imaginary body stands, as it were, between your real body and your psychology, influencing both of them with equal force. Step by step, you begin to move, speak and feel in accord with it; that is to say, your character now dwells within you (or, if you prefer, you dwell within it).

. . . But in any case, your whole being, psychologically and physically, will be changed—I would not hesitate to say even possessed—by the character. When really taken on and exercised, the imaginary body stirs the actor's will and feelings; it harmonizes them with the characteristic speech and movements, it transforms the actor into another person![16]

The imaging technique that Chekhov proposes here, and its effect on the sensitive actor, come as no surprise to those who have taken the plunge into mask improvisation. In our case, the mask with its mirroring body "stands between" the actor and her body, "influencing both of them with equal force." The specific image of the actual mask and its felt presence and pressure on the face of the wearer prompt the bodymind imagination to respond with power. Working with masks, students have learned the value of this technique in an indelible manner.

Directors and actors can also find the techniques of visualizing a character from the description in a text very useful as a way to begin a rehearsal concerned with character development.

These nonanalytic imaging exercises should be understood as only a starting point for developing a characterization. A characterization must never be "fixed" in the actor's bodymind from an isolated moment in the play. A complete characterization must come from a profound subjective and objective investigation into, and understanding of, the character's words, actions, motivations, and relationships throughout the entire play. The actor must also understand the historical and cultural context, the genre and style, of the play as well as the character's dramatic function.

Finding the Vocabulary of the Character's Mask: Self-Study

EXERCISE 8: READING THE VOCABULARY OF THE CHARACTER'S MASK

OBJECTIVE: to discover the vocabulary of a character's mask from a close reading of a playscript.

PARTICIPANTS: full group, working individually.

INSTRUCTIONS: Take a modern play and examine it carefully for any descriptions that the playwright gives concerning the vocabulary of the character's mask: the way the character looks, moves, and dresses. Try "stepping into" either the total image of the character or putting on each aspect of the character as described: physicalization, qualities, costume, and so on.

Anticipate and catch the beginning formations of images of the character that appear in the mind's eye. These fragments will always be a key aspect of the character. Let these image fragments inform your total sensibilities.

OBSERVATIONS/DISCUSSION: How much of the vocabulary of the character's mask did you discover through your visualization and physicalization of the character's mask of actions?

Discovery of the vocabulary of the character's mask in the text is also of the utmost importance for actors performing in the Brechtian style. Carl Weber writes, "Sorting out of clues, setting of priorities, evolving of appropriate gestic patterns, i.e. the experimentation with variants of character conduct as it manifests itself in gait, carriage, gesture, pitch and inflection of voice, rhythm or speech, and so forth, tends to quickly engage the actors' imaginations and stir their creativity. . . . In this mode, actors assemble a 'catalogue of gestures' [vocabulary] feasible for each segment of a scene and eventually make their choices in consensus with the director."[17]

Discovering the Character as Other

Another important benefit for the actor in understanding the character in a text as a mask is that this conception allows the actor to see the character initially as outside her Self, as other-than-me. Such a technique prevents the actor from immediately assuming that the character is identical-to-me. In this way the actor can effect the "meeting" with the mask or character, as Brook recommends, and be rescued from automatically perceiving every role she plays through what Peter Frisch calls her "own neurotic self-image."[18] Anna Deavere Smith calls this condition an actor's "self-based" focus: "The spirit of acting is the *travel* from the self to the other. This 'self-based' method seemed to come to a spiritual halt. It saw the self as the ultimate home of the character. To me, the search for character is constantly in motion. It is a quest that moves back and forth between the self and the other." [19]

Techniques of visualizing the character's mask, along with the realization of the character as other-than-me, though they are not emphasized in many classes in the realistic acting style, have been tremendously important for many successful actors in the process of their character development. Michael Chekhov writes:

> Seeing and hearing the character thus in my mind's eyes and ears, as the playwright saw and heard him, studying him in every detail as he lives out his half life on the stage, I am better able to absorb the qualities which will transform me into the character; I am better able to alter my body, my voice, and my emotions to conform with those of the character instead of forcing his to conform to mine. By so doing, I become the character's instrument for conveying his life to the audience, as the playwright saw it. I do not make the character just another instrument for conveying my own personality. [20]

Francis Sternhagen says, "I am the kind of person who tends to work from the outside in. I like to think of the way a person looks, and how I'm going to fit into her walk and mannerism. Then I start building the character's inner self within that framework." [21] Laurence Olivier describes his creation of a character: "I first visualize a painting; the manner, movement, gestures, walk all follow. It begins to come. Pictures and sound begin to form in my mind, subconsciously at first, but slowly working their way to the surface. You keep the image in the heart and then project it onto the oil painting. I say 'oil' rather than 'water-color' because for me, acting will always be in oils." [22]

As these statements illustrate, an imagined "painting" or visualization of the character as Other, like an actual mask, can function as a potent creative gestalt for the actor's psychophysical being.

Finding the Vocabulary of the Character's Mask: Rehearsal

At the first reading of a play with a cast, ask the actors to read a role other than their own. In this way they get impressions of their characters from a double perspective: from the outside by hearing another read it, and from the inside as they are conscious that the part being read is their own. This approach also prevents the cast from getting trapped into "performing" the role for each other to justify their casting this early in the process. They are all hearing the full text spoken aloud for the first time together.

During a rehearsal of a two-character scene, ask the actors to reverse roles so they can see and hear their own characters from another point of view. This also gives the actor a double perspective on her character.

Actors should also learn to visualize a compelling image of their characters—either seeing their portraits and/or their figures in movement—in the moments before rehearsing a scene or performing.

It is important to reemphasize that the primary way an actor shares her character's mask—her embodiment and enactment of the character—with the audience is through the externals of voice, gesture, movement, costume, and makeup. The audience must have a physical experience of the character as well as an ideational one. As Michael Goldman has stated, "A character in the theater, the created self, is identical with the actor's deed." [23]

Acting in the style of psychological realism, the actor must find a way in which her bodily intentions onstage match her character's psychological need. The latter must inform the former, unless the character is lying, is playing a role, or, like Quasimodo, is a countermask! Or, in the Brechtian style, the actor must find a way in which to step aside and manipulate the mask of her character so that the distinction between her own physical life and that of her character reveals the alienation and dialectical contradictions between them. Her task is to unmask her character and the situation for the audience, but not to unmask herself as actor.

In actor training we may need to separate the internal and the external approaches into two distinct training practices. Unfortunately, there is little training in the "externals," in nonrealistic styles, or in Brechtian-type acting in our theatre schools today. To be adequately prepared for the variety of performance modes needed in today's theatre, however, students should be trained in as many approaches as possible.

Additional techniques that are sometimes useful in assisting an actor in discovering the mask of the character include sketching a mask of the character on paper, sculpting a mask of the character in clay, and creating a collage portrait of the character using magazine photographs.

Finding the Vocabulary of the Character's Mask: Mask and Countermask

A character's persona, modeled on the understanding of a human persona, can be written to present either a conscious or an unconscious playing out of a pattern of behavior ("mask of actions") that is intended to show a sense of itself to others. Tartuffe, in Molière's play, is a character that, depending upon the actor's interpretation, can be a superb example of either the conscious or the unconscious presentation of a persona for its material advantage. An actor always needs to discover the seeming contradiction, if any, between the character's public face and its private face. As we have seen, these two faces—mask and countermask—are best understood either as part of a dynamic relationship of opposites or as complementary.

This raises the intriguing question for us again about the nature of fictional characters onstage. Tom Driver, in his influential book *Romantic Quest and Modern Query,* proposes that

> the character is the form of something other than itself—deeper, more mysterious, more mutable. If the playwright removes the character's mask, revealing what it hides [a countermask], he will move the dialectic to a new level, but he will not resolve it. The character newly exposed will prove to be another mask, negating and being negated by what it hides. And so on. A human being can be represented in the theater only by a set of masks, one inside the other, all of them worn by an invisible presence. The character as such is only a stereotype (what else are minor characters in most plays?). The person is revealed in the tension between the fixity of his character and the mobility of his inner life. This tension reappears on each successive level of analysis.[24]

What Driver expresses in this statement speaks to the heart of the matter. If the character's mask of actions (public face behavior) is understood by the actor only as the character's instrument of concealment behind which the character's "true being" (its private face) hides, then she should also realize that when the playwright lets the public face slip in order to uncover the "authentic core" of the character's being, that which is revealed is always another mask. In theatre the "invisible presence" of the person of the character can only be revealed through a mask or a series of masks!

What is Hedda really doing in the opening scene with Aunt Julianna? Is she trying to impress her in a particular way and for a particular reason? Does this mean that she herself is knowingly playing a role? Is she "other" than what she presents herself as being? If so, where in the play does Ibsen allow us to see Hedda's private face?

What about Hamm? Does his external physical reality represent his mask or his countermask? Does it represent his public face or his private face?

ASSIGNMENT: Think of a number of plays that you have recently read, seen, or performed and apply these concepts of mask and countermask, public face and private face, to the major characters in those plays. Here for consideration are some famous characters from a wide variety of plays: Oedipus, Medea, Hamlet, Cleopatra, Tartuffe, Phaedra, Nora, Solness, Major Barbara, Galileo, Willy Loman, Arlie/Arlene. Reflect on these questions:

1. What did you discover? Do many playwrights use this concept of the public face versus the private face as a method of suggesting character development or revelation?
2. When and how did the playwrights reveal the private face of the character behind the public face?
3. Did the public face reveal character traits that remained fixed throughout? Did the private face? Which character traits were fluid?

Imagine, then, what complexity of representation occurs when a character plays a character in a play-within-the-play. Sometimes even masks wear masks! What layers of characterization does the actor then have to reveal? These masking and unmasking moments can be some of the most exciting times onstage—and the most challenging for the actor to perform. Mask improvisation training, more than any other approach, illuminates ways in which actors can perform this layering, or nesting effect, of one character inside another.

Capstone Exercises

Margo Jefferson writes, "Scientists call it 'kinesthetic-visual matching'; we call it mimicry and imitation. They say that when we engage in it we learn empathy for others. We know that when we watch it—watch an actor alone on a stage that advertises its own bareness, for instance, watch him reshape his face, voice and body to become 5, 10 or 15 other people—we experience acute pleasure and wonder."[25]

A human being's ability to transform at will into multiple characters is the singular glory of the acting art. Numerous plays, from the ancient Greek tragedies and mimes to the recent *Travels with My Aunt,* require and celebrate the actor's talent for playing multiple roles. With the triumph of realism as the dominant theatrical style in the West, however, the vision of a theatre where actors could transform into more than one character in any production (except, of course, for economic reasons) was lost.

Solo performance, however, has a long and proud heritage in contemporary world theatre, from the Bhands in Rajasthan, India, and the Topeng Pajegan performers in Bali to the Rakugo storytellers in Japan. And modern and contemporary drama has also had its brilliant practitioners. Solo performers such as Ruth Draper, Cornelia Otis Skinner, and, more recently, Lily Tomlin, Eric Bogosian, and Anna Deavere Smith, among others, have carried on this ancient acting tradition to popular acclaim. Mask improvisation offers excellent training for anyone interested in creating solo performances or for actors required to play multiple roles.

The following exercises, like those described at the end of chapter 15, challenge the student to demonstrate the lessons learned in mask improvisation and to apply them to the creation of multiple characters in a nonmasked performance. For general instructions, see the section entitled "Final Projects: Solo Performances of Multiple Characters" in chapter 15. Some additional guidelines will also be helpful:

Find an interesting way to introduce your characters to the audience.

Consider which of the characters start talking with their public faces and then reveal in their monologues, without knowing it, their private faces. Which of the characters, if any, reveal their private faces directly?

Develop an appropriate physicalization and vocalization for each character. Work to create characters, not caricatures. The silhouette of each character should be filled in with the character's personal, idiosyncratic behavior. But keep it simple and believable!

Locate each character's movement center. Choose and develop characters that have different centers. Does the character's center move or change during the monologue? If so, why?

What element, or combination of elements, reflects each of the characters? What substance? What color? What animal? How does contemplation of these possible correspondences help you to imagine and create the characters?

What tempo or rhythm does each character have? Does this basic pulse stay the same or change during each of the monologues? Is there a difference between a character's inner tempo and rhythm and an outer one?

What emotional states do the characters experience during their monologues? Do these change?

Instead of having a complete costume for each character, wear a simple, plain outfit that can be used for all the characters or adapted with accessories such as a hat, jacket, or scarf.

EXERCISE 9: MULTIPLE ROLE PERFORMANCE WITH A PREEXISTING TEXT

PARTICIPANTS: individual or duo.

INSTRUCTIONS: Take five or six of the many fine character monologues from a preexisting text such as Edgar Lee Masters's poetry collection *Spoon River Anthology,* or plays such as Jaston Williams, Joe Sears, and Ed Howard's *Greater Tuna,* Jane Wagner's *Search for Signs of Intelligent Life in the Universe,* or Giles Havergal's adaptation of Graham Greene's *Travels with My Aunt.* Apply the lessons from the Neutral and Character Masks to a performance of the monologues.

EXERCISE 10: SOLO PERFORMANCE WITH A PREEXISTING TEXT*

PARTICIPANTS: individual.

INSTRUCTIONS: Choose a well-known play that has a number of interesting and challenging characters. After reading and studying the text, decide on the group of characters to present and the subject matter for the series of monologues.

This assignment is not meant to allow you to comment on or to parody the text through your presentation, or to create a miniplay in which the characters speak to each other. Some characters could evoke other characters and comment on their remarks as if they overheard them, however.

Do not assume that the audience knows the play or the central event or figure that is being focused on. Provide enough background information and context so that the presentation will make sense and function as a dramatic whole in its own right.

Write the monologues using as much of the actual text of the play as possible. Create any new dialogue in the style of the play and the diction of the different characters. How does the characters' diction reflect who and what they are? How do the characters' monologues reveal as much about the characters as they do about the subject matter?

EXAMPLES: One of my students chose Shakespeare's *Tempest* and then developed a series of character monologues portraying Caliban, Prospero, and Miranda, returning to Caliban again for a final commentary. Another student chose Lillian Hellman's *Little Foxes* and developed a portrayal of Regina, Birdie, and Horace (speaking from the dead about the suspicious circumstances of his death).

EXERCISE 11: SOLO PERFORMANCE WITH AN ORIGINAL TEXT*

Combining the guidelines given above with those found in the section "Final Projects: Solo Performances of Multiple Characters" in chapter 15, create an original performance piece.

Reflections on the Process of Acting

In Molière's *Tartuffe,* Cleante asks,

There's a vast difference, so it seems to me,
Between true piety and hypocrisy:
How do you fail to see it, may I ask?
Is not a face quite different from a mask?" [26]

Poor Cleante! He imagines that it is easy to tell the difference between a face and a mask. But if an actor is good at playing her role, it can be extremely difficult for the audience to know the difference. To see a mask only as an agent of concealment is to have a limited vision of what a mask is. We know from the experience of the workshop that the more important function of a mask is not to conceal but to reveal.

In Michael Redgrave's book *Mask or Face,* the British actor makes an important point about the correspondence between an actor's private and public face: the two cannot be separated. To clarify what he means about this divisible, yet indivisible, union that transpires between the actor and her own mask, Redgrave examines the difference between the "mask" and the "face" of the actress Edith Evans. He writes about "the essence of her emotional experience and the residuum of a life philosophy. This is the actress' Face. The rest, her appearance, her voice, her techniques, her mannerism, are the Mask, but without the perfect discipline of the latter, the former would not be visible to us." [27]

From our discussion so far, we should understand Redgrave's term *mask* as being roughly equivalent to our phrase *mask of actions.* The experience in mask improvisation demonstrates that, like the "face" and "mask" of a human being, the character's face and its mask should be intimately connected. Through careful presentation of the externals of appearance, voice, and habitual behavior, the "invisible presence" of the Other is revealed.

Our perception of what a person is is certainly dictated by what a person does and vice versa. The same is true of fictional characters. We project what Hedda Gabler does as emerging from what she is, and our perception of what Hedda Gabler is arises from what she does. But an actual person's invisible presence is more-than, or other-than, the sum of her mask of actions. The fictional Hedda Gabler's invisible presence may not be more than the sum of her actions, except as the living presence of the actor in the role bodies forth that illusion.

Are there attributes or qualities of a person and of a character's face and mask that are seemingly permanent, persistent, and even perhaps fixed and unchanging, and those that are seemingly in constant flux, adapting to change? [28] What Redgrave and others have suggested is that both the seemingly persistent and the seemingly fluctuating qualities or attributes of a person undergo a continual process of becoming. We are always in the process of becoming who we are.

We may understand someone else's face only in and through time—through the external mask of actions that she performs. Or as Driver stated it, "The person is revealed in the tension [or dialectic] between the fixity of his character and the mobility of his inner life." [29] We are, then, beings who are in the process of becoming through our doing.

A fictional character, however, may be somewhat different in this regard. For Bert States, a character must have a "gene structure" that projects "a more or less continuous and reliable personality." The challenge for a living actor embodying the ongoing life through time and space of a fictional character in a play is something else again. States says, "You certainly cannot act a character without a proper and consistent character-base. The moment an actor cannot find a self to play, however deluded his character may be about what selves are, the character is gone and the actor is alone on stage, as it were, by himselves." [30]

Interestingly enough, not only is the face of the actor herself in the process of becoming with her own personal mask of actions, but the actor's job in psychological realism is usually to portray a character's face that is also in the process of becoming through its mask of actions—those that the playwright has prescribed for it. There is, as Driver suggests, a dialectic at the heart of every actor's character creation. Actually, when an actor plays a character, there are at least three possible sets of corresponding dialectics nested one within the other: between the actor's face and her mask of actions, between the fictional character's face and its mask of actions, and between the actor's face and mask of actions and the fictional character's face and mask of actions. The first two sets of transactions are intrapsychic, existing within the actor and within the fictional character; the third is interpsychic, between the evolving actor and the evolving character.

In psychological realism the actor's task, then, is to give the illusion of resolving these dialectical relationships through the persistent presence of her bodymind while embodying and enacting the character's becoming. In Brechtian acting, the dialectic is to be made apparent but not resolved.

Outside or Inside? Two Approaches to Characterization

The old nagging argument about sequence and precedence in the acting process always reasserts itself: What should come first in the work of the actor on a role, the work on the externals or the work on the internals of the character?

By examining key statements from a number of successful actors about their own working methodologies, we will note that acting training has tended to create a false dichotomy where there should be none. Neither the inner nor the outer methodology is to be privileged. It is never a singular, one-way process. So it doesn't matter where you start, but considering the style and purpose of the playing, it does matter where, and how, you end up. Stanislavski says:

When I was working on the part of Stockmann, it was Stockmann's love and his craving for truth that interested me most in the play and in my part. It was by intuition, instinctively, that I came to understand the inner nature of Ibsen's character, with all his peculiarities, his childishness, his short-sightedness, which told me of Stockmann's inner blindness to human vices, of his comradely attitude to his wife, and children, of his cheerfulness and vivacity. I fell under the spell of Stockmann's personality, which made all who came in contact with him better and purer men and revealed the better sides of their natures in his presence.

It was my intuition that suggested to me Stockmann's outward appearance: it grew naturally out of the inner man. Stockmann's and Stanislavski's body and soul fused organically with one another. The moment I thought of Dr. Stockmann's thoughts and worries, his short-sightedness appeared by itself; I saw the forward stoop of his body and his hurried gait. The first and second fingers were thrust forward by themselves as though with the intention of ramming my feelings, words and thoughts into the very soul of the man I was talking to.[31]

Vanessa Redgrave describes her evolution of the character of Miss Jean Brodie:

How I eventually found her was finding out what she wanted to be like. She longs to be like Garbo, Pavlova, Thorndike. And so we made her dress in colours and materials and designs that were, to a certain extent, successful realizations of her dreams. It wasn't until I was in those damned clothes on the stage, four days from going out on tour, that I suddenly knew that what was vital was that Brodie is and looks like a dried-up spinster; that what makes her ironic and pathetic is that she is not, *not* for any single minute of her breathing life, what she wants to be. So then we found the plainness—you know, simple, neat clothes— and just added an Eastern bangle or Eastern belt from her voyages. We got to Torquay on the tour and I still had a completely different wig, a Sybil-Thorndike-in-*Saint-Joan* wig. But we had a smooth wig hanging by, which had been rejected. I suddenly thought one night, I'm going to put the other wig on. And I thought of Anna Pavlova making up in her dressing-room, and so I did my hair trying to be as near to the classical ballerina line as I could. Thinking of that, I suddenly found I *was* Brodie; that was when I got nearest to Brodie, because that was all that Brodie could want to be like.[32]

Morris Carnovsky wrote:

The whole matter of what we call identification with the image is the business of the actor's working to incorporate what he has *seen* in the eye of his imagination with what

he can *do* in his own body, mind, and spirit. It's a kind of double activity. In first attempting Falstaff, for example, and certainly Lear, I would *look* at him: there he is out there, and sooner or later I know I am going to have to incorporate him into this body of mine. To be sure, with the help of the padding which I get from the costume department, but it's more than that. It's a spirit, something which I see out there and which I desire to merge with, and eventually hope will become one with me—a double activity: back and forth, back and forth. . . . The creation of the role is not only induced by the quality of the image that we see, but we also impose our own qualities on the character itself as it emerges . . . the kind of qualities which are drawn out of you in order to support your own image of Sir Walter Blunt.[33]

Mask improvisation training teaches that the process of constructing a characterization is not an "either/or" experience but a "both/and" experience. The process involves a ready oscillation between multiple layers of consciousness, accessing the psychophysical imaging powers of the dark consciousness, until the two merge in the actor's bodymind imagination into one compelling image—the character's gestalt—the character's *mask and face*. Michel Saint-Denis calls this co-conscious process the true "chemistry of acting."

The connection between the subjective and the objective, the absolute necessity of constant exchanges between these two attitudes, conditions the entire progression of the work [on a role]. It is through the experience of this connection, this exchange, that the interpreter, having started from his instinctive way of working, gives himself the chance to go beyond himself. Through this he can raise his imagination to the level of the most demanding texts instead of remaining miserable, dependent on his own subjective identity, however profound it may be.

Yet, ultimately, in order to bring life to a part, the actor will have to move from his objective attitude to a concentration on himself. It is only from within himself, and through physical actions inspired by or drawn from his own inner resources, that the character can be realized, can finally be born. This requires a subjective attitude. From the conflict and reconciliation of these two attitudes, one can gradually obtain an interpretation which will be both faithful to the text and vitally alive.[34]

Masks and Faces: The Transformative Actor

The central paradox in acting has always been "whether the character which the actor portrays is a mask which he only wears, or whether (or to what degree) it becomes his own face."[35]

In 1888 William Archer published his book *Masks or Faces?* as a response to Denis Diderot's *Paradox of Acting*. Archer investigated the validity of Diderot's claim that the actor should not become emotionally identified with the character. His conclusion is consistent with what we have already discovered, that one cannot separate the actor's subjective emotional involvement in a role from the actor's ability to stand aside and objectively portray the character's life.

> The poet—say Shakespeare—fecundates the imagination of the actor—say Salvini—so that it bodies forth the great passion-quivering phantom of Othello. In the act of representation this phantom is, as it were, superimposed upon the real man. The phantom Othello suffers, and the nerve-centres of the man Salvini thrill in response. The blood courses through his veins, his eyes are clouded with sorrow or blaze with fury, his lips tremble, the muscles of his throat contract, the passion of the moment informs him to the fingertips, and his portrayal of a human soul in agony is true to the minutest detail.[36]

It is not only the actor's emotional life that is affected by the character's; her physical and mental life is affected also. Even Brecht had to admit that before his actors could "alienate"

their characters properly, they had first to identify with them in order to understand their inner lives.[37]

It is in the mysterious "meeting" that takes place in the interstices between the bright and dark consciousness of the actor where the chemistry of acting takes place. It is the body-mind of the transforming actor that effects the continuity and correspondence between the actual and fictional realities. And it is under the compelling influence of a mask, actual or imaginary, that the actor experiences and creates her "double": the mask transforms the actor into an Other, while the actor, in turn, brings the mask to life.

One cannot talk about a immutable separation between two sets of incompatible entities in the actor, or between the living actor and the fictional character—internal or external, subjective identification or objective detachment, masks or faces. One must talk about an intimate, inspiring, and inseparable connection: a fusion of masks *and* faces.

If the actor has undergone mask improvisation training and has learned its lessons well, then she can visualize each role she plays as a mask. She will understand that the character's mask will be created only through her own bodymind, which seemingly stands aside so that the character's bodymind can evoke an appropriate physical, vocal, emotional, mental, and spiritual life through her to complete it. She will know how to discover and live in and through the compelling image of the mask.

Mask Theatre

It is as absurd to declare, "One must only perform in a mask," as it is to state, "One must never perform in a mask." If there are cases, modes, circumstances, where the actor must perform in a mask, there are others where the use of the mask is senseless and an absurdity. . . .

Sometimes the use of the mask can serve to hide the weakness of a work or of an interpretation, to give a certain dramatic interest to that which doesn't have it. It is nothing more than a subterfuge on the part of the director.
— Léon Chancerel, "Notes personnelles"

Introduction

Chancerel's words stand as a warning about the use of masks in theatre. The desire to use masks for performance must show the proper respect and the proper motive. Masks are not to be used in the theatre as a way of being original or gimmicky. If they are treated this way, they will not give off their potency in performance. They will not live for those who want to use them but are unwilling to undergo their discipline.

Even with the proper rehearsal work and the best of intentions, mask theatre performances sometimes go awry. The comments of two major reviewers on a production of Aeschylus's *Oresteia* by the National Theatre of Great Britain are typical reactions to many mask theatre productions. Michael Billington wrote:

> The first problem is that of the masks. You can rationalise till you're blue in the face (and some very strange arguments are used in the programme to justify the masks) but the blunt Emperor-has-no-clothes truth is that masks make language very difficult to hear and deny the actor one of his most basic weapons. Of course they were used in the Greek theatre. . . .
>
> To employ them today (whatever the intellectual motive) seems to me as perverse as making a movie without sound or doing Shakespeare in a mock Elizabethan playhouse. What was an accepted convention for the Greeks for us becomes an arty device.[1]

In a similar vein, Milton Shulman wrote:

> Jocelyn Herbert's masks not only convert the entire cast into gesticulating puppets but force personalities upon the main characters which are disconcerting and inconsistent. . . .
>
> Also mitigating against one's ability to be gripped by the words is the difficulty of sorting out who was actually speaking them. I found concentrating on their Adam's apples was some help though it rather diminished one's involvement.[2]

Keeping these admonitions firmly in mind, let us proceed to consider the possibilities of mask theatre. By *mask theatre* I mean all modes of masked performance. My intent in this chapter is not to provide an extensive treatment of the techniques of mask theatre. Such a project would require another full text, if, indeed, it were possible. As chapter 2 disclosed, our Western mask performance traditions were only recovered through research and experimentation by sculptors and performing artists during the twentieth century.

But non-Western masked theatre traditions are alive, and we can learn much from them. At the same time, it is im-

UMO ensemble in the "T. Vangelist" scene from Midnight Comix. *Photo by Philip Brautigam.*

Arthur Blumberg and Tom Luce in a production of Fernando Arrabal's Architect and Emperor of Assyria. *Masks by Kathy Czar. Justin Morrill College, Michigan State University, 1968. Photo by David S. Brown.*

portant to acknowledge that each culture's masks and masking traditions contain and convey the resonances of its specific cultural contexts, so we must look at non-Western masks and masking practices with great respect and with prudence. We may be able to learn from their concepts, methods, and techniques, but we had best be cautious about appropriating their iconography for "exotic" ends.

One notable resource for the recovery of lost mask theatre performance techniques is puppet theatre. An important correlation exists between training for puppet theatre and training for mask theatre, as artist-performers like Peter Schumann of the Bread and Puppet Theatre know. Of course there are also important differences, but pertinent observations from puppeteers can illuminate masking techniques.

This chapter will offer a compendium of statements on the concepts, methods, techniques, and challenges of mask theatre. It makes no pretensions about being complete, and clearly, not all people working with masks agree on their use, meaning, and performance techniques. All this advice should be understood as provisional, not absolute, since in the arts there are no absolute rules anyway! But the comments are based on solid experience and will be helpful for experiments with mask performance. New exercises for mask theatre training and rehearsal are included where appropriate.

First, though, we need to examine some half-truths about the purpose and function of the mask in theatre. Masks are limited, some assert, in their range of expression and ability to communicate a complex character. That the mask is more limited in its range of expression than the human face is, of course, true. But that condition should not be seen as inhibiting the actor's range of expression; the boundaries of the mask actually release the actor into a different performance style and creative reality. Through mask improvisation training, actors discover that masks are not as limited as many people believe.

Another half-truth is that the presence of masks on actors alienates the emotional involvement of the audience. Russell Graves, for example, writes:

> *The mask places a barrier between the actor and the spectator.* An aesthetic barrier, if you will. The spectator is discouraged from—indeed he is not permitted to—identify with the character. He can only study him objectively. When freed of the responsibility for identification, he is also freed from the need to defend his own ego by withdrawing some of his emotional commitment for fear of psychological trauma.
>
> The spectator at the masked performance is a god watching men of more limited range of emotion than himself driven to the limits of their humanity. He is freed from fear by the presence of the mask.[3]

I am convinced that the mask does not free the spectator from fear; paradoxically, the "barrier" of the mask allows the spectator to be more deeply affected in ways not possible with the actor's naked human face. Aristotle's famous comment about *catharsis* concerned an audience's reaction to the

Bread and Puppet Theater, rehearsal of Domestic Resurrection Circus, *Goddard College, 1973. Photo by Sears A. Eldredge.*

enactment of material by actors wearing masks. This may help explain his use of a medical term to describe the audience's strong emotional and psychophysical response.

Why Mask Theatre?

The first question that must be asked and answered when thinking about creating a mask theatre piece is "Why?" Some movers and shakers of twentieth-century theatre and dance have answered, "Why not!" They have justified their fascination with the mask and its value for the theatre in various ways. Eugene O'Neill said, "Looked at from even the most practical standpoint of the practising playwright, the mask is dramatic in itself, *has always* been dramatic in itself, *is* a proven weapon of attack. At its best, it is more subtle, imaginatively, suggestively dramatic than any actor's face can ever be."[4] Bertolt Brecht wrote that "the theatre's main task is to express the 'fable' and communicate it with a certain estrangement. . . . The function of the mask is thus to reveal aspects which invite the spectator to judge what he sees, and to help, by visual

means, to pinpoint the characters in society, by establishing their way of thought and their behavior. All this must be in conformity with the 'fable' and the spirit of the play and in harmony with the acting."[5] Mary Wigman wrote: "The mask can hide and reveal, can erase the dancer's sex or underline it. The mask tries to blur the demarcation between the realistic and irrational levels. It can wipe out the shape of a human face and turn it into ghostlike features through schematic interpretations, or it can conjure up demonic features of man's darkest fantasy in its exaggeration of any meaningful form. The mask knows transfiguration and horror, the inexhaustible theme of its devices embraces everything human and everything demonic."[6] Tyrone Guthrie and Tanya Moiseiwitsch said,

Suddenly we apprehended that the only way we could get the feeling of universality, as opposed to particularity, of all men and yet no man was by hiding the faces of the actors, suppressing their own individual traits, obliterating their small particularities behind the impersonal, but not inexpressive, features of a mask. Suddenly we realized that this was one reason, if not the dominant one, why the Greek actors were masked—to obliterate particularity. Negatively, the actors must *not* suggest particularity; no detail of personality must intervene between the audience and the tragic symbol. Positively, they must preserve the anonymity, the aloofness, of a priest celebrating mass. So far as possible they must be mere channels through whom the effluence of something greater than ordinary human stature might pass.[7]

Finally, Nina Vidrovitch wrote,

The mask, which in certain languages has no word to designate it, can do more than create a character. It can create by itself other times and other spaces so necessary to the theatre. As a clear image, it catches light better than the face, which is erased by light. The stability of its features, when animated by the actor, expresses the desires of men more violently than any grimace. "It makes our face blaze forth in our whole body," says Jean-Louis Barrault.

Allied with music, it is machinery of motion, catalyst of instinct, creator of rhythms. The dark hole of its eyes delivers the most piercing of glances, the most inward. The beauty of its form united with other means of artistic expression in theatre—poetry of word which it purifies, poetry of gesture which it frees—makes it one of the most necessary tools of future theatre, following the devout wish of Yeats, of Gordon Craig, and of Jacques Copeau.[8]

Half Masks or Full-Face Masks?

In planning a mask theatre performance, one must decide whether to use full-face masks or half masks. Léon Chancerel was clear in his beliefs about what should be done: "In drama, comedy, or farce—everywhere that the actor has 'a text' to speak, the half-mask should be used. The full-face mask should be exclusively reserved for dumb-shows and for dance."[9]

While most Western performers would agree with Chancerel's comments, not all theatre artists throughout the world would. Full-face masks were used in the ancient Greek theatre. They are also used in the Japanese Noh theatre and in most other Asian mask theatre forms. But in Balinese Topeng, when the solo actor plays a comic character—a character who is required to improvise verbally within the structure of the play—he wears a half mask. Most modern experiments in the revival of ancient Greek plays have used half masks. But if full-face masks are to be used and it is critical for the audience to hear and understand the text, then the masks must be made of a permeable material so that the actor's voice can be heard clearly.

The Masked and the Unmasked

Should masked and nonmasked actors be used in the same production? It is, perhaps, a matter of taste. But if we say the mask is the reality, then what is the unmasked face? If the face is the reality, then what does the mask represent? The use of masked and unmasked faces in the same production may emphasize a modern psychological concept of the mask as a false face or persona that protects the vulnerable person within. This was part of Eugene O'Neill's rationale for the use in his experimental play *The Great God Brown*. But that fascinating play is deeply flawed because of O'Neill's confusion about what his masks (put on, taken off, and switched between characters) and his faces are finally meant to signify to his audience.

If masked and unmasked characters are employed in the same production, as in Noh drama, the effect is frequently that of otherworldly creatures (the masked characters) appearing as visitors from another reality. Two orders of being are onstage together. Strangely enough, the masked characters are not seen as masked by the unmasked characters and frequently appear "more real" to the audience.

Whatever the mix, masks in masked performances should be there to conceal the actor and to reveal the character!

Mask Theatre's Demands

To those who have undergone the mask improvisation training detailed in this book, it is obvious that many of the masks used for actor training—the Beginning Character Masks, the Life Masks, the Totem Masks, the Found Object Masks, the Complex Character Masks, and so on—could also be used for performance. Some of the exercises push the participants toward that end, especially those that suggest final project presentations. The Neutral Mask, however, since it is not a character, is only appropriate for abstract movement pieces.

The concepts and training procedures presented in this text are the fundamental basis for any work in mask theatre. When one moves from improvisation in masks for actor training to mask theatre, however, then one must acknowledge and deal with unique demands that go beyond the brief life of workshop improvisations, which have more of a diagnostic and instructional function. Mask theatre involves the demands of performance—rehearsal, repetition, and refinement—in order to produce a compelling image that will affect others.

Mask theatre is not realism! The characters and situations are more heightened, more intensely who or what they are. They are automatically more archetypal, more mythic, more representative, and metaphorical.

Mask Theatre and the Production Team

The whole production team needs to be initiated into the concept and theory of masks and mask theatre. It is essential that everyone involved in the performance understand the ways in which the needs and demands of mask theatre are different from those of other types of theatre.

The director especially must have had experience with masks, or he will not be able to guide his actors or the production through the process. He must plan a longer rehearsal schedule so that the actors can be trained in mask work, and he must be involved with the actors in working out the specific and appropriate vocabularies of their masks.

The design team should understand that decisions about the style of the masks come first. All other design decisions follow from these decisions.

Do not assume that there is a direct correlation between an excellent set or costume designer and an excellent mask designer or maker. My own early experience taught me that this is not necessarily so. The mask designer or maker must be involved in the discussion of the play, the characterizations, and the design concept from the beginning. The mask-maker must create the masks based on the dominant qualities or traits of the characters as found in the text, combined with, and in relationship to, the dominant qualities or traits of the actors who will play the parts. To do this most effectively, the mask-maker should observe the actors and make sketches for the masks based on the actors' personalities and abilities before sculpting the masks. This process can occur during the mask improvisation training, which uses other masks. I do not mean to suggest that the mask designer or maker simply reinforces the actors' qualities. But he must know what they are, either to reinforce or to work against them.

The mask designer or maker also needs to observe rehearsals when the masks in their base coat are first explored, and again after the masks are fully painted. The mask designer or maker must understand that the masks are not to be used as static wall decorations, but for performance on the stage. The sculptural qualities need to inspire the actor and must not be wiped out by fanciful surface decorations or the final painting. Simple, clean lines, planes, and angles for the sculpture and unfussy colors are necessary. Sculptural style, detail, and painting must always be judged in relation to the distance from the actor to the audience as well as the amount and quality of light. The actors, too, need to brought into the discussion of the final painting of their characters' masks.

The costume designer must also realize that mask theatre involves unique problems. The design and style of the costumes must harmonize with the design and style of the masks.

Some designers prefer to use makeup on that part of the actors' necks and faces not covered by the masks to complete the masks. Others do not, recognizing that seeing the rest of the face and hands of the actor does not distract from the experience. The actor's body either becomes transformed through the illusion or becomes part of the aesthetic doubling experience.

The lighting designer has to understand the unique challenges in working with masks in an indoor theatre. Masks need light, but the right kind of light for the sculptural style of mask that is being used. Strong, directional light can be a problem for some masks; these often look better with a general wash of lighting, similar to outdoor light. The actors must know the angle of the light and how to exploit it to reveal their characters. Leave time in the rehearsal schedule for experimentation!

The set designer needs to make sure that the set designs complement the style of the masks.

Masks in Casting, Rehearsal, and Performance

The joy of mask theatre is that color-blind, gender-blind, and age-blind casting is really possible. The casting director must only ask whether the actors' energy, as well as their physical and vocal abilities, are appropriate for the roles.

Each mask is a character, a history, an emotional shape, a choreography. Each mask generates its own energy field. It dances to its own rhythm, demands its own space.

Masks in performance are like searchlights on the faces of the actors. The masked actor must know when and where to focus at all times, or he will lose the attention of the audience. In silence and stillness masks have great ability to suggest powerful concentration, meditation, and thought, if they are being lived from the inside! Then the audience is moved into the heart and mind of the character.

Masks make unique demands on the actor: the demands for total control and mastery, as well as the precision necessary for each moment in performance, require tremendous concentration, discipline, and ensemble spirit on the part of the actor.

The actor in mask theatre must also adjust to limitations on his vision and audibility. Dario Fo said: "First and most importantly, performing with the mask is an agonizing experience for the actor, not only because of the complexities of its use but because of the limited visual field and acoustic plane it imposes. Your voice bounces back inside, distorting itself, and until you have got used to it, you can't breathe properly, thus ruining your concentration. The other reason is of a more mystical nature. When you remove your mask you feel as though a part of your face remains irretrievably stuck to it." [10]

Mirrors. Actors find the character in the mask in the same way as in mask improvisation: through watchful contemplation and working with mirrors. Now, however, there must also be intense work with an external observer (the movement coach, perhaps at first, but finally the director). The actor has to know how the angle of his head affects the play of light and shadow over the surface of the mask, and how the relationships between his head, neck, and upper torso affect the viewer's perception of his character.

Some masked theatre practitioners, like the Mummenschanz, think it is best to work without actual mirrors.

> This is difficult work and cannot be done alone. The one who is rehearsing must be aided by the other two. We hate mirrors—never work for the mirror. If we would control the work in a mirror and then play, we would always think about the picture we do, the picture we make. And that would close the circuit and we wouldn't reach any more the public. So even if we're not quite sure what it looks like, we need the public's reaction to be the mirror. Or if we were sure-sure, it would be cold and closed and the public wouldn't do *his* work.[11]

Even those who do not wish to use actual mirrors, however, must still work with mirrors of some sort. If you use actual mirrors, then, as in mask improvisation, only use the mirrors at the beginning, to get a start for the exploration. Otherwise they can become a crutch. If you choose to work without actual mirrors, then your mirrors must be the others working with you and, finally, your audience. (It is interesting to note that dancers use mirrors all the time to perfect their positions and movements but are not damaged by them in performance. It's all in how you understand the role of the mirrors in the creative process.)

Sightlines. Masks, like puppets, communicate best when seen 90 percent of the time from the front. Even so, as Noh actors understand, if the mask fully informs the body of the actor, then the members of the audience that sit on the sides imagine that they are seeing the character from the front. Masked actors need to learn the lateral and vertical range of their masks in relation to their audience in a particular theatre. The optimum extreme positions are 45 degrees up, down, right, and left from an imaginary center line drawn on the actor's body, facing front. This positioning, of course, will differ depending upon the frontality or three-dimensionality of the actual mask. And the actor should not tilt the mask so far up that the audience loses the face of the mask and sees the separation between the actor's face and the mask. Nor should the actor tilt the mask so far down that the audience cannot read it.

Thus, actors have to learn to play more to the front rather than to their partners onstage. In extreme cases, they may never actually look at another character onstage with them but appear to be doing so by a slight turn or inclination of the head. The mask, not the actor, has to see the other character.

Maintaining a Consistent World. It is important that the actor maintain the reality of the world of the mask. The actor therefore must not touch the mask with bare hands while performing or have the mask touch actual objects or surfaces, such as a handkerchief. The illusion of the unique reality is broken when the mask comes in contact with the actual. Gloved hands are therefore frequently employed in mask theatre in order to match the style and character of the world of the mask.

Music. Percussion instruments can provide a steady beat or tempo for the actors to work with and against while improvising. The live musicians should also interact with the improvisers, both leading them and following their lead.

Finding and Incorporating the Vocabulary of the Mask

Walter Sorell described a conversation with Mary Wigman: " 'The dancer who does not love his mask cannot properly wear it,' she told me. 'Moreover, he must know it even better than his own face, must know what it looks like *en face*, in profile, when he bends and turns.' "[12]

Most of the exercises explored previously in this book have focused entirely on the actor's personal objective and subjective response to the masks. In mask theatre this exploration can only be part of the actor's creative process. Now the external gaze of the audience must be acknowledged and controlled as much as possible. The audience's imaginations must be engaged to complete the transformation. The audience needs to see the fluctuations of the mind of the mask. The actor must realize that the mind of the mask is other than his own, but it must become his own.

Not only does every action need to register physically, but every subtext reaction also. The movement, however minimal —a slight tilt or turn of the head, an impulse seen in a hand or the half raising of an arm—must proceed or follow the verbalization of the thought and point to it in an isolated mini-unit. "Listening" is also an action that needs to be physicalized. The actor should always lead any movement with the nose of the mask and then let the rest of the body follow.

Of utmost importance in mask theatre is the inner stance that the actor takes toward his performance in masks. Because the mask covers the actor's face, he must be willing to give over his need to express himself and let the mask express itself through him. Robert More's comments on the unique placement of the Self in puppet performance apply equally well to the actor in mask theatre:

> The source of this energy is the total "presentness" of the manipulator, whose primary challenge during performance is to function with the alertness and receptivity of neutral mask. This means that the puppet animator's job is to exist in present time, without judgement, with a completely outward focus, in a condition wholly responsive to necessity, at all times letting himself be led by the mask of the puppet, by the script (the first mask). . . . It is the manipulator's lack of self-focus, of self-concern, transcending ego and placing himself "in the service of" the art of performance, that liberates all his or her powers to support the action of the play.[13]

But an actor primarily trained in nonmasked theatre may be more amenable to this behavior in class improvisations than in performance. What More discovered in puppet manipulation is also true of masked performance: "Once the personal self is given up, the creative self can thrive for a total presence on stage."[14]

The actor's selflessness in the mask does not restrict his creative abilities but enhances them. More says: "In a seeming contradiction, they will express the tremendous sense of freedom that they enjoyed and explain their whole involvement—at the very centre of their emotions, and yet, they claim to have felt quite 'detached' . . . simultaneously 'hot' and 'cool' while feeling completely in control and totally spontaneous at the same time."[15]

The Japanese Noh actor Kunio Komparu also talks about this selflessness in the context of a "double denial" performed by the actor, through which the mask is brought to life in the imaginations of the audience:

> By first denying all raw facial expressions in the act of donning the mask and then denying the existence of the mask, the performer constantly seeks a higher degree of sensitivity in the presentation of an infinite number of sentiments.
>
> . . . On the basis of the denial of the self . . . movements are highly symbolic and suggest much. The combination of this simplicity of expression with the mask and economy of movement of the body, however, calls up a wealth of images deep within the heart and mind of the viewer and makes the internal drama possible.[16]

The Basic Vocabulary

Mask theatre usually requires a greater use of isolation, pointing, and punctuation, such as head turns or gestures before or after key words and phrases. All movements, including those of the head, must have definite beginnings and endings, clear starting and stopping places.

The actor must find the basic *pulse* of the character and the range of tempos that the mask can handle. There is a need for variety, a mix of bold and subtle movements. Actors can work on basic movement and gestural rhythms and patterns without masks, in order to master them. The addition of the mask gives the rhythms and patterns their specificity, their unique color, texture, and character. Movement might even take a shape or pattern of its own—a dance based on the behavior of the character, which could bring its own aesthetic pleasure.

Size, clarity, and *appropriateness* of movement and gesture are the rule. These aspects are controlled by the sculpting style and features of the mask. *Scale* and *energy levels* of the movement and the resultant *spatial needs* of the character also originate in the general and particular sculpting qualities of the mask.

Actors should strive for *economy* of movement and gesture. Refine movements to only those that are essential. Because good masks are so powerful in their own right, the actor has to do less. Learn stillness.

The actor should also explore the *status* of the character. To what social class does the character belong? What does the character think about himself in relation to other characters?

Vocabulary Areas

The Head. The position of the mask on the face and head of the actor, and the position of the head of the character, are crucial to success in mask theatre. The Japanese Noh actor Shigeyama Sengoro gives important instructions about head movements in a mask: "The basic vocabulary of movements is of tilts of the head: up, down, left, and right; of sharp movements left and right; and rolling figure-eight movements."[17] Note that the "figure-eight" movements rotate the head through important diagonals and combinations of diagonals, with tilts up and down. These combinations can be very effective.

Komparu confirms these movements and provides some additional information:

> The actor's techniques for using the Noh mask are clear and simple. He can brighten the mask (*omote o terasu*) by tilting it slightly upwards, which usually expresses joy. He

can cloud over the mask (*omote o kumorasu*) by tilting it down and putting it into shadow, which expresses sadness. He can turn the mask from side to side, either quickly (to cut the mask, *omoto o kiru*), showing strong emotions like anger, or slowly and perhaps repeatedly (to use the mask, *omoto o tsukau*) for a number of deep meanings. There are other mask movement patterns, but all are related to these basic three.[18]

The Noh actor understands that tilting the head up and down can change the emotion expressed by his mask, while rotating the head right or left intensifies the basic expression of the mask.

The actor in a mask performance can use a tiny tic of the head up or down to punctuate the head movement before the movement begins and after the movement has been completed (tic up if the head is to move down, and vice versa).

The Neck. One body part usually ignored in acting training and performance is the neck. Its expressive capabilities, however, are crucial in mask theatre. Explore moving the neck forward and back at right angles to the body. Try shooting the neck forward to a stopping place. Try pulling the neck back quickly and holding. Try combinations of this movement using different tempos, tilts, and diagonals.

Head, Neck, and Torso. The manipulation of the mask on the face and head must not be isolated from the rest of the body. The Kyogen actor Takabayashi Koji discusses this interrelationship:

The whole body, not just the mask, expresses the emotions read as being in the mask. When one lowers the face (*kumorasu*, "cloud mask"), one lowers not only the head, but the whole upper torso. When such a pattern is meant to express sadness (as opposed to looking into the depths of a river) the chest also caves slightly. Looking up (*terasu*, "brighten mask") likewise involves a lifting of the upper torso. Therefore one might say that the audience, influenced by the words, melody, rhythms, and body posture, sees the feelings it is experiencing as if they emanated from the mask.[19]

The American mask-mime performance artist Leonard Pitt also understands this interrelationship of parts: "The most emotionally expressive part of the torso is the chest. . . . The eyes or mouth [of the mask] will express the character's level of energy, whereas the emotion invested in this energy will be subconsciously perceived from the chest and the way it is held. The eyes or mouth, in conjunction with the chest, give a precise indication of the character's inner state."[20]

Gestures. Gestures should be simple, direct, and broad.

Use the whole arm; use the hand as an extension of the arm. Only those gestures that are essential should be used. Complete all gestures. Even hesitant half gestures need definite stopping places. Joachim Tenschert, one of Brecht's designers, was aware of these demands: "Great simplification of all gestures, a restraining of too broad gestures, or, on the contrary, a single sweeping movement embracing several smaller ones, all that must be examined and established for each case in point."[21]

But Dario Fo, the great Italian mask performer, expresses another point of view: "While performing with the mask, the actor's gestures must be grandiose and exaggerated. The movement and dynamic of the body determine the impact of the mask: underneath the face remains passive, expressionless, a kind of counterreaction to the superactive body."[22] Not everyone would agree with Fo's statement about mask performance. Here he is referring specifically to the exaggerated style of commedia and comic masks. Whether the actor's face should remain impassive under the mask is also debatable. In many traditional mask theatre performances this is so, but not in all. This technique supports a Brechtian understanding that the actor needs to keep the distinction clear between himself and the character.

Legs. Leonard Pitt writes, "Although the character walks with the whole body, the walk itself originates in the legs. The way in which the legs relate to the ground creates the energy that gives life to the whole character. If the mask's sense of comedy or tragedy is not first reflected in the walk then the torso will have nothing firm on which to build. A mask with a spirited expression needs strong legs in a strong walk. To see it combined with a weak walk, by default, only tells us there is more to be done."[23]

Character Traits and Emotional States. The actor must identify and incorporate the character's dominant qualities, emotional states, and motivational needs within the total physicalization. Look for opposites or complementary qualities, such as happy versus sad, thoughtful versus active, and so on. In Sophocles' plays, Oedipus repeatedly fluctuates between the polarities of hope and despair; Electra, between grief and joy.

The actor should identify the dominant qualities, traits, and emotional states of his character in the script; discover any contrasting qualities; determine and rehearse the scale, or changing scale, of the different emotional states; and rehearse the sequence of emotional states within a scene and within the play.

In an article for *World Theatre*, the great French actor Jean-Louis Barrault commented on mask theatre's different demands, based on his experience with masks in a production of Aeschylus's *Oresteia:*

The mask has a deeper significance: it externalizes inner life, it extracts from the human being the second existence of his instincts and, hence, when an actor no longer has the subtle expressions of the features at his disposal, he must discover a deeper system of expression like so many taps which are suddenly turned on. The techniques of acting change. For instance, a pause between the uttering of two phrases may no longer be made effective by its duration, but more quickly and violently, more "vertically" by a change in the vocal pitch. Another example: under the mask, you no longer look with your eyes, but with your neck: under the mask you are no longer yourself, you are the character. Timidity disappears and one gains a much greater capacity for expression. Even one's toes rediscover their personality, the muscles of the abdomen find their *raison d'être*, the body regains its whole theatrical function. . . . it is the mask which helps us to regain the human being's totality of expression.[24]

Speech. The performer's speech in mask theatre should be simple, clear, and forceful. The principles here are the same as for movement and gesture.

Use the techniques of isolation and pointing in combination with movement and gesture. That is, say the line and then do the movement; do the movement and then say the line. The silence or pause before or after the utterance of a line can be effective in making the audience either anticipate the next line or sense the reaction after it has been spoken.

Learn to point the speech with a preceding gesture or movement, to signal who is to speak next. As in puppet theatre, the speaking actor must be in movement or draw the audience's attention with a movement or gesture in the moment just before speaking, or the audience will not be able to tell who is talking. If not, audience members, like the London reviewer, will be searching for the movement of the actor's Adam's apple.

Vocal Qualities. The vocal quality must also be in harmony with the style of the mask. Vocal patterns can be developed that are unique to the character or situation, such as the expressive ones employed in the Japanese Kabuki theatre. Dario Fo has discovered that the mask itself can assist in developing the vocal quality: "Every mask is a musical instrument that possesses a unique resonance. Employing various devices, it is possible to achieve a vast range of tonality, from falsetto to hissing and whistling noises, thus permitting one actor to portray several different characters."[25]

The Eyes. It is the eyes of the mask that must see, so if the eye holes for the actor are elsewhere than behind the mask's eyes, then the actor must imaginatively look out of the mask's eyes, thereby ensuring that the mask's eyes are looking, seeing, and reacting. Use the nose of the mask to orient the focus of the eyes on a new object of attention rather than leading with the eyes. Actors whose own eyes will be seen as part of the mask need to do eye-limbering exercises for mask performance.

Seeing Double. We know that the mask sculptor has sculpted definite qualities into the mask. Before the actor commits to a total identification with his character, he needs to identify these potential expressions. The actor has to know what possible expectations of personality traits and emotions the mask may suggest to an audience so that he can control the images flowing from his mask. To do that, he must gain not only an internal, subjective knowledge but also an external one. He must learn to see double; he must see his performance from the inside and outside simultaneously. Thus he will need to work with an observer. One of the highest goals of a Japanese Noh actor is to see his own performance from the audience's perspective, to see his own back.

Applying the Neutral and Character Mask Improvisations to Mask Theatre

Actors in mask theatre need to have some training in body articulation exercises in order to familiarize themselves with the expressive possibilities of different part of the body. Exercises in the Neutral Mask and the Character Masks, including the countermask, can be brought to bear in the development of characterizations for mask theatre. Use the Beginning Character Masks as preliminary training for actors new to mask theatre. The exercises that follow will provide additional techniques for discovering and developing a mask's vocabulary, after each actor has had sufficient time to improvise in his assigned mask. These exercises allow actors to see their masks objectively, enhancing their subjective response.

The movement coach or director is an important participant in these exercises. For the complete success of the characterization in its final presentation, it is extremely valuable for the costume designer to observe these explorations also.

EXERCISE 1: CONTEMPLATING AND WATCHING THE MASK
The actor needs to spend time contemplating and watching his mask. This activity is not to be rushed, as the actor must absorb the image of his mask into his "dark consciousness" before he can play with it improvisationally. Sometimes it is important for the actor not to put the mask on until the second rehearsal.

EXERCISE 2: BREATH
Once the actor has donned his mask, he should first find its breath. Do not rush this exploration. The physicalization of a

masked character must start in the diaphragm—in the breath or breathing of the character. All strong and important gestures must originate from that center.

EXERCISE 3: IMPROVISATION

Once he has found the breath of the character, the actor in a half or three-quarter mask should find the mouth or jaw that completes the mask. When a mouth or jaw has been found, he should explore the simple movement exercises. These spontaneous improvisations should be watched closely by the director or movement coach to see what character qualities are being projected.

EXERCISE 4: TWO-WAY MIRROR

OBJECTIVE: to discover the vocabulary of the mask.

PARTICIPANTS: the performer and the director or movement coach.

INSTRUCTIONS: After the actor has had time to improvise freely in his designated mask and make some discoveries about its bodymind (but before setting the physicalization), he presents himself to the director or movement coach for sidecoaching.

The actor-participant does not attempt to physicalize the masks on his own but only in response to succinct sidecoaching suggestions from the observer-coach. The participant's reactions and adjustments to the observer's sidecoaching will heighten the participant's as well as the observer's awareness of the possibilities in the mask. During this process, the wearer visualizes how he looks from the outside.

By this means, a reciprocal two-way mirror perspective is inscribed into the subjective and objective consciousness of the wearer. He gains an even more compelling image of the mask or character before he finally begins to "fix" it in his embodiment.

SIDECOACHING: Sidecoach the actor to try a series of specific movements, emotional states, and attitudes based on your previous observation and your analysis of the character in the text. In your sidecoaching, always try to be led by the mask; do not impose on it from the outside. This means that you should pick up clues for further intensifications from suggestions the mask is giving you. If you are in rehearsal with a specific text, then explore your knowledge of what the mask or character must project—its personal qualities, behaviors, and states of being—both for its mask and its countermask manifestations. Keep notes on the specific positions and movements for the mask and countermask so they can be recalled later.

Explore head tilts, angles, rotations, and forward and back neck placements. Try quick, sharp movements and slow, steady movements. Can the mask make eye contact with you? Can the mask show that it notices and reacts to things around it?

Explore different stances, movements, and gestures that seem appropriate for the mask and its countermask. Sidecoach the physicalizations to expand, to become larger in size. Coach them to contract and become smaller in size. Try different tempos and rhythms of movement. What dynamic range can the mask handle?

With half or three-quarter masks, explore different placements of the mouth or jaw. What range of possibilities are there in the mask? What is suggested when the mouth is open as wide as possible? What is suggested when the mouth is as small as possible?

In order to discover the range of the mask, explore different and contradictory attitudes and emotional states. Sidecoach the emotional states to increase or decrease in intensity: joy, sorrow, fear, anxiety, anger, happiness, pride, serenity, assertiveness. Use other emotional states as prompted by the mask or by the text.

EXERCISE 5: INSCRIBING THE IMAGE

Now that the actor has begun to acquire a double vision of his mask and its countermask, he needs to rehearse, with his mask both on and off, the movements and gestures needed for the characterization. (See the section "Movement Study" in chapter 8.) He might also record his performance of a speech or scene on audio tape and then work on the physicalization of it silently as he plays the tape back.

Traditional Western Mask Theatre Forms

Greek Tragedy. Greek tragedy is not a hegemonic edifice, with the form, structure, and characterizations more alike than different. The plays differ widely in each of these areas. Anyone who wants to direct a Greek tragedy must research the successes and failures of these previous productions: Barrault's *Oresteia* (1955), Guthrie's *Oedipus the King* (1954) at Stratford, Ontario, and *The House of Atreus* (1967) at Minneapolis; and the National Theatre of Great Britain's *Oresteia* (1981).

As part of the dramaturgical and character analysis for each play, it is important to examine the mental and emotional structure of the characters' masks and countermasks in the play. Ask, for example, what is the mental and emotional state of the Chorus when Oedipus makes his first entrance? What is Oedipus's mental and emotional state when he makes his first entrance? Does he support the emotional climate that he finds when he enters, or does he change it? When does Oedipus's countermask appear? What mental and emotional qualities does it have, and how are they manifested physically?

The architecture of the script must be matched by the architecture of the acting style: there must be a choreography of the whole as well as of the parts. The plays demand economy: precision in movement and gesture, including the movement of the head.

The Chorus in Greek tragedy is both a "one" and a "many." In training the protagonists and Chorus in a Greek tragedy, first identify and play the sequence of emotional states for each character and the Chorus separately. Note especially the emotional state at the beginning and ending of each episode or ode. Note where turning points occur, shifting from one emotional state to another. Then explore how the emotional states of two characters in the same episode modulate against each other like instruments in a musical performance.

Jacques Lecoq's training regimen incorporates a number of exercises for training a Chorus. One series has actors in Neutral Masks identifying collectively with elements or substances. Another series, specifically keyed to Greek tragedy, places the Chorus against the protagonist in establishing and maintaining an equilibrium within the space.[26]

I have found the following simple exercises useful:

EXERCISE 6: BUZZWORDS I

OBJECTIVE: to explore the sound and movement relationship inherent in onomatopoeic words.

PARTICIPANTS: full group, working individually without masks.

INSTRUCTIONS: When all participants are in the space in a neutral stance, the teacher calls out an onomatopoeic word and asks the students to move immediately throughout the space, physicalizing and vocalizing the word.

Some buzzword possibilities include *buzz, ping, clang, thud, pop, whisper, scratch, pong, bong, tinkle, plop, crash, pow, flicker, click, jingle, scrape, whir, knock, smack, slurp.*

Exercise 6a: Buzzwords II

PARTICIPANTS: full group.

INSTRUCTIONS: In this extension of the Buzzwords I exercise, the students start off by individually physicalizing and vocalizing each word. When the teacher claps his hands, the participants must start to evolve a common way of vocalizing and physicalizing the word.

Exercise 6b: Buzzwords III

PARTICIPANTS: either the protagonists or the Chorus of a Greek tragedy.

INSTRUCTIONS: Now identify the buzzwords that best characterize specific sections of the text and do a verbo-physicalization of them in isolation and in sequence. Discover the appropriate buzzwords for each of the protagonists separately and then together in the same scene. For the Chorus, the exercise should be done individually at first and then collectively.

OBSERVATIONS/DISCUSSION: How did it feel to change your individual interpretation and physicalization of each word into a group interpretation? What was lost? What was gained?

Exercise 6c: Buzzwords IV

Repeat the Buzzwords III exercise with actors in their masks. How does the mask change the way the buzzword is physicalized?

Commedia dell'Arte. The masks in commedia dell'arte refer to character rigidities: fixed personality traits and predictable behaviors. Fulfilling or upsetting the audience's expectations is part of the fun in commedia!

Do not begin rehearsals with a history lesson on commedia dell'arte or a description of the various masked characters. And do not begin by showing the actors the historical paintings and drawings of commedia dell'arte characters as a way to help them find the characters' body positions. As with any other mask, let them explore the characters' masks first through improvisation.

Look at the historical paintings and drawings late in the process of creating the characterization. Note how exaggerated they are. They were not intended as photographic representations, but as the artists' way of capturing and expressing in two dimensions the extremes of personality and energy of the three-dimensional commedia performers. The commedia masks, especially Arlecchino, demand extraordinary energy in performance.

An actor playing a commedia character must be willing to accept its boundaries upon his range. As Russell Graves observes, "In the *commedia dell'arte,* the isolation of avarice in Pantalone, or of intellectual pretension in the Dottore, is completely crystallized in their masks. The actor cannot escape into the complexities of personality. In a sense, he is the prisoner of the mask, and he must play out his part in terms of the statement *it* makes, rather than in terms of some complex of emotions that go beyond that statement."[27]

As in the totem mask exercises, the following exercises first ask each actor to identify with an animal that seems appropriate to the mask. Then the actor brings those animal qualities back into the physicalization of the character. The mask also identifies with an opposite animal, so that the actor can ex-

Christopher Reigel as Pantalone in Carlo Goldoni's Servant of Two Masters. *Commedia dell'arte mask by Aprylisa Snyder. Macalester College, 1986. Photo by Dan Keyser.*

plore comic opposites and conflicts within the mask (mask and countermask). For Pulcinella, for example, an actor might explore a turtle and a rabbit. See chapter 2 for additional comments on animal identifications and correspondences in the commedia masks.

EXERCISE 7: DISCOVERING THE ANIMALS
IN COMMEDIA MASKS

Use this exercise only after the actor has had time to work improvisationally in his commedia mask and has established some basic physical, emotional, and mental behaviors. This exercise is done with the actors in their commedia masks.

INSTRUCTIONS: Assume your masks and rediscover your commedia characters.

SIDECOACHING

(Time lapse) Freeze! When you come out of the freeze, you will physicalize the animal that the mask suggests to you.

Explore your territory. Hunt and find food.

(Time lapse) Explore the variety of sounds your animal makes.

(Time lapse) What other basic needs do you have? How will you fulfill them?

(Time lapse) Freeze! When you come out of the freeze, you will switch to your human character but incorporate movement and vocal qualities found in the exploration of the animal. Ready? Go!

(Time lapse) Freeze! Switch to your animal again. Ready? Go!

(Time lapse) Freeze! When you come out of the freeze, you will switch to your human again, keeping movement and vocal qualities you have found in the animal. Ready? Go!

(Time lapse) As you continue to improvise, find the triggers that release the more animal side of your nature—the private face—and the more human side—the public face.

(Time lapse) Freeze! Close your eyes, relax, and come out of the mask.

Exercise 7a: Exploring a Countermask Animal

Follow the procedures outlined in the previous exercise but ask the actor to improvise a countermask animal and discover its habits and sounds. After this exploration, the actor needs to see how each animal's energy, movement, and vocal qualities may be useful to him in creating the commedia mask.

The Mask of Theatre

The potentials for mask theatre are only limited by the restrictions we place on our imaginations. In this age of cultural diversity and globalization, the continuing penchant for realism only frustrates and exacerbates the ethnic and gender politics inherent in "color-blind" or "nontraditional" casting, creating enormous handicaps on a performer's ability, regardless of race, ethnicity, or gender, to be cast in any role for which he has the vocal, physical, and spiritual qualifications. But from the beginning, theatre artists have refused to let boundaries of time, space, and materiality limit their imaginations, or those of their audience, in the creation of new forms of theatre to challenge, to comfort, and to celebrate. Mask theatre frees us from this predicament.

The gift of theatre is the gift of Dionysus: double vision. Theatre is the place, and the event, where multiple layers of consciousness, as well as multiple perspectives, are simultaneously created and experienced by, and between, actors and audiences.

Theatre is a *mirror*. It reflects and refracts all who look into it. It is a two-way mirror. From the spectators' seemingly protected location, they gaze into another world, only to discover that they are looking at themselves as actors in the theatre of life.

Theatre is a *frame*. Its boundaries contain and privilege what is seen through it or within it.

Theatre is a *mediator* between interior and exterior worlds, between this world and other worlds.

Theatre is a *catalyst*. It stimulates desire and gives momentary illusion to some of our deepest longings, that all boundaries between this and that, subjective and objective, male and female, Self and Other, are dissolved.

Theatre is a *transformer* of outward appearances and inward perceptions.

Theatre is the locus where the material and the fictive worlds converge toward a center point of individual and collective meaning. It is itself the compelling image of the mask.

Mask Design and Construction

Mask Design

Design Principles. Not many mask-makers have shared their secrets about mask design and sculpting processes. Here, however, is a catalog of comments gleaned from well-known mask-makers and others about some design principles to consider in sculpting masks. These have been grouped under four key design concepts: suggestion, simplification, rhythmic coordination, and ambiguity and dimensionality.

Suggestion. E. H. Gombrich wrote, "I have proposed to call Toepffer's law, the proposition that any configuration which we can interpret as a face, however badly drawn, will *ipso facto* have such an expression and individuality."[1] Paul McPharlin said that "a mask must be an essence and not a substance, a type and not a typification."[2] Everett P. Lesley Jr. remarked: "Therefore, in an oddly subtle way, maker and wearer must complement each other; within each should be, if only latent, a susceptibility to the impersonation, if caricature is not to result. . . . so that once finished and put on, the mask will transfigure the human, internally and externally: he becomes a living work of art, and a working archimage."[3] Mask-maker Hector Ubertalli said that "into any mask I make, I pour my experience and my own sentiments about the particular character I am trying to represent. It is very important that I be familiar with the feelings behind the face, the symbolism, the motivation, so that the mask can come to life in my hands, regardless of how fantastic the creature might be."[4]

Simplification. Henri Cordreaux wrote: "The lines of a mask must be simple and few; abundance of detail renders the mask illegible at a distance. . . . A mask which appears for thirty seconds on a silent character can, if absolutely necessary, be complicated [in design], but a mask which must be inhabited by an actor embodying a character who speaks, behaves, listens, and reflects must have simple lines, clean intersecting planes, and precise contours."[5] "Anyone who has worked with masks," wrote Peter Arnott, "knows that in performance they are not rigid or impassive; rather, they form a blank screen on which the audience may project the emotions that the words suggest to them; and for this reason, in modelling, it is safer to put in too little than too much."[6]

Rhythmic Coordination. W. T. Benda wrote: "But at times a single feature, a certain peculiarity, may become a theme for a mask in which, around this one characteristic, the rest of the face shall be logically developed according to all the principles of rhythm and coordination. As a simple example, we may take the case where an unusually prominent and peculiarly shaped nose is the theme. The rest of the face has to be built in conformity with its characteristics; its lines must find support and balance in their rhythmic continuity through all parts of the face in order to achieve harmonious ensemble and semblance of life."[7] Benda said elsewhere that "we must feel the bone construction of the face, the tenseness or relaxation of the facial muscles and the quality of the skin."[8]

Ambiguity and Dimensionality. "We tend," wrote Gombrich, "to project life and expression onto the arrested image and supplement from our own experience what is not actually present. Thus the portraitist [and mask-maker] who wants to compensate for the absence of movement must first of all mobilise our projections. He must so exploit the ambiguities of the arrested face that the multiplicities of possible readings result in the semblance of life. The immobile face must appear as a nodal point of several possible expressive movements. As a professional photographer once told me with a pardonable overstatement, she searches for the expression which implies all others."[9]

Lesley wrote that "by modifying, to a greater or lesser degree, the parts of the face which we connect with character, the mask inflects the associative tone. Eyeless, it becomes vacant or secretive; a nose exaggerated or twisted or beaked will excite comparisons with humors and animals friendly or rapacious; and the mouth, smiling, sensual, compressed or awry, can indicate every temper from malevolence to charity. Unless the wearer is to remain motionless, the mask should have three-dimensional versatility: a nod, a toss of the head, a turn to the right or left, should expose the modelling which substitutes, in a static countenance, for the play of expression."[10]

"In most cases," said Benda, "the expressions of my masks are not definite, but are complexes of subtle, hesitating suggestions of expressions which in action undergo more complicated changes."[11] McPharlin wrote that "light and shade playing over a mask give it a strange animation as it turns from side to side. This effect is telling, and should be heightened. Where one plane of the modelling joins another, the transition should be abrupt. Hollows should be deepened, projections raised. . . . The type of play orders the type of mask."[12]

Donato Sartori said,

> The mask is an exact object. Its every line emanates from a sense of beauty that cannot avoid dry, detailed questions, a beauty conditioned by usefulness. . . . The lines serve to engrave the face which must be free of minute details, for they define [too completely] a character, an age, an emotion. The lines that carve out the face are its language, a lan-

guage never verbose but essential, taut, and thus poetic. A distant spectator in the furthest section of the pit sees nothing but angles, planes, lights and shadows; through these he feels the vibrant nucleus of the character. Whereas minute detail drifts weakly and evaporates past the third row of stalls, disintegrating against the force of light and movement, engulfed by the distance. To make a mask means to ask yourself what will be left of it when the action begins. You must force yourself to avoid the trap of the pleasure of detail your fantasy has come to be fond of, the narcissism [*sic*] of the exaggerated touch, because only the essential will remain.[13]

Alberto Marcia wrote,

> The mask does not affirm, it eludes; it does not stabilize, it awakens impressions; it re-awakens by means of continual returns various sensations; it conducts thought in an elliptical way through secret passages.
>
> The language of the mask is a language made of lights and shadows; of silences and of violent sounds; of movement and of pauses harmoniously fused, proportionally contrasted with one another.[14]

Summary. All of these design principles can be summed up as follows: The mask must become for the actor and the audience an instrument of *transformation* and *participation*.

Further Considerations. The mask must be latent with possibilities of the dominant qualities of the character, its physical and emotional states, its behavior.

The sculpted mask will either reinforce or play against the actor's natural abilities, so you must know how you want to affect the actor and the audience. For instance, the mask for Arlecchino historically has different possible eyes shapes, two of which are a cat's-eye and a "lima bean" shape. In my production of *The Servant of Two Masters,* the original mask for Truffaldino (or Arlecchino) was sculpted with the cat's-eye shape and painted a bright red color. In performance we discovered that the eye shape and color choice reinforced the actor's own strong personal qualities of intelligence and analytic thinking, thereby transforming the character of Truffaldino into a conniving, scheming manipulator. Thus we lost the ability of the character to become endearing to the audience, which was important to us. In an attempt to remedy this situation, and with the actor's permission, I recut the eyes into the "lima bean" shape, so that the character would be a more bumbling innocent who fell into solutions rather than one who planned them—thereby playing against the actor's own natural qualities. I also repainted the mask a red-brown, to have a warmer, earthier tone. The effect on the actor was immediate,

and audiences during the next set of performances were clearly warmer and more receptive to the character.

Some people believe that the actor's face beneath the mask should be made up to harmonize with the mask, thereby creating a better merger between the mask and the face in the audience's eyes. It depends upon the effect you want. From your experience of mask improvisation, you should realize that this is not necessary, unless the mask has been painted an unusual nonhuman color.

Research and Observation. In sculpting your own masks, collect materials for a photo gallery for each type of mask you wish to make for the workshop. The photo gallery is a collection of photographs taken from magazines, newspapers, and other sources, sorted into various categories, and placed in an accordion-pleated file folder. These illustrations will assist you in the design and sculpting of your masks.

Complex Character Masks. Choose a gender classification. Then choose an age classification: infant, child, youth, young adult, middle-aged person, old person.

Select a face from the photo gallery that you want to use as a *basic idea* for your mask. You are not sculpting a portrait bust here, so you can combine features from two photos if you like. But your mask must be an "essentialization" of a face, not a photographic likeness.

Examine the face of your subject closely: Why does this face appeal to you? What is "affecting" about it? How have the life experiences of the person sculpted character into the face? What do we mean by saying that a face has "character"? Why in sculpting a face mask must we consider questions of "character" and "physiognomy" together? (See chapter 10.)

Analyze the face for its design features: Note the asymmetry of the face. Look for unique hills, valleys, crevices, bumps, and so on. See how the various features of the face are modeled on the basic underlying forms of circles, triangles, rectangles, and their various combinations.

Sketch the basic planes of the face using these underlying forms. Use a piece of tracing paper over the photograph of the face if your sketching skills are weak.

Totem Masks. An image gallery, corresponding to the photo gallery, could also be established for the Totem Masks if participants are sculpting their own.

Conceptualization Process. Before sculpting, consider these important questions:

1. What is the mask to represent? A human being? A supernatural being? An animal? Something else?

2. What style should the mask have? The style will fall along a continuum from more realistic to more abstract. The style of the mask must be reflected in the style of the acting and the

style of the total performance. Remember, the actor's very real body will betray a mask that is too abstract, unless the costuming hides the actual body by complementing the mask—even to the fingertips!

3. How should the human face be treated? The mask represents an elimination of minute idiosyncratic detail in order to capture a distillation or essence of the individual character within the type.

4. What aspects of the person are to be represented? Gender? Age? Ethnicity? Emotional state? Psychological or spiritual state? Weight? Height (i.e., relationship between the size of the head and face and the rest of the body)? Physical state? Intellectual ability? Socioeconomic background? Energy level? Status or "dignity" of the character?

5. What type of facial expression should be embodied by the mask? Facial expressions are located on continua from indeterminate state to fixed state and from neutral to exaggerated. The more fixed and exaggerated the expression of the mask, the less flexibility and adaptability to changing emotions and situations it will have, and the less time it can live onstage. A mask must be alive in silence and in stillness on the living actor; in one's hands or hanging on a wall, it must be filled with the potential for life. In other words, the mask should not become alive until inhabited by the actor.

6. What emotional state(s) should the mask represent? Facing full front, each mask should exhibit a definite permanent state, even if it is neutral. The mask should subtly change emotional states when tilted up and down: tilted up, it can lighten or smile, showing joy or happiness, level, it can indicate placidity and impassiveness; tilted down, it can show shadow, sadness, agony. When rotated from side to side the mask should change the intensity of its permanent emotional state.

The depth and sharpness of sculpting on the sides of the mask will affect the tempo of the expression changes possible in "cuts," that is, sharp head turns from side to side. All tilts, rotations, and cuts done at various tempos will be determined by character and situation within the sculpted possibilities of the mask. Certain sculptural features, such as slight smiles, grimaces, and dimples, can be highlighted and brought into focus with the tilts, rotations, and cuts.

7. Consider the treatment of the three planes and four quadrants of the face. The planes are the higher (brow and forehead), middle (eyes, cheeks, and nose), and lower (mouth, chin, and jaw). The quadrants are the four divisions of the face created by drawing imaginary lines halving the face vertically and horizontally.

8. Consider the areas of the face and their possible treatment.

Foreheads can be smooth to taut.

Brows can be larger or smaller; they can be furrowed, wrinkled, concentrated, smooth.

As far as eyes are concerned, masks have basically two types: masks with eyes and lids sculpted in, and masks with lids but no eyes (lids define the eyes).

If the mask will have eyeballs sculpted in, then each needs to focus at a (very) slightly different place so that the eyes will live and not just produce a vacant stare. If the mask is not to have eyeballs sculpted in, then the eyelids must be sculpted in or the eyes will be vacant. Eye openings with eyelids must be sculpted or cut large enough to reveal the actor's eyes for characters with whom the audience needs to make close contact. It this is not possible or desirable, then the eyeballs must be present.

The overall shape of the eyes can be rounded to angular or sharp, wide-open to almost closed (a slit formed by lids). Some pupils can be cut round, some cut square. The use of a metallic color (gold) in the eye indicates a supernatural being or a character who is possessed by an evil demon; the amount of gold or metal used determines the difference.

Carve an indentation on the top lip of the upper lid. This helps to define the eye because it catches the light and shadow.

Consider whether you want an inner or outer focus and concentration.

Consider the placement of the eyes within the middle facial plane. Do you want them to be normal, high, or low?

Cheekbones can be barely present to very prominent. The nasolabial fold can be deeply indented or lightly indented—corresponding to the fleshiness or gauntness of the cheeks.

The corners of the mouth can be neutral, taut, turned up (smiling), or turned down (sorrowful). The teeth can vary from not seen to bared.

9. Consider the relationship of parts of the face to the whole: Asymmetry is desirable between the right and left sides of the face. Tension is always most evident in brows, eyes, and lips and teeth. What area of the face of your mask will carry the dominant statement about the character: the eyes, the brows, the nose, the lips?

Mask Construction

The Neutral Mask. See the Neutral Mask template in Appendix B. This template needs to be photocopied onto a variety of neutral shades of three-ply Bristol Board. The masks should not be solid white. (You can also use a heavier-ply Bristol Board or other study paper, but make sure that it is flexible enough to bend to the curve of a face without creasing.) If it is not possible to photocopy the template on Bristol Board, then take pieces of the board and carefully trace the circumference, the eye holes, and the nose hole of the Neutral Mask template onto it. Assemble the Neutral Mask in the following manner:

1. Cut out the circumference of the Neutral Mask template, the eye holes, and the nose hole.
2. Cut out the nose piece and cut half-inch tabs along the outer right-angled edge (cutting in toward the slotted line).
3. Bend these tabs along the slotted line at their base, insert into the nose hole of the Bristol Board form, and glue in place with a good white paper glue.
4. Take a paper punch and punch holes on both sides (on a center one-half inch in from the edge) adjacent to the outer edges of the eyes. Put hole reinforcements on the inside of the holes.
5. Take a piece of elastic cord long enough to hold the mask firmly in place against the face. You can judge this by holding the elastic up to the back of your own head, ear to ear. Knot the ends of the elastic. Staple the elastic to the Bristol Board support form, adjacent to the outer edges of the eyes and on the inside (the wearer's side). Make sure that the knot in the elastic is on the inside of your staple and that the rest of the elastic can easily be stretched to the other side of the mask.

The Beginning Character Masks. The Beginning Character Masks are in two parts: a blank support form (the Neutral Mask) and the thin surface layer that contains the character designs. See the Beginning Character Mask templates in Appendix B. These character designs need to be photocopied onto a variety of shaded or flecked paper stocks so that the masks are not black or white. Use only very light shades, as we do not want the color of the masks to affect the wearers' responses. Assemble the masks in the following manner:

1. Once the templates have been copied onto the shaded paper, cut out the circumference, the eye holes, and the nose hole of each.
2. Cut out the nose piece and cut half-inch tabs along the outer right-angled edge (cutting in toward the slotted line).
3. Bend these tabs along the slotted line at their base, insert into the nose hole of the mask, and glue in place with a white paper glue.
4. Take a paper punch and punch holes on both sides (on a center one-half inch in from the edge), adjacent to the outer edges of the eyes. Put hole reinforcements on the insides of the paper mask holes.
5. Place the finished Beginning Character Masks over the

Bristol Board Neutral Masks, which will function as support forms.
6. Take paper fasteners and attach these paper masks to the Neutral Mask support forms.

The Life Masks. In order to construct the Life Masks, you will first need to make a plaster bandage negative mold of the actor's face. The following materials will be needed:

- plaster-impregnated bandage
- scissors
- cold cream
- small plastic receptacles
- mirror
- tweezers
- plastic wrap
- hair dryer
- paper towel
- newspaper
- masking tape
- sandpaper (all three grades)
- old towels
- releasing agent/Vaseline
- plastic drop cloth(s)

This work is best done in the dressing room in front of the makeup mirrors. Students should be told to come to this session in old clothes and to bring old towels. They should remove all makeup from their faces before the plastering begins.

The process of making the negative mold uses plaster-impregnated bandage, which can be obtained at an art supply store. The subjects are sitting up rather than lying down on a table, so the resultant mold will show a living face. The other approach results in a mold that suggests a death mask.

The following preparatory steps will ensure a good session:

1. Cover the work area with newspaper before beginning. Tape it down. It is also wise to put plastic drop cloths or newspapers on the floor under you. Tape them down.

2. In a separate area, unroll the plaster-impregnated bandage and cut it into different lengths: one-inch squares, half-inch squares, one-inch by three-inch rectangles, one-inch by five-inch rectangles. The smaller pieces will be used for the smaller areas of the face; the longer for the larger areas. You will need a good supply. *Caution:* Keep the bandage dry! If water gets on these pieces of bandage before you want to use them, the plaster will start to set up.

3. The subject sits on a chair or stool in front of the work area, brushes her hair away from her face, and applies Vaseline or cold cream to her face. Make sure that the eyebrows are well greased, as well as any hair in front of the ears. It is important to emphasize that in making plaster of paris masks of the human face (or any other body part, for that matter), *you*

must always use a non-water soluble release agent! If you don't, you will find yourself in a hospital emergency room having the mask cut off your body—quite a painful process.

4. Put an old towel around the subject's shoulders, under her chin, and in her lap, as the plaster bandages will drip. Tape the towel together in the back across the shoulders.

5. Cover the hair with plastic wrap. Tear a large piece of plastic wrap and put it across the forehead and down over the ears, taping it at the nape of the neck. Fold the center peak of it down over the head and tape it down. This will prevent plaster from getting into the hair. Try to make the piece across the forehead as smooth to the forehead as possible, or the wrinkles of the plastic will show in the negative mold. Tiny wrinkles are acceptable and can be taken care of later.

6. Put lukewarm water in the receptacle in which you will dip the bandage pieces. The warmer the water, the faster the setup time of the plaster. Remember, though, that you will not want the plaster to set too quickly.

Now it's time to get plastered! Subjects should be informed that once the plastering begins, they must keep their faces neutral, as any change in facial expression will ruin the negative mold being made on their faces, and they will have to start all over again.

Getting plastered is a good trust exercise for the group. Those getting their faces plastered must trust those working on them. Some students will find this a frightening experience, but they will discover that it is not as scary as they imagine. In fact, it can be wonderfully meditative. The group not being plastered must be careful to earn the trust of those that are. Horsing around or making jokes during this process is extremely inadvisable.

The goal in making the negative mold is to create a plaster-bandage cast of the front half of the subject's head. To determine the edges of your plastering area, draw an imaginary line from in front of the ears down under the chin and up over the head.

The teacher should start the work by showing a group of students how to do the plastering by working on one subject in front of them. Then the teacher supervises students doing this to each other. Two students can work on a third, so a number of stations can be set up around the dressing room. Make sure that one or two students are on the bandage-cutting detail, so there will be a steady supply of bandage pieces.

Follow these procedures in making the mold:

1. Take a medium-sized piece of the plaster bandage, dip it in water, flop it onto a piece of newspaper to take away the excess water, and apply it to a cheek area.

2. Rub the piece into the cheek, making sure that you eliminate the air holes. As you smooth it on the surface, you are also smoothing it on the inside (on the face side). You want the negative mold to be as smooth and filled in *on the inside* as possible, so this first layer has to be done as thoroughly as possible.

3. Keep applying new pieces of bandage. As you do, make sure that you always *overlap* with a previous piece, as this bond makes for a sturdier mold. You will finally apply *three* layers of bandage all over the face, with a *fourth* layer around the outer perimeter of the plaster mold for further support.

4. Always inform your subject when you are ready to cover her eyes. Ask the subject to close her eyes and then start applying the bandages, working them in gently.

5. Use tweezers, if necessary, to place the smallest pieces: in the corner of the eye and around the nose holes. Make sure that you do not cover up the nose holes completely, as subjects seem to have a need to keep breathing. But you will need to capture in the negative plaster mold the curves of the nostrils going into the nose.

6. The lips also need good definition, so work slowly and carefully here. You will need to use medium-sized pieces.

One good practice is to have the two students who are plastering a third change places about halfway through the process. In this way they can check on each other's work—as well as stretching out the cricks they've got in their backs by bending the other way!

7. After you have covered the entire face with at least three layers, and a fourth on the outer perimeter of the mold, lead the subject by the hand to another section of the dressing room where the hair dryer is located. Have the subject sit there, and with the dryer set on *medium,* blow-dry the plaster. Do not aim the dryer up the nostrils or into the ears of the subject! The drying process will take five to ten minutes. You can tell that the mask is ready to remove when the surface plaster feels dry to the touch.

8. When the plaster is dry, unfasten the tape that holds the plastic wrap at the nape of the neck and at the top of the head, so the plastic wrap will come off with the mold. Take the mold in both hands, with your fingers splayed out along the perimeter of the mold. Inform the subject that when you say "Go!" she should start making faces inside the mold. At the same time you will start pulling the mold off the face, using a motion that tilts the mask *outward* and *downward* simultaneously.

This is the moment of truth! Now you will find out whether the subject put enough Vaseline in her eyebrows, in her eyelashes, and on any hair by the ears. It is wise to have blunt scissors handy to cut any stragglers that didn't get greased.

9. Caution the subject to be careful about opening her eyes, as plaster pieces may be around the edges. After the mold is off the face, the subject should wash her face well.

10. The inside of the mold is still very damp and vulnerable

to damage, so be careful about touching it. Using scissors, trim the edge of the mold evenly.

11. After the subject has cleaned up, she can finish off her negative mold. Take small pieces of wet plaster bandage and cover the nostril holes *from the outside* of the mold. Hold the mold up to a light source, and looking from the inside, identify any thin places in the mold that need reinforcement. Take other pieces and cover these thin spots in the mold, again *from the outside*. Then take a series of small wet plaster bandage pieces and seal the outer edge of the mold that was just trimmed, pressing the pieces down on both sides of the mold (inside and outside). Overlap slightly as you go around the perimeter of the mold.

12. Set this shell-like mold aside, face down, in a safe place. Let it dry for two days.

13. In cleaning up, DO NOT dump the containers with water and plaster down sinks or toilets, as the plaster WILL clog the pipes. Having the pipes fixed is a very expensive process. Also be careful not to overload large garbage containers with plaster, since these can become extremely heavy.

Constructing the Life Mask. Read all the instructions in this section before you proceed! Pay particular attention to the time required to complete all this work.

You will need the following supplies:
- shellac
- Exacto knife
- acrylic paint (in tubes)
- newspaper, paper towels, etc.
- paint brushes
- elastic
- water containers
- plasticine
- Vaseline
- needle
- thread
- Flex Glue or white glue
- aluminum wire
- wire cutters
- container with glue and water mixture

After the plaster bandage negative mold is thoroughly dry, paint it on the *inside only* with shellac. This will help seal the mold. Never mind about being fancy with your paint job. A good, simple base coat will be fine. Then place the mold in a dry place and allow two days for the shellac to dry.

Then, to prepare the Life Mask for paper-lamination, follow these steps:

1. Check the inside of your negative mold for any blemishes that may have occurred in the plastering of your face, such as those caused by wrinkled plastic wrap. Fill in these indenta-tions, holes, wrinkles, or folds with plasticine. You are aiming for a smooth interior for your negative mold (but not a reconstruction of your facial features).

2. Using Vaseline as a release agent, coat the inside of your negative mold, making sure the Vaseline forms a thin protective coating on all surfaces, including any crevices (but do not fill them in). Also make sure that you smear Vaseline on the top inside edge and at least one-half inch along the outside edge of the mold.

You are now ready to paper-laminate your Life Mask *inside* the negative plaster bandage mold. These steps will also be followed in making the Complex Character Mask. To paper-laminate your mask, follow these instructions:

1. Tear newspaper (or other kinds of porous paper) into approximately one-inch to one-and-a-half-inch square pieces. (As you learned in making the plaster bandage mold, you need larger pieces for larger planes and smaller pieces for smaller planes or areas of the face.) You will also need several pieces about one inch by three inches for the larger facial planes. Do not work with pieces larger than this.

2. Make a mixture of water and glue in a plastic container, with one part water to three parts glue. The mixture should be the consistency of a medium thickened cream. Dip the pieces of newspaper one at a time into the mixture and apply to the *inside* of the mask. It is a good idea to wipe the dipped paper along the edge of the container to remove the excess glue before placing the paper on the mask. Be sure you have applied your release agent (Vaseline) to the mask *before* you apply this glued paper!

3. Apply the pieces of paper one at a time, making sure that you overlap the pieces as you work. Work slowly and carefully, getting the newspaper worked into all the crevices. Completing the first layer takes the most time. Remember, your first layer will be the surface of the mask, so you want to do it particularly well.

4. Plan your laminating work time well. It is best if you set aside time to do all the paper-lamination at one sitting (usually two to three hours), as this will give you the best bonding. If that is impossible, then you must make sure that you finish one complete layer of the lamination in one session. Cover the entire mask with one layer of newspaper at a time.

5. You will need to laminate the mask with three or four layers of paper, depending upon the kind of paper you are using. Use four layers for newspaper; two or three for a heavier paper such as blotting paper.

6. Use different colors of newspaper (such as newsprint for one layer and the Sunday color comics for another layer) or a totally different kind of paper material, such as Handiwipes (or even cheesecloth), so that you can locate the previous layer

when applying the new layer. If you use only newsprint for each layer, it becomes very difficult to distinguish a previous layer from a new layer, and you will end up with a mask that has thin and weak spots that will need to be repaired later.

7. When you have finished laminating all the layers, set the mask aside to dry. Drying will take at least two days, depending upon the humidity level in the workroom. When the mask is dry, take a knife and pry around the edges of your mask, carefully lifting the mask away from the mold. Check to see if the inside paper is dry or wet. If it is wet, you will need to let the mask dry out more. Then ease, pry, and pull your paper mask away from the negative mold. When the mask is out of the mold, take a piece of paper towel or an old soft cloth and carefully wipe any excess Vaseline off the surface of your mask. Do not do this if the surface of the mask is still damp. Let it dry first.

8. Take a pair of scissors and trim around the edge of the mask. Let the mask dry for a day before you paint it.

9. Take an inexpensive flexible aluminum wire and cut it to fit the trimmed, or cut, edge of the mask. Laminate the wire onto the edge of the mask in the same way that you sealed the edges of your plaster of paris bandage mold. You will need to use two layers of paper here so the edge will be sturdy enough to take the stress of the elastic. The wire reinforces this edge and helps to keep the shape of your mask true.

To finish your Life Mask, follow these steps for painting:

1. Once the mask is dry, take a fine sandpaper and *very carefully* sand any rough surfaces of the mask. Remember, you are sanding paper, not wood.

2. Take a white or neutral paint and paint a base coat on the mask.

3. When the base coat is dry, take a neutral or lightly tinted paint and apply it to the mask.

4. After the painting is completed and you have allowed the paint to dry well, you will need to decide what you want to do about the eyes in your mask. Do you want to cut them out entirely? Do you want to cut only a slit or pupil? It is an artistic and aesthetic decision. What you do not want to do is change the way in which your Life Mask looks like you. Take a soft lead pencil and lightly sketch each option in turn on the surface of the mask. You can erase the previous sketch easily before you try another option. When you have decided what you want to do, take an Exacto knife and carefully cut out the eye area you want. Remember, you can always cut more, but you cannot cut less!

5. Place tiny dots of a darker shade of your tint on the tip of your index finger (or little finger), blot slightly, and rub lightly into the crevices and depressions of the mask. Here you are shading the mask slightly so that the sculptural features will be more prominent. This is called shadowing the mask.

6. Take tiny dots of white, or a shade lighter than your base color, and rub onto the high points of your mask, along the top of the cheekbone, the ridges of the nose—any of the most prominent places. This is called highlighting the mask.

Note at this point how asymmetrical your face really is. Is one eye larger than the other? Is your mouth uneven? Is one side of your face wider than the other side? No human face is symmetrical. That's what makes us interesting to look at.

7. Hold the mask up to your face. Ask someone else to take a pencil and mark an *x* just above the ear on both sides. Measure a wide elastic band and sew it on the *inside* of the outer edges of your mask just above your ear marks. Now your mask is ready to begin its improvisational life!

The Complex Character Mask. In order to construct the Complex Character Mask, you will first need to make a positive mold. The following materials will be needed:

- Vaseline
- plaster of paris
- water
- large container to mix plaster of paris and water
- long-handled spoon or stick for stirring

After you have made the Life Mask in the negative mold, it is time to make the positive mold that will act as a base for sculpting the Complex Character Mask. Follow these procedures:

1. Smear Vaseline on the inside of your negative mold again. Make sure the Vaseline coats the outer edge of the mask and all the crevices (but do not fill them in).

2. Use crumpled paper or a small box filled with sand or kitty litter as a support for your negative mold. Place your negative mold in it, with the inside facing up. Make sure the mold is level.

3. Mix plaster of paris according to the mix instructions.

4. When the plaster is the consistency of thick cream and drawing your finger across the top of it leaves an indentation, pour it quickly and carefully into your negative mold.

5. Gently vibrate the mold so that air bubbles will come to the surface.

6. Let the mask stand for a couple of days in a dry place.

7. Before trying to release the positive mold from the negative, pry the edges of the bandage mold gently away from the positive form to see if the form inside is dry.

8. If it is dry, start to pry the negative mold away from the positive. This can be tricky at times, and you will probably destroy your negative bandage mold in the process.

9. Once the positive mold is out of the negative, wipe off

the Vaseline and let the mold dry. If air bubbles inadvertently appeared in your positive mold, you can fill them in later with plasticine.

Sculpting the Complex Character Mask. To sculpt the Complex Character Mask, you will need the following supplies:
- Vaseline
- plasticine or klean clay
- sculpting tools
- aluminum foil

Do not invest in a lot of sculpting tools. Your fingers are your best sculpting tools. But one or two different tools will help you form crevices or create small places. Review the section "Mask Design," above.

To sculpt the Complex Character Mask, follow these procedures:

1. Place your positive mold on a board and give it a light coating of Vaseline.

2. Take a hunk of the plasticine and roll it between your palms until it is warm and pliable. Play around with it and see how it responds to your touch.

3. Flatten the softened plasticine into a pancake and press it onto the form, smoothing it down. This helps to anchor it to the form. Keep repeating this procedure until the whole form is covered with plasticine.

4. Remember that you want your mask to fit as tightly to your face as possible, so the thicker you sculpt the plasticine *away* from your positive mold, the further the final mask will be away from your face when you put it on. For instance, if you want your eyes to be seen in the mask, then you must sculpt the plasticine eye sockets back to the plaster form where your own eyes are located.

5. Sculpt the upper lip of your mask. Your own lower lip and chin will be used as part of the mask, so here again, make sure that you sculpt the plasticine in these areas back to the positive mold so the "flesh" of your mask will meet your face and not stand away from it.

6. As you sculpt, make the features of your plasticine mask slightly bolder (more sharply defined) than you finally want them to be, because the paper-lamination process will thicken the lines and wipe out sharp edges and tiny details. So any crevices you sculpt need to be a little wider and deeper than you will finally want, to compensate for the layering to come.

7. Wrinkled and furrowed brows are sometimes "in-sies" and sometimes "out-sies." Look at the images in your photo gallery carefully. Ask others to wrinkle and furrow their brows for you. Make faces in the mirror to find out how faces are sculpted in real life.

8. Make sure that you are modeling a "rounded" face—one that has depth as well as width and height. The features of the face do not sit on a flat plane on the front of the face, but curve around and back to the sides. As you work, examine your sculpture from the side as well as the front.

9. When you are finished, rub a light coating of Vaseline over your plasticine and the exposed portion of your mold to act as a release agent before you start paper-laminating your sculpture. You can also take small pieces of aluminum foil and cover the surface of the plasticine before doing the paper-lamination. The aluminum foil sticks to the Vaseline nicely and acts as an additional release agent.

10. Using the instructions given above for paper-laminating the Life Mask, start to cover your mask. In contrast to the Life Mask lamination process, this time the top layer of your lamination will be the surface of the mask, so do it carefully. Complete all the paper-lamination at one sitting, which could require two to three hours.

11. When all layers of the lamination process are complete, let the mask dry well.

12. Take a dull knife or a sculpting tool and start to pry your mask away from the plasticine and the base. Your own fingers are a good tool too. Work carefully around the edges, probing inward with your fingers and the dull knife or sculpting tool, applying pressure to lift the mask away from the plasticine. The mask is held onto the plasticine with the Vaseline and suction. You may destroy your plasticine sculpture during this process. Don't despair, though. Any rips can be mended.

13. When your mask is off the mold, clean the inside of it to remove the Vaseline and plasticine.

To paint and finish the mask, follow the instructions given above for the Life Mask. This time you should try to paint your mask in as lifelike a manner as possible. (Now is the time for you to use any knowledge you have of how to apply character makeup.) Trial and error is the best approach here. With acrylic paint, if you make a mistake or do something you don't like, you can always paint over it.

Remember, the painting style must reflect the sculptural style!

Mask Templates

The Neutral Mask Template

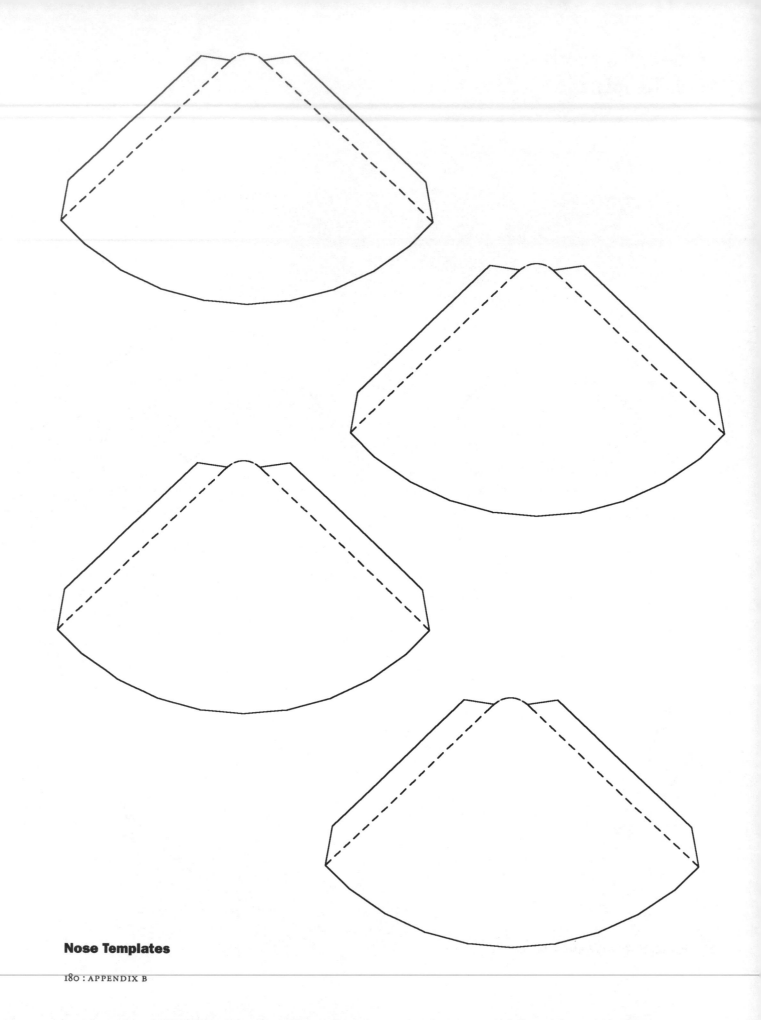

Nose Templates

The Beginning Character Mask Templates

Forms and Handouts

INDIVIDUAL MOVEMENT ANALYSIS FORM

Name:_____

A. Feet: Additional Comments:
——— turn out right/left
——— turn in right/left
——— walks on outside/inside of right/left foot

B. Walk/Stride:
——— fast/slow
——— uneven thrust right/left
——— grounding hard/light
——— stride long/short

C. Ankle, Knee, Leg:
——— weak inside/outside right/left ankle
——— right/left knee locked/loose
——— tight thighs

D. Pelvis, Hip:
——— thrust forward/cocked backward
——— belly/buttocks loose/rigid/tight
——— right/left hip high
——— lateral movement

E. Chest:
——— overexpanded/shallow
——— breathing shallow/constricted
——— breathing rapid/slow

F. Shoulders:
——— uneven, right/left high
——— drooping/drawn upward
——— pulled forward/backward

G. Arms/Hands:
——— uneven arm swing, right/left farther out
——— rigid/loose arm, right/left
——— right/left hand turns out/turns in

H. Head:
——— tilts forward/back
——— sits forward on neck
——— jaw in/out
——— tilts to side right/left

TOTAL BODY MOVEMENT:

A. ——— Right/Left Split ——— Diagonal Compensation
——— Top/Bottom Split ——— Front/Back Displacement

B. Lateral Line: * = forward of line; ** = back of line.
——— top of head, ——— middle of ear,
——— middle of shoulder, ——— midpoint of hip joint,
——— center of knee joint, ——— center of ankle joint

C. Tension Holding Areas
(areas between major segments of the body):

D. Personal Movement Center(s):
_____
For alignment, raise/lower movement center to: _____

E. Total Body Movement Qualities:

NEUTRAL MASK IDENTIFICATION-OBSERVATION FORM

Name:_____

Personal Element: _____

_____ . _____

FIRE: .WATER:
.
.
.
.
.
.
.
.
_____ . _____

AIR: .EARTH:
.
.
.
.
.
.
.
.
_____ . _____

Developing a Neutral Mask Movement Study

Develop your physicalization of each of the four elements into a movement study. A movement study is a brief embodiment of your identification with, and physicalization of, the element. Workshop time will be set aside for this. Two of the four elements will finally be presented to the rest of the group for comment. One of the elements will be chosen by the student for presentation; the other, by the teacher.

In each of the identification exercises, you were asked to visualize images of the four elements and, in the instant of visualizing them, spontaneously to become them without analysis. Now you need time to reflect on and refine the physicalizations of your specific images. Work on each of the aspects of the movement in isolation before recombining them and reidentifying with the image. Divide your research into three stages.

First, in the visualization and identification stage, go back into your Neutral Mask and innocent mind and rediscover the full identification with your original image. Next, in the reflection and experimentation/rehearsal stage, without assuming your Neutral Mask, work on isolated aspects of your physicalization of the image to clarify it, making it as specific as possible in all parts of your body.

Use the "Neutral Mask Movement Study Questionnaire" to help you clarify your physicalization. You want to make your physicalization of each element as distinct as possible, focusing on what makes it uniquely itself. Answer all of the questions in your journal, based on your experience of physicalizing the subject.

Finally, in the reidentification and presentation stage, you go back into the Neutral Mask, identify fully with it *as if for the first time,* and present your reembodiment of the element.

Neutral Mask Movement Study Questionnaire

1. What specific kind of fire/water/air/earth are you? How do the qualities of the specific image differ from the element's universal qualities? What you spontaneously imaged was, perhaps, a general kind of fire/water/air/earth that now needs to be made much more specific.

2. Sketch a picture of your image of each element in your journal. This will help you concretize your visualization of the image by exteriorizing the overall form, the shape, the direction, and the flow of the movement.

3. Make sure your identification and concentration are in the right place. For instance, with Fire, make sure that you identify with the element of Fire and not with the substance in which the Fire is burning. That is, you must be only a part of the Fire burning a match, not the match being burned by the Fire.

4. What are the unique physical properties or qualities of each of the elements? How will you convey these with your bodymind?

5. What are the distinctive movement properties or qualities of each element? Explore the following:

a) tempo/tempo changes

b) rhythm

c) weight/grounding

d) spatial needs/volume

e) breath/breathing pattern

f) boundaries

g) impulse for movement/movement center

h) energy/intensity level(s)

i) focus of attention

j) direction of movement: up, down, out, in, angled, straight (or combinations thereof)

k) inherent physical action (e.g., What does Air "need" to do physically?)

6. Don't personalize! It is important that you keep your own personal feelings and/or attitudes *about* the element out of the physicalization, or you will be commenting on it. This is looking at the element from the outside. You must work from the innocent neutral bodymind. But this does not mean that the visual-kinesthetic image has no emotional effect upon you. Ask yourself, What is the emotional "feel" of the movement of this image? What is the appropriate energy level or intensity of the movement? Then "live into" it fully with your bodymind.

7. Do not work on metaphorical associations that may be awakened in you by the subject. This transfer to a metaphorical level will come later. You are asked only to physicalize the element itself, not what you associate with it.

8. What problems did you encounter in connecting your respiration with your physicalization? For some identifications, you may need to have your respiration play against the tempo of your body movement so that you don't hyperventilate. Find the appropriate connection and relationship between your movement and your respiration so that you have enough breath to control the movement. This will vary for each identification exercise.

9. How can you use the techniques of stop motion and slow motion to help you be more effective in physicalizing your element?

10. Did you leave any part of your body out of the physicalization? You must be your specific type of fire/water/air/earth, from your scalp to your fingers and toes. Was your head connected to the movement, or was it watching the rest of you? Were your eyes connected, or were they watching?

Also be aware that the identification does not start somewhere in your body and then travel to other parts, eventually enveloping your whole being. You must be totally identified with the image from the beginning.

11. Where was the impetus for movement coming from: from inside your element, or from outside? How might this affect the connection of your breathing to your movement?

12. Where is the location of the movement center? Does it stay in one place or shift location during the physicalization?

Determining the Form and Structure of the Movement Study

In addition to researching the answers to the questions in the "Neutral Mask Movement Study Questionnaire" through your analysis and rehearsal, you must also consider giving *form* and *structure* to your final presentations.

Form. As you examine and develop your physicalization of the element, discover the typical beginning form and shape that you must establish before releasing the physicalization. Use the technique of the freeze-frame to fix your image in a single still frame before you begin. Ask yourself these questions:

1. What is the most effective and appropriate starting body position from which to start the physicalization of the element? Standing upright, crouching, lying on the floor, or something else? Have I explored all the possibilities to see which one gives me the most freedom and flexibility to express the image fully?

2. What internal and/or external pressures or force(s) condition the form and shape of the movement?

3. What sculptural shape should the silhouette of the element have?

The operating procedures to employ in completing the movement study are these: Establish the form. Then develop the movement!

Structure. In this movement study you will have to choose a dynamic phrase of the movement that captures your specific particularization of the element as completely as possible.

Avoid storytelling! The structure for your presentation does not tell a story, even one as apparently simple as the match is struck, it ignites, and then Fire burns down the match and goes out. That's a three-act play! Story development will come later. Here we are looking for a simple presentation structure that allows the element to be made manifest in its being and doing state. Working at developing the movement study will involve the use of your divided consciousness—your ability to be both outside and inside your work simultaneously.

This organic, dynamic, *becoming* phrase of your movement study should contain the following moments:

1. When you are ready, assume your Neutral Mask and move your body into neutral.

2. Find the neutral mind by concentrating on your breathing.

3. When your mind is clear, announce the image to yourself, visualize it again, as if for the first time, and then become it, transforming yourself into the beginning form and shape.

4. Establish the beginning form and shape as a starting point in a freeze-frame moment.

5. Then live the element through a moment of time.

6. Finally, establish an ending point. Hold this ending point in another freeze-frame for a three-count, and then relax out of the mask.

Consider the following overall structural patterns:

1. *Linear.* The movement begins at a certain point in time and space and develops toward a definite ending point, a conclusion or climax.

2. *Circular.* The movement begins at a certain point in time and space, swings outward to a point furthest away, or opposite, from the starting point, and then arcs back to the original beginning point.

3. *Vertical/epiphanic.* The movement is initiated and deepens/widens to reveal or become more what it is, with no clear starting point or ending.

4. *Spiral.* This is a combination of linear and circular patterns.

Of these structural patterns, only the vertical/epiphanic structure does not tell a story. Therefore, this is the one appropriate for the first Neutral Mask movement study. The other structures will be useful for later improvisations in the Neutral and Character Masks.

To complete the physicalization of the elements, you will want to return to a full identification with them, setting aside all your analysis and isolation work. Trust that your hard work in rehearsals will have inscribed the necessary kinesthetic image into your muscle memory as well as your imagination.

Time. The duration of your presentation of an element should be very brief—no more than twenty seconds!

Notes on Structure

You need to take into account the structure of your elemental dialogue interaction: How does it start? What relationship develops? How does it end? Does it have the structure of a journey? Does the structure tell a story? Along with the overall structures described under "Determining the Form and Structure of the Movement Study," you should consider a number of different internal structures, or methods of development, in order to fulfill this exercise.

An element, as you have discovered, always has a state of being. Sometimes that state of being evolves into a becoming, or into an action, a doing. Now it is important to develop these understandings further into the creation of an event (a doing) that reveals character, condition, theme, or idea. Possible methods for developing your dialogue include:

1. *Dramatic.* A relationship is established between two antagonistic forces. A "contest" develops in which one force tries to "win out" over the other.

2. *Dialectical.* A relationship is established between two antithetical entities. Each entity remains clearly separate at the beginning, but as the dialogue continues, an attempt at synthesis occurs.

The dramatic and the dialectical structures are closely related and are usually combined in a presentation.

3. *Collage.* Various contrasting aspects of a character, a relationship, or an event are presented in a series of disparate scenes to reveal different aspects or sides of the subject.

In any of the relationships called for by these exercises, take into account the amount of *tension* or *conflict* latent or inherent in the relationship at the beginning. Consider whether it increases or decreases as the relationship continues.

In considering the relationship as it can be manifested in physical movement, ask yourself whether the dialogue represents a movement toward (attraction), a movement away from (repulsion), or a movement into (merger, fusion). Later, when you deal with animate creatures, you may want to characterize these movement responses as fight, flight, or submission.

With the incorporation of tension/conflict, any story becomes dramatic!

TOTEM MASK INFORMATION SHEET

Name:_____

Subject:_____

1. In what ways does your animal move differently than you do? Where is its movement center? What movement dynamics does it have?

2. How are you trying to suggest the shape, size, and weight of your animal?

a) shape:

b) size:

c) weight:

3. How does your animal relate to its environment? Is your animal territorial?

4. How well did you explore the sounds your animal makes?

a) pitch:

b) range:

c) variety:

d) tempo:

e) rhythm:

f) tonal qualities:

5. On what senses does your animal depend for survival?

6. What did you discover about your animal in relating to the other animals?

7. How does your animal respond to danger?

8. What basic needs motivate your animal?

9. What thought processes and/or emotions does your animal have?

10. What mythic associations does your animal have in world cultures, if any?

If you are unable to answer any of these questions, go to the library and research the answers.

TOTEM MASK RESEARCH/FIELD TRIP LOG

Name:_____

Subject:_____

Instructions: Find your creature (or one as much like it as possible).

1. Notes on the Physical Properties of the Subject

a) color(s):

b) design(s):

c) texture(s):

d) simile/metaphor comparisons:

2. Movement Analysis

a) feet (hooves, paws, claws, etc.):

b) walk/stride:

c) ankles/knees/legs:

d) pelvis:

e) chest/respiration:

f) shoulders:

g) arms/hands (hooves, claws, paws, etc.):

h) head/neck:

3. Total Body Movement

a) movement center:

b) movement tempo(s):

c) movement rhythm:

d) symmetry/asymmetry:

e) What impressive and expressive qualities does your creature have that makes it uniquely itself? For example, does it exhibit strength or grace?

f) What are the characteristics of your animal when it is still?

4. Vocal/Sound Analysis

a) pitch(es):

b) dynamics:

c) range:

d) tonal qualities:

5. What kind of an environment does your animal inhabit? How does the animal relate to this environment?

6. What time(s) of day is your animal active? Doing what?

7. How does your animal relate to other animals?

8. What does your animal eat? How does it find food? If it is a carnivore, what kinds of creatures are its prey? How does it stalk its prey? What creatures, if any, prey on it?

9. What emotional states does your animal have? When are they activated?

    10. How territorial is your animal?

    11. On which of the senses does your animal rely most heavily? For what purposes?

    12. Sketch your animal in various poses and positions.

FOUND OBJECT MASK PROPERTIES/ QUALITIES CHECKLIST

Name:_____

Subject: _____

A. Physical Properties of the Found Object
    a) color(s)
    b) weight
    c) overall shape/structure (outline)
    d) size
    e) form
    f) texture (shiny/dull, rough/smooth, soft/hard, etc.)
    g) composition (opaque/transparent, etc.)
    h) flexibility (fluid/floppy/rigid/soft, etc.)
    i) design (simple/complex, pattern/solid, etc.)
    j) dimensionality (2D/3D, frontality/nondirectionality)
B. Movement Properties (real or suggested)
    a) opening
    b) closing
    c) unfolding
    d) tempo(s)
    e) rhythm
    f) energy level(s)
    g) boundaries
    h) spatial requirements
    i) impulse for movement (internal/external)
    j) direction of movement (in/out, up/down, single focus/multiple focus, etc.)
    k) levels (distance from floor)
    l) shape of movement through space
    m) dynamics (combination of the above)
C. Sound Qualities (actual or imagined)
    a) type   b) pitch   c) range   d)tone
    e) volume level(s)   f) tempo   g) rhythm
D. Emotional State(s) and Level(s) Suggested
    a) by shape and design features
    b) by physical properties
    c) by physicalization
Note: Do not assume that your Found Object is fixed in one emotional state or at one emotional level. It may very well have a dominant emotional state, but it will likely have other countermask possibilities also.

E. Motivational Needs: What are suggested by the physical properties, the physicalization, and the life you discover in the Found Object Mask?
F. Relationships
    a) to environment   b) to others   c) to self
G. Countermasks: Consider opposites to any or all of the above.
H. Setting, Locale, Environment: What is suggested by your manipulation of the object and its transformation?
I. Storyline
    a) suggested by your transformation(s)
    b) suggested by your series of masks

CHARACTER PSYCHOPHYSICAL PROFILE

Name:_____

Subject: _____

Record your observations on each Character Mask you explore. If you cannot answer a particular question, leave it blank.

_____

    1. Describe what your character looks like and how he or she moves through space.
    a) as mask:
    b) as countermask:
    2. What do you know about your character?
    a) name: b) age: c) gender:
    d) life history:
    e) attitude toward others/world as mask:
    f) attitude toward others/world as countermask:
    3. What personality traits or qualities appear to be fixed? Which ones are fluid?
    a) as mask:
    b) as countermask:
    4. Emotional/Psychological Needs
    a) as mask:
    b) as countermask:
    5. What thoughts, feelings, or images appear in your character's inner dialogue (subtext)?
    a) as mask:
    b) as countermask:
    6. Describe any conflict(s) your character experiences.
    a) as mask:
    b) as countermask:
    c) between mask and countermask:
    7. Which mask is your public face? Which one is your private face?
    a) mask:
    b) countermask:

Answer the following questions using M for mask, CM for countermask.

8. Where is your character's center? What part leads the movement?

_____ head   _____ chest/torso   _____ arms/hands

_____ stomach   _____ pelvis   _____ legs/feet

9. Character's breathing pattern? (Check one in each column.)

_____ slow   _____ even   _____ up/down

_____ moderate   _____ forward/back

_____ fast   _____ broken   _____ side/side

10. Energy Level:

_____ low   _____ moderate   _____ high

_____ variable

11. Direction of energy? (Check one or more.)

_____ outward   _____ upward   _____ forward

_____ inward   _____ downward   _____ backward

_____ twisting

_____ diagonal

12. Describe the placement of each part of your character's body.

    a) head and neck:

    b) torso/chest:

    c) stomach/pelvis:

    d) legs/feet:

    e) arms/hands:

13. Describe any recurring gesture(s) or movement patterns.

    a) as mask:

    b) as countermask:

PERSONAL PSYCHOPHYSICAL PROFILE

Name:_____

It is important for an actor to acknowledge what "habitual tapes" may automatically start to play when she or he begins to create a characterization. Reviewing your Character Psychophysical Profiles, record your observations on any recurring patterns of movement and behavior you now perceive in your Character Masks. These are observations, NOT an analysis.

_____

1. What age and gender do you gravitate toward in your masks?

2. What recurring pattern of movement or gesture, if any, have you noticed in your characters?

3. What recurring mental and/or emotional states of being, if any, have you noticed in your characters?

4. What recurring images, associations, and correspondences, if any, have you noticed in your characters?

5. What recurring needs, if any, do your masks express?

6. What recurring pattern of behavior, if any, toward others and/or the space have you perceived?

7. What area of the body, if any, have you repeatedly focused on to become the body center of your characters?

8. Does your critical voice talk to you in your masks? If so, what does it say?

9. Does your inner guide talk to you in your masks? If so, what does it say?

10. Review your answers to the questions above. What aspects of your characters' physical, emotional, and mental lives are not mentioned?

Notes

Chapter 1: The Ubiquitous Mask

1. Neither *he* nor *she* will be used universally throughout the text. But the awkward "he or she" alternative will also not be used. In order to be inclusive and resolve this dilemma in an equitable manner, generic pronoun references will change gender from chapter to chapter.

2. Harry Shapiro, "Magic of the Mask," *New York Times Magazine,* April 15, 1951, 26.

3. This figure is very difficult to see because parts of it are quite indistinct and painted across a crevice in the ceiling; therefore, what the figure actually represents is somewhat ambiguous. The reconstruction of the painting made in situ by one of the discoverers, the Abbé H. Breuil, has raised doubts in some scholars' minds about the reliability of the abbé's gaze. The name, "The Sorcerer," is one that was given it by its modern discoverers.

4. Mircea Eliade, "Masks: Mythical and Ritual Origins," in *Encyclopedia of World Art,* vol. 9 (New York: McGraw-Hill, 1964), 522.

5. John E. Pfeiffer, *The Creative Explosion* (Ithaca, N.Y.: Cornell University Press, 1982), 107.

6. Gaston Bachelard, "The Mask," in *The Right to Dream,* trans. J. A. Underwood (Dallas: Dallas Institute Publications, 1988), 157.

7. Henry Pernet, "Masks: Theoretical Perspectives," trans. Michele P. Cros, in *Encyclopedia of Religion,* ed. Mircea Eliade, vol. 9 (New York: Macmillan, 1987), 259.

8. Ibid., 262.

9. There are certainly other ways to classify the functions of masks. One classification groups them in four categories, according to function: the representational function, the emotive function, the indexical function, and the disguise (or "masking") function. See Greg Urban and Janet Wall Hendricks, "Signal Functions of Masking in Amerindian Brazil," *Semiotica* 47 (1983): 181.

10. Elizabeth Tonkin, "Masks and Powers," *Man* 14 no. 2 (June 1979): 242.

11. Marjorie Halpin, "The Mask of Tradition," in *The Power of Symbols,* ed. N. Ross Crumrine and Marjorie Halpin (Vancouver: University of British Columbia Press, 1983), 221.

12. Werner Muensterberger, "Man's Need to Change," *Persona Grata* (Houston: University of St. Thomas, 1960), n.p.

13. Ron Jenkins, "Two-Way Mirrors," *Parabola* 6, no. 3 (Aug. 1981): 18.

14. Ronald L. Grimes, "The Life History of a Mask," *TDR: The Drama Review* 36, no. 3 (Fall 1992): 66.

15. Margaret Mead, "Masks and Men," *Natural History* 55 (June 1946): 283.

16. Claude Lévi-Strauss, "The Many Faces of Man," *World Theatre* 10, no. 1 (Spring 1961): 18.

17. Tonkin, "Masks and Powers," 242.

18. Jenkins, "Two-Way Mirrors," 21.

19. A. David Napier, *Masks, Transformation, and Paradox* (Berkeley: University of California Press, 1986), xxiii.

20. Carl Kerényi, "Man and Mask," in *Spiritual Disciplines,* vol. 4 of *Papers from the Eranos Yearbooks,* Bollingen Series 30 (New York: Pantheon Books, 1960), 153; Muensterberger, "Man's Need to Change," n.p.

21. Jurgen Ruesch and Weldon Kees, *Nonverbal Communication* (Berkeley: University of California Press, 1956), 153.

22. Lévi-Strauss, "Many Faces of Man," 12; Charlotte Wolff, *The Psychology of Gesture,* trans. Anne Tennant, 2d ed. (London: Methuen, 1948), 65, 60.

23. Robert Brechon, *Michaud,* quoted in Eugenio Barba, "Theatre Laboratory 13 Rzedow," *Tulane Drama Review* 9, no. 3 (Spring 1965): 162n.

24. Max Picard, *The Human Face,* trans. Guy Endore (New York: Farrar and Rinehart, 1930), 3.

25. Lévi-Strauss, "Many Faces of Man," 12.

26. Bachelard, "Mask," 158.

27. E. H. Gombrich, "The Mask and the Face: The Perception of Physiognomic Likeness in Life and in Art," in *Art, Perception, and Reality,* by E. H. Gombrich, Julian Hochberg, and Max Black, (Baltimore: Johns Hopkins University Press, 1972), 13.

28. Stefan Brecht, *Peter Schumann's Bread and Puppet Theatre,* vol. 1 (New York: Routledge, Chapman and Hall, 1988), 312.

29. Tonkin, "Masks and Powers," 246.

30. Roger Caillois, *Man, Play, and Games,* trans. Meyer Barash (New York: Free Press, 1961), 87.

31. Pernet, "Masks: Theoretical Perspectives," 261.

32. Eliade, "Masks," 524–25.

33. Ibid., 524.

34. N. Ross Crumrine, "Masks, Participants, and Audience," in *The Power of Symbols,* ed. N. Ross Crumrine and Marjorie Halpin (Vancouver: University of British Columbia Press, 1983), 2, 3.

35. Tonkin, "Masks and Powers," 246, 247.

36. Bachelard, "Mask," 166.

37. Caillois, *Man, Play, and Games,* 87, 88.

38. Elias Canetti, *Crowds and Power,* trans. Carol Stewart (New York: Seabury Press, 1978), 377.

39. Quoted in Petr Bogatyrëv, "The Interconnection of Two Similar Semiotic Systems: The Puppet Theater and the Theater of Living Actors," *Semiotica* 47 (1983), 56–57. Bogatyrëv gives his sources as Carl Zuckmayer, *A Part of Myself,* trans. Richard and Clara Winston (New York: Harcourt, Brace, Jovanovich, 1970), 34, for the first paragraph and, for the second paragraph, his own translation of the original German edition of Zuckmayer's book *Als wär's ein Stück von Mir: Horen der Freundschaft* (Vienna: Fischer-Verlag, 1967), 43–45.

40. Walter F. Otto, *Dionysus: Myth and Cult,* trans. Robert B. Palmer (Bloomington: Indiana University Press, 1965), 210.

41. Richard Findlater, "Michael Redgrave with Richard Findlater," in *Great Acting,* ed. Hal Burton (New York: Bonanza Books, 1967), 105.

Chapter 2: Masks in Western Theatre

1. See Theodor H. Gaster, *Thespis: Ritual, Myth, and Drama in the Ancient Near East* (New York: Harper Torchbooks, 1961).

2. Renate Schlesier, "Mixtures of Masks: Maenads as Tragic Models," in *Masks of Dionysus*, ed. Thomas H. Carpenter and Christopher Faraone (Ithaca, N.Y.: Cornell University Press, 1993), 89.

3. Otto, *Dionysus*, 90.

4. S. Brecht, *Bread and Puppet Theatre*, 314.

5. F. B. Jevons, *Masks and Acting* (Cambridge: Cambridge University Press, 1916), 7.

6. Napier, *Masks, Transformation, and Paradox*, 8.

7. Henry Pernet, "Masks: Ritual Masks in Nonliterate Cultures," trans. Michele P. Cros, in *Encyclopedia of Religion*, ed. Mircea Eliade, vol. 9 (New York: Macmillan, 1987), 263, 264.

8. Ibid., 265.

9. John J. Winkler and Froma I. Zeitlin, eds., *Nothing to Do with Dionysus?* (Princeton, N.J.: Princeton University Press, 1990), 3.

10. Art historians have said that many of these artistic representations show actors observing their masks *after* performance. That may be true, although I fail to see how historians can identify the time as after performance rather than before. The practice of contemplating the mask *before* wearing it as a crucial part of the process of becoming the character is confirmed by Noh and Topeng practices.

11. A. M. Nagler, *A Source Book in Theatrical History* (New York: Dover Publications, 1952), 5.

12. Roger Caillois, *The Mask of Medusa*, trans. George Ordish (London: Victor Gollancz, 1964), 107, 106.

13. Ibid. 107.

14. Schlesier, "Mixtures of Masks," 94.

15. Ibid., 96.

16. Napier, *Masks, Transformation, and Paradox*, 8.

17. Ibid., 25–27.

18. Margot Berthold, *The History of World Theater: From the Beginnings to the Baroque*, trans. Edith Simmons (New York: Continuum, 1991), 308.

19. Bari Rolfe, personal interview, March 1, 1974, in Sears A. Eldredge, "Masks: Their Use and Effectiveness in Actor Training Programs" (Ph.D. diss., Michigan State University, 1975), 379.

20. Dario Fo, "Hands Off the Mask!" *New Theatre Quarterly* 5, no. 19 (Aug. 1989): 208.

21. For more information on commedia dell'arte, see John Rudlin, *Commedia dell'Arte: An Actor's Handbook* (New York: Routledge, 1994).

22. See Walter Sorell, *The Other Face: The Mask in the Arts* (Indianapolis: Bobbs-Merrill, 1973); Susan Harris-Smith, *Masks in Modern Drama* (Berkeley: University of California Press, 1984); and Eldredge, "Masks," 24–69.

23. Friedrich Nietzsche, *The Birth of Tragedy and The Case of Wagner*, trans. Walter Kaufmann (New York: Random House, 1967), 65–66.

24. Oscar G. Brockett and Robert R. Findlay, *Century of Innovation* (Englewood Cliffs, N.J.: Prentice-Hall, 1973), 143, 144.

25. Ibid., 265.

26. Carl Jung, "The Relations between the Ego and the Unconscious," in *The Portable Jung*, ed. Joseph Campbell, trans. R. F. C. Hull (New York: Viking Press, 1971), 105–6.

27. Christopher F. Monte, *Beneath the Mask: An Introduction to Theories of Personality*, 2d ed. (New York: Holt, Rinehart and Winston, 1979), 19.

28. Sorell, *Other Face*, 13.

29. Edward Sullivan, "There will be time, there will be time, to prepare a face to meet the faces that you meet," *Persona Grata* (Houston: University of St. Thomas, 1960), n.p.

30. John Balance [pseud. of E. G. Craig], "A Note on Masks," *Mask* 1 (March 1908): 11.

31. Quoted in John Cournos, "Gordon Craig and the Theatre of the Future," *Poetry and Drama* 1, no. 3 (Sept. 1913): 339–40.

32. Yvon Goll, "Two Superdramas," in *An Anthology of German Expressionist Drama*, trans. and ed. Walter H. Sokel (Garden City, N.Y.: Doubleday, 1963), 10.

33. Ibid., 11.

34. Sorell, *Other Face*, 15.

35. Eugene O'Neill, "Memoranda on Masks," *American Spectator*, Nov. 1932, 3; Kenneth MacGowan, "The Mask in Drama," *Greenwich Playbill*, Jan. 23, 1926, 1.

36. Sorell, *Other Face*, 77.

37. Napier, *Masks, Transformation, and Paradox*, 27.

38. Eugenio Barba, *The Paper Canoe*, trans. Richard Fowler (New York: Routledge, 1995), 11.

39. Canetti, *Crowds and Power*, 375; Bachelard, "Mask," 161.

40. Jean-Louis Barrault, *The Theatre of Jean-Louis Barrault*, trans. Joseph Chiari (New York: Hill and Wang, 1961), 76–77.

41. Lévi-Strauss, "Many Faces of Man," 20.

42. Robert Landy, "The Image of the Mask: Implications for Theatre and Therapy," *Journal of Mental Imagery* 9, no. 4 (1985): 55.

43. Sullivan, "There will be time," n.p.

Chapter 3: Mask Improvisation

1. Copeau himself soon discovered this when he moved his company of young actors to the country and created a series of mask theatre performances.

2. Gombrich, "Mask and the Face," 36.

3. Josette Féral, "Building Up the Muscle: An Interview with Ariane Mnouchkine," trans. Anna Husemoller, *TDR: The Drama Review* 33, no. 4 (Winter 1989): 91.

4. Ibid.

5. Clive Barker, "What Training—for What Theatre?" *New Theatre Quarterly* 11, no. 42 (May 1995): 108.

6. Theodore Roethke, "The Waking," in *The Collected Poems of Theodore Roethke* (Garden City, N.Y.: Anchor/Doubleday, 1975), 104.

7. Josette Féral, "Mnouchkine's Workshop at the Soleil: A Lesson in Theatre," trans. Anna Husemoller, *TDR: The Drama Review* 33, no. 4 (Winter 1989): 86, 87.

8. Shomit Mitter, *Systems of Rehearsal: Stanislavsky, Brecht, Grotowski and Brook* (London: Routledge, 1992), 116.

9. Ibid., 85.

10. In an educational institution, the most likely arrangement will be for a teacher to offer this class in mask improvisation for a number of enrolled students. So already there is a teacher-student relationship established, with all the unfortunate connotations and expectations such a relationship can imply on both sides. But I would encourage teachers to involve students in the observer-teacher role as much as possible, pairing them off with each other so that each student will function in both capacities. In this way the students will gain the most effective learning experience. The actual teacher, then, will not only guide the whole group through the learning process but also will be a participant-observer of the students in their roles as participants and as observers. A number of the exercises will require such a pairing arrangement.

11. Mask improvisation also serves the important purpose of training actors for mask theatre and other nonrealistic performance styles, as Copeau and his followers quickly discovered.

12. His "perceived Self" (his persona as he experiences it) and his "received Self" (the persona experienced by others) may not be the same. If this is true for anyone in the group, the discovery will be an invaluable one for him to make in the workshop, as it may be affecting work with others. It has generally proved true that those students who cannot set aside their own personas in order for the masks to give them new ones have the most difficult time in this course.

13. Herbert Blau, *Take Up the Bodies: Theater at the Vanishing Point* (Urbana: University of Illinois Press, 1982), 126.

14. Stephen Nachmanovitch, *Free Play: Improvisation in Life and Art* (Los Angeles: Jeremy P. Tarcher, 1990), 3.

15. Some requirements and criteria for evaluation that are more objective might include some of the following:

Attendance. There are no unexcused absences, and lateness does affect the final grade.

Completion and submission of written and performance assignments when they are due.

Completion of *x* number of well-constructed and finished masks. (This aspect of the evaluation is not based on the criteria of "well designed and well sculpted." Students will have differing abilities here, and it is not appropriate to require design and sculpting expertise. But it is possible to evaluate whether the student has made a serious attempt to apply the design and sculpting principles taught in this text.)

Submission of a photo and/or image gallery (similar to a makeup morgue) in preparation for sculpting.

Submission of a brief research paper on the methods of a famous "transforming actor." The paper should contain the actor's own comments on his or her process of transforming into a variety of characters, as well as the comments of others. Excellent candidates are actors like Glenn Close, Cecil Day-Lewis, Michael Gambon, John Giel-

gud, Helen Hayes, Jeremy Irons, Laurence Olivier, and Anna Deavere Smith.

Completion of a final project/presentation, demonstrating understanding of mask improvisation principles and practices and their application to acting without masks.

Submission of a thoughtful and well-written self-evaluation and workshop evaluation at the end of the course.

Chapter 4: Getting Started

1. Edward S. Casey, *Remembering: A Phenomenological Study* (Bloomington: Indiana University Press, 1987), 149.

2. Ken Dychtwald, *Bodymind* (New York: Jove Publications, 1983).

3. Thomas P. Kasulis, editor's introduction to *The Body: Toward an Eastern Mind-Body Theory,* by Yuasa Yasuo, ed. Thomas P. Kasulis, trans. Nagatomo Shigenori and Thomas P. Kasulis (Albany: State University of New York Press, 1987), 5.

4. Ibid., 5, 6. The term *dark consciousness* refers to a lower layer of consciousness, not to the unconscious. It has no pejorative denotations or connotations.

5. Harold Rugg, *Imagination* (New York: Harper and Row, 1963), 269.

6. Viola Spolin, *Improvisation for the Theater* (Evanston, Ill.: Northwestern University Press, 1963), 37.

7. Picard, *Human Face,* 46.

8. The participants should question why only the actor's face has been selected here, when they have all just observed with each other that *every* face is asymmetrical. What might be said, though, is that actors may be more conscious of and provoked by this fact. An actor can also use this knowledge to maximize her transformation into a character by highlighting one aspect over another when applying makeup.

9. Spolin, *Improvisation,* 63–64.

Chapter 5: The Lesson of the Mask

1. W. T. Benda, "My Talk on Masks," unpublished lecture notes, 1944–45, 6.

2. Rainer Maria Rilke, *The Notebooks of Malte Laurids Brigge,* trans. Stephen Mitchell (New York: Random House, 1983), 105–6.

3. Peter Brook, "Lie and Glorious Adjective," *Parabola* 6, no. 3 (Aug. 1981): 72.

4. Hal Burton, ed., *Great Acting* (New York: Bonanza Books, 1967), 133, 57.

5. Sam Shepard, "Language, Visualization, and the Inner Library," in *American Dreams: The Imagination of Sam Shepard,* ed. Bonnie Marranca (New York: PAJ Publications, 1981), 217.

6. Bob Ehlert, "Listening to the Voices," *Minneapolis Star Tribune Sunday Magazine,* Jan. 8, 1989, 8.

7. Lee Alan Morrow and Frank Pike, *Creating Theater: The Professionals' Approach to New Plays* (New York: Vintage Books, 1986), 16.

8. Judith Babnich, "In Search of William Mastrosimone," *Dramatics* 59, no. 8 (April 1988): 36.

9. Ehlert, "Listening to the Voices," 6.

10. Joseph Roach, *The Player's Passion: Studies in the Science of Acting* (Ann Arbor: University of Michigan Press, 1993), 190.

11. Quoted in William Archer, *Masks or Faces?* published with Denis Diderot's *The Paradox of Acting* (New York: Hill and Wang, 1957), 185.

12. H. Burton, *Great Acting*, 71, 72.

13. Laurence Olivier, *On Acting* (New York: Simon and Schuster, 1986), 26; Mike Steele, "Actor Janasz Enjoys Being a Character," *Minneapolis Star Tribune*, Sept. 20, 1991, 5E.

14. Yuasa's editor, Thomas P. Kasulis, also explains the interrelationship of the dark and bright consciousnesses within an individual by employing a driving analogy. It is most illuminating. See Kasulis, editor's introduction to *The Body,* by Yuasa Yasuo, 5.

15. Ibid.

16. Jenkins, "Two-Way Mirrors," 19.

17. Roach, *Player's Passion*, 16.

18. Kasulis, editor's introduction to *The Body,* by Yuasa Yasuo, 5, 6.

19. Yuasa, *The Body,* 62.

20. Michel Saint-Denis, *Training for the Theatre: Premises and Promises,* ed. Suria Saint-Denis (New York: Theatre Arts Books, 1982), 170.

21. Constantin Stanislavski, *Building a Character,* trans. Elizabeth Reynolds Hapgood (New York: Theatre Arts Books, 1949), 19.

22. Ibid., 27.

23. Ibid., 28; emphasis added. Chapter 3 of Stanislavski's book is a revelation about the types of acting students and their problems. These become very evident when working with masks. The mask reveals as it conceals! Stanislavski describes two major types of actors: the Personality Actors, who don't want to change or transform into their characters; and the Character Actors, who only want to change into their characters. The problem with the first is that they want to exhibit their own unique personalities onstage at all cost. Their characterizations shrink to a presentation of themselves. The problem with the second is that they do not fill their characterizations with their own lives. They keep themselves divorced from the characterization, so embodiment does not occur. In both cases these actors do not let the image live in and through them, as Kostya was able to do.

24. Quoted in Morrow and Pike, *Creating Theater,* 16.

25. Ronald Hayman, *Techniques of Acting* (New York: Holt, Rinehart and Winston, 1969), 36.

26. Rilke, *Notebooks,* 107.

27. Copeau, quoted and translated in Peter Burton and John Lane, *New Directions: Ways of Advance for the Amateur Theatre* (London: Methuen, 1972), 284.

Chapter 6: Masks and Countermasks

1. Mary Wigman, *The Mary Wigman Book,* ed. and trans. Walter Sorell (Middletown, Conn.: Wesleyan Univ. Press, 1975), 124.

2. Jacques Copeau, "Notes on the Actor," trans. Harold J. Salemson, in *Actors on Acting,* new revised ed., ed. Toby Cole and Helen Krich Chinoy (New York: Crown Publishers, 1970), 222.

3. Franco Ruffini, "Four Approaches: Theatre Anthropology," in *Approaching Theatre,* under the direction of André Helbo et al. (Bloomington: Indiana University Press, 1991), 89.

4. Kunio Komparu, *The Noh Theater: Principles and Perspectives,* trans. Jane Corddry (New York: Weatherhill, 1983), 230.

5. Max Picard, *The World of Silence* (Chicago: Henry Regency Co., 1952), 78.

6. This is Gombrich's term for our focus on the totality of the dominant features of a person's face, "the resultant of many factors which yet in their interaction make for a very particular physiognomic quality . . . some general dominant expression of which the individual expressions are merely modifications" ("Mask and the Face," 8).

Chapter 7: The Concept of Neutral

1. Rolfe, personal interview, in Eldredge, "Masks," 373.

2. The "Four Ages of Man" masks used in training programs initiated by Michel Saint-Denis are sometimes misidentified as Neutral Masks. They are wonderfully evocative masks but are not neutral. The better term for them would be *archetypal,* as they are used to explore heightened moments of awareness by larger-than-life figures that appear in myths, legends, or fairy tales.

3. Brook, "Lie and Glorious Adjective," 62.

4. Mitter, *Systems of Rehearsal,* 85.

5. Jacques Lecoq, personal interview, Aug. 6, 1974, in Eldredge, "Masks," 390.

6. Urban and Hendricks, "Signal Functions of Masking," 209.

7. Mitter, *Systems of Rehearsal,* 84.

8. Simon Callow, *Being an Actor* (London: Penguin Books, 1984), 166.

9. Quoted in Féral, "Building Up the Muscle," 93.

10. Peter Brook, "Knowing What to Celebrate," *Plays and Players* 23, no. 6 (March 1976): 18.

Chapter 8: The Neutral Mask Identifications

1. Gaston Bachelard, *The Poetics of Reverie: Childhood, Language, and the Cosmos,* trans. Daniel Russell (Boston: Beacon Press, 1969), 52.

2. Rosemary Gordon, "A Very Private World," in *The Function and Nature of Imagery,* ed. Peter W. Sheehan (New York: Academic Press, 1972), 79.

3. Ibid., 77.

4. Christine Edwards, *The Stanislavsky Heritage* (New York: New York University Press, 1965), 49.

5. Féral, "Mnouchkine's Workshop," 86.

6. Roach, *Player's Passion,* 39.

7. Sarah J. Sloane, "Close Encounters with Virtual Worlds," *Educator's Tech Exchange* (Spring 1994): 28.

Chapter 9: Continuing Identification Exercises

1. Lynn Garafola, "Variations on the Theme of Butoh," *Dance Magazine* 69, no. 9 (April 1989): 67.

2. Many haiku are available in English. One of the best collections I have found for this exercise is Peter Beilenson and Harry Behn, trans., *Haiku Harvest* (Mount Vernon, N.Y.: Peter Pauper Press, 1962).

3. I got the idea for this exercise from observing Bari Rolfe's work with students at the University of Washington in 1973. But Bari asked her students to handle the haiku quite differently.

4. Toshiski Munemura, program notes for a performance of Kazuo Ohno's *Water Lilies,* Walker Art Center, Minneapolis, Oct. 30, 1993.

5. Jean Viala and Nourit Masson-Sekine, *Butoh: Shades of Darkness* (Tokyo: Shufunotomo Co., 1988), 26.

Chapter 10: The Beginning Character Masks

1. These definitions come from *Merriam-Webster's Collegiate Dictionary,* 10th ed. (Springfield, Mass.: Merriam-Webster, 1993).

2. Bert O. States, *Hamlet and the Concept of Character* (Baltimore: Johns Hopkins University Press, 1992), xiv.

3. Cemrel, Inc., *The Five Sense Store: The Aesthetic Education Program* (New York: Viking Press/Lincoln Center for the Performing Arts, 1973). The permanent emotional states or sentiments of Indian theatre are the erotic, the comic, the pathetic, the furious, the heroic, the terrible, the disgusting, the marvelous, and the peaceful. See Edwin Gerow, "Sanskrit Dramatic Theory and Kalidasa's Plays," in *Theatre of Memory: The Plays of Kalidasa,* ed. Barbara Stoler Miller (New York: Columbia University Press, 1984), 324–25n11.

4. See Paul Ekman and Wallace Friesen, *Unmasking the Face* (Palo Alto, Calif.: Consulting Psychologists Press, 1984).

5. Denis Salter, "Hand Eye Mind Soul: Théâtre du Soleil's *Les Atrides,*" *Theater* 24, no. 1 (1993): 63.

6. Actually, this is not quite accurate, because the actor can make an identification and find a physicalization without using mirrors. But physicalizations using mirrors are more forceful and complete.

7. Mitter, *Systems of Rehearsal,* 31.

8. Gombrich, "Mask and the Face," 11.

9. Richard Schechner, "Aspects of Training at the Performance Group," in *Actor Training 1,* ed. Richard P. Brown (New York: Drama Book Specialists/Publishers, 1972), 53.

10. Robert Benedetti, "Notes to an Actor," in *Actor Training 1,* ed. Richard P. Brown (New York: Drama Book Specialists/Publishers, 1972), 72.

Chapter 11: The Countermask

1. States, *Hamlet and the Concept of Character,* 27.

2. Glenn Frankel, "Past Forged Streak of Steel in Britain's Major," *Minneapolis Star Tribune,* March 26, 1992, 4A [emphasis added].

3. Michael Chekhov, *To the Actor: On the Technique of Acting* (New York: Harper and Bros., 1953), 142–45.

Chapter 12: The Life Masks

1. *Merriam-Webster's Collegiate Dictionary,* 10th ed., s.v. "physiognomy."

2. Thomas R. Alley, "Physiognomy and Social Perception," in *Social and Applied Aspects of Perceiving Faces,* ed. Thomas R. Alley (Hillsdale, N.J.: Lawrence Erlbaum, 1988), 185; see also 168. I thank my colleague Charles Torry, in the Psychology Department at Macalester College, for bringing this valuable article to my attention.

3. Ibid., 174, 179–83.

4. Jenkins, "Two-Way Mirrors," 20.

5. This exercise was inspired by Kenneth Koch's wonderful book *Wishes, Lies, and Dreams: Teaching Children to Write Poetry* (New York: Vintage Books, 1970).

Chapter 13: The Totem Masks

1. *Merriam-Webster's Collegiate Dictionary,* 10th ed., s.v. "totem."

2. Ojima Ichiro, interview in *Ankoku Buto: The Premodern and Postmodern Influences on the Dance of Utter Darkness,* by Susan Blakeley Klein, Cornell East Asia Series 49 (Ithaca, N.Y.: Cornell University Press, 1993), 39.

3. Gombrich, "Mask and the Face," 35.

4. Antony Sher, *Year of the King: An Actor's Diary and Sketchbook* (New York: Limelight Editions, 1992), 122.

5. Ibid., 22, 75, 98, 102.

6. Gombrich, "Mask and the Face," 34.

7. Peter Brook, *The Empty Space* (New York: Avon Books, 1968), 12.

8. Blau, *Take Up the Bodies,* 150.

9. Here are some examples of student evaluations from previous workshops:

Student A continually developed characters that lacked energy. She also had trouble incorporating the lower half of her body into her characterizations. She was asked to develop a strong, active, "doer-type" character for her Complex Character Mask that was young, assertive, and energetic.

Student B had a penchant for strong characterizations, but their behavior was similar: they were all loners. So he was asked to develop an outgoing, gregarious character for his Complex Character Mask, a person who always needed to be in contact with others.

Student C's characters were always well considered and mature. She needed further challenge in abandoning herself to the role. She was asked to develop a character who was an energetic child, seven to nine years old.

Student D's characters tended to be loud and aggressive no matter what mask he wore. He also created characterizations that squatted down a lot. He was asked to create a tall, intelligent, quiet, and thoughtful character.

Student E's characters always worked hard to become the center of attention. Her physicalizations ate up space, with her body tilted forward and her arms sticking out and forward from the body. She was asked to create an anonymous member of the crowd.

Student F had a series of youthful characterizations that took advantage of his extensive dance training. His masks always moved well, frequently in fluid, circular motions. But he tended to keep his emotional commitment at a distance. He was asked to develop a final Complex Character Mask that was sharp, nonflowing, older-aged, and gutsy.

Student G's work was inhibited by the fact that she had such a strong persona that appeared in her classroom performance mode that she could not set it aside to let the mask take over and transform her bodymind. She was asked to note her personal psychophysical habits and then to work against them.

Chapter 14: The Found Object Masks

1. Renée Marcousé, *Using Objects* (New York: Van Nostrand Reinhold, 1974), 7.

2. Ruesch and Kees, *Nonverbal Communication*, 93.

3. Gombrich, "Mask and the Face," 35.

Chapter 15: The Complex Character Masks

1. It is possible, and sometimes desirable, to include a unique chin in the mask. If so, the mask must be a three-quarter mask with a chin attached to the side jaw or jowls with stretch fabric. The bottom lip of the mask remains the actor's.

2. This approach has been used successfully by Roland Meinholt at the University of Montana for a number of years. In one instance Meinholt used a book about the Donner Party, *Ordeal by Hunger*, as his source for a two-term mask improvisation project. Students designed and sculpted the masks for their assigned characters by combining descriptions given in the text with other photographic and visual art sources.

Chapter 16: Masks and Faces

1. Jennifer Dunning, "The New American Actor," *New York Times,* Oct. 2, 1983, sec. 6, p. 69.

2. Steele, "Actor Janasz," 5E.

3. John Willett, trans. and comp., *Caspar Neher: Brecht's Designer* (London: Methuen, 1986), 105. Brecht, of course, may have thought about neutrality quite differently from the way it is presented in this book.

4. Holly Hill, "Anthony Heald: Haven't I Seen Him Somewhere Before," *American Theatre* 4, no. 12 (March 1988): 46.

5. Anna Deavere Smith, *Fires in the Mirror* (New York: Anchor/Doubleday, 1993), xxiv. Here Smith is quoting her grandfather's sage advice.

6. Ibid., xxv–xxvi.

7. Sher, *Year of the King*, 207.

8. Peter Brook, "The Physical Life of the Actor," interview with Kenneth Rea, *Drama* 3, no. 153 (1984): 16.

9. Stanislavski, *Building a Character*, 3.

10. Brook, "Lie and Glorious Adjective," 64.

11. Peter Brook, *The Shifting Point* (New York: Harper and Row, 1987), 233.

12. Henrik Ibsen, *Hedda Gabler,* trans. Rolf Fjelde (New York: New American Library, 1965), 228.

13. Samuel Beckett, *Endgame* (New York: Grove Press, 1958), 1.

14. Jonathan Kalb, "Interview with Peter Evans, New York City, June 26, 1986," in *Beckett in Performance,* by Jonathan Kalb (Cambridge: Cambridge University Press, 1991), 42.

15. Stanislavski, *Building a Character*, 27.

16. Chekhov, *To the Actor*, 87.

17. Carl Weber, "The Actor and Brecht; or, The Truth Is Concrete," in *Brecht Performance,* ed. John Fuegi et al. (Detroit: Wayne State University Press, 1987), 69.

18. Peter Frisch, personal interview, July 11, 1973, in Eldredge, "Masks," 349.

19. Smith, *Fires in the Mirror,* xxvi–xxvii.

20. Michael Chekhov, *To the Director and Playwright,* comp. and written by Charles Leonard [pseud.] (New York: Limelight Editions, 1984), 21.

21. Morrow and Pike, *Creating Theater,* 164.

22. Olivier, *On Acting,* 153.

23. Michael Goldman, *Acting and Action in Shakespearean Tragedy* (Princeton, N.J.: Princeton University Press, 1985), 10.

24. Tom Driver, *Romantic Quest and Modern Query: A History of the Modern Theater* (New York: Dell Publishing Co., 1971), 406, 407.

25. Margo Jefferson, "Solo Actors Can Stretch So Far They Touch Us," *New York Times,* May 21, 1995, H5.

26. Molière, *Tartuffe,* trans. Richard Wilbur (New York: Dramatists Play Service, 1989), 24 (act I, scene v).

27. Michael Redgrave, *Mask or Face: Reflections in an Actor's Mirror* (London: Heinemann, 1958), 27.

28. The idea of "persistence" is one that Bert States uses in *Hamlet*

and the Concept of Character (xviii). There is a tremendous argument in critical, literary, and psychological thinking over the question of the reality or the illusion of an "authentic self." Some essentialist psychologists and literary critics believe there is such a self; others believe there is no such thing, or that there are only "authentic selves"—a cast of characters within. The debate gets even more complex when the question is applied to fictional characters, especially in performance when those characters are played by actors.

29. Driver, *Romantic Quest and Modern Query,* 407.

30. States, *Hamlet and the Concept of Character,* 205n12, 202n4, xviii.

31. Quoted in David Magarshack, introduction to *Stanislavsky on the Art of the Stage,* by Konstantin Stanislavsky, trans. David Magarshack (New York: Hill and Wang, 1961), 15.

32. Quoted in Hayman, *Techniques of Acting,* 35.

33. Morris Carnovsky, *The Actor's Eye* (New York: Performing Arts Journal Publications, 1984), 26, 27.

34. Saint-Denis, *Training for the Theatre,* 82.

35. Benedetti, "Notes to an Actor," 72.

36. Archer, *Masks or Faces?* 220.

37. Bertolt Brecht, *The Messingkauf Dialogues,* trans. John Willett (London: Methuen, 1965), 55.

Chapter 17: Mask Theatre

1. Michael Billington, "Masks That Obscure a Tragedy," *London Guardian,* Nov. 30, 1981, 11.

2. Milton Shulman, "Passion and the Puppets," *London Standard,* Nov. 30, 1981, 22.

3. Russell Graves, "The Psychological Effects of Masks," *Theatre Crafts* 5, no. 1 (Jan.–Feb. 1971): 15, 33.

4. O'Neill, "Memoranda on Masks," 3.

5. Bertolt Brecht, "Little Organon [sic] for the Theatre," in "The Mask at the Berliner Ensemble," by Joachim Tenschert, *World Theatre* 10, no. 1 (Spring 1961): 58.

6. Wigman, *Mary Wigman Book,* 124, 126.

7. Robertson Davies, "The Production of *King Oedipus,*" in *Thrice the Brinded Cat Hath Mew'd* (Toronto: Clarke, Irwin and Co., 1955), 123–24.

8. Nina Vidrovitch, "Introduction to the Mask," trans. Constance Wagner, University of Arkansas *Mime Journal,* no. 2 (1975): 23.

9. Léon Chancerel, "Le Masque," in *Prospero 11* (Paris: Publication du Centre Dramatique, 1947), 16, translated by Christopher Thor and Sears A. Eldredge.

10. Fo, "Hands Off the Mask!" 209.

11. Bari Rolfe, "Masks, Mime, and Mummenschanz," University of Arkansas *Mime Journal,* no. 2 (1975): 26.

12. Sorell, *Other Face,* 118.

13. Robert More, "Confessions of a Puppet Manipulator," *Canadian Theatre Review* 78 (Spring 1994): 20.

14. Ibid.

15. Ibid., 19.

16. Komparu, *Noh Theater,* 230.

17. Rebecca Teele, "The Kyōgen Actor and His Relationship with the Mask: An Interview with Shigeyama Sengoro," Pomona College *Mime Journal* 8 (1984): 168.

18. Komparu, *Noh Theater,* 229.

19. Monica Bethe, "Okina: An Interview with Takabayashi Koji," Pomona College *Mime Journal* 8 (1984): 99.

20. Leonard Pitt, "Mask Technique for the Actor," *Theatre Magazine* (Winter 1977): 83.

21. Joachim Tenschert, "The Mask at the Berliner Ensemble," *World Theatre* 10, no. 1 (Spring 1961): 57.

22. Fo, "Hands Off the Mask!" 209.

23. Pitt, "Mask Technique," 83.

24. Jean-Louis Barrault, "Greek Tragedy, its Production: The Foreign Producer's Point of View," *World Theatre* 6, no. 4 (Winter 1957): 276, 277.

25. Fo, "Hands Off the Mask!" 208.

26. Mira Felner, *Apostles of Silence: The Modern French Mimes* (Rutherford, N.J.: Fairleigh Dickinson University Press, 1985), 159–61.

27. Graves, "Psychological Effects of Masks," 15.

Appendix A: Mask Design and Construction

1. Gombrich, "Mask and the Face," 24.

2. Paul McPharlin, "To Make a Mask," *Theatre Arts Monthly* 9 (Sept. 1925): 593.

3. Everett P. Lesley Jr., *Alter Ego. Masks: Their Art and Use* (New York: Cooper Union Museum for the Arts of Decoration, 1951), 6.

4. Mirta T. Mulhare, "Hector Ubertalli: A Maker of Masks," *American Artist* 25 (Oct. 1961): 62.

5. Henri Cordreaux, *Fabrication du masque,* 2d ed. (Paris: Editions Bourrelier et Cie, 1946), 14; translation of quotation by Sears A. Eldredge.

6. Peter Arnott, *Plays without People* (Bloomington: Indiana University Press, 1964), 100.

7. W. T. Benda, *Masks* (New York: Watson-Guptill Publications, 1944), 23–25.

8. W. T. Benda, "Modern Masks and Their Uses," *Encyclopedia Britannica,* 1946, 15:15.

9. Gombrich, "Mask and the Face," 17.

10. Lesley, *Alter Ego,* 5.

11. W. T. Benda, "How Benda Revived the Use of Masks," *Boston Transcript,* April 17, 1926, 5, 7.

12. McPharlin, "To Make a Mask," 596.

13. Quoted in Alberto Marcia, *The Commedia dell'Arte and the Masks of Amleto and Donato Sartori,* trans. Cynthia Baker, Anne Marie Speno, and Brenda Porster (Florence, Italy: La Casa Usher, 1980), n.p.

14. Marcia, *Commedia dell'Arte.*

Bibliography

See also the extensive bibliography on masks, masking, and mask improvisation training in my "Masks: Their Use and Effectiveness in Actor Training Programs" (Ph.D. diss., Michigan State University, 1975).

Allan, Katherine. "Columbus and the Neutral Mask." *Canadian Theatre Review* 71 (Summer 1992): 20–25.

Alley, Thomas R. "Physiognomy and Social Perception." In *Social and Applied Aspects of Perceiving Faces,* ed. Thomas R. Alley, 167–86. Hillsdale, N.J.: Lawrence Erlbaum, 1988.

Archer, William. *Masks or Faces?* In *The Paradox of Acting,* by Denis Diderot, and *Masks or Faces?* by William Archer, 73–226. New York: Hill and Wang, 1957.

Arnott, Peter. *Plays without People.* Bloomington: Indiana University Press, 1964.

Babnich, Judith. "In Search of William Mastrosimone." *Dramatics* 59, no. 8 (April 1988): 34–41.

Bachelard, Gaston. "The Mask." In *The Right to Dream,* trans. J. A. Underwood, 157–66. Dallas: Dallas Institute Publications, 1988.

———. *The Poetics of Reverie: Childhood, Language, and the Cosmos.* Trans. Daniel Russell. Boston: Beacon Press, 1969.

Balance, John [pseud. of E. G. Craig]. "A Note on Masks." *Mask* 1 (March 1908): 9–12.

Barba, Eugenio. *The Paper Canoe.* Trans. Richard Fowler. New York: Routledge, 1995.

———. "Theatre Laboratory 13 R12dow." *Tulane Drama Review* 9, no. 3 (Spring 1965): 153–71.

Barker, Clive. "What Training—for What Theatre?" *New Theatre Quarterly* 11, no. 42 (May 1995).

Barrault, Jean-Louis. "Greek Tragedy, its Production: The Foreign Producer's Point of View." *World Theatre* 6, no. 1 (Winter 1957): 276–77.

———. *The Theatre of Jean-Louis Barrault.* Trans. Joseph Chiari. New York: Hill and Wang, 1961.

Beckett, Samuel. *Endgame.* New York: Grove Press, 1958.

Beilenson, Peter, and Harry Behn, trans. *Haiku Harvest.* Mount Vernon, N.Y.: Peter Pauper Press, 1962.

Benda, W. T. "How Benda Revived the Use of Masks." *Boston Transcript,* April 17, 1926, 5, 7.

———. *Masks.* New York: Watson-Guptill Publications, 1944.

———. "Modern Masks and Their Uses." *Encyclopedia Britannica,* 1946, 15:14–16.

———. "My Talk on Masks." Unpublished lecture notes, 1944–45, 1–10. Courtesy of Glena Benda Shimler.

Benedetti, Robert. "Notes to an Actor." In *Actor Training 1,* ed. Richard P. Brown, 65–95. New York: Drama Book Specialists/Publishers, 1972.

Berthold, Margot. *The History of World Theater: From the Beginnings to the Baroque.* Trans. Edith Simmons. New York: Continuum, 1991.

Bethe, Monica. "Okina: An Interview with Takabayaski Koji." Pomona College *Mime Journal* 8 (1984): 93–103.

Billington, Michael. "Masks That Obscure a Tragedy." *London Guardian,* Nov. 30, 1981, 11.

Blau, Herbert. *Take Up the Bodies: Theater at the Vanishing Point.* Urbana: University of Illinois Press, 1982.

Bogatyrëv, Petr. "The Interconnection of Two Similar Semiotic Systems: The Puppet Theater and the Theater of Living Actors." *Semiotica* 47 (1983): 47–68.

Brecht, Bertolt. "Little Organon [sic] for the Theatre." In "The Mask at the Berliner Ensemble," by Joachim Tenschert, *World Theatre* 10, no. 1 (Spring 1961): 50.

———. *The Messingkauf Dialogues.* Trans. John Willett. London: Methuen, 1965.

Brecht, Stefan. *Peter Schumann's Bread and Puppet Theatre.* Vol. 1. New York: Routledge, Chapman and Hall, 1988.

Brockett, Oscar G., and Robert R. Findlay. *Century of Innovation.* Englewood Cliffs, N.J.: Prentice-Hall, 1973.

Brook, Peter. *The Empty Space.* New York: Avon Books, 1968.

———. "Knowing What to Celebrate." *Plays and Players* 23, no. 6 (March 1976): 17–19.

———. "Lie and Glorious Adjective." *Parabola* 6, no. 3 (Aug. 1981): 60–73.

———. "The Physical Life of the Actor." Interview with Kenneth Rea. *Drama* 3, no. 153 (1984): 14–16.

———. *The Shifting Point.* New York: Harper and Row, 1987.

Burton, Hal, ed. *Great Acting.* New York: Bonanza Books, 1967.

Burton, Peter, and John Lane. *New Directions: Ways of Advance for the Amateur Theatre.* London: Methuen, 1972.

Caillois, Roger. *Man, Play, and Games.* Trans. Meyer Barash. New York: Free Press, 1961.

———. *The Mask of Medusa.* Trans. George Ordish. London: Victor Gollancz, 1964.

Callow, Simon. *Being an Actor.* London: Penguin Books, 1984.

Campbell, Joseph. *The Masks of God: Primitive Mythology.* New York: Viking Press, 1959.

Canetti, Elias. *Crowds and Power.* Trans. Carol Stewart. New York: Seabury Press, 1978.

Carnovsky, Morris. *The Actor's Eye.* New York: Performing Arts Journal Publications, 1984.

Casey, Edward S. *Remembering: A Phenomenological Study.* Bloomington: Indiana University Press, 1987.

Cemrel, Inc. *The Five Sense Store: The Aesthetic Education Program.* New York: Viking Press/Lincoln Center for the Performing Arts, 1973.

Chancerel, Léon. "Le Masque." In *Prospero 11,* 15–21. Paris: Publication du Centre Dramatique, 1947.

Chekhov, Michael. *To the Actor: On the Technique of Acting.* New York: Harper and Bros., 1953.

———. *To the Director and Playwright.* Compiled and written by Charles Leonard [pseud.]. New York: Limelight Editions, 1984.

Copeau, Jacques. "Notes on the Actor." Trans. Harold J. Salemson. In *Actors on Acting,* new revised ed., ed. Toby Cole and Helen Krich Chinoy. New York: Crown Publishers, 1970.

Cordreaux, Henri. *Fabrication du masque.* 2d ed. Paris: Editions Bourrelier et Cie, 1946.

Cournos, John. "Gordon Craig and the Theatre of the Future." *Poetry and Drama* 1, no. 3 (Sept. 1913): 339–40.

Crumrine, N. Ross. "Masks, Participants, and Audience." In *The Power of Symbols,* ed. N. Ross Crumrine and Marjorie Halpin, 1–11. Vancouver: University of British Columbia Press, 1983.

Davies, Robertson. *Thrice the Brinded Cat Hath Mew'd.* Toronto: Clarke, Irwin and Co., 1955.

Driver, Tom. *Romantic Quest and Modern Query: A History of the Modern Theatre.* New York: Dell Publishing Co., 1971.

Dunning, Jennifer. "The New American Actor." *New York Times,* Oct. 2, 1983, sec. 6, pp. 34–37, 68–70, 72, 74.

Dychtwald, Ken. *Bodymind.* New York: Jove Publications, 1983.

Edwards, Christine. *The Stanislavsky Heritage.* New York: New York University Press, 1965.

Ehlert, Bob. "Listening to the Voices." *Minneapolis Star Tribune Sunday Magazine,* Jan. 8, 1989, 6–9.

Ekman, Paul, and Wallace Friesen. *Unmasking the Face.* Palo Alto, Calif.: Consulting Psychologists Press, 1984.

Eldredge, Sears A. "Masks: Their Use and Effectiveness in Actor Training Programs." Ph.D. diss., Michigan State University, 1975.

Eliade, Mircea. "Masks: Mythical and Ritual Origins." In *Encyclopedia of World Art* 9:521–26. New York: McGraw-Hill, 1964.

Felner, Mira. *Apostles of Silence: The Modern French Mimes.* Rutherford, N.J.: Fairleigh Dickinson University Press, 1985.

Féral, Josette. "Building Up the Muscle: An Interview with Ariane Mnouchkine." Trans. Anna Husemoller. *TDR: The Drama Review* 33, no. 4 (Winter 1989): 88–97.

———. "Mnouchkine's Workshop at the Soleil: A Lesson in Theatre." Trans. Anna Husemoller. *TDR: The Drama Review* 33, no. 4 (Winter 1989): 77–87.

Findlater, Richard. "Michael Redgrave with Richard Findlater." In *Great Acting,* ed. Hal Burton, 99–110. New York: Bonanza Books, 1967.

Fo, Dario. "Hands Off the Mask!" *New Theatre Quarterly* 5, no. 19 (Aug. 1989): 207–9.

Frankel, Glenn. "Past Forged Streak of Steel in Britain's Major." *Minneapolis Star Tribune,* March 26, 1992, 4A.

Garafola, Lynn. "Variations on the Theme of Butoh." *Dance Magazine* 69, no. 9 (April 1989): 66–68.

Gaster, Theodor H. *Thespis: Ritual, Myth, and Drama in the Ancient Near East.* New York: Harper Torchbooks, 1961.

Gerow, Edwin. "Sanskrit Dramatic Theory and Kalidasa's Plays." In *Theatre of Memory: The Plays of Kalidasa,* ed. Barbara Stoler Miller, 42–62, 324–27. New York: Columbia University Press, 1984.

Goldman, Michael. *Acting and Action in Shakespearean Tragedy.* Princeton, N.J.: Princeton University Press, 1985.

Goll, Yvon. "Two Superdramas." In *An Anthology of German Expressionist Drama,* trans. and ed. Walter H. Sokel, 9–11. Garden City, N.Y.: Doubleday, 1963.

Gombrich, E. H. "The Mask and the Face: The Perception of Physiognomic Likeness in Life and in Art." In *Art, Perception, and Reality,* by E. H. Gombrich, Julian Hochberg, and Max Black, 1–46. Baltimore: Johns Hopkins University Press, 1972.

Gordon, Rosemary. "A Very Private World." In *The Function and Nature of Imagery,* ed. Peter W. Sheehan, 63–80. New York: Academic Press, 1972.

Graves, Russell. "The Psychological Effects of Masks." *Theatre Crafts* 5, no. 1 (Jan.–Feb. 1971): 12–15, 33.

Grimes, Ronald L. *Beginnings in Ritual Studies.* Lanham, Md.: University Press of America, 1982.

———. "The Life History of a Mask." *TDR: The Drama Review* 36, no. 3 (Fall 1992): 61–77.

Guss, David M. *The Language of the Birds.* San Francisco: North Point Press, 1985.

Halpin, Marjorie. "The Mask of Tradition," In *The Power of Symbols,* ed. N. Ross Crumrine and Marjorie Halpin, 219–26. Vancouver: University of British Columbia Press, 1983.

Harris-Smith, Susan. *Masks in Modern Drama.* Berkeley: University of California Press, 1984.

Hayman, Ronald. *Techniques of Acting.* New York: Holt, Rinehart and Winston, 1969.

Hill, Holly. "Anthony Heald: Haven't I Seen Him Somewhere Before." *American Theatre* 4, no. 12 (March 1988): 46–47.

Ibsen, Henrik. *Hedda Gabler.* Trans. Rolf Fjelde. New York: New American Library, 1965.

Jefferson, Margo. "Solo Actors Can Stretch So Far They Touch Us." *New York Times,* May 21, 1995, H5.

Jenkins, Ron. "Two-Way Mirrors." *Parabola* 6, no. 3 (Aug. 1981): 17–21.

Jevons, F. B. *Masks and Acting.* Cambridge: Cambridge University Press, 1916.

Jung, Carl. "The Relations between the Ego and the Unconscious." In *The Portable Jung,* ed. Joseph Campbell, trans. R. F. C. Hull, 70–138. New York: Viking Press, 1971.

Kalb, Jonathan. *Beckett in Performance.* Cambridge: Cambridge University Press, 1991.

Kasulis, Thomas P. Editor's introduction to *The Body: Toward an Eastern Mind-Body Theory,* by Yuasa Yasuo, ed. Thomas P. Kasulis, trans. Nagatomo Shigenori and Thomas P. Kasulis, 1–15. Albany: State University of New York Press, 1987.

Kerényi, Carl. "Man and Mask." In *Spiritual Disciplines,* 151–67. Vol. 4 of *Papers from the Eranos Yearbooks,* Bollingen Series 30. New York: Pantheon Books, 1960.

Kirby, E. T. "The Mask: Abstract Theatre, Primitive and Modern." *TDR: The Drama Review* 16, no. 3 (Sept. 1972): 5–21.

Klein, Susan Blakeley. *Ankoku Buto: The Premodern and Postmodern*

Influences on the Dance of Utter Darkness. Cornell East Asia Series 49. Ithaca, N.Y.: Cornell University Press, 1993.

Koch, Kenneth. *Wishes, Lies, and Dreams: Teaching Children to Write Poetry.* New York: Vintage Books, 1970.

Komparu, Kunio. *The Noh Theater: Principles and Perspectives.* Trans. Jane Corddry. New York: Weatherhill, 1983.

Landy, Robert. "The Image of the Mask: Implications for Theatre and Therapy." *Journal of Mental Imagery* 9, no. 4 (1985): 43–56.

Lecoq, Jacques. "Mime—Movement—Theatre." *Yale/Theatre* 4, no. 1 (Winter 1973): 117–20.

Lesley, Everett P., Jr. *Alter Ego. Masks: Their Art and Use.* New York: Cooper Union Museum for the Arts of Decoration, 1951.

Lévi-Strauss, Claude. "The Many Faces of Man." *World Theatre* 10, no. 1 (Spring 1961): 11–20.

MacGowan, Kenneth. "The Mask in Drama." *Greenwich Playbill,* Jan. 23, 1926, 1, 6.

Magarshack, David. Introduction to *Stanislavsky on the Art of the Stage,* by Konstantin Stanislavsky, trans. David Magarshack, 11–87. New York: Hill and Wang, 1961.

Marcia, Alberto. *The Commedia dell'Arte and the Masks of Amleto and Donato Sartori.* Trans. Cynthia Baker, Anne Marie Speno, and Brenda Porster. Florence, Italy: La Casa Usher, 1980.

Marcousé, Renée. *Using Objects.* New York: Van Nostrand Reinhold, 1974.

McPharlin, Paul. "To Make a Mask." *Theatre Arts Monthly* 9 (Sept. 1925): 593–96.

Mead, Margaret. "Masks and Men." *Natural History* 55 (June 1946): 280–85.

Mitter, Shomit. *Systems of Rehearsal: Stanislavsky, Brecht, Grotowski and Brook.* London: Routledge, 1992.

Molière. *Tartuffe.* Trans. Richard Wilbur. New York: Dramatists Play Service, 1989.

Monte, Christopher F. *Beneath the Mask: An Introduction to Theories of Personality.* 2d ed. New York: Holt, Rinehart and Winston, 1979.

More, Robert. "Confessions of a Puppet Manipulator." *Canadian Theatre Review* 78 (Spring 1994): 17–20.

Morrow, Lee Alan, and Frank Pike. *Creating Theater: The Professionals' Approach to New Plays.* New York: Vintage Books, 1986.

Muensterberger, Werner. "Man's Need to Change." *Persona Grata,* n.p. Houston: University of St. Thomas, 1960.

Mulhare, Mirta T. "Hector Ubertalli: A Maker of Masks." *American Artist* 25 (Oct. 1961): 43–47, 62–63.

Munemura, Toshiski. Program notes for a performance of Kazuo Ohno's *Water Lilies.* Walker Art Center, Minneapolis, Oct. 30, 1993.

Nachmanovitch, Stephen. *Free Play: Improvisation in Life and Art.* Los Angeles: Jeremy P. Tarcher, 1990.

Nagler, A. M. *A Source Book in Theatrical History.* New York: Dover Publications, 1952.

Napier, A. David. *Masks, Transformation, and Paradox.* Berkeley: University of California Press, 1986.

Nietzsche, Friedrich. *The Birth of Tragedy and The Case of Wagner.* Trans. Walter Kaufmann. New York: Random House, 1967.

Olivier, Laurence. *On Acting.* New York: Simon and Schuster, 1986.

O'Neill, Eugene. "Memoranda on Masks." *American Spectator,* Nov. 1932, 3.

———. "Second Thoughts." *American Spectator,* Dec. 1932, 2.

Otto, Walter F. *Dionysus: Myth and Cult.* Trans. Robert B. Palmer. Bloomington: Indiana University Press, 1965.

Pernet, Henry. "Masks: Ritual Masks in Nonliterate Cultures." Trans. Michele P. Cros. In *Encyclopedia of Religion,* ed. Mircea Eliade, 9:263–69. New York: Macmillan, 1987.

———. "Masks: Theoretical Perspectives." Trans. Michele P. Cros. In *Encyclopedia of Religion,* ed. Mircea Eliade, 9:259–63. New York: Macmillan, 1987.

Pfeiffer, John E. *The Creative Explosion.* Ithaca, N.Y.: Cornell University Press, 1982.

Picard, Max. *The Human Face.* Trans. Guy Endore. New York: Farrar and Rinehart, 1930.

———. *The World of Silence.* Chicago: Henry Regency Co., 1952.

Piggot, Juliet. *Japanese Mythology.* London: Paul Hamlyn, 1969.

Pitt, Leonard. "Mask Technique for the Actor." *Theatre Magazine* (Winter 1977): 81–83.

Redgrave, Michael. *Mask or Face: Reflections in an Actor's Mirror.* London: Heinemann, 1958.

Rico, Gabriele Lusser. *Writing the Natural Way.* Los Angeles: Jeremy P. Tarcher, 1983.

Rilke, Rainer Maria. *The Notebooks of Malte Laurids Brigge.* Trans. Stephen Mitchell. New York: Random House, 1983.

Roach, Joseph. *The Player's Passion: Studies in the Science of Acting.* Ann Arbor: University of Michigan Press, 1993.

Roethke, Theodore. *The Collected Poems of Theodore Roethke.* Garden City, N.Y.: Anchor/Doubleday, 1975.

Rolfe, Bari. "Masks, Mime, and Mummenschanz." University of Arkansas *Mime Journal,* no. 2 (1975): 24–35.

Rudlin, John. *Commedia dell'Arte: An Actor's Handbook.* New York: Routledge, 1994.

Ruesch, Jurgen, and Weldon Kees. *Nonverbal Communication.* Berkeley: University of California Press, 1956.

Ruffini, Franco. "Four Approaches: Theatre Anthropology." In *Approaching Theatre,* under the direction of André Helbo et al., 75–91. Bloomington: Indiana University Press, 1991.

Rugg, Harold. *Imagination.* New York: Harper and Row, 1963.

Saint-Denis, Michel. *Training for the Theatre: Premises and Promises.* Ed. Suria Saint-Denis. New York: Theatre Arts Books, 1982.

Salter, Denis. "Hand Eye Mind Soul: Théâtre du Soleil's *Les Atrides.*" *Theater* 24, no. 1 (1993): 59–74.

Schechner, Richard. "Aspects of Training at the Performance Group." In *Actor Training 1,* ed. Richard P. Brown, 3–64. New York: Drama Book Specialists/Publishers, 1972.

Schlesier, Renate. "Mixtures of Masks: Maenads as Tragic Models." In *Masks of Dionysus,* ed. Thomas H. Carpenter and Christopher Faraone, 89–114. Ithaca, N.Y.: Cornell University Press, 1993.

Shapiro, Harry. "Magic of the Mask." *New York Times Magazine,* April 15, 1951, 26–28.

Shepard, Sam. "Language, Visualization, and the Inner Library." In *American Dreams: The Imagination of Sam Shepard,* ed. Bonnie Marranca, 214–19. New York: PAJ Publications, 1981.

Sher, Antony. *Year of the King: An Actor's Diary and Sketchbook.* New York: Limelight Editions, 1992.

Shulman, Milton. "Passion and the Puppets." *London Standard,* Nov. 30, 1981, 22.

Sloane, Sarah J. "Close Encounters with Virtual Worlds." *Educator's Tech Exchange* (Spring 1994): 23–29.

Smith, Anna Deavere. *Fires in the Mirror.* New York: Anchor/Doubleday, 1993.

Sorell, Walter. *The Other Face: The Mask in the Arts.* Indianapolis: Bobbs-Merrill, 1973.

Spolin, Viola. *Improvisation for the Theater.* Evanston, Ill.: Northwestern University Press, 1963.

Stanislavski, Constantin. *Building a Character.* Trans. Elizabeth Reynolds Hapgood. New York: Theatre Arts Books, 1949.

States, Bert O. *Hamlet and the Concept of Character.* Baltimore: Johns Hopkins University Press, 1992.

Steele, Mike. "Actor Janasz Enjoys Being a Character." *Minneapolis Star Tribune,* Sept. 20, 1991, 1E, 5E.

Sullivan, Edward. "There will be time, there will be time, to prepare a face to meet the faces that you meet." *Persona Grata,* n.p. Houston: University of St. Thomas, 1960.

Teele, Rebecca. "The Kyōgen Actor and His Relationship with the Mask: An Interview with Shigeyama Sengoro." Pomona College *Mime Journal* 8 (1984): 156–70.

Tenschert, Joachim. "The Mask at the Berliner Ensemble." *World Theatre* 10, no. 1 (Spring 1961): 50–61.

Tonkin, Elizabeth. "Masks and Powers." *Man* 14, no. 2 (June 1979): 237–48.

Urban, Greg, and Janet Wall Hendricks. "Signal Functions of Masking in Amerindian Brazil." *Semiotica* 47 (1983): 181–216.

Viala, Jean, and Nourit Masson-Sekine. *Butoh: Shades of Darkness.* Tokyo: Shufunotomo Co., 1988.

Vidrovitch, Nina. "Introduction to the Mask." Trans. Constance Wagner. University of Arkansas *Mime Journal,* no. 2 (1975): 18–23.

Wardle, Irving. "An Outline of Grandeur: *Oresteia.*" *London Times,* Nov. 30, 1981, 13.

Weber, Carl. "The Actor and Brecht; or, The Truth Is Concrete." In *Brecht Performance,* ed. John Fuegi et al., 63–74. Detroit: Wayne State University Press, 1987.

Wigman, Mary. *The Mary Wigman Book.* Ed. and trans. Walter Sorell. Middletown, Conn.: Wesleyan University Press, 1975.

Willett, John, trans. and comp. *Caspar Neher: Brecht's Designer.* London: Methuen, 1986.

Winkler, John J., and Froma I. Zeitlin, eds. *Nothing to Do with Dionysus?* Princeton, N.J.: Princeton University Press, 1990.

Wolff, Charlotte. *The Psychology of Gesture.* Trans. Anne Tennant. 2d ed. London: Methuen, 1948.

Yuasa Yasuo. *The Body: Toward an Eastern Mind-Body Theory.* Ed. Thomas P. Kasulis. Trans. Nagatomo Shigenori and Thomas P. Kasulis. Albany: State University of New York Press, 1987.